The Symbolic and Connectionist Paradigms
Closing the Gap

The Cognitive Science Series: Technical Monographs and Edited Collection
Donald A. Norman, Andrew Ortony, and Roger Schank, Series Editors

---

The Symbolic and Connectionist Paradigms
Closing the Gap

Edited by
John Dinsmore
Washington University

LAWRENCE ERLBAUM ASSOCIATES, PUBLISHERS
1992   Hillsdale, New Jersey   Hove and London

Lawrence Erlbaum Associates, Inc., Publishers
365 Broadway
Hillsdale, New Jersey 07642

Library of Congress Cataloging-in-Publication Data
The Symbolic and Connectionist Paradigms: Closing the Gap / John Dinsmore,
editor.
    p.   cm.
    Includes bibliographical references and index.
    ISBN 0-8058-1079-X. — ISBN 0-8058-1080-3 (pbk.)
    1. Cognition. 2. Connectionism. 3. Mental representation.
I. Dinsmore, John, 1949–
BF311.C543 1992
153—dc20   91-30328
                                                          CIP

Printed in the United States of America
10 9 8 7 6 5 4 3 2 1

Contents

Preface

The modern study of cognition finds itself with two widely endorsed but seemingly incongruous theoretical paradigms. The first of these, inspired by formal logic and the digital computer, sees reasoning in the principled manipulation of structured *symbolic* representations. The second, inspired by the physiology of the brain, sees reasoning as the behavior that emerges from the direct interactions found in large networks of simple processing components. Each paradigm has its own accomplishments, its own problems, its own methodology, its own proponents and its own agenda.

What should one make of the gap between these two paradigms? To some, there is no conflict: They simply study different things at different levels, as do physics and zoology. To others, connectionism is the "new improved" cognitive science to which symbolicism must ultimately give way. Still others take an intermediate position that the gap can be closed by unifying or compromising the paradigms in one way or another.

This book records the thoughts of a number of researchers, both in computer science and in philosophy, on resolving the debate between symbolicism and connectionism. It addresses theoretical and methodological issues throughout, but at the same time exhibits practicing cognitive scientists' current attempts to solve real problems.

The audience for the book will be the general cognitive science community, especially researchers and students in connectionism, and in more traditional symbolic models who want to understand better the relation of their work to connectionist research. For the most part the presentation is relatively informal and takes care to provide enough background material, both philosophical and technical, to potentially serve as supplementary reading for an advanced course in connectionism, artificial intelligence, cognitive psychology or philosophy of mind.

OVERVIEW

The symbolicism/connectionism debate has many aspects and has been conducted at many different levels, from the abstract (such as, how have other sciences resolved analogous debates?) to the concrete (such as, what kinds of applications can be achieved in each paradigm?). This book attempts to be comprehensive yet develop some specific positions on the gap between the paradigms. John Dinsmore, in the introductory chapter "Thunder in the Gap," presents an overview of the symbolicism/connectionism debate and how the remaining chapters fit into that debate. I review the state of the art in each paradigm, including practical successes and weakness. I then survey, and introduce, some arguments concerning the gap between the paradigms.

One of the most difficult issues in studies of cognition is how it is possible for formal structures manipulated by cognitive processes actually to be meaningful. Dave Chalmers, in "Connectionism and the Chinese Room," uses Searle's well-known *Chinese Room* argument against the possibility of a computational account of meaning to bring out some critical distinctions between symbolic and connectionist systems. He concludes that the Chinese Room argument carries much less weight when applied to connectionist systems because connectionism disassociates the level at which processing takes place from the level at which meanings are assumed to attach, and gives representations a much richer internal structure.

Symbolic theories have been strongly influenced by computational (computerlike) systems. Some of these systems, like LISP and production systems, are actually implemented to run on modern computers, others, like Turing machines, are mathematically defined. However, real cognition occurs in the brain, which has an architecture more closely modeled by connectionist systems. The following question naturally arises: Is there something fundamentally different about computational and connectionist architectures that underlies the gap between the symbolic and connectionist paradigms? Fred Adams, Kenneth Aizawa, and Gary Fuller, in "Rules in Programming Languages and Networks," point out that the processes that occur in computationalism are generally assumed, in contrast to connectionist architectures, to be discrete, explicit, exceptionless and sensitive to compositional structures. Focusing on the concept of *rule* in *Turing machines* and in connectionism, they argue that the differences in the architectures are not as great as generally thought, by pointing out computational models that lack these properties and connectionist models that have them.

Connectionist models are inspired by brain architecture, yet at the same time are developed with functional applications in mind. Kenneth Aizawa, in "Biology and Sufficiency in Connectionist Theory," examines the degree to which current connectionist theories are successful in being simultaneously *physiological plausible* and *psychologically complete*. He points out that connectionist models often involve mechanisms that do not seem to have neural counterparts, that certain processes and structures found in the brain are not found in neural models, and that physiological motivation might be discovered at other than the neural level. He then shows a number of examples in which current connectionist models rely crucially on implicit, unreduced *black box* mechanisms in order to realize the cognitive function for which they are intended. He suggests that a proper methodology for connectionism is to develop models with such mechanisms, but then to attempt to reduce them through connectionist implementation. He illustrates how an explicit connectionist recall module can be added to a Bolzmann machine memory module in order to reduce one of these black box mechanisms.

Much of the debate between symbolicism and connectionism recapitulates the debate between *functionalism* and *reductionism,* a debate that has relevance to many sciences. On the one hand, it is argued that one level of description is autonomous and irreducible to the level that implements it. On the other hand, it is argued that a higher level of description can be explained away by the lower level. Justin Schwartz, in "Who's Afraid of Multiple Realizability?: Functionalism, Reductionism, and Connectionism," shows that things are not so simple. He points out how Mendelian genetics is at least in part reducible to, or explained in terms of, the structure of DNA, yet is at the same time a viable functional level of description. If DNA were different, then Mendelian genetics could well be different. If this is true of genetics, why can't it be true of cognition? Functionalism, he argues, is independent of multiple realizability.

A common criticism of connectionist systems is that they deal poorly with the *compositionality* of representations. Quite a lot of research currently addresses this deficit. Douglas S. Blank, Lisa Meeden, and Jim Marshall, in "Exploring the Symbolic/Subsymbolic Continuum: A Case Study of RAAM," discuss a means of learning and retrieving high-level compositional structures in a specific connectionist architecture. Although their experiments deal with sequences of symbols, the architecture they discuss is capable in principle of storing trees of symbols of arbitrary size. Their system relies on a technique of inducing a network to create a compact *holistic* representation of a larger input pattern. They then demonstrate that several manipulations and tests that would seem to require access to the individual components of the encoded sequence can actually be done on the compact holistic encoding itself. This chapter is at the same time an answer to an important symbolic challenge and an attempt to unearth the unique properties of *subsymbolic* connectionist representations.

Nevertheless, the complexities of representations a cognitive system should support go far beyond the simple relations current connectionist models are trying to handle. John Barnden, in "Connectionism, Generalization, and Propositional Attitudes: A Catalogue of Challenging Issues," surveys a variety of outstanding problems in representation and inference that an adequate connectionist account of cognition should be required to solve. These problems include the following: the need for *explicit* representations of generalizations, alongside the implicit generalizations that connectionist networks acquire naturally; analogical matching of short-term information structures; the handling of propositions involving anomalous combinations of ideas; and the embedding of reasoning within belief contexts. This chapter has a special focus on the problems of representing and reasoning about propositional attitudes, a matter that has so far been largely neglected within connectionism. Barnden concludes that the prospective ability of certain types of connectionist model to deal with the problems is very mixed.

A well-known criticism of connectionism has been that it allegedly fails to account for the profound *systematicity* of cognitive processes. Chan-Do Lee and Michael Gasser, in "Where Do Underlying Representations Come From?: A Connectionist Approach to the Acquisition of Phonological Rules," focus on natural language phonology with this criticism in mind. In traditional symbolic accounts the acquisition of underlying representations has been difficult to account for, and has in part motivated the idea of innate predispositions to certain linguistic structures. The existence of underlying representations that can be manipulated by rules had also been used to argue against the adequacy of connectionist systems specifically in providing an adequate account of phonology. Lee and Gasser show how *rules* and *underlying representations* as used in *symbolic* accounts of phonology arise in a natural way from a general underlying *connectionist* architecture in the process of generalizing over a set of training instances that exhibit the alternation between English plural and singular noun forms.

A common criticism of *symbolic* systems, on the other hand, is their relative brittleness when presented with unexpected or faulty input. For instance, much natural language input is in fact ungrammatical, but parsers, to the extent they account for such input at all, have traditionally relied on special mechanisms that specifically anticipate what types of mistakes are likely to occur. Stan Kwasny and Kaanan Faisal, in "Symbolic Parsing via Subsymbolic Rules," discuss a *hybrid* implementation of a *deterministic parser* for natural language, roughly of a kind previously described as a symbolic model. The symbolic components manage a lookahead buffer and apply rules that modify the contents of the buffer. The connectionist component decides which rules to apply on a best-match basis. In exploiting the natural best-match and generalization properties of connectionist networks, the system degrades gracefully in response to ungrammatical or unanticipated input without any special mechanisms.

In fact hybrid models that combine symbolic and connectionist components are increasing in popularity. Trent Lange, in "Hybrid Connectionist Models: Temporary Bridges Over the Gap Between the Symbolic and the Subsymbolic," justifies and illustrates the development of such hybrid models. For him hybrid models are temporary means of building prototypes or models until we understand better how to deal with a problem at the connectionist level. The goal of reducing to a more uniform connectionist system is for him the ideal. He illustrates this methodology in ROBIN, a hybrid system that combines distributed and localist connectionist components but succeeds in implementing some higher-level features, such as the ability to bind variables, and in SAARCS, a system that adds a symbolic marker-passing component to ROBIN.

ACKNOWLEDGMENTS

I would like, on behalf of all of the contributors, to thank all those who made this book possible. Many of the chapters that appear here are based on papers presented at the *Second Midwest Artificial Intelligence and Cognitive Science Conference* at the Touch of Nature Environmental Center in Southern Illinois in the Spring of 1990. This conference was organized by Tim Koschmann, Marie Malinauskas, and myself. The variety of perspectives on symbolic and connectionist processing expressed in presentations at the MAICSS conference, along with a general suggestion of Rob Jensen, helped inspire the concept of a book integrating such varying and interdisciplinary perspectives into a coherent and comprehensive discussion of the symbolicism/connectionism debate. Many of the authors also got together a year later and a few days before this writing at the *Third MAICSS Conference* to present and hash out much of this material in a special session.

The chapters were reviewed for the most part rather extensively by other contributors. I thank Ken Aizawa, John Barnden, Dave Chalmers, Lisa Meeden, Doug Blank, James Marshall, Stan Kwasny, Trent Lange, Chan-Do Lee, Fred Adams, Gary Fuller; and noncontributors Tim van Gelder and Chris Moehle for their help in this process.

The proposal for this book was reviewed and accepted by Don Norman and Andrew Ortony in consultation with people at Lawrence Erlbaum Associates. Judi Amsel of Lawrence Erlbaum Associates was very helpful in the editorial process and in handling the business end of the project, as was Kathleen Dolan.

I would personally like to thank all of the contributors themselves. The enthusiasm and enormous talent that they—many of them still very young researchers—have demonstrated have made this project rewarding to me far beyond my initial expectations.

—John Dinsmore

1 Thunder in the Gap

John Dinsmore
Washington University

This is the unfolding story of *symbolicism* and *connectionism,* the argumentative paradigms who inhabit the modern study of cognition, and of the gap that stands between them. The purpose of this initial chapter is to provide a general overview of the debate between the paradigms, and to show where each of the remaining chapters slices through this debate. It also provides the introductory background, both technical and philosophical, necessary for the comprehension of the remaining chapters. I begin by looking at symbolicism and connectionism independently, what each is and what each has accomplished or failed to accomplish. Then I look at ways in which the gap between them might be handled.

1. THE SYMBOLIC PARADIGM

Symbolic theories are *representation-oriented* in the sense that each begins by positing basic syntactic structures assumed to possess a transparent compositional semantics. Momentarily, we see that connectionist models, in contrast, are process-oriented. The greatest problems for symbolic theories begin in looking for the kinds of *processes* needed to produce the properties observed in human cognition.

In this section I try to characterize symbolicism a little more accurately, and give a general assessment of the many strengths but especially of the apparent limitations found in current work within the symbolic paradigm.

1.1. Symbolic Mechanisms

The central principles that characterize traditional work in the symbolic paradigm can be summarized as follows:

- there are such things as *symbols,* which can be combined into larger *symbolic structures* (or *expressions*),
- these symbolic structures have a *combinatorial semantics* whereby what a symbolic structure represents is a function of what the parts represent, and
- at the same time all cognitive *processes* (reasoning) are manipulations of these symbolic structures.

This position is represented by Fodor and Pylyshyn (1988)—one of the most cited references in this book—Pylyshyn (1984), and Newell and Simon (1976; Newell, 1982). The latter incorporate this position as the central idea of what they called the *physical symbol system hypothesis.*

Other properties have often been attributed to symbolic systems, but either do not adhere very firmly on closer inspection, or do not turn out to be of critical importance in the debate between the paradigms. Most of these involve the thesis that the symbolic paradigm is *computationalist,* that is, that it takes the *computer metaphor* very seriously in talking about human cognition. Newell and Simon in fact borrowed specific assumptions related to modern digital computers, such as *universality* (the ability to stimulate any other system), *discreteness,* and the ability to execute *programs.* But as Derthick (1990) pointed out, these assumptions seem to go by the wayside in Fodor and Pylyshyn's well-known arguments against the viability of a connectionist cognitive science. Another feature sometimes attributed to the symbolic paradigm is the assumption of *seriality,* but there are simply too many exceptions in modern artificial intelligence, such as *marker-passing systems* discussed later, to take this attribute seriously, and the advent of massive parallelism in computer architecture no longer supports seriality as characteristic of computers in any case. Nevertheless, I return later to the issue of whether the abstract concept of *computation* offers a principled distinction between the paradigms.

1.2. Examples of Symbolic Models

The principles listed earlier are central in the sense that symbolic theories tend to conform these principles, but, as becomes evident, systems often deviate from them in restricted ways. I look at a couple of kinds of symbolic models that come up most often in discussing contrasts between the paradigms.

1.2.1. Logic and Rule-based Systems.   Perhaps the prototype of symbolic models is the *logic-based system,* especially common in artificial intelligence, whereby a proposition is expressed discretely by a predicate (a symbol for a relation) and a linear sequence of arguments (each a symbol for an object). Inference procedures define manipulations of those structures, generally in a manner that preserves meanings or truth conditions. For example, such a procedure would allow the presence of the following expressions,

bird(Tweety)
bird(X) → feathered (X)

to result in the derivation of the following expression.

feathered (Tweety)

Alongside logic-based systems are *rule-based* or *production* systems, common in psychology and linguistics as well as artificial intelligence. These systems interpret *rules* (each of which has a *condition* that potentially matches some symbolic structure and an *action* that specifies some symbolic manipulations) by repeatedly selecting a rule (generally one of many) whose condition is satisfied and then executing the action. For instance, the following rule might cause the inference discussed earlier to be derived.

condition: bird(X)
action: add feathered (X)

1.2.2. Associative Networks.   Also known as *semantic networks,* these were introduced in psychology (Quillian, 1968) to model *associative memory.* We observe associative memory when the sound of a voice causes us to think about the person belonging to the voice. An associative network represents the concepts in an encyclopedic way, as a set of nodes interconnected with links labeled for the relations holding between concepts. The original semantic network models attributed to particular symbolic nodes *activations* that increased when a node was processed, but automatically *spread* to connected nodes. For instance, the kind of *semantic priming* that occurs in a sentence like *The astronomer married a star,* whereby the interpretation of *star* as a celestial object, strongly suggested by *astronomer,* confuses the interpretation, can be modeled in an associative network by activation spreading from the node for astronomer.

In many associative network models the passing of discrete symbolic *markers* in a much more controlled manner replaces spreading activation (see Lange, chap. 10 in this volume). Marker passing, however, is capable of achieving many specific inferences through graph-traversal instead of by rule application. The links serve as an indexing mechanism to facilitate matching one structure against another and finding intersections of sets or concepts.

Associative networks are of interest in the symbolicism/connectionism debate because they are perhaps the most connectionist of the symbolic models. In fact, although work in associative networks is generally assumed to belong firmly in the symbolic tradition, we doubtlessly find some stretching of some of the central premises of the symbolic paradigm in this framework: In associative networks manipulations are sensitive to current activation levels (or the presence of certain markers) yet these do not contribute to semantics. Thus processing in associative networks is not defined in terms of strictly symbolic structures. Lange (chap. 10 in this volume) and some others like to classify these as connectionist in a very broad sense to underscore these similarities while at the same time recognizing that they are at the same time fundamentally symbolic.

1.3. Representations in Symbolic Systems

Philosophers, linguists, psychologists, researchers in artificial intelligence, and many others have been comfortable with the languagelike expressive abilities provided in the symbolic paradigm, the clarity with which the symbolic paradigm treats reasoning in science or other conscious domains and its natural affinity for dealing with concepts at a level subject to conscious introspection. Almost all of the practical successes in artificial intelligence in implementing higher-level abilities in such domains as expert systems, language understanding, machine translation, goal-oriented planning, and mathematical reasoning, have relied on symbolicism.

The symbolic paradigm is in effect designed around its support for representation, and it is therefore hardly surprising that this is where its strengths lie. Fodor and Pylyshyn (1988) saw this strength in *systematicity* and *productivity* of cognitive representations, which arise from the way the compositionality of symbolic expressions allows for the decomposition and recomposition of representations. Barnden (chap. 7 in this volume) contrasts these representational advantages with those of connectionist representations.

1.4. Learning

What has been simple for symbolic systems is simply acquiring information already encoded in some propositional language, that is, *learning by being told*. However symbolic models are very poor at adapting or organizing themselves dynamically on the basis of experience. Although a lot of attention has been given within artificial intelligence to symbolic learning algorithms (Michalski, Carbonell, & Mitchell, 1983, 1986), each of these generally works in some specialized domain and does not reorganize the system in any profound way. The lack of generality in learning means that computational symbolic models are invariably *hand-coded* with a particular algorithm in mind. This contrasts very markedly with connectionist systems for which very general and powerful learning techniques exist, which make it unnecessary to explicitly program the networks for specific behaviors.

1.5. Mysterious Processes

There appear to be many cognitive processes that do involve symbolic manipulations, in the sense of mapping one symbolic structure, A, into another, B, but nevertheless resist symbolic analysis, in the sense of an explicit specification of what the relation of A to B must be strictly in boolean terms of the symbolic structures involved. Dinsmore (1991) called symbolic processes with this property *mysterious*. Let's look at a few processes that appear to be mysterious, given symbolic experience, at this time.

1.5.1. Holistic Processes.   As an example, face recognition might be seen abstractly as a mapping that takes a set of symbolic structures representing facial features, and returns a symbol representing some individual. Now, humans can recognize the same face in a variety of contexts, from different angles, under different illuminations, with parts obscured by shadows or other objects, and so on. No known boolean combination of features determines this mapping, yet a given face is recognized fairly reliably. Dreyfus and Dreyfus (1986) described such processes as *holistic,* resisting the explicit decomposition of objects into component features.

1.5.2. Noise and Unexpected Input.   Symbolic models are notoriously brittle when presented with unusual, unplanned, faulty, or noisy input. Even where the symbolic mapping is analyzable under ideal noise-free conditions, noise introduces a degree of complexity into the mapping that humans, but not symbolic models, are typically capable of overcoming.

Kwasny and Faisal (chap. 9 in this volume) discuss some examples in the context of parsing natural language. Symbolic parsers generally cannot successfully parse ungrammatical sentences like *John did hitting Jack,* even though they are close to grammatical sentences and can be processed by humans. The symbolic parsers that can handle such sentences do so by explicitly anticipating such anomalies, in effect making the grammar accepted by the parser more general to accommodate them. There is a problem because there are always new instances that will not be anticipated, so that the process involved must either become enormously complex or remain inadequate. Kwansy and Faisal in fact handle such cases by building in a connectionist component to account for the mysterious mapping.

1.5.3. Associative Memory.   Associations between concepts have proven particularly resistant to symbolic analysis. Such associations should allow the retrieval of a complete memory given a partial description of the content of the memory, such as *high-ranking government official who is not too bright.* Examples from natural language processing are semantic priming (discussed earlier), *metonymy* (the reference to one object or concept by means of an expression that stands for an associated object or concept) and the resolution of anaphoric, for example, pronominal, reference.

1.5.4. The Problem of Mysterious Processes for Symbolism.   In summary, mysterious processes can be seen to map symbolic representations to others as required in the symbolic paradigm, but the symbolic vocabulary often does not seem to allow us to fully analyze the mapping, not to the degree that we can predict which representations will get mapped onto which, or such that we could develop a purely symbolic artificially intelligent program that achieves behavior that depends on mysterious processes. It follows that there can never be a complete, strictly symbolic theory of cognition. Work in connectionism, to which we now turn, suggests that dropping down to a lower, *subsymbolic,* level allows mysterious processes to be analyzed more successfully in terms of a nonsymbolic vocabulary.

2. THE CONNECTIONIST PARADIGM

The connectionist paradigm is, in marked contrast to the symbolic paradigm, *process-oriented.* That is, it starts with the assumption that the basic objects posited in a theory of cognition will be processed in a simple and usually uniform way. Unfortunately, this orientation then leaves connectionist models with the rather daunting task of discovering how representations emerge from the simple processing components.

This section provides a brief description of connectionism and lists some of its accomplishments and problems. Keep in mind that not as much work has been done to date in connectionist theories as in symbolic theories. It is hardly surprising, therefore, that (a) connectionism has logged fewer substantial achievements than symbolicism, (b) fewer clear weaknesses in the connectionist paradigm have been demonstrated, and (c) researchers in connectionism tend to have very high expectations of future success.

2.1. Connectionism in a Nutshell

A connectionist system is a network of very simple processing *units* that stores knowledge in the *weights* of the *connections* between units and realizes computation in the dynamic global behavior that results from the local interactions among units. The following few pages give a basic introduction to the fundamentals of connectionism equivalent to a one-semester university course, and in particular introduces some of the terminology used in the other chapters of this book. The uninitiated will have to hold onto their hats, but in principle should come out with enough background to appreciate the rest of the book.

2.1.1. Units and Connections.   A *connectionist* model consists of a set of *units* linked together in a network by a set of *connections.* Units and connections are neurologically inspired by neurons and synapses respectively. At a given time each unit has an *activation* level and produces an *output,* which affects other units through connections to those units.

Typically certain units are assumed to communicate with the outside world. *Input units* are often *clamped* onto certain activation values (as if due to some environmental influence, much like receptors in the retina of the eye react to impinging light). *Output units* are monitored for their output values (as if producing effects in the outside world). Figure 1.1 illustrates the functioning of an intermediate unit.

The specific behavior of a unit varies from one connectionist model to another. Activations and outputs are either continuous or discrete scalar values. The output of one unit can affect the activation level of another unit if there is a connection between the two units. A connection has a *weight*, which determines the extent to which the output of one unit can affect the activation of the other unit. A weight typically assumes a continuous value in a scale between $+1.0$ and -1.0. A high positive weight and a high output from the source unit will tend to raise the activation level of the destination unit. A negative weight and a high output from the source unit will tend to diminish the activation level of the destination unit. Positively weighted connections are said to be *exitatory*, whereas negatively weighted connections are said to be *inhibitory*. The activation of a unit typically changes very rapidly, but weights on connections typically change very slowly over time as part of *learning,* described later.

A unit adjusts its own activation level in response to the input it receives from other units through incoming connections. How a unit does this is described by an *activation function*. Almost always the input to a unit is determined by a *sigma-pi* computation, that is, by summing up individual incoming signals, each of which is the output produced by the unit on the other side of a connection scaled down by the weight of the incoming connection. Activation functions vary from one connectionist model to another. Very often a *sigmoid* function is used to squish the activation down to fit in a range from 0 to 1. Often the activation function will take the previous activation of the unit into account such that, for instance, if the input signal drops the activation of the unit will only gradually *decay*. Often some kind of *bias* is added in to influence the value of the activation function.

A unit produces an *output level,* which is what other units see, as a function of the activation level. Again output functions vary from one connectionist model to another. Very often the output is simply identified with the activation level. Very often the output will be a discrete value, 0 or 1, while the activation will have a continuous value. Often the output is 0 until the activation level crosses some *threshold* value.

Often the output is a nondeterministic *stochastic* function of the activation value, such that even with a fixed activation level the output will toggle between 0 and 1 with a higher activation level making it more likely that at a given time the output will be 1 rather than 0. The analogy is drawn between these last models and the statistical behavior of *thermodynamic* systems. One such connec-

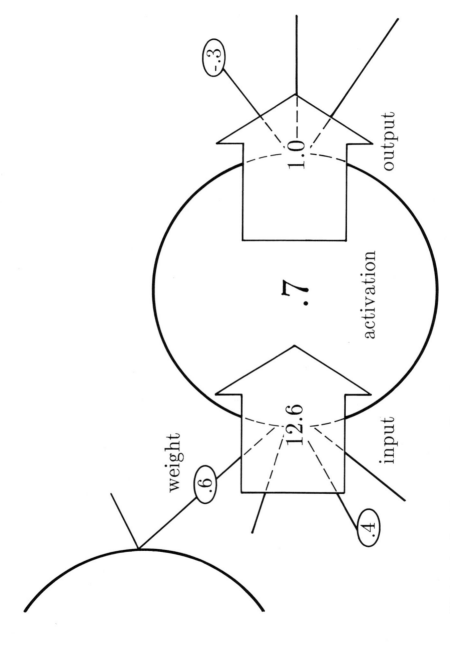

FIG. 1.1. A unit and its connections illustrating summation of input, adjustment of activation, and production of output.

tionist system is called the *Bolzman machine.* Often the stochastic function is varied so that it becomes increasingly deterministic as the global computation proceeds, much as a drop in temperature makes a thermodynamic system more predictable. The use of stochastic output functions with the element of decreasing temperature built in is referred to as *simulated annealing.*

    2.1.2. Configurations of Units and Connections. The computational properties of a connectionist network result not only from the particular activation and output functions used, but also—not surprisingly—of the way the units and connections are interconnected. Figure 1.2 illustrates a very common connectionist architecture, a *feed-forward network,* in which units are grouped into *layers,* with a connection running from each unit in one layer to each unit in the layer above. If the units in the input layer of Fig. 1.2 are clamped onto certain activation levels, activation changes will propagate upward through the hidden layers and the units in the output layer will converge on certain activation values. Effectively, some pattern of activation on the input will be mapped onto some pattern of activation on the output, with the mapping dependent on the connection weights and the particular activation and output functions used in the system. This configuration is thus being used as a *pattern associator.* A pattern

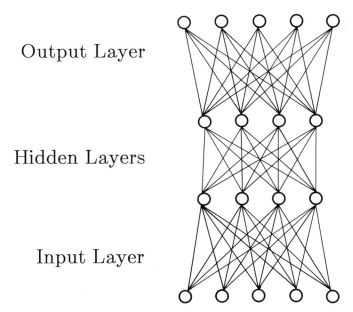

    FIG. 1.2. A simple feedforward network in which activation flows from the input layer and through hidden layers to produce a pattern of activation on the output layer.

associator that maps a pattern of activation on the input layer onto the same pattern on the output layer is an *autoassociator*. Autoassociators are interesting for reasons discussed later. The mappings can also be very complex. This can be appreciated intuitively if one thinks of each unit on the first hidden layer as serving to measure how closely some possible pattern on the input layer (which pattern depends on the weights of the incoming connections) is realized, each unit on the second hidden layer as serving to measure how well some possible pattern on the first hidden layer is realized and so on.

Many alternative configurations can be regarded as variations of that of Fig. 1.2. A common kind of variation forces a layer or some subset of units in a layer (sometimes called a *clique*) to assume a pattern of activation in which a *single* unit is *on* or highly activated and the remaining units are *off* or minimally activated. This effect can be produced by interconnecting the units within the clique by *inhibitory* connections, producing competition among units as the more highly activated units try to turn off the less activated, as well as each other. Such a subnetwork is a *winner-take-all* network. This is used in the McClelland and Rumelhart model of letter perception discussed by Adams, Aizawa, and Fuller (chap. 3 in this volume) and by Aizawa (chap. 4 in this volume). Another variation is the *simple recurrent network* discussed by Lee and Gasser (chap. 8 in this volume) and Blank, Meeden, and Marshall (chap. 6 in this volume), which makes use of connections from a hidden layer down to a clique in a lower layer to make the behavior of the network effectively dependent on the previous states of the network.

2.1.3. Learning. A real strength of connectionist networks is their ability to adaptively organize themselves to acquire appropriate behavior. A connectionist network can learn from experience through procedures that adjust weights gradually in the direction of more appropriate responses to environmental input. The most common learning method in layered networks like that illustrated in Fig. 1.2 is *backpropagation*. Backpropagation is a *supervised* technique that requires the presentation of a series of training exemplars, each of which represents an input pattern and a target output pattern. The backpropagation algorithm begins by comparing the output pattern actually produced with the target output pattern and propagates a series of error-correcting weight changes backward level by level from the output units to the input units. The connection weight changes are gradual so that the network can adapt simultaneously to a large number of training exemplars to produce the desired mapping with a low error rate.

2.1.4. Semantics. Connectionist networks are useful for low-level pattern recognition tasks, for instance those that might well fall within a housefly's capabilities as well as within a human's. Nevertheless, as Fodor and Pylyshyn (1988) pointed out, virtually all connectionists agree with symbolicists that postulating complex representational states is essential to a theory of cognition. Some connectionist models, called *localist,* assume that individual units stand for individual objects or concepts. For instance, one unit might represent your dog Fido, another your grandmother's rocking chair.

Other models, called *distributed,* make the more intriguing assumption that objects and concepts are represented as patterns of activity over many units, with each unit participating in many patterns. Distributed models exhibit many distinctive properties, to be described presently, whereas localist models tend to be more akin to symbolic models. Lange (chap. 10 in this volume) contrasts the differences between localist and distributed connectionist models in more detail.

For the most part the chapters in this book focus on distributed connectionist models. Processing in all connectionist models is realized only in direct, interactions among individual units, so under the assumption of distributed representations the level at which processing is described (individual units) is lower than the level at which representations are described (patterns of activation over many units). Distributed connectionist models are therefore said to make use of *subsymbolic* processing.

A very interesting aspect of distributed representations is that the acquisition of new representations seems to follow from general learning techniques like backpropagation. However, with localist models, or for that matter symbolic models, there is no obvious account of how the decision is made that some given node is now going to stand for your grandmother's rocking chair. Experiments with backpropagation in autoassociative networks (a specific kind of pattern associator defined earlier) reveal the ability of a network to acquire new distributed representations of locally encoded concepts. The idea is to train the network on the identity mapping, but set up the network so that the hidden levels have fewer units than the input and output layers. Each pattern of activation that appears on a hidden level can be viewed as representing the same thing as the autoassociated pattern—but more compactly—but is in effect invented by the network itself. This technique is exploited by Blank, Meeden, and Marshall (chap. 6 in this volume).

2.2.   Does Connectionism Take the Brain Seriously?

Much of the appeal of connectionism is doubtlessly its basis in brain architecture, which potentially gives it more of a hard science flavor. On the other hand, this basis tends to be quite tenuous. As Aizawa (chap. 4 in this volume) discusses, many connectionist mechanisms have no known neural counterparts. For instance, backpropagation, as its name suggests, requires the propagation of a signal backward along connections in a manner that is not generally observed physically. Also, less frequently observed, many neural mechanisms have no counterparts in connectionist models, for the most part because they are poorly understood. For instance, little in existing connectionist models correspond to hormonal and other chemical mechanisms, or to large-scale anatomical structures observed in the brain.

2.3. Limitations of Connectionist Learning

Although the availability of generalized learning techniques is one of the great achievements of connectionist research, these techniques have critical limitations. First, learning is generally achieved by providing highly reliable training instances in a very systematic way, normally iterating over all desirable input–output correspondences a number of times. The quality and systematicity of training by a more realistic, random sampling of the environment would fall far short of that achieved artificially. Aizawa (chap. 4 in this volume) discusses the problem of the absence of external sources of supervision.

Second, learning is generally achieved only after hundreds of thousands of training instances. The slow speeds of human neural architecture, in contrast to that of the computers on which simulations are run, make so many iterations infeasible.

Third, these techniques may have difficulty in scaling up tractably from the relatively small networks and relatively simple problems for which they have been tested. This is not only because the time required to train a network could well explode exponentially with an increase in the size of the network, but also because the learning algorithms for connectionist networks are in essence *hill-climbing* techniques, which have been shown in artificial intelligence to be of limited usefulness for problems of significant complexity (Minsky & Papert, 1988, epilogue).

But aside from the slow rate and lack of reliability of connectionism's standard learning techniques, the most pervasive and successful kind of learning in symbolic models is virtually unknown in connectionist models, that is, learning *by being told.* No mechanisms have been proposed for connectionist systems to account for the extremely rapid acquisition by humans of very complex information, found, for instance, in the interpretation of conscious rules, like *put the green ones over here and the red ones over there,* that begin to affect behavior immediately after acquisition.

2.4. Representing Things in Connectionist Models

Connectionism is often criticized for not being able to deal naturally with compositional representation structures (Fodor & Pylyshyn, 1988), or for simply providing *implementations* of structures properly described at the symbolic level without adding anything to symbolic descriptions. Representing things adequately is a one of the fundamental challenges to connectionism.

2.4.1.   Simple Compositional Structures.   Over the last decade quite a bit of progress has been made in representing simple relations like *Bif sees Matilda* in distributed connectionist networks. In symbolic theories this is easy: simply *concatenate* symbols. In connectionism it was not initially clear how this would be done: *Bif* might be represented by a pattern of activation, as might *Matilda* and the concept of seeing, but what would represent the whole thing?

Blank, Meeden, and Marshall (chap. 6 in this volume) present one very general approach to this that allows for the representation of arbitrary sequences of representations. This approach makes use of a technique of compressing a concatenative structure into a smaller hidden layer by training for autoassociation. The representation on the hidden layer can be used as one of the concatenated elements on the input layer in producing a compressed representation for a yet larger structure. The compressed representation is created by the system itself, through backpropagation, and does not have any transparent internal structure, yet can be easily translated into a concatentative structure, thus demonstrating that the original content is faithfully preserved. Blank, Meeden, and Marshall show additionally how many of the processing advantages of general connectionist models over symbolic models are preserved in their model.

Similarly, Lee and Gasser (chap. 8 in this volume) make use of the framework of a *simple recurrent network* in representing the sequences of phonemes that represent words in their system for learning the past tense. Simple recurrent networks represent concatenative structures as temporally ordered activation patterns.

2.4.2.   Rules.   We have seen that many symbolic systems are based on rules that match symbolic structures and typically produce new symbolic structures. By training a pattern associator like that in Fig. 1.2 the network can do a fairly good job, by simple cumulative connection weight adjustments, at picking up the generalizations expressed by a set of symbolic rules. Although it has behavioral properties like rules, the representation itself is implicit because in the connectionist model individual rules cannot be recognized (Rumelhart & McClelland, 1986). Lee and Gasser (chap. 8 in this volume) give a very good discussion of the acquisition of such rulelike behavior in natural language phonology.

Pinker and Prince (1988) pointed out that symbolic linguistic models not only depend on rules, but on ordering of rules and on the existence of hidden *underlying representations* on which these rules operate. For instance, the English past tense is expressed in a number of ways, each of them derived by the application of some rule to a common underlying form. Lee and Gasser (chap. 8 in this volume) show how an appropriately trained network might even create its own underlying representations as patterns on hidden units as it learns the implicit rules that manipulate those representations.

Barnden (chap. 7 in this volume), on the other hand, shows why explicit rules like those in symbolic models are needed in addition to the implicit rules realized by pattern association. For instance, he points out that a network might represent the sentence, *Most communists in town are atheists,* implicitly as a pattern associator that when presented with a pattern representing a *communist* (*in town*) on its input layer would produce a pattern representing *atheist* on its output layer. However, it is difficult to see how such an associator would be used in building a higher-level representation for *If most communists in town are atheists then the town is eligible for a grant from the Fundie Fund.*

2.4.3. Complex Relations/Propositional Attitudes. Then there are higher-order representations. For instance, given a complex distributed representation for *John loves Mary,* how does the connectionist network represent that the agent *knows* that John loves Mary? Barnden (chap. 7 in this volume) discusses the multitudinous problems that arise in connectionist attempts to represent individuals' beliefs. These problems, as the reader will see, are far greater than that of representing simple relations, which connectionism is just beginning to get a handle on.

2.5. Observations About Connectionist Semantics

One of the remarkable capabilities of distributed connectionist systems is the automatic creation of new representations. New representations in a symbolic system are just assumed when needed (for instance, by a call to *gensym*), leaving the question open of how the system fixes the referent of the symbol. The creation of representations is illustrated by the technique of inducing the system to create a more compact representation on the hidden layer through autoassociation previously described. Such representations tend to develop what Blank, Meeden, and Marshall (chap. 6 in this volume) call a *microsemantics* whereby representations that are learned in the same kinds of contexts tend to be similar activation patterns. Chalmers (chap. 2 in this volume) argues that this does a far better job at fixing referents than is found in symbolic models.

Also, because connectionism typically makes a clear break between processing and semantics, connectionist models are in principle immune to many of the criticisms already raised to symbolic models. First, although certain patterns of activation may denote things out there in the world, there is no requirement that all patterns of activation do this. Thus, processes without semantic counterparts, as found, for instance, in making aesthetic judgments, are entirely consistent with the connectionist paradigm (this is not to say that anyone has any specific idea at this time of how these would occur in a connectionist network).

2.6. Mysterious Processes from a Connectionist Point of View

We have seen how connectionist systems are able to organize themselves, developing their own distributed representations. This results in some remarkable properties, which are especially apparent when we look at processes that are mysterious from a symbolic point of view. These processes seem to emerge naturally as consequences of the connectionist architecture.

Connectionist models are very good at *generalizing* information. For instance, Lee and Gasser's (chap. 8 in this volume) system is trained to produce past-tense forms of a set of verbs. When presented with verb roots it has not been trained on, it will generally produce the correct form of the past tense; it has made generalizations equivalent, roughly, to linguistic rules of phonology. Representations created in similar contexts will also tend to be realized as similar patterns of activation. As a result, connectionist systems seem to naturally *classify* concepts. Blank, Meeden, and Marshall show how their system develops classifications like *aggressive animal* based on the sentences in which such concepts are mentioned.

Connectionist models have been especially successful in finding a *best match* when a number of competing interpretations are available. Kwasny and Faisal (chap. 9 in this volume) describe a hybrid (with symbolic and connectionist components) system that overcomes the brittleness normally associated with rule selection in symbolic systems by handling this decision in a connectionist component. In the presence of ungrammatical natural language input the system naturally selects the rule that matches best. In general, this illustrates the ability of connectionist systems to reach interpretations fairly reliably in spite of *noise* in the input.

Likewise, the most common mechanisms in symbolic models to access memories rely on knowing where to look for specific information. How to find a complete memory given a partial description of its content has been a problem. However, such retrieval occurs naturally in connectionist models. For instance Rumelhart, Smolensky, McClelland, and Hinton (1986) developed a model that learns generalizations about the objects that occur in different kinds of rooms. Given an input representing, for instance, a toaster and a sink, the network naturally completes the representation by filling in a refrigerator, an oven, and so on.

Another kind of task that connectionism seems to handle effortlessly is that of satisfaction of multiple simultaneous *soft constraints* as an interactive process that finds a compromise (Adams, Aizawa, & Fuller, chap. 3 in this volume). Rumelhart, Smolensky, McClelland and Hinton (1986) demonstrated how the system described in the previous paragraph naturally makes compromises among conflicting schemas for types of rooms when given an input representation, for instance, for a room with a bathtub and a toaster.

Connectionist networks tend to be relatively good at handling what are arguably holistic processes, such as recognizing faces. In fact, Blank, Meeden, and Marshall's (chap. 6 in this volume) show how a connectionist system actually develops holistic compositional representations. Fodor and Pylyshyn (1988) argued that compositional representations must be *concatenative,* that is, decomposable into parts such that structure-sensitive processes can manipulate the representation. Blank, Meeden, and Marshall's model for learning short sentences, on the other hand, actually translates a concatenative representation into a holistic encoding, in which subrepresentations cannot be individually isolated. This result is particularly interesting because they show that what in symbolic terms would be structure-sensitive processes can operate on the holistic representations themselves. First, the holistic representation can be translated back into a concatenative representation. Second, pattern associators can be trained that can determine from the holistic whether, for instance, an aggressive animal is mentioned in the original sentence. Third, syntactic transformations such as passivization can be performed directly over the holistic encodings.

2.7. High-Level Processing

There are a lot of high-level symbolic processes, and some not so high-level, that are not matched in existing connectionist systems. For instance, it is hard to get multiple instantiations of a generic representation in connectionist models and we don't know how to set up or forget complex associations between generalizations and specific instances quickly as is done through role and variable binding in symbolic models.

Especially focusing on propositional attitudes, Barnden (chap. 7 in this volume) offers an extended discussion of the kinds of problems that occur in high-level reasoning tasks that are particularly challenging to connectionism. Among these are the need to match different short-term information structures, the need to deal with anomalous combinations of concepts, and the need to perform embedded reasoning, for instance to reason about a particular person's beliefs.

More generally, full cognitive systems are complex. It has been very difficult for connectionist systems to move beyond modeling one component of a cognitive system. McCarthy (1988) called this deficient property *elaboration tolerance*. This is certainly largely a result of the fact that a pattern of activity created through weight adjustments by one connectionist network will generally not be interpretable by another.

Aizawa (chap. 4 in this volume) discusses the reliance of current connectionist models on outside intervention, and investigates the viability of adding additional connectionist modules to systems to make them more complete. For instance, the Bolzman machine's knowledge of the world is reflected in the relative frequency in which patterns of activation occur. However there is no immediate way to use knowledge in other processes, for instance in reporting beliefs. He proposes a special *recall module* that is able to summarize relative frequencies in order to proceed with such processes. But Aizawa worries that such a module would be entirely ad hoc, designed to acquire behaviors that do not emerge naturally from the underlying connectionist architecture.

2.8. Summary

There are some very basic differences between symbolic and connectionist systems, in the level at which processing is described, in the nature of representation, and so on. The capabilities of the systems seem to be quite different, in pattern matching, in holistic processing, in high-level compositional representation. What should we make of these differences?

3. THE GAP

Pinker and Prince (1988) discussed three different philosophies about the relationship of connectionism to symbolicism: *Implementational connectionism* describes the philosophy that connectionist networks simply provide an alternative means of implementing understood symbolic structures and processes. *Eliminative connectionism* describes the opposing, more radical, position that the symbolic level is not necessary at all to a complete description of cognition. Finally, *revisionist connectionism* describes a more subtle, intermediate position whereby connectionism will lead to different sets of symbols and operations and to new discoveries about the nature of symbolic processing, even while the levels remain distinct. I organize the discussion approximately around the first two possible positions and a generalization of the third.

3.1. Eliminativism

Eliminativism sees connectionism as the wave of the future, destined to sweep away symbolicism. Presumably no one seriously wants to eliminate connectionism itself (however much one may criticize the current direction of connectionist research, one must accept that the brain is a connectionist system of some sort and worth studying as such). The alternative to eliminativism would be a view in which the symbolic and the connectionist coexist, but at different *levels*. Let's look briefly at the case for and against eliminationism.

3.1.1. Profound Computational Differences?   A potential argument for eliminativism is that the symbolic paradigm is inextricably linked to computationalism and computationalism is capable in principle of only an inadequate account of cognition, that is, that the computer metaphor must fail. Chalmers (chap. 2 in this volume) answers this by pointing out that connectionist networks can be simulated by computational devices and computational devices can be simulated by connectionist networks and therefore cannot be distinguished as computational versus noncomputational. Adams, Aizawa, and Fuller (chap. 3 in this volume) attack this question without recourse to the simulation argument by comparing connectionist architectures with the most general computational architecture, the Turing machine, and reasonable extensions thereof, with respect to a number of alleged differences such as explicitness, discreteness, distributed representations, and structure-sensitivity. They discover that these are not criterial in distinguishing symbolic models from connectionist models.

One of the most outspoken critics of computationalism is Searle, whose

Chinese Room argument hinges on showing that "syntax is not sufficient for semantics." Chalmers (chap. 2 in this volume) argues that his criticisms actually only apply to symbolic theories, in which semantics is defined for the same level at which syntactic manipulations take place. While not endorsing Searle's arguments in their entirety, Chalmers points out that they fail in distributed connectionist models in which representations have a rich internal (subsymbolic) structure. The fundamental differences between symbolicism and connectionism is for Chalmers in the level at which semantics attaches.

3.1.2. Connectionism Needs Symbolicism. Clearly, connectionist networks with significant cognitive abilities will have to be far more complex then the simple computational models that now exist. But as models become more complex, they will become more opaque (recall also that connectionist networks are for the most part trained, not programmed). For this reason connectionist models cannot dispense with higher-level functional abstractions that summarize large parts of the network structure or behavior. Dyer (1988) imagined running a large connectionist network for 20 years and sending it to college and pointed out that there would be no way to understand what had been produced, even though the network might exhibit intelligent behavior.

Lachter and Bever (1988) suggested that symbolic principles are actually often snuck into the design of a connectionist network to achieve higher-level behavior. For instance, a certain model of speech production crucially arrays nodes at different levels of lexical and phonological representation. However, these levels are those originally posited in symbolic models as representations over which rules can operate. Pinker and Prince (1988) similarly argued that rulelike behavior is often achieved by putting a system into an unrealistic teaching environment tailored to result in behavior they wanted to see in order to make up for lack of explicit macrorganization. In short, the contribution of symbolic theories is not always properly acknowledged.

The recognition of higher-level structures is in no way inconsistent with the thesis that cognition emerges from connectionist principles. But like many kinds of physical systems, the connectionist architecture can be assumed to organize itself into higher-level structures and processes with their own properties that call for a higher level of description. We should always look for higher-level organizational principles.

3.2.   Implementationalism

Implementationalism sees the symbolic system as a virtual machine that in humans happens to be implemented on top of connectionist hardware, but could just as well have been implemented to run on some other machine. Symbolicism and connectionism for the implementationalist belong to strictly distinct levels of description.

3.2.1. The Justification for Separate Levels of Description. Implementationalism has traditionally been an ally of the symbolic paradigm (e.g., Marr, 1982). Putnam (1973) in developing the philosophy of *functionalism,* drew the analogy to computer systems. A high-level language like LISP can be implemented in any of a variety of hardware machines, and therefore has properties that are independent of any particular machine. A single programming language is therefore *multiply realizable.* Additionally, the same hardware machine can be used to implement any high-level programming language, for instance, PROLOG and SMALLTALK in addition to LISP. Another example of multiple realizability is the implementation of the same mathematics by the abacus, by an electronic calculator and by the brain (Schwartz, chap. 5 in this volume). In fact all of science—physics, chemistry, biology, zoology, sociology, and so on—seems to naturally fall similarly into relatively independent levels of description. Dinsmore (1991, chap. 1) discussed levels of description in more detail.

3.2.2. Symbolicism Needs Connectionism. Against implementationalism Smolensky's (1988) *subsymbolic hypothesis* states that the cognitive system cannot be adequately described at the symbolic level (Chalmers, chap. 2 in this volume). However, if implementationalism were correct there wouldn't be so much interest in connectionism among cognitive scientists brought up in the symbolic tradition. More precisely, we observe that connectionist models that perform low-level tasks such as pattern recognition exhibit a number of naturally emergent properties like graceful degradation, noise tolerance, ability to generalize, and so on. However, such properties are also observed in processing at the symbolic level, but are unexplained in the symbolic paradigm. Dyer (1988) pointed out that if traditional symbolic operations were simply implemented in connectionist models many of the significant and useful cognitive properties of connectionist models would simply be lost at the symbolic level, where they in fact fulfill a great need. This would include the natural account of *mysterious processes* into which symbolic models have not provided much insight. The fact is that connectionist models seem to provide natural solutions to many of the most serious problems that arise in symbolic models.

3.3. Interactions Between Levels

The alternative to eliminativism and implementationalism is an intermediate position that accepts symbolicism and connectionism as legitimate levels of description, but nevertheless does not regard them as strictly separate.

3.3.1. Functionalism Without Multiple Realizability. Schwartz (chap. 5 in this volume) argues that the separation of levels is much more complex than the philosophy of functionalism would suggest. In particular, he looks at Mendelian genetics (the functional level) and how it is implemented in terms of the structure of the DNA molecule. Schwartz asks, for instance, what if the DNA molecule had three instead of two strands. This would entail a corresponding difference in Mendelian genetics; humans would seem to require three parents. Schwartz argues at the same time for the nonautonomy of levels but also for the need for high-level functionalist descriptions.

Actually, many of the same points can be made immediately and directly with respect to cognition. For instance, a symbolic theory that proposes a process involving a long sequence of serial steps, as in search with backtracking, can certainly be dismissed if it is known that humans carry out the process very quickly. This is because of the demonstrated slowness of neural architecture. An alternative proposal that divides the original process into many parallel subparts is more likely to be consistent with connectionist evidence, since massive parallelism is supported by the underlying connectionist architecture.

3.3.2. Revisionism.   Revisionism is the position described by Pinker and Prince (1988) whereby symbolicism will remain its status as a functional level of description, but will nevertheless be influenced by connectionism. Thus, as they suggest, some complex symbol manipulations might be eliminated because of unanticipated computational powers of connectionism. There are probably many examples of mysterious processes for which this is likely. For instance, what is typically described as a rule application at the symbolic level is in distributed connectionist systems a process that exhibits properties of automatic generalization, best-match, noise tolerance, and so on. Knowing that these properties are accounted for in the connectionist implementation, the symbolicist might feel comfortable as accepting these as a primitive feature of rule application requiring no further analysis within the symbolic theory.

3.3.3. Limitivism.   I interpret Pinker and Prince's revisionism as a very controlled view of the interrelation between the different levels of description. Smolensky (1988) advocated a position, which he called *limitivism,* that also accords symbolicism legitimacy as a level of description, but a somewhat more tenuous one. A good symbolic account is an approximation of a more accurate connectionist account that is of predictive value within certain limits. An analogy can be drawn to statistical thermodynamics and statements about temperature and flow of heat.

3.4. Hybridism

The successful cognitive scientist of the future may well be one who can shift comfortably from one level of description to the next in accordance with which provides a better conceptual grasp of the problem at hand, recognizing that two complementary perspectives are more powerful than a single, uniform one.

Kwasny and Faisal (chap. 9 in this volume) describe a natural language parsing system that is based on symbolic work, but makes use of a connectionist component to make mysterious high-level decision about rule application. Basically, the symbolic component captures the systematicity that is captured in rules of grammar. The connectionist component, on the other hand, smooths the boundaries of what the parser can successfully process to include ungrammatical sentences or sentences with ambiguous or unknown words. It makes use of the generalization properties of the network to find a best match among the candidate symbolic rules.

Lange (chap. 10 in this volume) provides a general overview of a variety of hybrid systems and discusses a general framework for developing hybrid systems that combine distributed connectionist, localist connectionist, and symbolic marker-passing components. He considers the justification of hybrid systems to be in the development of temporary prototypes that can eventually be replaced with a single level. This replacement is desirable, he argues, because the difficulty of interfacing different levels in a natural way.

I feel that hybrid systems are a necessity and cannot in principle be replaced by single-level descriptions. Cognitive systems are complex, consisting of many component structures and processes. Looking over the range of these components we will often overextend the limits of the descriptive powers of symbolic models in two ways. First, connectionist processes may not have organized themselves into higher-level behaviors or structures that are subject to symbolic description. This may be the case, for instance, with emotional responses. Second, symbolic descriptions may simply be incomplete. This would be the case in mysterious processes like face recognition and associations between concepts.

Nevertheless, to the extent that connectionist networks have organized themselves into functionally motivated, systematic, high-level behaviors, symbolic descriptions can, and should, take over. Although parallel descriptions at the symbolic and connectionist levels may be possible, the symbolic description in this case is bound to be much simpler. Even when a full account in symbolic terms does not present itself, partial higher-level or functional descriptions of certain aspects of processes may be appropriate supplements to the connectionist description.

As the researcher moves through the various aspects of a cognitive problem moving up or down to the most useful level of description, a model will emerge that will look like a patchwork of symbolic and connectionist components. This will be a hybrid model.

4. CONCLUSION

Symbolicism and connectionism are not threats to one another. The success of one does not undermine the other. In fact, we should be happy when a problem makes sense from both perspectives. But failing this we should be free to exploit their complementary strengths. When we realize this, the gap between the paradigms will be closed.

ACKNOWLEDGMENTS

I would like to thank Fred Adams, Ken Aizawa, John Barnden, Doug Blank, Dave Chalmers, and Stan Kwasny for reading and commenting on an earlier draft. Jackie Muehler drew the figures.

REFERENCES

Derthick, M. (1990). [Review of *Connections and symbols*]. *Artificial Intelligence, 43,* 251–265.
Dinsmore, J. (1991). *Partitioned representations: A study in mental representation, language understanding and linguistic structure.* Dordrecht: Kluwer.
Dreyfus, H., & Dreyfus, S. (1986). *Mind over machine.* New York: Free Press.
Dyer, M. (1988). The promise and problems of connectionism. *Behavioral and Brain Sciences, 11*(1), 32–33.
Fodor, J., & Pylyshyn, Z. W. (1988). Connectionism and cognitive architecture: A critical analysis. In S. Pinker & J. Mehler (Eds.), *Connections and symbols* (pp. 3–72). Cambridge, MA: Bradford/MIT Press.
Lachter, J., & Bever, T. G. (1988). The relation between linguistic structure and associative theories of language learning: A constructive critique of some connectionist learning models. In S. Pinker & J. Mehler (Eds.), *Connections and symbols* (pp. 195–247). Cambridge, MA: Bradford/MIT Press.
Marr, D. (1982). *Vision.* San Francisco: W. H. Freeman.
McCarthy, J. (1988). Epistemological challenges for connectionism. *Behavioral and Brain Sciences, 11*(1), 44.
Michalski, R. S., Carbonell, J. G., & Mitchell, T. M. (Eds.). (1983). *Machine learning: An artificial intelligence approach.* Palo Alto, CA: Tioga.
Michalski, R. S., Carbonell, J. G., & Mitchell, T. M. (Eds.). (1986). *Machine learning,* (Vol. II). Palo Alto, CA: Tioga.
Minsky, M., & Papert, S. (1988). *Perceptions, (expanded ed.).* Cambridge, MA: MIT Press.
Newell, A. (1982). The knowledge level. *Artificial Intelligence, 18*(1), 87–127.
Newell, A., & Simon, H. (1976). Computer science as an empirical inquiry: Symbols and search. *Communications of the ACM, 19,* 113–126.
Pinker, S., & Prince, A. (1988). On language and connectionism: Analysis of a parallel distributed processing model of language acquisition. In S. Pinker & J. Mehler (Eds.), *Connections and symbols* (pp. 73–194). Cambridge, MA: Bradford/MIT Press.
Putnam, H. (1973). Reductionism and the nature of psychology. *Cognition, 2,* 131–146.
Pylyshyn, Z. (1984). *Computation and cognition.* Cambridge, MA: Bradford/MIT Press.
Quillian, M. R. (1968). Semantic memory. In M. Minsky (Ed.), *Semantic information processing* (pp. 227–270). Cambridge, MA: MIT Press.
Rumelhart, D., & McClelland, J. (1986). On learning the past tenses of English verbs. In J. McClelland, D. Rumelhart, & the PDP Research Group (Eds.), *Parallel distributed processing* (Vol. 2, pp. 216–217). Cambridge, MA: MIT Press.

Rumelhart, D. E., Smolensky, P., McClelland, J. L., & Hinton, G. E. (1986). Schemata and sequential thought processes in PDP models. In D. Rumelhart, J. McClelland, & the PDP Research Group (Eds.), *Parallel distributed processing* (Vol. 1, pp. 7–57). Cambridge, MA: MIT Press.

Smolensky, P. (1988). On the proper treatment of connectionism. *The Behavioral and Brain Sciences, 11*(1), 1–74.

2   Subsymbolic Computation and the Chinese Room

David J. Chalmers
Indiana University

1. INTRODUCTION

More than a decade ago, philosopher John Searle started a long-running contro-
versy with his paper "Minds, Brains, and Programs" (Searle, 1980a), an attack
on the ambitious claims of artificial intelligence (AI). With his now famous
Chinese Room argument, Searle claimed to show that despite the best efforts of
AI researchers, a computer could never recreate such vital properties of human
mentality as intentionality, subjectivity, and understanding.

The AI research program is based on the underlying assumption that all
important aspects of human cognition may in principle be captured in a computational model. This assumption stems from the belief that beyond a certain level,
implementational details are irrelevant to cognition. According to this belief,
neurons, and biological wetware in general, have no preferred status as the
substrate for a mind. As it happens, the best examples of minds we have at
present have arisen from a carbon-based substrate, but this is due to constraints
of evolution and possibly historical accidents, rather than to absolute necessity.

As a result of this belief, many cognitive scientists have chosen to focus not
on the biological substrate of the mind, but instead on the abstract causal structure that the mind embodies (at an appropriate level of abstraction). The view that
it is abstract causal structure that is essential to mentality has been an implicit
assumption of the AI research program since Turing (1950), but was first articulated explicitly, in various forms, by Putnam (1960), Armstrong (1970), and
Lewis (1970), and has become known as *functionalism*.

From here, it is a very short step to *computationalism*, the view that computational structure is what is important in capturing the essence of mentality. This step follows from a belief that any abstract causal structure can be captured computationally: a belief made plausible by the Church–Turing thesis, which articulates the power of simple computational structure. Some, nevertheless, have chosen not to make this step. Penrose (1989), for instance, seems to be a functionalist without being a computationalist, holding that certain causal properties of the mind cannot be captured algorithmically. Since Putnam's Turing-machine model of mental states, however, computationalism has been the most popular form of functionalism. In the eyes of many, the terms *functionalism* and *computationalism* are synonymous.

Searle's terms for the doctrine of computationalism is *strong AI*. This contrasts with *weak AI*, which holds merely that the computer can be used as a powerful tool for understanding the mind. Strong AI goes far beyond this, holding that the appropriately programmed computer really *has* (or *is*) a mind. In Searle's view, strong AI is thoroughly implausible, and his arguments attempt to discredit it, showing that nothing could ever possess true mentality merely by virtue of instantiating an appropriate computer program.

On the issue of computationalism, the artificial intelligence research community is unsurprisingly in near-universal agreement: There exists a certain class of computer programs (none yet written), such that anything that instantiates one of these programs can be correctly said to have (or be) a mind. There is nevertheless significant disagreement over just what this class of programs is. In recent years, artificial intelligence researchers have split into two polarized camps.

One camp, the *symbolic AI* school, has the weight of 3 decades' tradition behind it. The symbolic camp maintains that the correct level at which to model the mind is that of the *symbol*—that is, an entity in a computer program that is taken to refer to some entity in the real world. Programs that instantiate mentality, this camp claims, will be a subset of the class of programs that perform computation directly on such symbols. This view has been carefully articulated by Newell and Simon (1976), and is discussed in more detail later.

The *connectionist* school, by contrast, has only recently become a serious contender, although it has grown out of less visible research from the last few decades. On the connectionist view (Rumelhart, McClelland, & the PDP Research Group, 1986), the level of the symbol is too high to lead to a good model of the mind. We have to go lower: Instead of designing programs that perform computations on such symbols, design programs that perform computations at a lower level. The correct level is sometimes taken to be the level of the neuron, as the basic unit of many connectionist models has a causal structure reminiscent of the neuron, although Smolensky (1988) cautioned us against making too much of this similarity. It may be that going to the level of the neuron is going deeper than necessary. Some connectionist models, and certainly the related models of Holland (1986) and Mitchell and Hofstadter (1990) are better taken as working at the *subsymbolic* level. This is a level below that of the symbol—unlike symbolic models, these models have no direct correspondence between the entities computed upon and entities in the world—but not necessarily as deep a level as that of the neuron. These systems still follow rules, but the rules are well below the semantic level. It is hoped that as a consequence of following rules at this low level, semantic properties will emerge—that is, manifest themselves in the processing and behavior of the program—without having been explicitly programmed in. Consequently, when viewed at the semantic level such systems often do not appear to be engaged in rule-following behavior, as the rules that govern these systems lie at a deeper level.

Searle views each of these enterprises as misguided. Both hold that some computational structure is sufficient for mentality, and both are therefore futile. Searle's position is that his arguments show that neither of these schools of research could produce a truly cognitive system. In this chapter, I examine Searle's arguments carefully to see how they apply to both schools of artificial intelligence research. We find that Searle's arguments provide at least a plausible criticism of the symbolic AI research program, but that connectionist models are less vulnerable to his arguments.

In fact, it turns out that some of Searle's arguments are almost equivalent to those put forward by some members of the subsymbolic school as criticisms of their more traditional colleagues. It seems that perhaps Searle should desist from his blanket condemnation of the entire AI research endeavor, and instead sign up for his connectionist calling-card as soon as possible. This seems a little unlikely, however.

2. SEARLE'S ARGUMENTS

2.1. The Chinese Room

Searle first propounded his arguments against computationalism in terms of the Chinese Room thought-experiment. The argument, briefly, goes something like this: Assume, along with AI researchers, that it is possible to write a computer program that is an accurate model of the mind. In particular, such a program would then be an accurate model of human behavior, and would be able to pass the Turing test, producing verbal behavior indistinguishable from that of a human. For added color, Searle asked us to imagine a program that produces fluent linguistic behavior in Chinese.

Proponents of strong AI claim that such a program, when implemented, would produce all the essential properties of mentality, including intentionality, consciousness, and so on. In particular, any implementation of such a program could fairly be said to understand Chinese in the same way that a human speaker of the language would. This is the claim with which Searle took issue.

To convince us of this, Searle asked us to imagine a run of the program being simulated by a human who speaks no Chinese. The instructions in the program are formulated as a set of rules (in English) for the human to follow, stepping through the program by hand. The human is isolated in a secure room, and batches of Chinese writing are passed into the room. The human understands no Chinese, but using the supplied rules (representing the program), undertakes a series of manipulations involving symbols on paper, yielding as an end-product certain other shapes on paper, which are in fact Chinese symbols that represent the output of the program. Those outside the room are unaware of the internal details—they see only a room that is somehow passing a Chinese Turing test.

It is clear, according to Searle, that the human does not understand Chinese. To the human, the manipulated symbols are simply meaningless squiggles and squoggles. This is intuitively clear, and few have disputed this point. From here, Searle concluded that a computer running the same program would understand Chinese no better. In this way, strong AI is refuted.

Many problems have been pointed out with Searle's argument. The most common reply has been to note that whereas few would suggest that the human understands Chinese, it is not implausible that the system as a whole does. Searle dismissed this idea, finding it ridiculous that a system of pens, paper, and human could ever understand anything, but this may be a limit of Searle's intuition. (It has been pointed out that in practice, such a Chinese Room would almost certainly be tortuously complex, with one input-output sequence taking days, months, or years on the part of the human. Faced with such complexity, our intuitions tend to break down.) Searle defended the argument against this reply, the so-called *Systems Reply,* but many have found his defense unconvincing. It seems to many that Searle committed the mistake of confusing two different systems that have a common location.

2.2. Syntax and Semantics

Faced with such criticisms, Searle streamlined his argument to its essence, as follows (Searle, 1984, p. 39; Searle, 1987, pp. 231–232):

Axiom 1: Syntax is not sufficient for semantics.

Axiom 2: Minds have contents; specifically, they have semantic contents.

Axiom 3: Computer programs are entirely defined by their formal, or syntactical, structure.

Conclusion: Instantiating a program by itself is never sufficient for having a mind.

This is the form of the argument on which this chapter focuses. The original Chinese Room thought-experiment is a rich source of intuitions, and it is not impossible that some of the force of the original argument might be lost in this bare-bones reformulation. (I discuss some other aspects of the Chinese Room argument in Chalmers, 1991.) Nevertheless, the syntax/semantics argument is Searle's preferred formulation, and it seems to capture a significant intuition behind the original thought-experiment. It is toward this argument, and toward the corresponding intuition, that my remarks are addressed.

Each of the axioms in this argument is superficially plausible. To determine just how compelling the argument is, however, we will need to examine exactly what is meant by *syntax* and *semantics,* and see how the truth of the axioms depend on the definitions of these terms.

The key axiom is the first: "Syntax is not sufficient for semantics." This seems plausible indeed: Have we not all learned from our explorations in folk linguistics that syntax and semantics are very different things? It is probably safe to assume that Searle's motivation for this axiom comes directly from linguistics. It says, effectively, that the way in which objects (words in language, computational entities in artificial intelligence) obey formal rules is independent of the way in which they have meaning.[1]

This axiom, it seems, represented for Searle a distillation of the main thrust of the Chinese Room argument. When the human in the room is manipulating symbols on paper, all she sees are "meaningless squiggles and squoggles." Although she is able to follow the (syntactic) rules perfectly, she has no idea what the symbols *mean,* and so she cannot be said to have any true understanding of the Chinese language.

The way this argument can be used against computationalism is clear. Computer programs may manipulate symbols labeled **RESTAURANT, ELEPHANT,** and so on, but they will still have no idea what a restaurant is, and they will not understand the concept *elephant.* The entities manipulated by the computer, in Searle's view, are hollow, empty symbols, devoid of meaning. The symbols, and therefore the program, possess no intrinsic semantics.

Before proceeding any further, it is important to clarify precisely to which brand of semantics this argument applies. Meaning comes in a variety of guises. One sort of meaning is externalist, *extensional* semantics. Under this construal, something possesses meaning only if it picks out some definite object or set of circumstances in the external world. Here, meaning is essentially a world-involving notion. A symbol or mental state has meaning only in virtue of a relation to some external object—an *extension*—and such an extension can only be acquired by appropriate causal interactions with the external world.

Searle's notion of semantics is not, however, an externalist notion. When Searle claimed (in Axiom 2) that "Minds possess semantic contents," he is referred to *internalist* semantic contents. These are semantic contents that the

---

[1]More accurately, the rule-following behavior does not determine the meaning. Recent work in linguistics (e.g., Lakoff, 1987) has demonstrated that syntax and semantics are not completely independent.

mental states possess independent of specific environmental details. Roughly, they are *intensions* rather than extensions. Searle (1980b) made this internal-' ism very clear, arguing that even a disembodied brain possesses semantic content:

> If I were a brain in a vat I could have exactly the same mental states I have now; it is just that most of them would be false or otherwise unsatisfied. Now this . . . is designed to make clear what I have in mind when I say that the operation of the brain is causally sufficient for intentionality, and that it is the operation of the brain and not the impact of the outside world that matters for the content of our intentional states, at least in one important sense of "content". (p. 452)

Searle's notion of content is what is referred to in the philosophical literature as a *narrow* notion of content: Content that is possessed by an individual merely in virtue of physical properties of that individual, and not in virtue of properties of the environment. This contrasts with *wide,* or environment-involving content.[2] In fact, Searle's notion of content is sufficiently internalist that according to this notion mental states only count as truly semantic if they are conscious or potentially conscious, as a recent article (Searle, 1990) has made clear.[3]

This internalist/externalist distinction serves to cut off a potential escape route from the syntax/semantics argument. If externalist semantics were under discussion, one might argue that certainly purely syntactic computation, operating in a vacuum, cannot give rise to semantics; but if we simply hook up the computer to the real world in the right way, then its states will acquire semantic content in virtue of their causal interaction with the world, must as human mental states acquire extensional content in virtue of causal interaction with the world. This escape route, which Searle dubbed the *Robot Reply,* will not work for internalist content, as this kind of content is independent of environmental factors. If a system cannot possess internalist content on its own, environmental hook-up will not help.

The thrust of Searle's argument, then, is that computers can manipulate symbols, but there is nothing internal to the system that gives the symbols any meaning. If this is true, then computers stand in clear contrast to humans, whose mental states possess intrinsic meaning.

---

[2]The literature on narrow and wide content started with Putnam (1975), and has been developed by Fodor (1980) and Burge (1984), among many others.

[3]It should be noted that an internalist view on content does not preclude content from being a referential notion. A mental state may possess internalist semantic content by virtue of reference to some object or concept in a subject's notional world (Dennett, 1982), rather than by virtue of reference to the external world (as is the case for externalist content). A subject's notional world will usually match up quite well with the external world, but need not, as evidenced by the case of the brain in the vat.

3. SYMBOLIC AND CONNECTIONIST AI

3.1. Symbolic AI

Before we can determine how well Searle's arguments apply to the symbolic and connectionist artificial intelligence endeavors, we must outline and compare the fundamental assumptions and commitments of these two schools. We start with the symbolic AI, whose underlying assumptions have been well stated by Newell and Simon, two of the founders of the field.

Newell and Simon (1976) explicitly stated the assumptions on which the symbolic AI research program rests, and group these under the name of the "Physical Symbol System Hypothesis." This states, simply: "A physical symbol system has the necessary and sufficient means for general intelligent action" (p. 19). To Newell and Simon, an entity is potentially intelligent if and only if it instantiates a physical symbol system: a system, embodied physically, that is engaged in the manipulation of symbols.

The most important property of a symbol, according to Newell and Simon, is that it *designate*. A symbol is not a symbol unless it symbolizes something. Further, symbols are *atomic*. Symbols may combine together to form expressions, but they may not be broken down. The most obvious example of such symbols comes in a programming language such as LISP. Symbols, such as **CLYDE, ELEPHANT** and **TREE** are implemented as LISP atoms. These refer to objects or concepts, in these cases those of *Clyde, elephant,* and *tree* respectively. The symbols may be combined to form complex structured expressions, which refer to more complex entities. A complex entity may be represented to by a property list, for instance: as a simplistic example, a circus might be represented by **(CIRCUS (NUMBER-OF-PERFORMERS 23) (ELEPHANT CLYDE) (LOCATION BIG-TOP))**. There is some room for debate, within the symbolic tradition, over just which mental representations are symbols and which are expressions. For instance: *bachelor* is presumably a compound concept (formed out of lower level expressions such as *unmarried* and *male*), but is *elephant*? Might this be an expression rather than an atomic symbol, formed out of basic concepts such as *gray, animal,* and *trunk*? Whatever the correct level for atomic symbols, however, no question is raised that this level is a *semantic* one. Atomic symbols must carry a representational burden.

A symbol, then, is an atomic entity, designating some object or concept, which can be manipulated explicitly by a physical symbol system, leading to intelligent behavior. Symbolic AI deals with the class of programs that perform computations directly on such symbols.

3.2. Connectionist AI

Connectionism, by contrast, eschews atomic symbols. Connectionism is usually taken not to be symbolic, but subsymbolic. The best account of the assumptions underlying connectionism has been given by Smolensky (1988). Smolensky offered the following *Subsymbolic Hypothesis* as "the cornerstone of the sub-symbolic paradigm": The intuitive processor is a subconceptual connectionist dynamical system that does not admit a complete, formal, and precise conceptual level description (p. 7).

The second clause here is important, for it is what establishes connectionist and symbolic AI as distinct endeavors. The Physical Symbol System Hypothesis holds that all mental processing consists in computation on atomic symbols. If this hypothesis is true, then there exists a complete description of mental processing at the level of the atomic symbol. A description in these terms will necessarily be a description at the conceptual level, as atomic symbols are by definition representations of concepts. The Subsymbolic Hypothesis explicitly holds that no such description exists. Rather, to give a full account of mental processes, one must invoke processes that lie beneath the conceptual level.

There is certainly computation in connectionist systems, but such computation lies below the conceptual level. Computation takes place at the level of nodes and connections between nodes, and the individual nodes and connections are not intended to carry any semantic burden alone. The semantic burden of the system lies at a higher level, that of the *distributed representation* (Hinton, McClelland, and Rumelhart, 1986). Such a representation consists of a pattern of activity over a number of different nodes. In virtue of this distributed pattern, the representation has a complex internal structure that plays an important causal role. A distributed representation, then, is certainly not atomic. Neither is it a complex *expression* in the symbolic style, made up of simpler atomic representations. The components of the representation—the individual nodes or connections—carry no semantic burden and are therefore not representations in their own right. Connectionist systems therefore avoid the use of atomic symbols, and the connectionist endeavor consequently rejects the Physical Symbol System Hypothesis.

3.3. Connectionist and Symbolic Systems: A Comparison

It is important to clarify precisely how the symbolic and connectionist endeavors differ. Some have tried to isolate the differences between symbolic and connectionist systems purely in virtue of their architecture. The connectionist endeavor might be distinguished solely by its reliance on neuromorphic processing, with neuron-like units and synapse-like connections between units, whereas the symbolic endeavor is identified by its reliance on von-Neumann-style processing, or by architectures based on the Turing machine, or by the use of programs formulated in programming languages. Such a distinction is unlikely to be useful, however. For a start, both von Neumann and the neural-network architectures are *universal:* Anything that one can do, the other can do also (Franklin & Garzon,

1990). Indeed, connectionist models are typically formulated in high-level programming languages, and implemented on von Neumann machines, but this does not make them any less connectionist.

Adams *et al* (Chap. 1 in this volume) compare the capacities of programming-language and neural-network architectures, and find no significant differences. This should not be too surprising. Both kinds of architecture should be regarded as tools with which various kinds of cognitive models can be implemented. Even within the symbolic school, high-level programs on von Neumann machines have for years been used as implementation bases on which other virtual architectures—such as production systems, script-based memories and so on—have been overlaid. The situation with neural networks is no different. Like production systems, connectionist models can be implemented equally well on a Turing machine or a neural-network base. Connectionist models no more imply a rejection of the Turing machine model of computation than do production systems or blackboard architectures.

It follows that the connectionist and symbolic schools should not be distinguished by *syntactic* criteria alone. The styles of formal computation used may appear identical. Rather, the relevant criteria are *semantic*. It is the way in which representations are used that is fundamental. To be precise, the schools are distinguished by the way in which their computational (syntactic) features relate to their representational (semantic) features. To see this, consider the role of syntax and semantics within symbolic and connectionist systems.

Consider syntax first. In any computational system, the fundamental syntactic entities are *computational tokens:* These are the atomic objects that are manipulated in order for the computation to take place. In a neural network, the computational tokens—the elementary indivisible units—are individual nodes and connections. In a typical symbolic system, the computational tokens might be LISP atoms.

The fundamental semantic entities of any system, on the other hand, are *representations:* By definition, these are the objects that carry the semantic burden of the system. In a connectionist system, a representation is typically a distributed pattern of activation over a set of nodes. In a symbolic system, a representation might be a LISP atom or expression.

Both connectionist and symbolic systems, then, possess both computational tokens and representations, so the two classes cannot be distinguished by the possession of either of these features alone. They can, however, be distinguished by the relationship they suppose between the two. In symbolic systems, representations and computational tokens coincide. Every basic representation is an atomic computational token, and other representations are built by compounding basic representations. A LISP atom, for instance, serves simultaneously as a computational token and as a representational vehicle. This is precisely the import of the Physical Symbol System Hypothesis. A *symbol,* in Newell and Simon's usage, is an object in a computational system that (a) is atomic, that is, is a computational token, and (b) designates, that is, is a representation.

In connectionist systems, by contrast, representations and computational tokens are quite separate. Individual nodes and connections, the computational tokens, lie at a completely different level of organization from representations, which are distributed patterns of activity over such tokens. This is the most important distinguishing feature of connectionist systems: the level of computation falls below the level of representation. This distinction, philosophically, is much more important than the choice of any particular architecture. Some connectionists have proposed that this feature be the defining feature of connectionism, but for many the term *connectionism* is too closely bound to the neural-network architecture, hence the coining of the term *subsymbolic*. A subsymbolic system is precisely one in which the level of computation falls below the level of representation.[4]

We may enshrine this distinction into the two distinct philosophical commitments of the symbolic and subsymbolic schools. These commitments define symbolic and subsymbolic cognitive models.

> *The Symbolic/Subsymbolic Distinction:* In a symbolic system, the computational level coincides with the representational level. In a subsymbolic system, the computational level lies beneath the representational level.

There are a couple of points worth clarifying. First, we do not want to assume in advance that either kind of system possesses intrinsic semantics, in Searle's sense. So at least for now, talk of representations should be regarded as *interpretational* talk. An object within a computational system is a representation if it is an object of our semantic interpretation. Perhaps such an object of interpretation possess honest-to-goodness intrinsic semantics, and perhaps it does not. That remains to be seen. In these terms, another way of phrasing the relevant distinction is as follows:

> *The Symbolic/Subsymbolic Distinction* (alternative version): In a symbolic system, the objects of computation are also objects of semantic interpretation. In a subsymbolic system, the objects of computation are more fine-grained than the objects of semantic interpretation.

Second, the symbolic/subsymbolic distinction completely cross-classifies the architectural distinction between Turing machines, say, and neural networks. Turing machines can be used to implement both symbolic and subsymbolic

---

[4]The term *subsymbolic* is perhaps best viewed as modifying the noun *computation*, so that *subsymbolic system* is shorthand for *system utilizing subsymbolic computation*. The computation is subsymbolic in virtue of falling below the representational level. Perhaps a better term would be *subrepresentational*, due to the many connotations of the word *symbol*, but the term *subsymbolic* seems to be around for the long haul.

models, as can neural networks. Indeed, the well-known *localist* neural-network models, in which concepts are represented by single nodes, have representations that coincide with computational tokens. Such localist models are therefore better regarded as symbolic than subsymbolic, despite their use of a neural-network architecture. On the other hand *distributed* neural-network models, which lie at the core of the connectionist endeavor, are paradigm examples of subsymbolic computation. In future, when I use the term *connectionist* alone, I will be referring to distributed, and therefore subsymbolic, connectionist models.

Finally, some might argue that even traditional symbolic models can be construed as engaging in subsymbolic computation. In a typical symbolic system, a basic representational token—a LISP atom, say—might be implemented as a pattern of bits within the circuitry of the computer. One might argue that the real computation is going on at the bit level, and not at the level of this LISP atom. If this was the case, then the level of computation would fall below the level of representation, and we would have subsymbolic computation on our hands.

In response to this argument, it should be pointed out that whereas such bits might be entering into a computation, they are not individually causally efficacious. Whenever they enter a computation, they enter as a chunk—for instance, the eight bits that implement the atom **ELEPHANT** are always manipulated together. For all intents and purposes, these eight bits form an atomic unit. They stand in a strictly *implementational* relationship to the computation at LISP-atom level, and so do not have any significance of their own. The eight bits merely form an arbitrary label for the LISP atom; any collection of bits would do as well. This contrasts clearly with the connectionist case. In a connectionist network, a representation is made up of a collection of activated nodes, but each of these nodes plays a separate and significant causal role. We could not replace this particular configuration of active nodes by another configuration without radically altering the causal role of the representation. The distributed representation, unlike the LISP atom, cannot be treated as an atomic object.

The moral here is that the computation at stake in distinguishing symbolic from subsymbolic computation must be causally efficacious. If a computation is merely implementing a separate algorithm at a higher level of description, then we should move to that higher level. For a model to be truly subsymbolic, it must not only be the case that it engages in subsymbolic computation: It must also be the case that it cannot be redescribed as engaging in symbolic computation at a higher level. Otherwise the subsymbolic computation of the model would be a merely implementational, causally irrelevant feature. This coheres well with Smolensky's Subsymbolic Hypothesis, which states that mental processes form a subconceptual dynamical system, and cannot be completely described at the conceptual level. This hypothesis, translated into the language that we have been using, states that the mind engages in truly subsymbolic computation, and therefore cannot be redescribed as engaging in symbolic computation.

4. SEARLE'S ARGUMENT
AND SYMBOLIC/SUBSYMBOLIC COMPUTATION

Now that we have our distinctions clear, we may apply them to Searle's argument, and see how successfully the argument applies to the two distinct brands of AI. We have seen that the symbolic and subsymbolic schools take very different views of the relationship between syntax and semantics, so it would not be surprising if Searle's argument applied differently in each case.

Before proceeding, there is one overly simple view of the application of Searle's argument to connectionism that we can readily dismiss. This view holds that the argument should not be construed as even attempting to apply to connectionism; rather, the argument is a critique solely of symbol-manipulating systems. This argument is fallacious: Searle's argument is aimed at computational systems in general, and connectionist systems are computational systems. Indeed, almost all connectionist models are implemented as programs, so the argument applies directly.

The fallacy in this argument trades on an ambiguity in the term *symbol*. Sometimes, the term *symbol* is taken to be synonymous with *computational token*—as, for example, when one regards a one or zero in a Turing machine as a symbol irrespective of whether it carries any representational content. In this sense, Searle's argument indeed is aimed at only symbol-manipulating systems—that is, systems that manipulate computational tokens—but this is not much of a restriction. More frequently, however, the word *symbol* is used to mean something intended to possess representational content—most typically, a computational token that also represents, as we saw above. In this sense, the only symbol-manipulating programs are those of symbolic AI. This does not mean that Searle's argument is directed only at symbolic AI, however, as the term *symbol-manipulating* is being used differently in different parts of the argument.

4.1. Searle and Symbolic AI

Symbolic models, as we have seen are distinguished by their manipulation of atomic symbols—primitive computational tokens that are intended to carry semantic content. This leaves them vulnerable to Searle's argument in a very direct way. In virtue of what do such tokens posses intrinsic content?

First, *interpretational* content alone is not enough. To be sure, we may interpret such tokens as possessing content, but the possibility of such interpretation cannot guarantee intrinsic semantics, as witnessed by the case of words on a page. The word *dog*, written on a page, is interpreted by an observer as referring to the concept of dog, but such a word surely does not possess intrinsic semantic content. Rather, its semantic content is derived entirely from the semantic content of the observer, and is therefore merely extrinsic content.

Furthermore, we cannot argue that such tokens accrue content by virtue of a causal relationship to an object in the external world. One might wish to argue that the token *dog* represents the concept *dog* in virtue of the fact that the token is activated by the presence of real dogs, but such an argument would only work if it was externalist content that was at stake. As we saw earlier, however, Searle's argument is directed at internalist content, and so environmental properties are irrelevant.

We therefore need to find some intrinsic property by virtue of which a computational token can possess content. But here, we come up against the basic problem: these tokens are *atomic*. They possess no relevant internal structure. A token representing the concept *elephant* may be labeled **ELEPHANT,** but it might equally be labeled **APPLE** for all the program cares. Internal to the computation, such a token might consist of some pattern of bits, but any pattern of bits will do equally well. For all intents and purposes, a computational token is a featureless chunk, coming only with an arbitrary label that only serves to distinguish it from other computational tokens. Nothing intrinsic to the **ELEPHANT** token makes it any more closely related to the *elephant* concept than to the *apple* concept.

This seems to be precisely the import of the intuition behind Searle's argument. As far as system is concerned, the token **ELEPHANT** is meaningless. To the computer, such a token no more carries semantic content than do Chinese symbols to the English-speaker in the Chinese Room. It is a featureless object that is shoved around within the system, with nothing, apart from an arbitrary label, to distinguish it from other tokens within the system. As a syntactic primitive, there is nothing about it that qualifies it for meaning.

Searle's argument that "syntax is not sufficient for semantics" is effectively claiming that no amount of syntactic manipulation of such an object can endow it with true meaning. I should make clear that I am not necessarily endorsing this argument. One possible reply, for instance, might be that such a token does not represent in virtue of any intrinsic properties, but instead in virtue of its relationship to other tokens. Searle would argue that such relational properties cannot help—that an extrinsic relation between one primitive token and another cannot endow either token with meaning. However, the concern here is not to evaluate the ultimate success of this argument. Instead, I am pointing out that symbolic systems may be vulnerable to the argument in a way that subsymbolic systems may not be. Searle's argument derives its force from a set of powerful intuitions; I am trying to isolate these intuitions, and to see how they apply in various cases. The chief intuition behind Searle's argument appears to be that manipulation of tokens cannot endow these tokens with meaning. If this intuition is correct, then it certainly applies strongly to symbolic models.

4.2. Searle and Subsymbolic AI

In contrast to symbolic AI, connectionism eschews the usage of atomic symbols altogether. In connectionist models, and in other subsymbolic models, the level at which rule-following manipulation occurs is not a semantic level at all, and makes no claims to be. The fundamental idea behind connectionism, as we have seen, is to engage in algorithmic processes at a lower, nonsemantic level. The hope is that a semantic level will be emergent from this level, not unlike the way in which the laws of thermodynamics are emergent from the motion of individual particles.

One key property of connectionist systems, as we saw earlier, is that in these the meaning of the term *symbol* has come apart into two pieces. In such systems there are representations, and there are computational tokens, but the two classes are quite separate. This separation goes a long way toward safeguarding these systems from Searle's argument. To see this, let us try to run the argument through against these models. The argument, recall, is that symbol manipulation cannot give these symbols meaning. As the term *symbol* has now split into two, we may concentrate on either of the two relevant concepts: computational tokens or representations.

First, consider computational tokens, such as nodes and connections. It is true that these are primitive, featureless entities in connectionist systems, with nothing to distinguish them except perhaps a numerical degree of activation. Therefore, running Searle's argument through, such tokens cannot possess any intrinsic semantic content. But this is no problem for the connectionist! Such tokens were never intended to possess content; unlike their counterparts in symbolic models, these tokens are only intended to be syntactic objects. As is made clear by the symbolic/subsymbolic distinction, the computational level in connectionist systems is not a representational level. Therefore Searle's argument, applied to computational tokens, tells us nothing that we did not already know.

Second, let us consider representations. Representations in connectionist systems, unlike those in symbolic systems, are not primitive, featureless entities. Rather, a connectionist representation is a complex distributed pattern of activity, emerging from computational activity at a lower level. Representations are not manipulated directly, but rather are the indirect result of low-level manipulations. Most importantly, connectionist representations have a rich *internal* structure. Unlike symbolic representations, connectionist representations have their own intrinsic organization, by virtue of their consisting in a complex pattern of activation; it is impossible to treat such a representation as a featureless chunk. Because of this internal structure, Searle's argument does not go through. According to the connectionist claim, distributed representations carry content precisely in virtue of their rich internal structure. In the terms of Dyer (1990), connectionist representations have a *microsemantics*—internal pattern that systematically reflects the meaning of the representation.

The internal structures of symbolic representations, we saw, are entirely interchangeable. Any token will serve as well as any other, and there is nothing about the label **ELEPHANT** that makes it serve any better as a label for the atomic representation of the *elephant* concept than as a label for the *dog* concept. By contrast, the internal structure of a connectionist representation is of central importance. If we take the representations of two concepts—say *elephant* and *dog*—and attempt to exchange the relevant patterns of activation, the system will not function properly. If we attempt to modify the system of weights from these representations to compensate for this exchange, all the other representations in the system will be interfered with. The internal structure of a connectionist representation is essential to the system's function, and it is not the case that any old pattern of activity will do. The specific pattern of activity within a representation is responsible for making it represent what it does.

We can therefore see that Searle's intuition is not nearly as applicable in the connectionist case as in the symbolic case. There are both syntactic objects (computational tokens) and semantic objects (representations) in a connectionist system, but the syntactic objects are not semantic objects and vice versa. In this way the syntax/semantics argument is avoided.

4.3. Is Syntax Sufficient for Semantics?

Searle would doubtless be unimpressed by this argument. He might point to his axioms and say: (a) connectionist models are computational, consisting in syntactic manipulation of computational entities; (b) syntax is never sufficient for semantics; therefore (c) connectionist models can possess no true semantics. Even though distributed representations are not primitive tokens, they result entirely from syntactic manipulations, and so can carry no true semantic content.

We must therefore consider whether it is possible for syntactic systems to possess semantic content at any level. First, what might it mean for a system to be syntactic? Presumably, this means that the system functions by following rules, whether at a low level, such as the level of the node and connection in a connectionist system, or at a high level, such as the level of the representation in a symbolic model. Second, what does it mean here for a system to possess semantic content? As we have seen, the notion of content at stake here is internalist, intensional content. Putting these together, we may translate the statement about syntax and semantics approximately as follows: "No system that consists entirely of rule-following behavior can possess internal content."

Unfortunately, this axiom as it stands is false, as we may see by considering the example of the human brain. The brain surely possesses internal content, if any system does. Yet the brain can in principle be described as following a set of iron-clad rules: namely, the laws of physics. On the highest level, the human mind seems extremely flexible, producing the very antithesis of rule-following behavior; yet at the bottom level, it is made up of a physical substrate, consisting of such entities as elementary particles and electrical charges, whose actions are determined by the laws of physics. Of course, in our current state of knowledge we do not have complete knowledge of these laws, but it is a tenet of modern science that a complete set of such laws exists. At the lowest level, neural processing is not sensitive to any semantic properties; rather, each neuron fires or not depending only on content-free properties of input signals from other neurons. At some level, then, the brain is a rule-following, syntactic device. Nevertheless, it certainly possesses internal content, so Searle's "axiom" is false.

Consequently, it is simply not true that no syntactic system can possess content. Nevertheless, we have seen that there is some strong intuition behind the claim that "Syntax is not sufficient for semantics" that might be worth saving. If we modify the force of this axiom appropriately, we might be able to arrive at a formulation that applies to the cases where the intuition is most compelling, while at the same time excluding the obvious counterexamples such as the human brain.

Where does the motivation for the "Syntax is not sufficient for semantics" axiom come from? It seems clear that it comes from linguistics: The syntactic rules that words obey are not enough, alone, to endow these words with semantic content. For a *sentence,* then, it is true that syntax is not sufficient for semantics. We must therefore find some relevant difference between brains and sentences in virtue of which syntax is sufficient for semantics in one case but not in the other. A plausible answer immediately suggests itself: While it is true that brains are syntactic, their syntax lies at an extremely low level. The syntactic properties of atoms, molecules, even neurons seem almost irrelevant when we are talking about the conceptual level. Such syntax lies so far down that it does not diminish any semantic properties of *concepts.* In the case of the sentence, by contrast, the syntax and the intended semantics lie at precisely the same level, the level of the word. It is words that are manipulated syntactically, and it is words that are the object of semantic interpretation.

We might therefore patch up Searle's axiom as follows. Instead of the blanket pronouncement "Syntax is never sufficient for semantics," we might instead make the more limited conjecture: "Syntax, at a certain level, is never sufficient for semantic content at the same level." This conjecture comes much closer to capturing our intuitions, about linguistic cases for instance. To be able to formally manipulate nouns and verbs in sentences like "The cat sat on the mat" does not automatically endow us with an understanding of what the same nouns and verbs mean. Similarly, the formal manipulation of Chinese squiggles and squoggles in the Chinese Room may not necessarily lead to an understanding of the meaning of these symbols.

When syntax and semantics lie at the same level, the objects of syntactic manipulation—atomic tokens—and the objects of semantic interpretation coincide. We may therefore regard the above reformulation of Searle's axiom as equivalent to the statement: "Manipulation of atomic tokens is never sufficient to endow these tokens with meaning." This statement seems to be at the heart of the intuitions behind Searle's argument.

With this formulation of the relationship between syntax and semantics in place, the application to symbolic and subsymbolic AI is quite clear. By definition, in symbolic models the computational (syntactic) and the representational (semantic) levels coincide. When a symbolic system such as LISP manipulates an expression such as (**IS-A CLYDE ELEPHANT**), both the syntax and the intended semantics lie at the level of the LISP atom. From our reformulated axiom, if correct, it then follows that the semantics at this level cannot be true semantics. At best, it is extrinsic semantics, thrust upon the symbols by observers. In a connectionist system, on the other hand, the computational and representational levels are quite separate. The fact that there is syntactic manipulation going on at the level of the individual node does not stop there being semantic content at the level of the distributed representation any more than the fact that the cells in a human brain obey iron-clad laws of physics stops there being semantic content at the level of the concept. Because the levels of syntax and semantics are distinct, connectionist networks are safe from the argument.

4.4. Symbolic Replies

This argument, despite its refinement, is not necessarily a knockdown argument against symbolic models. These have various resources up their sleeve. I examine a few objections that proponents of symbolic models might make, some perhaps valid, some invalid.

1. Symbols in a symbolic system do not get their semantics by being manipulated, but rather by being connected to the world in the right way.

Response: As we have seen, this can give only an account of externalist content, and not an account of internal content (such as conscious mental content), and internal content is what is at stake here. If a system possesses internal content, it does so solely in virtue of its intrinsic properties, and the presence or absence of particular objects in the environment makes no difference. Even a brain in a vat might possess internal content. So this reply is not relevant.

2. Even in a symbolic system, it is not necessarily true that syntax lies at the same level as the semantics. A LISP atom, for instance, may consist of a complex pattern of bits in the system's machine language. The bit-level syntax lies below the atom-level semantics.

Response: As we saw earlier, the computation at the level of the bits is not *causally efficacious* computation. The bits are manipulated as a chunk, and merely serve as an arbitrary label for the atom. They are no more intrinsically important to the atom's functional role within the system than are the individual letters *C, H, A, I,* and *R* in the word *CHAIR* relevant to the word's semantic function within language. Both the word and the atom effectively enter into computation as atomic wholes. In contrast, the pattern of activity within a distributed representation is causally efficacious: each node plays an autonomous role. There is no way in which the representation can be interpreted as atomic. In the symbolic case, the bit-level story is mere implementational detail; in the connectionist case, the node-level story plays a vital role.

3. Perhaps the argument applies to atomic representations in symbolic systems, but what of the complex expressions that are formed from such atoms? Like distributed representations, these have complex internal structure, and so might possess intrinsic content.

Response: There is something to this argument. It is true that the compositional properties of an expression such as (**IS-A CLYDE ELEPHANT**) are represented by intrinsic features of the representation. The trouble is that *only* the compositional properties are so represented. Such a complex expression, if it has meaning at all, derives most of its meaning from its components, and as we have seen, the components—that is, the atoms **CLYDE** and so on—do not possess intrinsic meaning. Consequently, neither can the complex expression possess full intrinsic meaning. The fact that the expression is about *elephants,* rather than apples, is not represented by any intrinsic feature of the representation. Only the compositional structure of the proposition "Clyde is an elephant" is represented intrinsically, and although this is something, it is not enough.

4. Perhaps symbolic representations do not possess *intrinsic* content, that is, content intrinsic to the tokens themselves. Nevertheless, it is possible that the tokens possess content by virtue of the way in which they interact with each other. Such content would be extrinsic to the individual tokens, but still intrinsic to the system as a whole.

Response: This is the most promising symbolic reply, I believe. Perhaps the requirement that content be represented by internal properties of the representation itself was indeed too stringent. Rather, what is required is that content be represented internally to the system as a whole; but this is consistent with content being extrinsic to individual tokens. Indeed, the theory of functional-role semantics (Block, 1986) suggests that tokens acquire their meaning in virtue of their interactions with the rest of the system. This is certainly a coherent possibility, although it might require a slight rethinking of the symbolic commitments. In particular, if content accrues to a system only in virtue of a particular pattern of causal interactions between tokens, then what sense is there in ascribing content to single tokens alone? It might seem more logical to ascribe content to the patterns of interaction themselves. If we did this, the problem that symbolic representations lack internal structure would be removed. These patterns of interaction would possess internal structure not unlike that of a connectionist pattern of activation.

This reconstrual of symbolic systems might seem to be one way to bridge the conceptual gap between symbolic and connectionist systems. It would, however, require a rethinking of such fundamentals as the Physical Symbol System Hypothesis. If we hold that representation is carried by a pattern of interaction, and not by individual tokens, then the notion that atomic tokens designate would have to be stricken from the hypothesis, in favor of a more complex notion of representation. In some ways, this rethinking might move the foundations of the symbolic endeavor closer to those of the connectionist endeavor, but this might not be such a bad thing.

5. FURTHER REMARKS

5.1. Symbol Grounding

The argument I have put forward is closely related to the enterprise of *symbol grounding,* as described by Harnad (1990). The project of symbol grounding starts from the observation that computation consists in the manipulation of meaningless symbols. The meaning of these symbols, it is held, is only projected onto them by an observer. For the symbols to possess true semantic content, they must somehow be grounded in some nonsymbolic base.

In talking about symbol grounding, one must be careful here not to fall into the old trap of conflating the two quite separate meanings of *symbol,* that is, *computational token* and *representation.* When one argues that computation consists in the manipulation of meaningless symbols, this is a point about computational tokens. When one asks how symbols can be grounded, this is essentially a question about representations. Computational tokens do not necessarily need to be grounded, as they are not necessarily the object of semantic interpretation in the first place. Harnad (1990) drew the conclusion that no purely computational system can understand, but this may be due to the conflation of computational tokens with representations. The fact that no computational token is grounded does not immediately imply that no representation is grounded.[5] It might therefore be clearer to talk about the *representation grounding* problem: how can a representation in a computational system possess true meaning?

This problem is precisely the problem we have been talking about in this chapter. As the problem stands, there are two possible answers, depending on whether the kind of meaning in question is an internalist or an externalist notion. If one is concerned with how our symbols can possess externalist, extensional content, then one will engage in the project of *causal grounding.* This is the enterprise of hooking up computational systems to the external environment, and thus connecting representations directly to their referents. Proponents of causal grounding hold that there can be no reference in a vacuum, and true representation must be grounded in sensorimotor interaction with the environment. For instance, if the representation **DOG** is triggered by the presence of actual dogs in

---

[5]This conflation, incidentally, may also be responsible for much of the appeal of Searle's argument as an argument against the entire AI endeavor. Superficially, there is something quite compelling about the argument: "Computers can only engage in formal symbol manipulation. These symbols are meaningless. Therefore computers cannot understand." But such an argument draws its force entirely from the conflation of representations with computational tokens, under the term *symbol.*

the environment, then one might fairly claim that the representation really does have *dog* as its external referent.

Causal grounding is an extremely interesting project, but it is not quite so central to this chapter due to its concern with externalist, extensional content. When one asks the question "How can representations be grounded?" about internal content, a different project suggests itself. This is the project of *internal grounding*: ensuring that our representations have sufficient internal structure for them to carry intrinsic content. This is the project that immediately suggests itself from a consideration of symbolic models. In such models, the basic representational units are computational tokens, and such tokens have all the problems with lack of intrinsic meaning that we have already seen.[6]

The goal of internal grounding, then, is to find a vehicle for representational content that is richer than a primitive computational token, and therefore has some chance of possessing intrinsic content. Harnad (1990) has suggested one solution: Ground our representations internally in *sensory icons*. This is perhaps a plausible suggestion, but it may be further than we need to go. An alternative possibility, suggested by connectionism, is to ground our representations in distributed patterns of activity. In this way, as we have seen, the internal structure of a representation can systematically reflect the semantic features that it is intended to represent. Connectionism, then, is highly consistent with the goals of this aspect of the symbol grounding project. Connectionist distributed representations are perhaps the best tools currently available through which we can achieve the grounding of representations in their internal structure.

5.2. Representations as Patterns

The roots of the vulnerability of symbolic models to the Chinese Room argument lie in the lack of internal structure in basic symbolic representations. Not only has this atomicity of basic representations long been a core assumption of symbolic AI, but it has also had considerable philosophical support. According to Fodor's (1975) influential theory, the mind is nothing but a computational system operating syntactically on structured representations, which have innate, atomic concepts as building blocks. These building blocks (which are of course intended to be semantically interpretable), form the foundation for the "language of thought."

Searle has not been the only one to oppose this view. Much of the impetus for the connectionist movement came from the view that atomic symbols in such a

---

[6]The projects of causal grounding and internal grounding are certainly not competing with each other. Rather, each has a different goal. Through the pursuit of both projects, we might be able to come up with adequate accounts of both externalist and internalist content. Taken together, the projects would thus support a "two-factor" theory of meaning (Block, 1986), which many have argued can be the only kind of complete theory of meaning.

system must necessarily be brittle, rigid, and even empty. Hofstadter, who certainly did not accept Searle's main argument, nevertheless found himself in agreement when it comes to atomic symbols: "Formal tokens such as 'I' or 'hamburger' are in themselves empty. They do not denote. Nor can they be made to denote in the full, rich, intuitive sense of the term by having them obey some rules" (Hofstadter 1985, p. 645). Such criticisms are reminiscent of the interpretation of Searle that we have made herein. Unlike Searle, however, Hofstadter did not make the leap to an anticomputationalist position. Instead, he considered how these problems might be constructively addressed within a computationalist framework.

The emptiness of these such symbolic tokens, according to Hofstadter, arises from their passivity. They are "dead, lifeless" tokens, which are only manipulated by some overlying program. There is nothing about the tokens themselves that indicates their reference. Even Newell and Simon (1976) concede this point (happily, it seems): "A symbol may be used to designate any expression whatsoever. That is, given a symbol, it is not prescribed a priori what expressions it can designate" (p. 116). According to Newell and Simon, such symbols get their designation only in virtue of how they are manipulated by a program, and how they interact with the outside world.

Hofstadter envisaged instead *active symbols*—representations that carry content in their own right. Such representations would be "statistically emergent" from a computational substrate, and would be rich enough to carry their own meaning with them. They would not be formally manipulated by a computer program, but instead emerge from computational manipulations on a lower level.

Connectionism may not as yet have achieved symbols that are fully active in this sense, but it seems to be moving in the right direction. In the sense in which connectionism has symbols, these are not at all atomic, but instead emerge from a multitude of activity at a lower level. These representations have active internal structure in a distributed pattern of activity. Such a patterned internal activity seems to be an important step toward truly active symbols.[7] The idea of *representation as pattern,* at the heart of the connectionist endeavor, may ultimately prove to be the secret of content. Atomic symbols, lacking any internal structure, are content-free. Connectionist distributed representations, however, have so much information carried by the pattern of the representation itself that they are much more plausible candidates to be meaningful.

Connectionist representations have this rich internal pattern precisely because the syntactic structure lies below the symbolic level. If syntax lies at the level of semantics, then symbols are doomed to be atomic, and mental representations are at best a simple compositional combination of such symbols. It is interesting

---

[7]Kaplan, Weaver, and French (1990) argued that connectionist representations are not yet fully active, due to their not being functionally autonomous. They also offered suggestions about how truly active representations might be achieved in a connectionist framework.

to note that Fodor and Pylyshyn (1988) based their criticisms of connectionism on the idea that connectionist representations do not possess sufficient internal structure. The correct story, it seems, is precisely the opposite: Connectionist representations have so much internal structure that they hold much more promise as true representations than do the simple compositional representations of traditional AI.

Fodor and Pylyshyn accused connectionist models of lacking systematicity in representation. Here, too, it is not impossible that the boot may be on the other foot. Symbolic models, it is true, possess a certain kind of *compositional systematicity*—compositional properties of a represented entity are reflected by internal properties of a representation. But recent results seem to demonstrate that connectionist models can possess equal compositional systematicity (Blank, Meeden, and Marshall, chap. 6 in this volume; Chalmers 1990; Pollack 1990). What connectionist models possess, and symbolic models lack, is general *semantic systematicity*. In symbolic models, compositional properties are the only semantic properties that are reflected by internal properties of a representation. The semantic properties of basic (noncompositional) representations are not reflected at all. By contrast, in a connectionist model any semantic attribute of an entity is fair game for reflection in the internal structure of a distributed representation. Consequently, such representations can represent any semantic property systematically.

It is precisely because of this semantic systematicity that connectionist models possess many of their most desirable properties, such as automatic generalization. When a number of examples have been presented to a connectionist network, and an appropriate representational framework has been learned by the tuning of connection strengths, a novel example when presented will be systematically slotted into an appropriate representational form. The internal structure of the representation will be relatively similar to the structure of representations of objects to which this example is semantically similar in relevant respects, and quite different from the structure of semantically different objects. Because of this reflection of semantic properties in internal properties, appropriate behavior is generated for the novel example. Without such semantic systematicity, generalization between semantically similar objects is much more difficult, and indeed automatic generalization is rare in symbolic systems. Such similarity-based generalization is just one example of the advantages achieved by the use of representations with rich internal structure.

6. CONCLUSION

Searle's original arguments treated the field of artificial intelligence as a single endeavor, and the arguments were put forward as applicable to any computational system. But as we have seen, AI is far from unified, and it is vital to draw careful distinctions between different approaches before issuing blanket statements. The "Syntax is not sufficient for semantics" argument, superficially very appealing, may well apply strongly to traditional, symbolic AI. If one's intuitions about AI are derived entirely from the consideration of traditional models, one might take the argument as a condemnation of the entire field. But this would be to ignore the fact that other approaches are possible.

In this chapter, I have tried to analyze the intuitive force of the argument against AI. The argument plays on a fundamental weakness in computational systems: the fact that primitive tokens cannot carry intrinsic content. Instead of treating this intuition as a destructive argument against AI, however, it is perhaps better to view it as a constructive criticism which AI might be able to overcome. It turns out that AI research, chiefly through the connectionist endeavor, may be well on the way to dealing with this problem. I have argued that if we use representational vehicles that are not primitive tokens, but instead possess rich internal pattern, the problem of intrinsic content might be solved.

We should not pretend that there is no difficulty with the idea that semantics might somehow be emergent from syntax, even if the semantics lie at a much higher level. This is indeed a mystery. It is a mystery with which we have been faced with for years, however, in the guise of the human mind. A priori, it would seem implausible to suggest that a mechanical system such as the brain could possess semantics, have understanding, be conscious. Yet it does. The problem of how such a semantic, mental level can emerge from a mechanical substrate is one of the thorniest aspects of the mind–body problem. It should not be surprising that the emergence of semantics from syntax in computational systems should be equally difficult to understand.

Consequently, we might ask Searle to stop proclaiming that "syntax is never sufficient for semantics," and instead join in the investigation of how, possibly, semantics at a high level might emerge from syntax down below. This question will not be resolved overnight, but it seems that connectionism is playing its part in clarifying the issues.

ACKNOWLEDGMENTS

I would like to thank Bob French, Douglas Hofstadter, and two referees for their helpful comments.

REFERENCES

Armstrong, D. M. (1970). The nature of mind. In C. V. Borst (Ed.), *The mind/brain identity theory* (pp. 67–79). London: Macmillan.
Block, N. (1986). Advertisement for a semantics for psychology. In P. French (Ed.), *Midwest Studies in Philosophy,* Vol. 10 (pp. 615–78). Minneapolis: University of Minnesota Press.

Burge, T. (1984). Individualism in psychology. *Philosophical Review, 95,* 3–45.

Chalmers, D. J. (1990). Syntactic transformations on distributed representations. *Connection Science, 2,* 53–62.

Chalmers, D. J. (1991). *In and out of the Chinese Room.* Manuscript in preparation.

Dennett, D. C. (1982). Beyond belief. In A. Woodfield (Ed.), *Thought and object* (pp. 1–95). Oxford: Oxford University Press.

Dyer, M. G. (1990). Distributed symbol formation and processing in connectionist networks. *Journal of Experimental and Theoretical Artificial Intelligence, 2,* 215–239.

Fodor, J. A. (1975). *The language of thought.* Cambridge, MA: Harvard University Press.

Fodor, J. A. (1980). Methodological solipsism considered as a research strategy in cognitive psychology. *Behavioral and Brain Sciences, 3,* 63–109.

Fodor, J. A., & Pylyshyn, Z. (1988). Connectionism and cognitive architecture: A critical analysis. *Cognition, 28,* 3–71.

Franklin, S., & Garzon, M. (1990). Neural computability. In O. Omidvar (Ed.), *Progress in Neural Networks,* (Vol. 1., pp. 127–145). Norwood, NJ: Ablex.

Harnad, S. (1990). The symbol grounding problem. *Physica D, 42,* 335–46.

Hinton, G. E., McClelland, J. L., & Rumelhart, D. E. (1986). Distributed representations. In D. Rumelhart, J. McClelland, & the PDP Research Group, *Parallel Distributed Processing* (pp. 77–109). Cambridge, MA: MIT Press.

Hofstadter, D. R. (1985). Waking up from the Boolean dream, or, subcognition as computation. In *Metamagical themas* (pp. 631–665). New York: Basic Books.

Holland, J. H. (1986). Escaping brittleness: The possibilities of general purpose machine learning algorithms applied to parallel rule-based systems. In R. Michalski, J. Carbonell, & T. Mitchell (Eds.), *Machine Learning* (Vol. 2, pp. 593–623). Los Altos, CA: Morgan Kaufmann.

Kaplan, S., Weaver, M. E., & French, R. M. (1990). Active symbols and internal models: Towards a cognitive connectionism. *AI and Society, 4,* 51–71.

Lakoff, G. (1987). *Women, fire, and dangerous things.* Chicago: University of Chicago Press.

Lewis, D. (1970). Psychophysical and theoretical identifications. *Australasian Journal of Philosophy, 50,* 249–258.

Mitchell, M., & Hofstadter, D. R. (1990). The emergence of understanding in a computer model of concepts and analogy-making. *Physica D, 42,* 322–334.

Newell, A., & Simon, H. A. (1976). Computer science as empirical inquiry. *Communications of the Association for Computing Machinery, 19,* 113–126.

Penrose, R. (1989). *The emperor's new mind.* Oxford: Oxford University Press.

Pollack, J. B. (1990). Recursive distributed representation. *Artificial Intelligence, 46,* 77–105.

Putnam, H. (1960). Minds and machines. In S. Hook (Ed.), *Dimensions of mind* (pp. 138–164). New York: New York University Press.

Putnam, H. (1975). The meaning of "meaning". In K. Gunderson (Ed.), *Language, mind, and knowledge* (Minnesota Studies in the Philosophy of Science, Vol. 7, pp. 131–193). Minneapolis: University of Minnesota Press.

Rumelhart, D. E., McClelland, J. L., & the PDP Research Group (1986). *Parallel distributed processing.* Cambridge, MA: MIT Press.

Searle, J. R. (1980a). Minds, brains and programs. *Behavioral and Brain Sciences, 3,* 417–424.

Searle, J. R. (1980b). Intrinsic intentionality. *Behavioral and Brain Sciences, 3,* 450–457.

Searle, J. R. (1984). *Minds, brains, and science.* Cambridge, MA: Harvard University Press.

Searle, J. R. (1987). Minds and brains without programs. In C. Blakemore & S. Greenfield (Eds.), *Mindwaves* (pp. 209–233). Oxford: Blackwell.

Searle, J. R. (1990). Consciousness, explanatory inversion, and cognitive science. *Behavioral and Brain Sciences, 13,* 585–596.

Smolensky, P. (1988). On the proper treatment of connectionism. *Behavioral and Brain Sciences, 11,* 1–74.

Turing, A. M. (1950). Computing machinery and intelligence. *Mind, 59,* 433–460.

3 Rules in Programming Languages and Networks

Fred Adams
Kenneth Aizawa
Gary Fuller
Central Michigan University

Debates concerning the relative merits of programming languages and connectionist networks frequently discuss the role of rules in the different computational devices (Fodor & Pylyshyn, 1988; Gasser & Lee, chap. this volume; Horgan & Tienson, 1988, 1990; Lachter & Bever, 1988; Pinker & Prince, 1988; Rumelhart & McClelland, 1986a, 1986b). Among the specific questions that arise are

1. Do models formulated in programming languages use explicit rules where connectionist models do not (Gasser & Lee, chap. this volume; Rumelhart & McClelland, 1986)?
2. Are rules as found in programming languages hard, precise, and exceptionless, where connectionist rules are not (Horgan & Tienson, 1988, 1990; Smolensky, 1988b)?
3. Do connectionist models use rules operating on *distributed representations* where models formulated in programming languages do not (Horgan & Tienson, 1988, 1990; Smolensky, 1988a, 1988b)?
4. Do connectionist models fail to use structure sensitive rules of the sort found in "classical" computer architectures (Fodor & Pylyshyn, 1988; Smolensky, 1988b)?

In this chapter we argue that the answer to each of these questions is negative. We argue that hard, explicit, exceptionless, structure-sensitive rules are only contingently associated with programming languages, such as Turing machines, production systems, LISP, FORTRAN, Pascal, and only contingently excluded from connectionist models.[1] In other words, although there is some truth in saying that a particular connectionist model does not use explicit rules, or does use soft rules, and so forth, there appear to be other connectionist models that do use explicit rules, do use hard rules, and so forth. Similarly, whereas there are particular programs in programming languages, such as Turing machines, production systems, and so forth, that do use explicit rules, and so forth, there appear to be other programs that do not use explicit rules and so forth. We conclude, therefore, that it is possible to dissociate the various questions concerning rules from the issues separating programming languages and networks of units and connections. Part of what emerges in the course of this chapter is that there are networks that are symbolic processors and networks that are subsymbolic processors, and there are programs that are symbolic processors and programs that are subsymbolic processors (See Dinsmore (chap. 1 in this volume) and Blank, Meeden, and Marshall (chap. 6 in this volume) for more on the symbolic-subsymbolic distinction).

Having found these numerous failed attempts to contrast networks and programming languages in terms of rules, we are moved to question the motivation underlying these attempts. What reason is there to suppose that there is some grand difference between connectionist models and programming language models in their use of rules? Why have people thought it important for there to be greater differences between networks and Turing machines than there are between, say, Turing machines and LISP programs? Why are we not merely being deceived by the fact that units and connections do not look like computer programs?

We should note at the outset that the issue of the use of rules is not to be settled merely by appeal to standard proofs of the equivalence of Turing machines and connectionist networks. These simply show that any Turing-computable function is also computable by a network. They are input–output equivalent. The claims concerning the use of rules are not about differences in the functions computed by the two types of devices, but about differences in the way in which these functions are computed. Programming languages compute functions using explicit rules, where connectionist networks do not.

Our case for this view begins with a brief review of the basics of connectionism and Turing machines. For many purposes, Turing machines will provide a simple means of generating clear counterexamples. If the various *rule-based* distinctions between programming language models and activation propagating/weight changing networks are to be vindicated, at the least, they should separate networks from Turing machines. Such a separation would appear to be a necessary condition for making good the "rule-based" distinction between programming language and connectionist models. After this review, we treat explicit

---

[1]*Programming language* is here taken in the standard sense from computation theory, for example, what Machtey and Young (1978, chap. 3) referred to as an acceptable programming system.

rules, *soft* rules, rules operating on distributed representations, and rules operating on *structured representations*.

1. THE NUTS AND BOLTS OF CONNECTIONISM AND TURING MACHINES

For a more accessible introduction to connectionism (one whose philosophical analyses we do not necessarily endorse) the reader should refer to the editor's introduction to this volume. Here we offer only a bare bones sketch to fix terminology and specify what we mean by connectionism. Our introduction to Turing machines is somewhat longer than our introduction to connectionism, because we need to remind our readers of a number of features of Turing machines that are important for subsequent discussion.

We describe connectionism in terminology taken from Rumelhart, Hinton, and McClelland (1986). A connectionist model consists of a set of units with positively and negatively weighted connections between them. In the Rumelhart, Hinton, and McClelland vocabulary, each unit has an associated activation value and output. The activation value of unit i determines the output of unit i by a so-called *output function*. In many models, the output of a unit is simply its activation value, so that the output function is merely the identity function. The output of unit i is weighted as it is sent out along various connections and joins with the weighted outputs of other units to determine the net input to other units j. This functional relationship is specified by a *propagation function*.[2] The net input to unit j, possibly in conjunction with earlier activation values of unit j, determines a new activation value for j.[3] This functional relationship is specified by an *activation function*. Thus, units, connections, weights, activation values, outputs, and net inputs, form the basic ontology of connectionism. Their interrelations during their "computational" mode is specified by the activation functions, propagation functions, and output functions. Learning takes place in networks via procedures that specify changes in weights as a function of the results of preceding computations. Learning will not figure in our later discussion so we do not elaborate any further. Notice that we are indifferent here to the particular functional relationships between activation values, and so forth, and the manner in which units are arranged into networks. For us these are all connectionist networks. The Boltzmann machine (Hinton & Sejnowksi, 1986), Hopfield nets (Hopfield, 1982), interactive activation models (McClelland & Rumelhart, 1981; Rumelhart & McClelland, 1982), networks that use the stan-

---

[2] Actually, Rumelhart, Hinton, and McClelland (1986) used *propagation rule*, but because of the present topic, we choose to change the terminology slightly.

[3] In stochastic models, such as the Boltzmann machine, this net input determines the probability distribution over different possible activation values of j.

dard back-propagation feedforward computation phase (Rumelhart, Hinton, & Williams, 1986), the RAAM model (Blank, Meeden and Marshall, chap. 6 in this volume) are all examples of networks.

A Turing machine may be divided into two distinct parts, a finite state control unit and an infinitely long tape divided into squares. Consider, first, the tape and what appears there. Each square contains a letter from an alphabet over which a Turing machine computes. The alphabet may consist of any arbitrarily chosen finite set of symbols. Two examples of alphabets are the letters in the set {0,1} and the set of English letters along with punctuation marks such as the comma, the period, and the question mark. In addition to the arbitrariness in the choice of alphabet, there is latitude in the choice of language conventions one uses in computations. First of all, the items on the tape may denote nothing at all.[4] More commonly, however, they are assumed to denote, represent, or refer to various things. For example, the number one may be denoted by the string "1," two may be denoted by "11," three may be denoted by "111," and so on. Alternatively, the number one may be denoted by "11," two may be denoted by "1111," three denoted by "111111," and so on.

The finite state control unit has a so-called *read-write head* that scans a single tape square at a time. It also contains a program consisting of a set of instructions. A Turing machine instruction is an ordered four-tuple consisting of

1. a state symbol s_i,
2. a tape symbol t_j,
3. another tape symbol t_k or a direction symbol from the set {L,R}, and
4. a second state symbol s_m.

So, one Turing machine instruction might be "q_5 1 0 q_1," and another "q_{12} 1 L q_3," and another "q_{31} 1 L q_{33}." The first instruction may be read in English to mean, "If the finite state control unit is in state q_5, scanning a '1,' then it should write a '0' and change to state q_1." The second may be read "If the finite state

---

[4]We do not here mean simply that it is possible to have names or descriptions for nonexistent objects, such as Pegasus or the golden mountain. That is, of course, true, but it is not our point. We mean that none of the tape symbols, or combinations of tape symbols, need denote; they need not even "purport to denote." For example, when Turing machines are construed as *acceptors* of recursive languages, one may say that they accept a type of string in virtue of accepting an instance of the string. So, a Turing machine may accept the string type "000" in virtue of accepting a token of the string "000" written on its tape. In this account, no mention is made of the denotation, or reference, or meaning relation. It uses the instantiation relation; something obviously distinct from the denotation, reference, or meaning relation. For example, Descartes is an instance of a philosopher, but he does not denote (refer to, mean) a philosopher. We, thus, reject Pylyshyn's maxim "No computation without representation" (Pylyshyn, 1984, pp. 62f).

control unit is in state q_{12}, scanning a '1,' then it should move one square to the left and change to state q_3."

It is well known that the mathematics of Turing machines can, in principle, describe a great diversity of physical, chemical, and biological processes. Here it is perhaps worth noting an important caution this fact suggests, namely, that we must not construe such phrases as *read-write head* and *symbol manipulation* too narrowly. To describe an object as the read-write head of a Turing machine, one need not mean that the object literally writes, as with pen and paper or with laser printing technology. Nor should one think of symbol manipulation as necessarily akin to something like having the finite state control unit lifting labelled blocks or tickets from one square of the tape and carrying them to another (cf. Feldman, 1981, pp. 53–54). Symbol manipulation can describe such processes, but it may describe others. For example, if one were to suppose that the brain is a Turing machine, a biologically inspired suggestion as to the instantiation of, for example, the 0s and 1s of a Turing machine tape would be that the quiescence of a neuron corresponds to a particular square of the tape having a "0" in it, while the firing of the neuron could correspond to the square having a "1" in it. A biologically inspired suggestion as to the instantiation of a larger alphabet might have different firing frequencies corresponding to different letters. Although this picture of the instantiation of Turing machines may sound vaguely like connectionism, certainly some such biological instantiation of programming language ideas must have been in the back of investigators' minds all along.

Here we suppose that computation theory and Turing machines provide a mathematical theory that may be used to describe various physical objects. These physical objects may be electronic, chemical, biological, or whatever. This is analogous to the way in which one might suppose that differential geometry or a particular set of geometrical objects might be used to describe various sorts of masses distributed throughout a spacetime. As with computation theory and Turing machines, the objects described by differential geometry may have various electronic, chemical, or biological properties. In general practice, scientists and philosophers do not bother to distinguish the mathematical apparatus for describing the physical world and the physical world. Thus, spacetime is often said to be a differentiable manifold or an object is said to be a point mass. This casual manner of speech is generally unproblematic, but because it is potentially misleading here, we draw attention to it. This much said, we add that we adopt a similar treatment of connectionism. Units, connections, weights, and so forth, are mathematical objects that may be used to describe various physical, chemical, or biological objects. Thus, we take the usual assumption that units and connections are somehow instantiated by neurons or clusters of neurons to be an assumption over and above the assumptions concerning the mathematics that will ultimately describe (sub)cognitive processing. Although this may seem surprising to some, it in fact appears to be a view tacitly held by important practitioners of connectionism.

2. EXPLICIT RULES

With technical matters aside, let us consider one possible rule-based line of demarcation between connectionist networks and Turing machines. Sometimes *rule* is used to mean simply an input–output mapping. Rumelhart and Mc-Clelland (1986b) used rule in this sense at one point, when they speak of the "rule of 78." Lachter and Bever (1988, pp. 196, 216) also described a related sense when they speak of a rule as a physical object that computes an input–output mapping. This, however, is not the sense of rule at issue. When one asserts that a Turing machine uses explicit rules where a network does not, one might mean that there is something in a Turing machine that *instantiates an instruction,* where there is nothing in a connectionist model that does. More specifically, there are instructions in the Turing machine finite state control unit, but there is nothing like an instruction in a network. We are not sure if any connectionist explicitly holds such a view. We consider it primarily for the sake of completeness and expository clarity.

An instruction, here, means something like the primitive changes that are to be made as defined by the basic ontology of a computational device. But, it is clear that connectionist models specify primitive changes in the basic ontology. They are the equations relating activation values, outputs, and weights. Standard back-propagation learners, for example, use instructions such as the following:

1. if unit i is an input unit and the net input is 0, then the activation value of unit i is 0,
2. if unit i is a hidden unit or an output unit and the net input is $x,$ then the activation value of unit i is $1/(1 + \exp(-x))$, and
3. if unit i is an input unit or a hidden unit and its activation value is $y,$ then the output of unit i is $y.$

Clearly these instructions govern the behavior of standard back-propagation networks during their computation phase, just as four-tuples, such as "q_0 1 L q_3" and "q_3 0 1 q_8," govern the behavior of Turing machines, and whereas the back-propagation instructions differ from Turing machine instructions, Pascal instructions and FORTRAN instructions differ from Turing machine instructions and are nonetheless instructions.

Here it may be thought that network equations specify something like laws of nature governing the interactions of activation values and outputs, where the instructions in the finite state control unit of a Turing machine can be multiply instantiated in a great diversity of physical, chemical, and biological objects. But, as was mentioned in the previous section and as many advocates of connectionism realize, the basic ontology of networks consists of the mathematical units, connections, and so forth, which may also be used to described things constructed from something other than neurons or clusters of neurons.

Consider, now, a second possibility, the possibility we think most investigators have in mind. Let us admit that both networks and Turing machines instantiate instructions, that the four-tuple instructions of Turing machines are comparable to the equations relating activation values, outputs, weights, and net inputs, but in the face of this maintain that nets do not consult rules in their processing like programming language models. To use an explicit rule is, thus, to consult a rule. This seems to be the view found in Rumelhart and McClelland (1986a, 1986b), Davies (1990), and Gasser and Lee (chap. 8 in this volume). We might clarify this idea using Turing machines. A physical object that corresponds to the program of a Turing machine instantiates a set of instructions. An explicit rule, however, is instantiated by a physical object that corresponds to the data that appears on the tape of a Turing machine. A Turing machine with a program for checking the spelling of English words that has the string of symbols, "i before e, except after c," written on its tape might be said to consult a rule in the course of its computation. Of course, not every piece of data that appears on the Turing machine tape constitutes a rule. Consider a Turing machine that computes over the alphabet $\{0,1\}$, that uses the language convention that "1" denotes one, "11" denotes two, "111" denotes three, and so on, and begins its computations on the leftmost "1," if there is one, in a finite string of 1s surrounded by 0s. If this Turing machine has the program,

$$s_0 \ 0 \ 1 \ s_1$$
$$s_0 \ 1 \ L \ s_2$$
$$s_2 \ 0 \ 1 \ s_3,$$

for computing the successor function, $S(x) = x + 1$, it evidently does not consult rules written on its tape when computing $S(x)$. Neither "$S(x) = x + 1$," nor an equivalent, appear on the tape. All that appears on the tape are unary representations of numbers. Rules are part of the data a program uses in order to process information, whereas instructions process the information. To use a rule, that is, to consult a rule, is thus to use a certain type of data.

This account brings us to the truth in the connectionist's claims that particular models do not use explicit rules. A number of connectionist models, such as the Rumelhart–McClelland past-tense model (Rumelhart & McClelland, 1986b) and the Gasser–Lee phonological model only instantiate instructions (Gasser & Lee, chap. this volume), but do not use explicit rules in the sense that they do not consult rules. The data they receive as input, the input pattern of activation, do not constitute rules such as i before e, except after c. Instead, the data consist of codings of such things as a representation of the present tense of English verbs. The data are, thus, like that for the Turing machine that computes the successor function, rather than our spellchecker. It codes things other than rules.

Although we believe that Rumelhart and McClelland, Gasser and Lee, and Davies are correct in asserting that particular connectionist models do not consult rules, our point is to specify the significance of this observation. It is important to note that just as some Turing machines may consult explicit rules where others do not, so some networks may consult explicit rules where others do not. There is no reason to suppose that one cannot produce a large network with a module that takes as input a pattern of activation constituting a rule. That is, one can feed patterns of activation representing *i* before *e,* except after *c* into networks. Exactly how and why one might produce a network of this sort is an open question, but there is nothing in the connectionist literature that justifies what would be an astonishing discovery, namely, that the class of all networks cannot use explicit rules in this sense.[5,6]

We have approached this last sense of using explicit rules, the sense of consulting a rule, from a somewhat technical direction. It is, however, possible to approach it from a more intuitive direction as well. We have found what we take to be this more intuitive approach in (Rumelhart & McClelland, 1986b, p. 217), as well as in conversations. It seems natural to say that humans differ from rocks and planets in an important way. Rocks and planets may be governed by Newton's laws, but they do not follow or use a representation of Newton's laws to determine how they shall move. Humans, in contrast, often appear to use representations of rules, such as, "When driving a car, merge right after passing only after you see the headlights of the passed car in the rear-view mirror," or "In English spelling, *i* before *e,* except after *c.* "[7] As commonly as this view is heard, it is evidently a nonstarter for the desired characteristic difference between connectionist models and programming language models. It would seem that no advocate of connectionism would wish to say that it is a good thing that connectionist models as a class do not use explicit rules in just the way rocks and planets do not use explicit rules. That would ensure that networks are necessarily like inanimate objects, rather than humans. The reasonable theorist would seem to want to maintain, as we do, that although there are some networks that do not use explicit rules, there are some that do.

3. HARD, PRECISE, EXCEPTIONLESS RULES

The preceding section considered distinguishing connectionism and programming language models in terms of the use of explicit rules. An alternative rules

---

[5]We would point out that if PDP networks can use explicit rules in this sense, this undercuts the motivation Davies (1990) offered for his *intermediate* theory of rules.

[6]It might be thought here that we have made the connectionist claim too strong. Rather than suppose the connectionist to believe that nets cannot use rules, we should take them to believe that nets need not use explicit rules. This claim, however, would apply equally to Turing machines. Turing machines, like nets, need not use explicit rules. Our example of the Turing machine for computing the successor function is but one example. This alteration, therefore, does not save the connectionist's position.

[7]The rule is, of course, not strictly correct as evidenced by, say, *weigh* and *neighbor.*

approach is to admit that both types of computing device use rules, but they differ in the types of rules used. In this section we examine the connectionist's claim that programming language models use "hard," precise, and exceptionless rules, where connectionist models use "soft" rules (For example, Horgan and Tienson, 1988, 1990; Smolensky, 1988a, 1988b).

To begin, we cannot accept Smolensky's (1988b, p. 138) suggestion that *soft* means stochastic and *hard* means deterministic and that the difference between Turing machines and connectionist networks is that nets are stochastic, whereas Turing machines are deterministic. This is, first, because there are both deterministic and stochastic networks; backpropagation learners, interactive activation nets, and perceptrons, for example, are deterministic, whereas Hopfield nets, the Boltzmann machine, and Harmony theory models are stochastic.[8] The stochastic models are sometimes treated as Markov random fields. Moreover, we observe that it is possible to define both nondeterministic and probabilistic Turing machines alongside deterministic Turing machines. A nondeterministic Turing machine is like a deterministic Turing machine save for the fact that it is permitted to have two or more instructions beginning with the same state symbol s_i and the same tape symbol t_j. Such nondeterministic computing devices are at the heart of the vast computer science literature on NP-completeness. A probabilistic Turing machine is, then, like a nondeterministic Turing machine, but each instruction has a fifth element specifying the probability of taking that instruction when given the chance. Probabilistic Turing machine instructions might then look like this:

$$q_0 \ 1 \ L \ q_3 \ 0.25$$
$$q_0 \ 1 \ R \ q_3 \ 0.25$$
$$q_0 \ 1 \ R \ q_4 \ 0.50.$$

When the Turing machine with these instructions is in state q_0 scanning a 1, it will move left and go into state q_3 25% of the time, it will move right and go into state q_3 25% of the time, and it will move right and go into state q_4 50% of the time.

We also challenge Smolensky's suggestion that *soft* means *fuzzy,* as in fuzzy logic (Zadeh, 1965, 1975, 1983), and in this sense connectionist systems are soft (Smolensky, 1988b, p. 139). Although some networks, such as say the interactive activation models, may be treated as fuzzy models, McCulloch–Pitts nets are not fuzzy. Similarly, whereas the Turing machine programs one usually thinks of for computing number theoretic functions do not use fuzzy values, there are Turing machines programs that could work with them.

Another sense of hard rules versus soft rules may be found in the distinction between *constraints* and *costs* (Hinton & Sejnowski, 1986, p. 284). Here the

---

[8]We might note that it is possible to generate stochastic networks that use standard backpropagation or perceptron convergence learning, as is done in Rumelhart and McClelland (1986).

distinction is between rules that must be satisfied and those that are usually good or helpful to satisfy. There is a difference between rules that must be obeyed and those that it is in some sense usually better to obey. The distinction may be made using an example from chess. A hard rule, or hard constraint, is a rule that must always be obeyed, for example, that a rook cannot move diagonally. Another hard rule is that the King may not move into check. A soft rule, a rule of thumb that is usually wise to follow, is that one ought to attempt to control the center of the board. Another soft rule is that it is wise to get your pieces out early. Horgan and Tienson (1988, 1990) suggested this sense of soft rules when they suggested that the cognitive processing found in professional basketball players involves the simultaneous satisfaction or consideration of multiple soft constraints.

It is worth noting that the distinction between rules of the game and rules of strategy, if you will, is not the same as the difference between rules with exceptions and rules without exceptions. There may, for example, be rules of strategy that are always, without exception, good rules. Perhaps making one's first move taking the center square is such a rule in tic-tac-toe.

In order to investigate the previous suggestion, we should see how it is implemented in some connectionist models. In nets, the weights between units may be thought of as weak constraints between two hypotheses. Many network models might serve to illustrate this point, but we will consider the principles of interactive activation and a concrete example of its application, the interactive activation model of letter perception (McClelland & Rumelhart, 1982; Rumelhart & McClelland, 1986b). In *interactive activation theory,* the activation values of units may be considered a sort of measure of the credibility of an hypothesis, the credibility of the hypothesis associated with the unit.[9] The equations relating activation values, outputs, and weights are such that, if unit i is connected to unit j with a positive weight, a large activation value for unit i will support a large activation value for unit j. In other words, a high degree of credibility for the hypothesis associated with unit i will confer a high degree of credibility on the hypothesis corresponding to unit j. The equations are also such that if unit i is connected to unit j with a negative weight, a large activation value for unit i will support a small activation value for unit j. In other words, a high degree of credibility for the hypothesis corresponding to unit i confers a low degree of credibility for the hypothesis corresponding to unit j. A small activation value for unit i means that it will have little effect on j either way.[10] In the interactive activation model, all the constraints are weak in the sense that all weights are finite, and whereas the credibility of hypothesis i supports hypothesis

---

[9]The measure of credibility embodied in the activation value is not always a probability measure insofar as it sometimes ranges from -0.2 to 1, as in the interactive activation model of letter perception.

[10]We might note that there is a slight interpretive problem with this theory when we come to negative activation values of the sort found in the model of letter perception, because the hypotheses with negative credibility will end up supporting hypotheses with which they are inconsistent.

j, the credibility of *j* may be undermined by other hypotheses, so that although *i* supports *j*, *j* does not end up being very credible. The constraints in the network (e.g., if the hypothesis associated with unit *i* is credible and consistent with the hypothesis associated with unit *j*, then hypothesis *j* should be credible) are soft in the sense that, while this constraint is actually true and useful in coming to a conclusion about the hypothesis associated with unit *j*, the weights and activation values with units *k*, *l*, *m*, and *n*, may lead to a low activation value for unit *j*, so that unit *j* is not credible.

We might make these ideas more concrete by appeal to McClelland and Rumelhart's model of letter perception. In this model, there are three levels of units: *feature* units, *letter-position* units, and *word* units (See Fig. 3.1). Thus, at the lowest level, there are units that register the presence of parts of letters, such as the lower left leg of the letter *A*. The set of possible features and ways in which they may be organized into letters is shown in Figs. 3.2 and 3.3. At a higher level, the letter-position level, there is a unit representing the letter *A* occurring at the first position in a word being scanned, a unit representing the letter *B* at the first position in a word being scanned, and so forth for each letter. There is a similar array of 26 units for each of the four positions in a fixed visual field. At the highest level, the word level, there is also a unit for the word *read*, a unit for

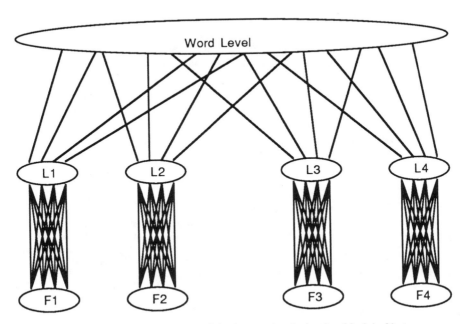

FIG. 3.1.   General structure of the Interactive Activation Model of Letter Perception.

FIG. 3.2. The set of features constituting letters in the Interactive Activation Model of Letter Perception.

the word *bead,* and so forth, for various four-letter words of the English language. In this model, there is a positively weighted connection between the unit corresponding to *B* at the first position and the unit corresponding to the word *bead,* and a negatively weighted connection between the unit corresponding to *B* at the first position and the unit corresponding to the word *read.* Each of the weights in an interactive activation model, such as the model of letter perception, constitutes a soft constraint. If there is something corresponding to the lower left leg of the letter *A* in the first position of the visual field, this makes it more credible to suppose that the first letter in the visual field is an *A.* So, the net has the constraint: If there is something in the position of the lower left leg of the letter *A* in the visual field, then the object in the visual field is an *A.* This constraint is soft, because it may be outweighed by the other feature units. Thus, if the two units indicating the line along the bottom of a *B* both have high activation value, then their negative weights to the letter-position unit *A* may outweigh the single unit for the *A* letter-position unit, and the model will not believe that there is a letter *A* at the first position in the visual field.[11]

We think this theory of soft constraints makes perfect sense, but again this difference does not fall along the line between Turing machines and connectionism. Existing chess-playing programs use soft constraints when they take into account various features of a situation in order to decide on a move. Turing machines that use the same system of evaluating moves would, then, presumably use the same soft constraints as the available chess-playing programs. Perhaps the important general point to make is that there is no inconsistency between determinism and the use of soft rules. The interactive activation model is deter-

---

[11]We note in passing that Horgan and Tienson suggested that programming languages cannot be used to model the play of professional basketball players because of "the need to deal simultaneously with numerous constraints and the resultant threat of computation explosion. Anything having to do with basketball might appropriately be a factor, and it is at least a practical impossibility to list all of the factors." The passage appears in the context of the difficulty of the frame problem. It is not at all clear, however, that the existing connectionist constraint satisfaction picture offers a solution to the problems. No reason is given for thinking that, whereas there is not enough time to take all the relevant constraints into account, there are enough brain cells to take all the relevant constraints into consideration. In other words, what reason is there to think an explosion in *spatial* complexity is any less a problem than an explosion in *time* complexity?

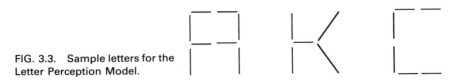

FIG. 3.3.   Sample letters for the
Letter Perception Model.

ministic, but it uses soft rules or soft constraints, so the mere fact of the determinism of a Turing machine does not preclude the use of soft constraints.

Another way of drawing attention to the fact that soft constraints may be
implemented in conventional computing devices is to note the large literature in
nonmonotonic reasoning (See, for example, Kimbrough & Adams, 1988, for
numerous references). In work on nonmonotonic reasoning, the principal idea is
to develop an inferential system that accommodates the defeasibility of various
inferences.

It might be objected, here, that we still have not correctly interpreted the
claims about the soft nature of connectionist inferences. One might claim that
while Turing machines fundamentally use hard constraints, but can be programmed to use soft constraints, networks are fundamentally soft. That is, the
fundamental operations of programming language models are exceptionless,
where the fundamental operations of networks are not exceptionless. This may
be what Smolensky had in mind when he talked of traditional expert systems that
use many, many lines of code in such a way that "softness emerges from
hardness," where in networks, "the cognitive system is fundamentally a soft
machine that is so complex it sometimes appears hard when viewed at higher
levels" (Smolensky, 1988b, pp. 139–140). This response, however, is belied by
the observation that the relations between the activation values, outputs, and
weights in existing network models are as hard, exceptionless, and precise as you
please. The equations for backpropagation learners introduced earlier, for example, clearly show this. Interactive activation and perceptron equations also show
this. Note that even taking *fundamentally soft* to mean *fundamentally probabilistic* does not work for the reasons cited earlier: Both connectionist models and
Turing machines admit of probabilistic and deterministic strains.

4. RULES OPERATING
ON DISTRIBUTED REPRESENTATIONS

Advocates of connectionism frequently assert that their models use distributed
representations, often with the suggestion that programming language models do
not. One might then say that both connectionist models and programming language models use rules, but the rules in connectionist models operate on distributed representations, where the rules in programming language models oper-

ate on localist representations. The phrase *distributed representations* has a number of meanings. Four of these are relevant to the present discussion. We discuss these in turn. First, representations may be said to be distributed in the sense that many units are used in the representation of a concept from ordinary language discourse. The concept of a chair, for example, might involve the activation values of a set of units, rather than only a single unit. Although it is true that various connectionist models use distributed representations in this sense, it would be a mistake to conclude that this is an essential characteristic of connectionism. There are obviously models that use localist representations in the sense that for each concept or hypothesis the model might be said to possess, there is a unit. In the interactive activation model of letter perception described earlier, there are single units for words such as *read* and *bead*. Each of these units corresponds to a proposition such as *The word "read" was seen* with the activation value of the unit constituting a sort of measure of the confidence in the hypothesis. This sort of understanding is implicit in the very theory of interactive activation.

From well-known examples, it is clear that there are networks that use both localist and distributed representations in the sense of using many units per concept or proposition. It is also clear that Turing machines can use the equivalent of distributed or localist representations, that is, several tape squares per concept or proposition. Distributed representations in Turing machines have markers in numerous tape squares to denote objects or stand for propositions. For example, suppose we wish to have a representation of chairs. One way to prepare a Turing machine to have these representations would be to use a Turing machine that computes over the standard alphabet of English with a few punctuation marks thrown in, that is, {A, a, B, b, . . . , ?, ,, ., "}. To perform computations concerning chairs the Turing machine might manipulate strings consisting of a *c,* an *h,* an *a,* an *i,* and an *r,* where *c, h, a, i,* and *r* each appear in a distinct tape square. Propositions could be given a similar treatment with sentences written in the tape squares. These sorts of representations would apparently count as *distributed Turing machine representations.* A Turing machine using a localist representation might compute over a different alphabet, for example, letters from the set {dog, cat, house, chair, boy, girl, . . . }. Each of these representations is a letter in the sense that each occupies only one tape square. Propositions might be treated similarly using sentences. Thus, whereas particular connectionist models may use rules defined over distributed, rather than localist, representations it is also possible to have Turing machines that use either distributed or localist representations in the sense sketched earlier.

Second, *distributed representations* at times, means something like *redundant representations.* In the Rumelhart–McClelland past-tense model, for example, *went* is represented by many different real-valued activation values of a set of output units. Turing machines, however, can also avail themselves of redundant representations. To take a simple example, it is possible to write a computer program that will compute the successor function given the language convention that "1," "11," and "111" denote one, that "1111," "11111," and "111111," denote two, and so on.[12]

Third, sometimes one means by distributed representations, representations in which the same units and activation values can be used to represent different objects. Thus, for example, an activation value of 0.95 on unit i could be part of the representation of the color of a cat when it is part of one pattern of activation and then later be part of the representation of the weight of an automobile when it is part of another pattern of activation. The distinct representations are thus *superimposed* on the same activation value for the same unit.

Granted there can be this sort of superimposition. But it should also be granted that nets need not have this sort of superimposition. The activation values of units can be assigned meanings in such a way as not to vary with context. So much for connectionism. Turing machines, likewise, can have letters whose denotations do not vary with their context. But, of course, the letters can vary from context to context. For example, the letter a has no meaning of its own in certain contexts—it means *not* in its first occurrence of *atypical* but nothing at all in its second occurrence. Larger strings of symbols have this property as well. The string *bank* could be given different meanings in different contexts a programming language uses.

Finally, representations may be said to be *spatially distributed* that is, the symbols are spread diffusely through space. In connectionism, the neurons serving to support a mental representation are spread throughout the cortex in such a way that a lesion of a small cluster of cells will not completely obliterate the representation, hence causing loss of memory about the object represented. This

---

[12]A program for doing this is the following:

$$s_0 \ 0 \ 1 \ s_1$$
$$s_0 \ 1 \ R \ s_2$$
$$s_2 \ 0 \ 1 \ s_4$$
$$s_2 \ 1 \ R \ s_3$$
$$s_3 \ 0 \ 1 \ s_9$$
$$s_3 \ 1 \ R \ s_0$$
$$s_4 \ 1 \ R \ s_5$$
$$s_5 \ 0 \ 1 \ s_6$$
$$s_6 \ 1 \ R \ s_7$$
$$s_7 \ 0 \ 1 \ s_8$$
$$s_9 \ 1 \ R \ s_{10}$$
$$s_{10} \ 0 \ 1 \ s_{11}.$$

The read-write runs across the input string of 1s noting blocks of three 1s. When it comes across a block of less than three 1s, it rounds the total number of 1s up to an even multiple of three, then adds a single additional 1.

sense of distributed representations, representations spatially spread out, does not contrast networks with programming languages, because the object described with the mathematics of Turing machines can be diffused through space just as easily as can units, or the neurons underlying units. There is no reason to suppose that neurons underlying a "1" on a tape square cannot be spread throughout the cortex. This sense of distributed representations is perhaps a less popular means of contrasting networks and programming languages than the senses considered earlier, but we include it for completeness.

For these reasons, we believe there is no difference between the class of Turing machines and the class of connectionist networks when it comes to rules that apply to distributed versus localist representations.

5. STRUCTURE-SENSITIVE RULES

It might be thought that Fodor and Pylyshyn (1988) put forth a view that is at odds with the sort of view we have so far developed, namely, that connectionist models do not use rules sensitive to the structure of representations, where programming language models do. This way of putting things is not entirely satisfactory. The Fodor–Pylyshyn view is a bit more subtle, and is in fact very much in keeping with the view we have taken of other purported contrasts between programming languages and connectionism. Fodor and Pylyshyn do not reject the idea that what takes place in human brains may involve something like the activation propagation and weight change processes described in section 1. Rather, they take exception to a particular view of mental representation that has contingently grown up around networks and conflicts with a way of using Turing machines and their kin, those that have what may be called *classical cognitive architecture*. By a *classical* architecture, Fodor and Pylyshyn meant a computing device working with certain constraints on the way symbols, or markers, are manipulated and on the way the manipulated markers denote objects. In other words, Fodor and Pylyshyn did not offer a distinction between activation propagating/weight changing devices on the one hand and programming languages on the other.

According to Fodor and Pylyshyn, a computing device with a classical architecture has (a) representations with a combinatorial syntax and (b) rules that are sensitive to that combinatorial syntax. In Turing machines, for example, (a) amounts to the assertion that tape symbols are organized in such a way that all representations are either atomic or built up by combinations of atomic symbols. Thus, one may be denoted by "1," two by "11," and so on, with representations of larger numbers built up from representations of smaller numbers. Claim (b) amounts to the assertion that the instructions in the finite state control unit are sensitive to the way in which the symbols are organized on the tape. Thus, it matters to the computation of the successor function how symbols fill the tape squares. If the language conventions a program presupposes are not used, then the program may compute a different function. So, if we change one of the language conventions mentioned earlier so that "111" denotes four rather than three, then a program for computing successor that adds a single "1" to the left of the string "11" will not compute the successor of two, but the successor of three.

It is clear from the following passage that Fodor and Pylyshyn (1988) did not believe that activation propagation and weight changing models are inconsistent with a classical architecture,

> But we are not claiming that you can't reconcile a Connectionist architecture with an adequate theory of mental representation (specifically with a combinatorial syntax and semantics for mental representations). On the contrary, of course you can: All that's required is that you use your network to implement a Turing machine, and specify a combinatorial structure for its computational language. (p. 28)

According to Fodor and Pylyshyn, if a network were outfitted with a classical architecture then it would have the resources they believe necessary in order to account for what they call productivity, systematicity, compositionality, and inferential coherence.

So, it is fairly clear on inspection, that Fodor and Pylyshyn thought there is no contradiction in speaking of an activation propagating/weight change network that has a classical architecture. Moreover, it is also rather clear that Fodor believed that there can be Turing machines that do not use classical architecture. He discussed these in Fodor (1987). There he distinguished between representational theories of mind that postulate a language of thought from representational theories of mind that reject a language of thought.

6. CONCLUSION

In this chapter we have surveyed the leading attempts to draw a contrast between the class of programming language models and the class of network models in terms of the use of various types of rules. In each case, we have found the purported distinction to be spurious. We have not, of course, proved that there can be no such distinction; that was not our aim. Nor was it our aim to show that there is no difference at all between networks and programming languages. Our point has been merely that existing explications of the differences between nets and programming languages made in terms of rule use are inadequate.

It is, of course, inevitable that someone will try to invent a new characterization of the difference between nets and programming languages in terms of rules, but we wish to discourage such attempts. First, we note that it may or may not be possible to come up with an accurate rule-based distinction between nets and programming languages. In either case, however, there remains a further hurdle that must be overcome. If one finds a difference between networks and programs in terms of rules, we should like to know why it is a difference that makes a difference. What empirical, rather than purely philosophical, reason is there to suppose that a purported difference is not a trivial difference and in fact a key to understanding what takes place in the human brain? Why would a difference in rule use be an empirical difference that makes a difference? Second, we observe that much of the philosophical work on networks and artificial intelligence, by both cognitive scientists and by philosophers, has been preoccupied with efforts to draw deep distinctions between networks and programming languages. The appeal to talk of rules constitutes one such attempt. We must, however, ask ourselves why deep distinctions are necessary here. Why suppose that there is some great divide between networks and, say, LISP programs on the one hand, yet no great divide between LISP programs and production systems? If there need be no such divide, then perhaps there need be no rule-based distinction.

REFERENCES

Davies, M. (1990). Knowledge of rules in connectionist networks. *Intellectica, 9–10*, 81–126.

Feldman, J. A. (1981). A connectionist model of visual memory. In G. E. Hinton & J. A. Anderson (Eds.), *Parallel model of associative memory* (pp. 49–82). Hillsdale, NJ: Lawrence Erlbaum Associates.

Fodor, J. A. (1987). *Psychosemantics*. Cambridge, MA: MIT Press.

Fodor, J. A., & Pylyshyn, Z. (1988). Connectionism and cognitive architecture: A critical analysis. In S. Pinker & J. Mehler (Eds.), *Connections and symbols* (pp. 3–71). Cambridge, MA: MIT Press.

Gasser, M., & Lee, C. (This volume). Where do "underlying representations" come from?

Hinton, G. E., & Sejnowski, T. J. (1986). Learning and relearning in Boltzmann machines. In D. E. Rumelhart, J. L. McClelland, & the PDP Research Group, (Eds.), *Parallel distributed processing: Explorations in the microstructure of cognition* (Vol. 1, pp. 282–317). Cambridge, MA: MIT Press.

Hopfield, J. J. (1982). Neural networks and physical systems with emergent collective computational abilities. *Proceedings of the National Academy of Sciences, 79*, 2554–2558.

Horgan, T., & Tienson, J. (1988). Settling into a new paradigm. In T. Horgan & J. Tienson, (Eds.), *Spindel Conference 1987: Connectionism and the philosophy of mind* (pp. 97–114). Memphis, TN: Department of Philosophy, Memphis State University.

Horgan, T., & Tienson, J. (1990). Representations without rules. *Philosophical Topics, 17*(1), 147–174.

Kimbrough, S. O., & Adams, F. (1988). Why nonmonotomic logic? *Decision Support Systems, 4*, 111–127.

Lachter, J., & Bever, T. G. (1988). The relation between linguistic structure and associative theories of language learning: A constructive critique of some connectionist learning models. In S. Pinker & J. Mehler (Eds.), *Connections and symbols* (pp. 195–247). Cambridge, MA: MIT Press.

Machtey, M., & Young, P. (1978). *An introduction to the general theory of algorithms*. New York: North Holland.

McClelland, J. L., & Rumelhart, D. E. (1981). An interactive activation model of context effects in letter perception: Part I. An account of basic findings. *Psychological Review, 88*, 375–407.

McClelland, J. L., Rumelhart, D. E., & Hinton, G. E. (1986). The appeal of parallel distributed processing. In D. E. Rumelhart, J. L. McClelland, & the PDP Research Group (Eds.), *Parallel distributed processing: Explorations in the microstructure of cognition* (Vol. 1, pp. 3–44). Cambridge, MA: MIT Press.

McClelland, J. L., Rumelhart, D. E., & the PDP Research Group (1986). *Parallel distributed processing: Explorations in the microstructure of cognition* (Vol. 2). Cambridge, MA: MIT Press.

Pinker, S., & Prince, A. (1988). On language and connectionism: Analysis of a parallel distributed processing model of language acquisition. In S. Pinker & J. Mehler (Eds.), *Connections and symbols* (pp. 73–193). Cambridge, MA: MIT Press.

Pylyshyn, Z. (1984). *Cognition and computation.* Cambridge, MA: MIT Press.

Rumelhart, D. E., Hinton, G. E., & McClelland, J. L. (1986). A general framework for parallel distributed processing. In D. E. Rumelhart, J. L. McClelland, & the PDP Research Group (Eds.), *Parallel distributed processing: Explorations in the microstructure of cognition* (Vol. 1, pp. 45–76). Cambridge, MA: MIT Press.

Rumelhart, D. E., Hinton, G. E., & Williams, R. J. (1986). Learning internal representations by error propagation. In D. E. Rumelhart, J. L. McClelland, & the PDP Research Group (Eds.), *Parallel distributed processing: Explorations in the microstructure of cognition* (Vol. 1, pp. 318–362). Cambridge, MA: MIT Press.

Rumelhart, D. E., & McClelland, J. L. (1982). An interactive activation model of context effects in letter perception: Part 2. The contextual enhancement effect and some tests and extensions of the model. *Psychological Review, 89*, 60–94.

Rumelhart, D. E., & McClelland, J. L. (1986a). PDP models and general issues in cognitive science. In D. E. Rumelhart, J. L. McClelland, & the PDP Research Group (Eds.), *Parallel distributed processing: Explorations in the microstructure of cognition* (Vol. 1, pp. 110–146). Cambridge, MA: MIT Press.

Rumelhart, D. E., & McClelland, J. L. (1986b). On learning the past tense of English verbs. In J. L. McClelland, D. E. Rumelhart, & the PDP Research Group. *Parallel distributed processing: Explorations in the microstructure of cognition* (Vol. 2, pp. 216–271). Cambridge, MA: MIT Press.

Rumelhart, D. E., McClelland, J. L., & the PDP Research Group (1986). (Eds.). *Parallel distributed processing: Explorations in the microstructure of cognition* (Vol. 1). Cambridge, MA: MIT Press.

Smolensky, P. (1988a). On the proper treatment of connectionism. *Behavioral and Brain Sciences, 11*, 1–74.

Smolensky, P. (1988b). The constituent structure of connectionist mental states: A reply to Fodor and Pylyshyn. In T. Horgan & J. Tienson (Eds.), *Spindel conference 1987: Connectionism and the philosophy of mind* (pp. 97–114). Memphis, TN: Department of Philosophy, Memphis State University.

Zadeh, L. A. (1965). Fuzzy sets. *Information and Control, 8*, 338–353.

Zadeh, L. A. (1975). Fuzzy logic and approximate reasoning. *Synthese, 30*, 4-7–428.

Zadeh, L. A. (1983). Role of fuzzy logic in the management of uncertainty in expert systems. *Fuzzy sets and systems, 11*, 199–227.

4 Biology and Sufficiency in Connectionist Theory

Kenneth Aizawa
Central Michigan University

Models that explain human cognition in terms of units and connections and models that explain human cognition in terms of processes in computer programming languages, such as Turing machines, LISP, and production systems—what we might call *computationalist* models, have been thought to differ in a number of respects.[1] Many of these differences are real and important; others are real but not important, and still others are simply not real. In an effort to narrow the apparent gap between connectionist and computationalist models, the contributions of myself and my colleagues focus on many of the popular distinctions we take to be unreal. In the chapter by Adams, Aizawa, and Fuller in this volume, my colleagues and I examine some alleged *rule-based* differences. This chapter, on the other hand, focuses on two additional areas that might be thought to separate computationalist models and network models, (a) the use of biological evidence and (b) a computational sufficiency restriction. The first of these ideas

---

[1]Note that the use of *networks* and *programming languages,* rather than *symbolic* and *subsymbolic,* has a philosophical point. A network, or net, or connectionist model, is any model consisting of nodes with weighted connections between them. It is a model that fits within the framework articulated by Rumelhart, Hinton, and McClelland (1986). A programming language is any computational device that computes the partial recursive functions. (See Machtey & Young, 1978, for the definition of a programming language.) For definitions of *symbolic* and *subsymbolic* see Dinsmore (chap. 1 in this volume) or Blank, Meeden, and Marshall (chap. 6 in this volume). The relation between the two sets of terminology is crudely that symbolic and subsymbolic are two ways of using networks and programming languages. That is, both networks and programming languages admit of symbolic and subsymbolic processing in the sense described by Dinsmore, Blank, Meeden, and Marshall. The focus on connectionism versus programs makes this chapter run counter to the central issue in the title of this volume, but nevertheless, I believe, it constitutes an important alternative perspective that is intimately related to the central topic of this book.

purports that network models take the brain seriously where computationalist models do not (Rumelhart & Norman, 1981, p. 2). The second suggests that connectionists place principled limitations on the mechanisms that they will use to explain behavior, where computationalists do not. This suggests that when supposing the mind to run a computer program, one simply postulates whatever mechanisms one needs to get the job done; but with connectionism this is not done (Rumelhart & Norman, 1981, p. 2). Thus, nonconnectionists are playing fast and loose with the idea that the computational processes found in a computer program are sufficient to produce cognition. As in Adams, Aizawa, and Fuller, (chap. 3 in this volume), this chapter narrows the gap between the connectionist and computationalist approaches to cognition by indicating that there is less to these alleged differences than might appear at first glance.

Section 1 examines the various senses in which one might say that network models embody a different attitude toward biological evidence than do computationalist models. For those who are indifferent to biological evidence and study networks only for their computationally interesting, or computationally useful, properties, this section may seem otiose. In response, it should be noted that their perspective is not universally shared; there are efforts under way among some connectionists to bring together biology and psychology (See, for example, Gluck & Rumelhart, 1990; and Nadel, Cooper, Culicover, & Harnish, 1989). Moreover, there is an additional justification for examining the biological issue: We should consider whether or not there are reasons for being indifferent to biology, other than mere personal taste. Are there reasons why certain attitudes toward the biological facts will not move a theorist toward one computational approach rather than another? Certainly both a connectionist and a computationalist can share an indifference to biological data, but what more can be said? What we find, perhaps not surprisingly, is that connectionists and computationalists actually agree, or can agree, on a number of views about the significance of biological facts in psychological theorizing. There is room for further articulations of ways in which connectionists might differ from computationalists in their attitudes toward biology, but nonetheless the gap between nets and programming languages on the biological front is smaller than one might have expected.

Section 2 examines the idea less frequently articulated in connectionism that we must place principled limitations on the mechanisms we postulate in connectionist cognitive science. What this amounts to is the claim that connectionist models can use only units, connections, weights, and so forth. The various subsections of section 2.1 indicate numerous ways in which connectionism fails to live up to this methodology, so that the idea that connectionists restrict their ontology in principled ways where computationalists do not will be undermined. The subsections of Section 2.2 explain two ways of handling the violations of the sufficiency condition: eliminating the offending processes and actually reducing the mechanisms to units and connections. This second approach is illustrated in the elaboration of an incomplete Boltzmann machine memory model.

1. TAKING THE BRAIN SERIOUSLY IN CONNECTIONISM AND COMPUTATIONALISM

The issues concerning the relationship between biology and psychology are complex, but they seem rarely to fall along the lines separating connectionist models from computationalist models. That is, it is often possible to adopt a given attitude toward biological facts, without being thereby committed to supposing that cognitive processing is connectionist processing or program execution. The following subsections consider various senses in which it might be thought that a connectionist attitude toward biological evidence differs from the computationalist's attitude. Due to this focus, we set aside the connectionist attitude of indifference to biological facts.

1.1. Connectionists Aim for Biological Confirmation Where Computationalists Do Not

To say that connectionists aim for biological confirmation where computationalists do not seems implausible on the basis of general principles of scientific rationality. It seems to be a canon of scientific practice that scientists want support for their theories wherever it can be had, from biology or elsewhere. At the least, they do not wish to be inconsistent with accepted facts. For this simple reason, it seems that we must admit that computationalists and connectionists wish biological confirmation (or consistency) for their theories. To suggest otherwise would be to suggest that they are somehow unscientific. It might, however, be suggested that where both computationalists and connectionists both wish to have biological confirmation for their theories, only connectionists are able to get it. The units and connections in a network are biologically plausible. It is more or less easy to see how to relate them to the structure and function of networks of neurons, but not so the computational structures postulated in typical computer programs.

To evaluate this second suggestion, we must lay down a bit of groundwork. First, we introduce the supposition that there is more to confirmation than mere consistency. That is, evidence e can be consistent with hypothesis h, without necessarily confirming h. For example, the fact that there are more than five neurons in my head is consistent with my thinking I'm hungry, but it does not seem to confirm the fact that I'm hungry. Given this last observation, it seems that one would much prefer to have evidence confirm a hypothesis rather than have evidence merely be consistent with a hypothesis. *Confirmation* is more valuable than *consistency*.

Our second bit of preparatory work involves a review of three popular, but nonetheless sketchy, biological interpretations of the mathematics of units and connections. These are three accounts of how one is to understand units and connections in biological terms. First, there is the *subneuronal interpretation* according to which a unit and its incoming connections should be thought of as a dendritic spine with various synapses onto it (Sejnowski, 1986). Second, there is the *neuronal interpretation*. On this view, a unit is to be identified with a neuronal cell body and the connections identified with individual axons and dendrites. Furthermore, an activation value is to be understood as the membrane potential in a nerve cell body and an output is to be understood as some property of the firing of action potentials, say, the firing or quiescence of the neuron or its rate of firing. Hopfield (1984), had this view in mind in his refinement of his original model in Hopfield (1982). Third, we have the *supraneuronal interpretation* according to which each unit corresponds to a cluster of neurons.

With preliminaries aside, we return to the suggestion that connectionists provide confirmation for their models where computationalists only wish they did. If we adopt either the subneuronal or neuronal interpretation sketched earlier, far from receiving confirmation, existing connectionist weight change procedures come into conflict with the standard conception of neuronal function. For example, the standard backpropagation weight change procedure given by Rumelhart, Hinton, and Williams (1986), would require sending signals in both directions across synapses, which is generally not possible. Synaptic transmission usually involves presynaptic release of a chemical neurotransmitter that diffuses across the synapse to be bound on the postsynaptic side. Only one side of the synapse releases the transmitter and only one side binds it. Thus, the vast majority of synapses in the cortex are unidirectional. Second, both the standard backpropagation procedure, as described by Rumelhart, Hinton, and Williams, (1986), and the Boltzmann machine weight change procedure, as described by Hinton and Sejnowski (1986), involve changing excitatory synapses into inhibitory synapses, and vice versa, which is again not possible. A synapse generally produces only one type of chemical transmitter that usually has either an excitatory or inhibitory effect. Finally, both backpropagation and Boltzmann machine weight change permit a single unit to have both excitatory and inhibitory connections emanating from it when, in general, a single neuron has either all inhibitory or all excitatory synapses. These facts should be evident from any neuroscience text (e.g., Kandel & Schwartz, 1985; Shepherd, 1988). To repeat, the hypothesis that the brain is a backpropagation or Boltzmann machine learner is, on either the neuronal or subneuronal interpretation, disconfirmed.

The preceding arguments are usually conceded by all, but it is frequently suggested that this means that we should adopt the supraneuronal interpretation of units and connections for networks using these weight change procedures.

This move spares backpropagation and Boltzmann machine weight change from outright refutation, at least for now, but it still leaves them in an unsatisfying situation. That is, they are now consistent with the biological facts, but they are also presently unconfirmed and unconstrained by biological evidence. Units and connections following the backpropagation and Boltzmann machine learning procedures could turn out to be made of neurons, but there is no positive evidence for this hypothesis.

The difference between confirmation and consistency may seem like a small difference on the face of it, but to put it in a better perspective, we might look at an analogous case. The case is one of the most frequently suggested failings of computationalist models of cognition (Churchland & Sejnowski, 1989, pp. 24–25).

> Anatomically and physiologically, the brain is a parallel system, not a sequential von Neumann machine. The neural architecture is highly interconnected. Neurons such as Purkinje cells may have upwards of 80,000 input connections, and neurons in cerebral cortex can have upwards of 10,000 output connections.

Similar objections to the von Neumann computer architecture may be found in Rumelhart and Norman (1981). I doubt that anyone really supposes that the brain is a von Neumann computer, so that Churchland and Sejnowski are in fact just attacking a straw man. In any case, the biological facts brought forth by Churchland and Sejnowski fail to knock down this straw man in just the way that the earlier points that synapses are unidirectional, that synapses do not change from inhibitory to excitatory or vice versa, and that all synapses of a given neuron are usually all excitatory or all inhibitory fail to refute the hypothesis that the brain is a Boltzmann machine or backpropagation learner. If we take the hypothesis that the brain is a serial von Neumann computer to imply that individual neurons fire one at a time, or some other such low-level interpretation, then the straw man hypothesis will be refuted. So, subneuronal or neuronal interpretations of the von Neumann hypothesis are refuted. But, what about the supraneuronal hypothesis, the hypothesis that, at the level of clusters of neurons, the brain is a von Neumann computer? Is this consistent with the biological facts adduced? It would seem so. Thus, if we move to the supraneuronal interpretation for either backpropagation, the Boltzmann machine, or the von Neumann computer, there is no biological refutation of the hypotheses. The hypotheses are consistent with the available biological facts.

The point here is not to argue that the brain is a von Neumann computer. The brain is almost certainly not. The brain and the von Neumann computer are the products of radically distinct design processes working with wildly different physical constraints. But, the hypothesis that the brain uses backpropagation at some level and the (straw man) hypothesis that the brain is a von Neumann computer at some level are both consistent with the available biological evi-

dence, but not confirmed by it. So, connectionists, of at least the backpropagation or Boltzmann machine persuasion, appear to have no greater claim to biological dedication than do the computationalists, who assert the very strong claim
that the brain is a von Neumann computer, when both hypotheses are given
supraneuronal interpretations. So much then for the connectionist idea of taking
the brain seriously.

1.2. Connectionists Are Preoccupied with Mere Implementation Details Where Computationalists Are Not

Computationalists often argue that biological facts only pick out contingent
features of the way cognition happens to be instantiated in brains, so biological
facts do not really form a part of cognitive science. This general attitude is turned
into an attack on connectionism by saying that network models only pick out
contingent biological features of the way cognition is instantiated in the brain,
hence connectionist networks do not belong in cognitive science.

Connectionists have responded to this line in diverse ways. A common line is
to indicate agreement with the computationalist view that a theory of cognition
should be pitched at the level of rules operating on representations, but to offer a
challenge to the computationalist's theory of rules and representations. So, for
example, Smolensky, (1988), spoke of "soft" and "hard" rules and distributed,
rather than local representations. Alternatively, connectionists have rejected the
rules and representations picture for talk of "subthings." The rules and representations of computationalism are not really to be found in the head, but are merely
useful descriptions. Smolensky, (1988), also spoke this way. These stories are
played out in much more detail in other chapters in this collection, so they are not
discussed here (Blank, Meeden, & Marshall, chap. 6 in this volume, Chalmers,
chap. 2 in this volume, Dinsmore, chap. 1 in this volume).

In addition to the various subthing strategies one might try in defense of the
connectionist enterprise, connectionists should also point out that they too wish
to ignore irrelevant implementation detail. Connectionists certainly wish to leave
out of their psychological theories biological facts that are only contingently
associated with cognition. Thus, connectionists are likely to be indifferent to
exactly which chemical molecules make up the cell membrane of neurons, the
molecular weight of the transmembrane proteins responsible for action potentials
and membrane potentials, or the particular ions that are responsible for the
potential gradient across the neuronal membrane. Connectionists are obviously
indifferent to many such implementation details.

Of course, while connectionists and computationalists share the view that
irrelevant chemical, biological, and physical detail is to be ignored, there is still
room for them to disagree on what facts are cognitively relevant. Certainly
connectionists are more likely to see the properties of neurons as relevant to

cognition than are computationalists. Computationalists, however, may well find other sources of evidence more relevant to their models than to connectionist models. Filling out this suggestion is the topic of the next subsection.

1.3. Connectionist Models Are More Easily Confirmed by Biological Data Than Are Computationalist Models

Although the claim that connectionist models are more easily confirmed by biological data than are computationalist models may have some intuitive plausibility, it is not entirely clear that it can be maintained. When connectionist models are given a neuronal interpretation, it is fairly easy to get some sorts of facts to bear on the theory. If, however, we adopt the subneuronal or supraneuronal theories, then confirmation and disconfirmation are much harder to come by, as was mentioned earlier. Moreover, there are cases where computationalist models admit of rather straightforward biological confirmation or disconfirmation. These cases may be found in the vast literature on the effects of lesions on cognitive processing. They offer a wealth of examples in which the biological fact that a person or animal has a lesion in a particular region of the brain is used as evidence, albeit weak evidence, concerning the functional role of that region of the brain, hence as evidence concerning the functional decomposition of tasks in the cerebral computer. To get a feel for this, consider an example based on the behavioral neuropsychology of the rat. (For one of a multitude of possible examples, see Harrell, Barlow, and Parsons, 1987. For a randomly selected example of the lesion studies in humans in a clinical setting, see Farah, 1984.)

Suppose a neuroscientist found that after removal of a particular portion of the brain a rat loses a cognitive capacity. It cannot learn to find a piece of food that may always be found in a particular location in a maze. Moreover, control rats learn where the food is kept in the maze with no difficulty. One way this phenomenon might be explained would be to suggest that the rat possesses at least two types of memory, memory for spatial facts and memory for other types of facts, and these are located in different regions of the brain. The lesion in question removes the region of the brain dedicated to spatial memory, so the test rats cannot remember where the food is kept, whereas the control rats can. This sort of theorizing certainly counts as computational insofar as it is concerned with the rat's computational resources, the way information is stored in the rat's brain. It is, of course, to be conceded that neuropsychological observations of the effects of lesions are extremely difficult to interpret, are sometimes difficult to reproduce, and involve a large number of variables. However, that lesion studies provide a valuable instance in which biological evidence can easily be brought to bear on computationalist hypotheses. Thus, it is far from clear that connectionist models are more easily confirmed by biological evidence than are computationalist models.

The point of the observations in the previous subsections has not been to say that connectionists and computationalists are in complete agreement on the role of biological facts in psychological theorizing. Instead, it is to support the growing belief that attitudes toward biological facts do not make for a great gap between those who work with networks and those who work with computationalist models of cognition.

2. COMPUTATIONAL SUFFICIENCY IN CONNECTIONISM

One of the common aims of both computationalist and connectionist models is to provide a set of mechanisms that is sufficient to explain cognition (McClelland, Rumelhart, & Hinton, 1986, p. 11; Pylyshyn, 1984, p. 74f; Rumelhart & Norman, 1981, p. 2). Computationalist models suggest that the sorts of processes that are adequate for defining a computer programming language are sufficient for explaining cognition. Or, as Pylyshyn (1984) put it,

> The term *sufficiency* refers to the theory's ability to explain how actual instances of behaviors are generated. Further, the explanation of the generation of such behaviors must be constructive, that is, effectively computable or realizable by a formal mechanism, for example, a Turing machine. (p. 75)

In connectionism, on the other hand, units, connections, and weights are supposed to be sufficient. There appears to be no doubt that the sufficiency condition is important in connectionism, yet there are numerous instances in the literature where connectionists use more than the canonical complement of units, connections, and weights. The subsections of subsection 2.1 explain four of these instances involving standard backpropagation weight change (Rumelhart, Hinton, & Williams, 1986), Boltzmann machine weight change (Hinton & Sejnowski, 1986), the interactive activation model of letter perception (McClelland & Rumelhart, 1981; Rumelhart & McClelland, 1982), and a Boltzmann machine theory of memory (Hinton & Sejnowski, 1986). Subsection 2.2 examines some strategies for bringing connectionism into line with the sufficiency requirement. Here at the outset we should note that the sufficiency condition is independent of any theory of the biological interpretation of units and connections, subneuronal, neuronal, or supraneuronal. All connectionists want computational sufficiency, regardless of their attitudes toward biological facts.

2.1. Examples of Insufficiency

2.1.1. Standard Backpropagation Weight Change. The standard backpropagation weight change procedure is an *error-correction procedure,* that is, it performs computations on inputs, then compares the actual outputs of the computations with the desired outputs, then uses the differences to make changes in weights. Sometimes this is called *supervised* learning. There is an obvious and well-known problem with these sorts of procedures because as a matter of psychological fact there does not always appear to be an external source of supervision. This is a problem, but not a violation of the sufficiency condition. Where a violation of sufficiency does occur, however, is when we note that, even assuming the availability of a supervisor, no units-and-connections mechanism is specified for comparing the actual output with the desired output.

Consider a second violation of the sufficiency condition. In backpropagation weight change, the network runs feed-forward computations on a set of input patterns noting the differences between the actual outputs of the computations and the desired outputs of the computations. In other words, it performs computations of, say, 100 input–output pairs. The sum of the differences found on all of these computations must be saved until the network has run through the entire training set, then weight changes are made on the basis of the sum of all the differences (Rumelhart, Hinton, & Williams, 1986, pp. 324ff). However, there is nothing in the general connectionist framework of units, connections, activation values, outputs, or weights for recording and preserving these differences. There is no units-and-connections account of this memory facility.

2.1.2. Boltzmann Machine Weight Change. Weight change in the Boltzmann machine model faces some similar problems. Weight change here consists of alternating learning and unlearning phases. In the learning phase, the network is given an input, annealed, and the network run through a sample of global states. While the sample is being taken, there must be some mechanism that determines the frequency with which each pair of units in the network simultaneously has an activation value of 1 during the sample of states. This sample is referred to as a set of *co-occurrence statistics*. For a network with n units, this means that there must be a mechanism that collects a set of $n(n - 1)$ learning co-occurrence statistics. In the unlearning phase, the network is given no input and again operated so as to yield a set of $n(n - 1)$ unlearning co-occurrence statistics. Finally, the difference between the learning co-occurrence statistics and the unlearning co-occurrence statistics are used to make weight changes. Thus, in addition to the mechanism(s) for collecting the co-occurrence statistics for the learning and unlearning phases, there must be some sort of memory resources for holding the learning and unlearning co-occurrence statistics after they have been collected and until they are used for weight changes. Here we have three important computational tasks of Boltzmann machine learning left in the background, unaccounted for in terms of activation values, outputs, weights, units, and connections: (a) There is no units-and-connections mechanism for comparing inputs and outputs, (b) there is no mechanism for collecting co-occurrence statistics, and (c) there is no mechanism for remembering the co-occurrence statistics.

2.1.3.   The Interactive Activation Model of Letter Perception.   The two problems we have described in backpropagation and Boltzmann machine weight change infect every model that applies these weight change procedures. In contrast, the problems to be described with the interactive activation model of letter perception are specific to the model of letter perception. They are impressive, however, for their number. The interactive activation model of letter perception was developed to accommodate a number of phenomena associated with the perception of letters in various contexts (McClelland & Rumelhart, 1981; Rumelhart & McClelland, 1982). For example, there is the *word advantage effect,* wherein it appears that it is easier to perceive letters in the context of words than in isolation. The effect is observed when human subjects are briefly shown targets consisting of either four-letter words or single letters in isolation, for example, *BEAD* or *B* _ _ _ . After the presentation, the targets are covered with a mottled mask and subjects are prompted with, for example *R* _ _ _ or *B* _ _ _ . The subject must then answer which of the two alternatives is the correct partial description of the briefly presented targets.

The model used to account for this phenomenon may be thought of as having two parts, one formulated in terms of the interactions of units and connections using the principles of interactive activation and the other as a black box. The network portion of the model, outlined in Fig. 4.1, consists of three layers of units:

1.   64 (= 4 × 16) *feature* units—16 units for each of four positions—that correspond to propositions asserting the presence of parts of letters, such as the lower left leg of the letter *A* or a part of the horizontal bar in the letter *H,*
2.   104 (= 4 × 26) *letter-position* units that correspond to propositions asserting the presence of 1 of 26 letters at one of four positions in a visual field, and
3.   *word* units corresponding to propositions asserting that a particular word is present.

In the model, the activation values indicate a sort of credibility that is assigned to each of the propositions. Connections between units corresponding to mutually consistent hypotheses are positively weighted, connections between units corresponding to mutually inconsistent hypotheses are negatively weighted. These are the central ideas of interactive activation.

Attached to the letter-position units of this network is a black box responsible for a number of tasks. The real-valued activation values of the letter-position units serve as the outputs of the explicitly described network. These outputs vary over time, thus the first thing the black box must have is some mechanism that knows when to read the output of this network so as to use it as the input to

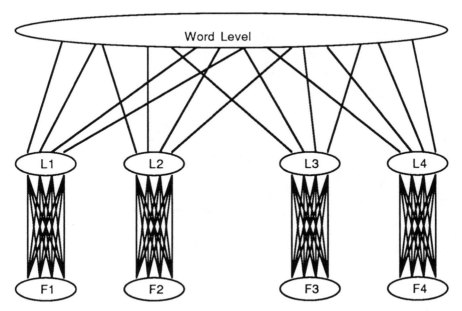

FIG. 4.1. General structure of the Interactive Activation Model of Letter Perception.

further processing (McClelland & Rumelhart, 1981, p. 382). Second, McClelland and Rumelhart postulated a mechanism that converts the activation values of the letter position units into four probability distributions: One distribution assigns a probability of occurrence to each letter that could have occurred at the first position, a second distribution assigns a probability of occurrence to each letter that could have occurred at the second position, and so on (McClelland & Rumelhart, 1981, p. 381). Third, after the distributions have been computed, the black box must read in the forced choice between, say, R _ _ _ and B _ _ _ , and use this along with the probability distribution for the first position to compute a choice. The black box uses the probe to select a position, then finds the most probable letter for that position. If the most probable letter is one of the two offered in the probe, that letter is selected. Otherwise, the black box conjectures one or the other randomly (McClelland & Rumelhart, 1981, p. 382). Here the black box portion of the model would appear to do no mean feat of processing, yet is not explained in terms of the actions of units and connections.

2.1.4.   The Boltzmann Machine as a Memory Module for Probabilistic Beliefs.   A somewhat more subtle case of incompleteness may be found in a particular use of the Boltzmann machine. Hinton and Sejnowski (1986) suggested that it is possible to use a Boltzmann machine as a "stochastic generative

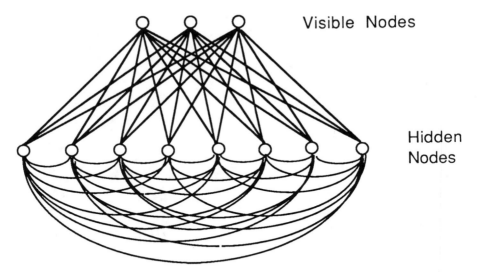

Visible Nodes

Hidden
Nodes

FIG. 4.2.   Structure of the Boltzmann Machine Memory Module.

model of the environment," or as what we call a *memory module*. In this use of
the Boltzmann machine, the units in the network are divided into two groups, the
visible and the hidden, as shown in Fig. 4.2. We suppose that there are v visible
units and 2^v hidden units connected so that (a) every visible unit is connected to
every hidden unit, (b) every hidden unit is connected to every other hidden unit,
and (c) no visible unit is connected to any other visible unit.

Although the mathematical details of the Boltzmann machine will be omitted in
the present account, the interested reader may refer to Hinton and Sejnowski
(1986). When in use as a memory module, the network operates in its normal
fashion so that each global state of the network will appear with a fixed limiting
relative frequency. This *equilibrium* probability distribution over global states defines an equilibrium marginal distribution over the states of the visible units of the
network. This marginal distribution may be used to represent probabilities of
events in the environment. Thus, if the pattern "000" appears on the set of visible
units with a limiting relative frequency of 0.3, the network assigns a probability of
0.3 to the environmental state denoted by "000".[2]

We suppose that the network learns the probabilities of events, or changes the
probabilities it assigns to events, using the Boltzmann machine weight change
procedure. As described earlier, the procedure has two phases, the learning phase

---

[2]Note that the limiting relative frequency is not a philosophical interpretation of the concept of
probability; it is only a network's way of representing the probabilities it assigns to events, whatever
probabilities may be. Thus, in principle, one could hold a subjectivist interpretation of probability
while also holding that a person's subjective probabilities are represented as the limiting relative
frequency of states of the visible nodes of a Boltzmann machine.

and the unlearning phase. It is hoped that, through learning, the difference between the marginal distribution over the visible units during the learning phase and the marginal distribution over the visible units during the unlearning phase will approach 0, hence that, during learning, the limiting relative frequency of states of the visible units will approach the probability of the corresponding states in the environment. In other words, we ultimately wish to have the two distributions be the same.

We should note that it is this learning theory that suggests intensional descriptions of the operation of the memory module in spite of the fact that Hinton and Sejnowski declined to use this vocabulary and speak only of a "generative model of the environment." We say that the distribution on the visible units of the network constitutes the model's *beliefs* about the probabilities of events in its environment. If, in addition, the probabilities the model assigns to events equal the probabilities of the corresponding events in the environment, the model's beliefs are true. We may also wish to say that the model's beliefs are approximately true insofar as the probabilities the model assigns to the events are close to the environmental probabilities. These are the things to say because the most plausible rationale for wanting the marginal distribution on the visible units to come to match (or approximate) the distribution over environmental states is that one wants successful learning to lead to (approximately) true beliefs.

We have assumed that memories will be stored using the Boltzmann machine weight change procedure, but we must now ask how they will be accessed. How can a network use the limiting relative frequency with which a pattern of activation appears on the visible units of a Boltzmann machine as the basis for verbal reports of beliefs or other actions? How can we recall the probability of an arbitrarily selected event, say, the event denoted by "000," in the form of a single pattern of activation suitable for use by other modules for other tasks, such as verbal reporting or decision making? Certainly we cannot "wait for the limit." We need to use a sample of the behavior of the network. Hinton and Sejnowski provided no account of how this might be done, much less an account in terms of units and connections. Note that the problem here is not one of making implicit beliefs explicit. The problem is how the network can act on probabilistic beliefs that are not stored in the canonical form of a single pattern of activation. Overt verbal report of its beliefs is one way in which the model might act on its beliefs, but certainly not the only one. It might use its belief, or tacit belief if you will, to decide on a course of action, such as whether or not to buy home fire insurance or whether or not it is reasonable to try to steal second base in a game of baseball. Both decisions may well rely on implicit estimates of the probabilities of events that the agent cannot articulate.

It is worth noting that a mechanism for recall is essential to having a genuine memory. Two examples of systems lacking a mechanism for recall will illustrate this point. The first involves cases of amnesia induced by electroconvulsive therapy (ECT). After ECT, persons for a time lose the ability to recall events shortly preceding the therapy, but thereafter recover this ability. Apparently, in these cases, during the state of amnesia the person has the information about the events stored in memory, but cannot access it. During the time in which the person cannot recall the information, the person does not really have a memory of those events. This is exactly what is going on in a Boltzmann machine memory network lacking a recall procedure. The information is in the model in the sense that the probability is coded as a limiting relative frequency, but for lack of a system of recall that converts the information into usable canonical form the model is permanently *amnesic*. A permanently amnesic "memory" model, however, has no memory at all.

A second example comes from the use of registers in von Neumann computers. In these machines, one can store a piece of data in a register and keep track of it by the register's address. If, however, one loses the address, the information in the register will be unchanged, but it will nonetheless not be recoverable. In an important sense, the information is no longer stored in memory; a computer program can no longer act appropriately on the basis of that information. A program may inadvertently access the information, but that would likely be an accidental, inappropriate use of the information. As we said in the case of the human that is permanently prevented from recalling information, a machine that can never access the information in its registers, in an important sense, never remembers anything. So, in particular, a Boltzmann machine memory network without a way to recover stored probabilities is not really a memory network at all.

2.2. Strategies for Meeting the Sufficiency Condition

There seem to be two principal strategies for dealing with aspects of connectionist models that do not conform to the sufficiency condition. First, one might show that in fact the hypothesized mechanisms one thought to be necessary are not in fact necessary. This has happened to some extent with the storage of error terms in backpropagation and Boltzmann machine learning. Although the original "derivation" of the backpropagation weight change rule in Rumelhart, Hinton, and Williams (1986) presupposed that weight changes were not to be made until all the input patterns had been presented, actual simulation results have shown that this is often not necessary in order to achieve acceptable computational results. In other words, it is not necessary to save the sum of errors until all patterns have been tested, so a memory facility for this is not necessary. Similar developments have taken place with Boltzmann machine learning.

The second strategy is to construct a network that performs the tasks that were previously left undone. This seems to be the strategy that is needed to bring the interactive activation model into line with the computational sufficiency criterion. It also seems to be the strategy that needs to be employed with the Boltzmann machine memory module. The next subsections of the chapter indicate how this might be done for the Boltzmann machine memory module. They describe the construction of a recall module. It should be noted before we begin that there is a sense in which the addition of units for specific functions is easy and a sense in which it remains hard. It is easy in the sense of getting a set of units and connections to do the job. It is hard, however, to make the solution seem natural and elegant. We discuss this point in a bit more detail in subsection 2.2.2.

2.2.1.   *A Boltzmann Machine Recall Module.*   To recall probabilities stored in the model, we simply add units and connections to form a *recall module* that recalls a probability stored in memory by statistical inference based on a sample of the changing states of the visible units. The design of the recall module involves the solution of two principal difficulties. First, we assume that more than one event and its associated probability may be stored in memory at one time, so we will need some mechanism that will allow us to recall the probability of one event as opposed to the probability of another. That is, we need a units-and-connections mechanism for recalling the event denoted by, say, *000* on one occasion and the event denoted by *111* on another. A network with the structure shown in Fig. 4.3 can do this. Suppose we wish to recall the probability of the event denoted by *000*. This pattern of activation is given as input to the *query units*. This pattern of activation remains on the query units while the units in the Boltzmann machine continue to be evaluated, say, 1,000 times, so that the global

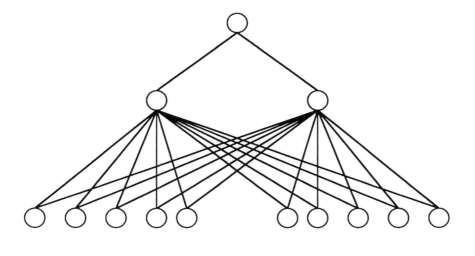

Query Nodes   Visible Nodes in
                                Memory Module

FIG. 4.3.   Portion of the Recall Module dedicated to transforming specific patterns to be recalled into a sequence of 0's and 1's.

states of the network may change. Any time the pattern of activation on the query units matches the pattern of activation on the visible units of the Boltzmann machine memory module the so-called *sample frequency unit* produces an output of 1. This pattern matching network, therefore, transforms a sequence of states of the visible units into a sequence of 0s and 1s on the sample frequency unit. The structure and weights for the recall module are taken from an example presented by Rumelhart, Hinton, and Williams (1986) for solving the symmetry problem.[3]

The preceding portion of the recall module transforms the various patterns of activation appearing on the visible units of the Boltzmann machine into a string of 0s and 1s. The second major problem is then to transform the temporal sequence of 1s and 0s on the sample frequency unit into a single pattern of activation that can be used by other network modules. This, after all, is the current canonical form of representation in connectionism. To effect this transformation, we add an output array of, say, 100 units and connections to the network shown in Fig. 4.3. This produces the network shown in Fig. 4.4. Each of these connections has a weight of $+1$ and the thresholds are such that the units output a 1 after a sufficient number of 1s appear on the sample frequency unit. Thus, if a 1,000-member sample of global states is taken, the threshold of the first unit in the output array is equal to 9, so that if the sample frequency unit comes on 10 or more times in the 1,000-member sample, the first unit in the output array comes on. Similarly, the threshold of the second unit is equal to 19 so that if the sample frequency unit comes on at least 20 times in the 1,000-member sample, the second unit in the output array comes on. In general, then, we let the i-th unit have a threshold of $(10i - 1)$, so that it comes on just in case the sample

---

[3]The details of this network are rather tedious, so we relegate them to a footnote. The nodes in the recall module are not Boltzmann machine nodes, they are deterministic binary threshold nodes. Consider the first query node and the first visible node in the Boltzmann machine. Both send a connection to the two hidden nodes, both of which have thresholds of 0. The query node sends a positive weight to the first hidden node and a negative weight to the second hidden node. The visible node, however, sends a negative weight to the first hidden node and a positive weight to the second hidden node. For convenience, suppose the magnitude of all four weights is 2. The second query node and the second visible node will be connected to the hidden nodes in the same way, except that the weights on the connections will be twice that on the first pair. That is, the second query node will send a positive weight of 4 to the first hidden node and a negative weight of 4 to the second hidden node, while the second visible node of the Boltzmann machine sends a negative weight of four to the first hidden node and a positive weight of four to the second hidden node. It is left to the reader to verify that both hidden nodes will have activation values of 0 just in case the entire pattern on the query nodes matches the entire pattern on the visible nodes.

This accounts for the connections from the visible nodes of the Boltzmann machine and the query nodes to the hidden nodes. Consider now the connections from the hidden nodes to the sample frequency node. This node has a threshold of -1, so that it is on unless it is inhibited by the hidden nodes. The weights on connections coming from both of the hidden nodes are -1, so if either hidden node is on, the sample frequency node will be turned off. With this configuration, the sample frequency node will be on just in case the patterns on the query nodes and the visible nodes match.

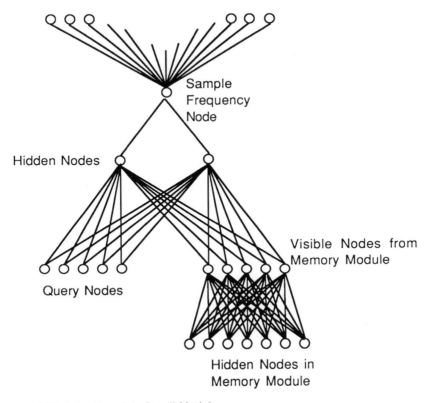

FIG. 4.4.   Complete Recall Module.

frequency unit comes on at least 10i times during the sampling. This allows a recall of the probabilities of events accurate to the nearest percentile. This last array of units sums the inputs it receives over an interval of time; it uses what might be called *temporal integration*. This contrasts with the typical network use of *spatial integration*, where the activation value of a unit at a given instant is determined by the net input to the unit (plus, perhaps, the activation value of the unit at the previous instant).[4]

We have added a recall module to the basic Boltzmann machine memory module, but of course, one need not stop here in building additional structure onto the Boltzmann machine memory module. One might embed the memory unit just described into a larger network for other cognitive tasks. One possibility

---

[4]We should note that although the terminology of spatial and temporal integration is borrowed from neurobiology, the borrowing is merely for expository purposes. There seems to be no reason to think that spatial and temporal integration in neural systems is used in anything like this model.

that has been described in detail involves modifying the recall unit and combining it with additional units and connections so as to accommodate some aspects of decision making under risk (Aizawa, 1989). The suggested network implements a portion of Kahneman and Tversky's (1979) prospect theory. It models aspects of the way humans choose between two courses of action when there are two possible states of affairs with known probabilities of occurrence.

2.2.2. Remaining Difficulties with the Boltzmann Machine Memory Unit.   It should also not be thought that the modification just offered brings the Boltzmann machine model of probabilistic memory into tremendous agreement with empirical data or philosophical intuitions about human cognition. As a general point, for example, we may note that the choice of structure for the whole memory is underdetermined by available biological and behavioral evidence. There would appear to be a multitude of possible networks for bringing about the desired phenomenon. On a more specific point, the model as laid out earlier has no means for expressing probabilistic beliefs of different degrees of precision, where humans can have both very precise and very imprecise probabilistic beliefs. Humans can believe that there is a 1 in 1,024 chance of tossing 10 heads in a row on a fair coin or that it is unlikely that it will rain tomorrow. The present system, in contrast, always has quite precise beliefs, it is the real number between 1 and 0 corresponding to the limiting relative frequency with which a pattern of activation appears on the visible units. As a more philosophical objection, because it may frequently happen that the sample frequency of a state of the visible units does not equal the limiting relative frequency of the state, the model will often produce as output a belief that it does not really have. The model will not say, or act on, what it believes. It will have one probabilistic belief, represented by the limiting relative frequency of the state of the visible units, but it will report, or act on, another, represented by the sample frequency of the state.

One continuing problem with the model arises because it remains empirically inadequate in ways such as those just sketched. There is also a deeper problem, however, because the models fail to come to grips with sufficiency in a "nice" way. One wishes to have the additional structure fit in with the existing structure in a "natural" way. The additional structure must be added in a principled way; it cannot be tailored to fit in an ad hoc manner. The additional structure in the recall module is ad hoc. It does not have the principled elegance that seemed to be found in the original memory module. Connectionists seem to aspire to this sort of elegance, even in cases where they arguably do not have it. For example, it is commonly felt that one of the attractive features of the Rumelhart–McClelland model (1986) of the acquisition of the past tense of English verbs is the fact that overregularization falls out as a natural consequence of just the representational system, the structure of the net, and the weight change procedure. There is a certain elegance to this. The naturalness of the network has been challenged by Lachter and Bever (1988), but it is nonetheless clear that naturalness is a genuine connectionist aspiration. And, of course, it is a proper aspiration. The methodological challenge for connectionism lies not just in respecting the computational sufficiency condition, but in meeting the computational sufficiency condition in ways that preserve, or create, the naturalness that is such an appealing feature of scientific models in general.

3. CONCLUSION

Contrary to most philosophical discussions centering on connectionism and more traditional computer-based approaches to cognition, this chapter stresses the difference between computationalism and connectionism, rather than symbolism versus subsymbolism. This is to focus on the mathematics of the two approaches, rather than the philosophical commentary that has been contingently attached to them. This is as I believe it should be. Despite the difference in focus, however, it should be clear that this broader difference in intellectual perspective does not affect the present concerns with biology and computational sufficiency. If one is a subsymbolist one should still be concerned, first, with the role of biological facts in subsymbolism (even if this means ignoring biological facts) and, second, with respecting the sufficiency of units and connections. This chapter indicates that there is less in the biological arena separating the subsymbolist and the symbolist, the connectionist and the computationalist, than one might have expected. Moreover, we have rejected the claim made by Rumelhart and Norman (1981), that connectionists are concerned with computational sufficiency where computationalists are not. We cited Pylyshyn's (1984) work that explicitly endorses the importance of computational sufficiency. Moreover, we indicated ways in which connectionism flouts sufficiency at times and some of the ways in which connectionist modelling must change in order to meet the sufficiency condition shared by connectionists and their rivals.

REFERENCES

Aizawa, K. (1989). *The promise of parallel distributed processing.* Unpublished doctoral dissertation, University of Pittsburgh.

Churchland, P. S., & Sejnowski, T. J. (1989). Neural representation and neural computation. In L. Nadel, L. Cooper, P. Culicover, & R. Harnish (Eds.), *Neural connections, mental computation* (pp. 15–48). Cambridge, MA: MIT Press.

Farah, M. (1984). The neurological basis of mental imagery: A componential analysis. In S. Pinker (Ed.), *Visual cognition* (pp. 245–271). Cambridge, MA: MIT Press.

Gluck, M., & Rumelhart, D. (1990). *Neuroscience and connectionist theory.* Hillsdale, NJ: Lawrence Erlbaum Associates.

Harrell, L. E., Barlow, T. S., & Parsons, D. (1987). Cholinergic neurons, learning, and recovery of function. *Behavioral Neuroscience, 101,* 644–652.

Hinton, G., & Sejnowski, T. (1986). Learning and relearning in Boltzmann machines. In D. E. Rumelhart, J. L. McClelland, & the PDP Research Group (Eds.), *Parallel distributed processing: Explorations in the microstructure of cognition* (Vol. 1, pp. 282–317). Cambridge, MA: MIT Press.

Hopfield, J. J. (1982, April). Neural networks and physical systems with emergent collective computational abilities. *Proceedings of the National Academy of Science, USA, 79,* 2554–2558.

Hopfield, J. J. (1984, May). Neurons with graded response have collective computational properties like those of two-state neurons. *Proceedings of the National Academy of Science, USA, 81,* 3088–3092.

Kahneman, D., & Tversky, A. (1979). Prospect theory: An analysis of decisions under risk. *Econometrica, 47* 263–291.

Kandel, E. R., & Schwartz, J. H. (1985). *Principles of neural science* (2nd. ed.). New York: Elsevier North Holland.

Lachter, J., & Bever, T. G. (1988). The relation between linguistic structure and associative theories of language learning: A constructive critique of some connectionist learning models. In S. Pinker & J. Mehler (Eds.), *Connections and symbols* (pp. 195–247). Cambridge, MA: MIT Press.

Machtey, M., & Young, P. (1978). *An introduction to the general theory of algorithms.* New York: North Holland.

McClelland, J. L., & Rumelhart, D. E. (1981). An interactive activation model of context effects in letter perception: Part I. An account of basic findings. *Psychological Review, 88,* 375–407.

McClelland, J. L., Rumelhart, D. E., & Hinton, G. E. (1986). The appeal of parallel distributed processing. In D. E. Rumelhart, J. L. McClelland, & the PDP Research Group (Eds.), *Parallel distributed processing: Explorations in the microstructure of cognition* (Vol. 1, pp. 3–44). Cambridge, MA: MIT Press.

Nadel, L., Cooper, L. A., Culicover, P., & Harnish, R. M. (1989). (Eds.). *Neural connections, mental computation.* Cambridge, MA: MIT Press.

Rumelhart, D. E., Hinton, G. E., and McClelland, J. L. (1986). A General Framework for Parallel Distributed Processing. In D. E. Rumelhart, J. L. McClelland, and the PDP Research Group, (Eds.), *Parallel distributed processing: Explorations in the microstructure of cognition* (Vol. 1, pp. 45–76). Cambridge, MA: MIT Press.

Pylyshyn, Z. (1984). *Computation and Cognition.* Cambridge, MA: MIT Press.

Rumelhart, D. E., Hinton, G. E., & Williams, R. J. (1986). Learning internal representations by error propagation. In D. E. Rumelhart, J. L. McClelland, & the PDP Research Group (Eds.), *Parallel distributed processing: Explorations in the microstructure of cognition* (Vol. 1, pp. 318–362). Cambridge, MA: MIT Press.

Rumelhart, D. E., & McClelland, J. L. (1982). An interactive activation model of context effects in letter perception: Part 2. The contextual enhancement effect and some tests and extensions of the model. *Psychological Review, 89,* 60–94.

Rumelhart, D. E., & McClelland, J. L. (1986). On learning the past tense of English verbs. In J. L. McClelland, D. E. Rumelhart & the PDP Research Group (Eds.), *Parallel distributed processing: Explorations in the microstructure of cognition* (Vol. 2, pp. 170–215). Cambridge, MA: MIT Press.

Rumelhart, D. E., & Norman, D. A. (1981). Introduction to G. E. Hinton, & J. A. Anderson (Eds.), *Parallel models of associative memory.* Hillsdale, NJ: Lawrence Erlbaum Associates.

Sejnowski, T. J. (1986). Open questions about computation in cerebral cortex. In J. L. McClelland, D. E. Rumelhart, & the PDP Research Group (Eds.), *Parallel distributed processing: Explorations in the microstructure of cognition* (Vol. 2, pp. 372–389). Cambridge, MA: MIT Press.

Shepherd, G. M. (1988). *Neurobiology* (2nd. ed.). New York: Oxford University Press.

Smolensky, P. (1988). On the proper treatment of connectionism. *Behavioral and Brain Sciences, 11,* 1–74.

5

Who's Afraid of Multiple Realizability?: Functionalism, Reductionism, and Connectionism

Justin Schwartz
Ohio State University

1. INTRODUCTION

The current orthodoxy among cognitive scientists and philosophers of mind holds that reductive materialism has been decisively refuted by Fodor (1981) and Putnam (1975). Because mental states are in principle *multiply realizable* in a variety of physical ways, for example, in humans and computers, it is widely held that "If functionalism is true, physicalism is probably false" (Block 1980, p. 270). *Functionalism* is a disputed notion, often identified with multiple realizability—mistakenly, it is argued here. For our purposes it is the view in philosophy of mind that mental states are characterized by their causal or computational role in producing behavior. *Physicalism* here means the metaphysical thesis that every kind of mental state is identical with some kind of physical state. The corollary epistemological thesis is *reductionism,* the doctrine that the mental can in principle be systematically explained in terms of or reduced to the physical in virtue of these identities.[1] A similar multiple realizability argument dismisses the relevance to psychology of *connectionism,* sketched in the next section. This is a reductive materialist program if we identify connectionist networks with neural networks. According to the argument, even if cognition is implemented in the "brainlike" way connectionists urge, this has no explanatory bearing on psychology because it is only one possible implementation.

The multiple realizability of the mental, according to Fodor and Putnam,

---

[1]Smart (1971) and Armstrong (1968) are the classic statements of these positions. A different form of physicalism (constitutive materialism) which does not rely on identity is sketched in the body of the present chapter and further developed in Schwartz (1991).

shows that such reductionist claims are false because the mental and the physical unsystematically cross-classify each other. The same type of mental state (e.g., a belief that p) can be realized in a variety of physical states; thus, we must reject the classic identity thesis (strong or *type* physicalism). In addition, because the same mental state can have a variety of types of physical realizations which may have no scientifically interesting commonalities, the reductionist program of explaining mental properties and processes in physical terms must go by the board. The orthodoxy accepts a weaker identity thesis (weak or *token* physicalism), according to which each token or instance of any mental state is identical to some token of a physical state, but no type of mental state is identical to any type of physical state. The token identity is a merely metaphysical fact that does not underwrite any explanatory connection between the mental and the physical. Psychology is autonomous and irreducible. Call this view *autonomous functionalism*.[2] As Block's remark shows, some even hold that the expression autonomous functionalism is redundant: functionalism implies the autonomy of the mental.

I argue that this view is radically mistaken. If valid, the argument proves too much. A functional state of a system is one intrinsically characterized by its causal or computational role in mediating between inputs (e.g., sensory stimulation) and outputs (e.g., behavior), as well as by the internal relations among the functional states themselves. Multiple realizability is a property of any functionally characterized state, so the argument would establish the irreducibility of any theory that appeals essentially to such states, such as transmission genetics, which adverts to the states and properties of genes. *Gene* is a functional term. To say *x is a gene* is to characterize it in terms of its functional role in transmitting hereditary information. Genes are therefore multiply realizable. But if the multiple realizability argument for autonomy denies the reducibility of genetics, this is a reductio: transmission genetics is in part reduced to molecular genetics.

What has gone wrong? One diagnosis focuses on the empiricist notion of reduction invoked by the multiple realizability argument, which fails to capture many actual explanations of less basic by more basic sciences (see Schwartz 1991). A deeper diagnosis, though, holds that autonomous functionalism, while not perhaps bound to an untenable empiricist account of science and of reductive explanation, has an inappropriate conception of psychology as a priori universal, applying in the same way to all cognizers. This is no more plausible than a universal biology. I suggest that psychology, like biology, be *provincialized,* giving us different psychologies for different classes of cognizers. The potential universal applicability of psychology may be reconstrued as a consequence of its

---

[2]The autonomy is a matter of irreducibility. It has nothing to do with the psychological individualism presupposed by Stich's "autonomy principle," or Fodor's similar "methodological solipsism" (Fodor, 1981, pp. 225–256) according to which only what's inside the epidermis is admissible in an explanatory psychological theory (Stich, 1983, pp. 160–170).

idealized character. This move permits species-specific or, more precisely, provincial, reduction of psychologies.[3] A reduction of merely human psychology would count as satisfying reductive materialism, whether or not it reduced the psychology of any possible cognizer. Whether any such reductions take the form of establishing classical type-identities or some different relation of constitution (as suggested in sections 6 and 7) depends on the facts and on theoretical convenience. Whether any reduction of psychology at all is forthcoming is an empirical question, but I wish to remove the idea that multiple realizability is an impediment.

2. CONNECTIONISM AND GOFAI

The discussion bears on more than the fate of the identity theory and materialistic reductionism. Almost exactly the same issues emerge in the context of the current debate over the relation between the competing programs of GOFAI (Good Old-Fashioned Artificial Intelligence, in Haugeland's [1985] expression) and connectionism as accounts of human cognitive processes.[4] Very roughly, advocates of GOFAI maintain that such processes must invoke explicit rules operating on syntactically structured representations. Connectionists urge that these processes be understood instead in terms of the activation of nodes or patterns of nodes in neural nets that are not governed by explicit rules nor have any syntactic structure. Fodor and Pylyshyn (1988) argue that while GOFAI models may be implemented in a connectionist manner, they need not be, and therefore whatever the implementation, it is not explanatorily interesting in understanding cognition. The claim is essentially that GOFAI is multiply realizable in different implementations, and so autonomous with respect to them.

Here the issue is not directly the reduction of functionally characterized mental states to physical ones but of one functional model, GOFAI, purportedly of cognition, to another, connectionism, which Fodor and Pylyshyn maintain is not a model of cognition at all and the connectionists claim is the correct model of cognition. I do not attempt to adjudicate who, if either, is right. My point is more restricted, namely, that multiple realizability arguments against reduction of

---

[3]Species-specific is not the right term, as we can see in view of the biological analogy. All forms of terrestrial life appear to use DNA as the hereditary material (viruses are a primitive precursor of this system). So we have at least a planet-specific genetics shared by different species on Earth. (It may be in part because of this that the physiological basis for psychology also appears to be shared widely among different terrestrial species.) So I use the term *provincial*, explained more fully later, where that indicates any group of species or class of entities that shares a sort of structural basis for a higher-order functional system, biological or psychological.

[4]It is debatable how different the programs are and whether they really are in competition. See Bechtel (1988) for discussion. I believe but will assume without argument that they really do compete.

GOFAI or psychology to connectionism are as defective as those against reduction of the mental to the physical. Therefore, if GOFAI is the correct account of cognition and if GOFAI architecture has a connectionist implementation in humans, then connectionism provides a reduction of GOFAI in humans.[5]

The parallel between the mental–physical case and GOFAI-connectionism case may be closer than mere analogy. As Churchland (1989, pp. 153–196) observed, part of the attraction of connectionism is precisely its promise of offering a more realistic account than GOFAI does of neural processing in human brains. Connectionists hope that their networks will be revealed to be networks of neurons. If so, then, GOFAI aside, connectionism might provide a physical reduction of human cognition. It is still too early to say whether connectionism is more than merely promising as an account of the functional architecture of cognition, much less whether it is also the correct account of the neural architecture. Whether or not connectionism is the correct account of how cognition is implemented in any cognizer, however, my point is that if it is nonetheless the correct account for human beings, that is good enough for provincial reductive explanation of human cognition. And that would be good enough for reductive materialism.

3. ANTI-CHAUVINISM AND AUTONOMY

Underlying autonomous functionalism is the intuition that psychology, like arithmetic, is not tied down to the physical structures in which it may be instantiated. Just as the same mathematics applies whether we use electronic calculator, a wooden abacus, or a human brain,[6] so (it is said) psychological explanations must apply equally and in the same way to humans, thinking computers, or Martians. Our provincial physical constitution is highly contingent. Martian neurophysiology might even be silicon-based (like a computer) rather than car-

---

[5]Connectionism enthusiasts (I am a moderate fan of the program) tend to deny the two antecedent clauses. They think that GOFAI is wrong and connectionism right as an account of cognition. They typically hold that the correct relation between the two models is not that the latter reduces the former, but rather replaces it. This is a sort of eliminativism about GOFAI rather than any sort of reductionism about it. Many connectionists, however, think of connectionism as a program for reducing commonsense psychology if not GOFAI; although some, like Churchland, conceive of it (if *conceive* applies here) as a replacement for commonsense psychology, and therefore are full-fledged eliminativists about the mental, not just about GOFAI.

A different possibility is suggested later: even if GOFAI is wrong as an account of much of cognition, as I suspect, it may be construed as an idealization of connectionist mechanisms, which therefore (as I understand reduction) reduce it. At this point I do not think we know enough to say, although I suspect that this may be the best way to look at it. In Schwartz (in press) I urge that this sort of ideal type reductionism is the best way to understand propositional attitude psychology and our ordinary folk theory of mind.

[6]Cummins and Schwartz (1988) explore this analogy, which is common, but problematic. See Schwartz (in press, section 10.3) for more discussion.

bon-based. But these differences cannot be that important when it comes to psychological explanation. To do psychology at all, we must abstract from the material constitution of beings whose behavior we seek to explain. To deny this is chauvinist, refusing to attribute mentality because of irrelevant differences in physical realization (Block 1980, p. 270).[7] This intuition may be expressed by the claim that beings who vary widely physically can have identical mental states, just as calculators that vary widely physically can have identical computational states. That is to say, psychological states, like arithmetic or computational ones, are capable of multiple physical realizations.

The multiple realizability argument presupposes that psychology has to fit any possible intelligent beings, even ones *ex hypothesi* different from us physically. Is this a reasonable demand? Humans are the only class of beings that we know has a full-blown intentional psychology, and who, therefore, could be objects of empirical psychological study as things now stand. We are interested in non-human intelligence, of course; and if we knew any thinking computers or intelligent aliens, we would be very interested in them, too. But so far as we know, there aren't any. Below I suggest some things we might say if there were. This chapter argues that functionalism and multiple realizability are independent theses.

The orthodoxy holds that multiple realizability, so construed, together with a number of supposedly uncontroversial claims about the nature of reductive explanation, shows that distinct disciplines will cross-classify their predicates so that there will be no clean correlations among their terms (Fodor, 1981, p. 145). The same belief that p would be realized by physical state P1 in humans, P2 in Martians, P3 in some type of computer, and so forth. Type-type correlations (implied by the classic identity thesis) are a necessary condition for reduction on the empiricist model invoked by Fodor, so nothing would count as a proper explanation of psychological phenomena in physical terms. Such phenomena will have physical descriptions, allowing us to a degree to save our materialist inclinations, but this materialism (token physicalism) will do no scientific work.

Fodor's presentation of the argument relies on the logical empiricist deductive-nomological (D-N) account of explanation as *nomic subsumption*.[8] To ex-

---

[7]Liberalism, the opposite vice, is the attribution of mentality to beings which plausibly do not have it.

[8]Logical empiricism was the reigning philosophical account of the structure of science from the 1930s to the mid-1960s. See Nagel (1961) for a comprehensive account. It has succumbed to 40 years of withering criticism. Empiricism may be understood, roughly, as the doctrine that science systematizes into laws statements about observable regularities in experience, enabling us to predict the course of experience from statements of these lawlike regularities. Explanation on the empiricist account is exactly symmetrical to prediction. In contrast, scientific realism—the view of science I share with Fodor and (the old) Putnam—regards science as the description of the real nature of phenomena and their explanation by elucidation of the causal mechanisms that produce or (in cases of reduction) constitute them. Scientific realism accords no special status to observed phenomena and is not committed to seeking laws.

plain an event, a law, or a theory, according to this view, is to derive it logically from a more general law or theory. A reduced law or theory T_1 is fully explained by or reduced to a reducing law or theory T_2 just in case every theoretical term F of T_1 is linked by biconditional "bridge laws" to a term G of T_2 (so that [F iff G])—thus reducing the terms referring to entities or properties. With such links, the laws, and ideally the whole of T_1 would be deductively derivable from T_2. Fodor's argument denies that the terms and laws of psychology have the "right" kind of coextensions (lawlike ones) at the physical level.

Fodor (1981) illustrated the point with Gresham's Law—roughly, "Bad money drives out good"—an example of a purported law from economics, a non-basic science. With respect to any physical explanation of such a generalization, he says:

> A physical description which covers all [monetary exchanges] must be wildly disjunctive. Some monetary exchanges involve strings of wampum. Some involve dollar bills. And some involve signing one's name to a check. What are the chances that a disjunction of physical predicates which covers all these events . . . expresses a physical kind? (p. 134)

To put it formally, at the level of psychology or economics, we have interesting explanatory laws of the idealized form

$$(x)(Fx \rightarrow Gx) \tag{1}$$

where F and G stand for psychological or economic type terms, identifying real properties which are related as they are because of their intrinsic nature. These generalizations are real laws in part because their arguments are kind terms, reflecting the way the world is actually cut up. The properties to which F and G refer may be realized or implemented at the physical level in various ways, so that F and G correspond in some physical theory to a *disjunction* of complex physical terms; one has F just in case one has (U or V or W); one has G just in case one has (X or Y or Z), where U-Z are terms in physical theory, or at least are physical descriptions. These disjunctions are not (are not likely to be?) kinds. The disjunction (U or V or W)] is not a type term. There are then no type-type correlations among the terms of T_1 and T_2. The physical generalization corresponding to (1) is then

$$(x)([Ux \lor Vx \lor Wx] \rightarrow [Xx \lor Yx \lor Zx]). \tag{2}$$

But nothing of this form, Fodor says, can be a law or an explanatory generalization just because the arguments of the conditional are not type terms.[9]

---

[9]Fodor's insistence that the arguments of a *proper law* must designate natural (or social?) kinds sits poorly with an empiricist account of reduction, given empiricist skepticism about kinds. Fodor insists on kinds because he is a scientific realist who thinks that things enter into causal and other relations with each other in virtue of their objective properties, including causal powers, but realists should not use the D-N model, which is motivated by an antirealistic empiricism. On the D-N model explanatory force is a linguistic feature of the theory (that the explanation is a valid argument) and not due to intrinsic characteristics of the phenomena, as a realist would like.

As the informal presentations previously sketched suggest, the force of the argument does not depend on the details of the D-N model, so Fodor's use of it may be regarded as heuristic. Be that as it may, because the disjunctions will not be type terms,

> whether the physical descriptions of the events subsumed by [interesting psychological generalizations] have anything in common is, in an obvious sense, entirely irrelevant to the truth of the generalizations, or to their interestingness, or to their degree of confirmation, or indeed to any of their epistemologically important properties. (p. 133)

Disjunctive generalizations like formula (2) will not properly explain laws like formula (1), and therefore the more basic theories which describe the realization or implementation of less basic theories will not reduce those theories. The two levels are autonomous. We must accept "the disunity of science as a working hypothesis" (Fodor, 1981, p. 120).

Fodor and Pylyshyn's (1988) critique of connectionism as an account of cognition reveals the same structure of argument and may help to make its force more manifest. They argue that psychology qua cognition must be understood, in view of the evidence, as rule-governed manipulation of syntactically structured symbols (that parallel a semantic interpretation of those symbol strings). The classical computer architectures of GOFAI, whose algorithms perform just such manipulations, provide the best model of psychological theory. Connectionist models, which do not operate with rules or structured representations, may be regarded as implementing GOFAI models (insofar as they can do so). But the implementation is at best irrelevant to psychology and at worst misleading and impoverished. First, irrelevance:

> the *implementation,* and all properties associated with the particular realization of the algorithm . . . in a particular case, is irrelevant to the psychological theory; only the algorithm and the representations on which it operates are intended as a psychological hypothesis. (p. 65)

Tienson correctly reads this as invoking a multiple realizability argument. "If we found Martians who satisfied the GOFAI cognitive theory, but not the connectionist implementation, we would (and should) say that the Martians were cognitively, psychologically, like us" (Tienson, 1988, p. 13). Connectionism may or may not be right, but "it couldn't be *psychology*" (Fodor & Pylyshyn, 1988, p. 66).

Second, and quite differently, misleadingness and impoverishment. These objections have nothing to do with the concern about mere implementation. If, taken by the apparently closer analogy of connectionism to brain processes, we regard connectionism as a model of cognition and not a mere implementation of GOFAI programs, they say, we are driven back on a "largely discredited Associationist psychology" (Fodor & Pylyshyn, 1988, p. 63), which cannot account for the most important features of cognition. These include: *productivity* (our unbounded capacity to represent indefinitely many propositions), *systematicity* (the way our ability to produce and understand some propositions is intrinsically connected, in virtue of the syntax, to our ability to produce and understand others); and *compositionality* (that each representation makes an approximately similar semantic contribution wherever it occurs). Connectionism, which views mental representation and processing as the activition of interconnected nodes of the unstructured connectionist net, suffers from the same weaknesses in explaining these phenomena as classical empiricist associationist psychology, which used "ideas" or mental images instead of nodes and relations of "similarity" among ideas instead of the connectionists' (presumably electrochemical) links activitating or inhibiting nodes (presumably neurons). "The current attempt to . . . 'take the brain seriously' . . . lead[s]," say Fodor and Pylyshyn, "to a psychology not readily distinguishable from the worst of Hume and Berkeley" (Fodor & Pylyshyn, 1988, p. 64). My concern is not whether connectionists can answer these latter objections, which are good if they can be made to stick,[10] but with the moral of the first objection from mere implementation: physical realization or functional implementation doesn't matter and isn't psychology any more than a calculator's computations are arithmetic.

4.   PROVINCIALISM AND REDUCTIVE EXPLANATION

Four avenues of reply show that we could have reduction despite (or instead of) multiple realizability. Strictly they involve rejecting the multiple realizability of the mental as construed by autonomous functionalism.

1. One might doubt, with Kim (1980, pp. 234–236), that "vast heterogeneous disjunctions" would have to be as arbitrary as Fodor suggests. Here we reject Fodor's a priori strictures on admissible natural kinds: What kinds are admissible is a matter for scientists to decide.

2. We might deny that kinds or laws are necessary for reduction, so the heterogeneity of the disjunction would be irrelevant. It can be shown that the

---

[10]Each side of the GOFAI-connectionist debate spends a great deal of time emphasizing the weaknesses of the other and playing up the rather different areas in which each is strong rather than trying to address the problems for their own accounts that emerge in that discussion. Consequently I am unclear on how well connectionists can answer charges like Fodor and Pylyshyn's—or for that matter, how well GOFAI advocates can answer connectionist objections. It seems to me early in the day to say that connectionist models cannot account for the sort of phenomena that concern Fodor and Pylyshyn; less so to say that GOFAI models, which have been around much longer, can deal with the sorts of problems that impel cognitive scientists to connectionism. I predict, though, that the correct account of cognitive architecture will be gerrymandered, with some models dealing better with some processes and other models with others.

reduction base of a natural kind need not itself be a kind; nor that of a law itself a law. The thermodynamic kind term entropy, for example, reduces to a complex set of non-nomological and non-kindlike statistical mechanical facts about the probabilistic tendency of Bolzmann's H to decrease.

3. We might question whether, as a matter of fact, there are that many physical ways of making minds. The plausibility of the multiple realizability argument depends on certain science fiction suppositions that turn out to be questionable, for example, that silicon-based minds are nomologically possible. The usual analogy to silicon-based life suggests that they may not be (see Smart, 1968, p. 111).

These alternatives address whether psychology might have a physical reduction base of the appropriate sort. Avenue (2) turns on rejecting the D-N model of explanation; avenues (1) and (3) grant it for the sake of argument. In Schwartz (1991) I offer more extended criticisms of the D–N model as an account of reduction in particular. In what follows I focus on avenue (4), challenging the conception of psychology invoked by autonomous functionalism. I deny that psychology need be universal or structure-independent. The mental and its physical explanation may be *provincial,* bound to particular physical realizations. Reduction of mentalistic kinds to (kind or nonkind) multiple reduction bases, and even identification of the former with the latter, is legitimate. Generality is *only* a desideratum. It is destructive to make it constitutive of a realm of inquiry.

Because functional predicates pervade every science, the multiple realizability argument should establish the irreducibility of any science that appeals essentially to functionally characterized states. Indeed, it should establish the irreducibility of parts of physics widely regarded as in part already reduced to other, such as thermodynamics, with its functionally characterized notion of temperature, to statistical mechanics. So if such sciences are irreducible in virtue of multiple realizability, many accepted reductive explanations will fail to be either reductive or explanatory. The unity of science will come apart, not only between the social and natural sciences, but among and within the natural sciences.

5. A TALE OF TWO SPECIES

Here I pursue the analogy of psychology with genetics.[11] Watson and Crick's demonstration that the genetic material is a double helix composed of two strands of deoxyribonucleic acid (DNA) bound by complementary pairs of amino acids (bases) is widely thought to be a reduction-sketch of Mendelian genetics. As Hull (1974) said, "given our preanalytic intuitions about reduction, it *is* a case of

---

[11]Richardson (1979) deploys the analogy to similar effect, using, however, real-life cases of multiple realizability in transmission genetics rather than my science-fiction case of Martian genetics. Moreover, he offers no diagnosis of the appeal of the multiple realizability argument.

reduction, a paradigm case" (p. 44). The double helix model accounts for the major features of Mendelian genetics in purely molecular terms. DNA replicates itself when the strands of the helix separate and each acts as a template for forming a new double helix, allowing for inheritance. Each strand can act as a template for forming other molecules, such as ribonucleic acid (RNA), carrying genetic instructions to cells in the metabolism of a given organism.

If reduction of a function means at least its explanation in terms of its physical structure, Mendelian genetics is in part reducible to physics and chemistry. We can construct, however, an autonomy argument for Mendelian genetics exactly parallel to Fodor's argument for the irreducibility of psychology or for the irrelevance of connectionist implementation. Genes, as noted, are functionally characterized by their causal role; genetic states are functional ones. Human genes are DNA molecules, but this is just a contingent fact reflecting special conditions on earth. Silicon-based Martians have a xeno-molecular genetics. Mendelian transmission genetics applies to them even though their genes are made of ABC. (ABC is chemically distinct but functionally the same as DNA.) So genes are multiply realizable as (DNA or ABC or . . .). Thus genetics cross-classifies physics and chemistry. Say that (DNA or ABC or . . .) is neither a kind nor displays any relevant nonkind de facto commonalities. If we need kinds or de facto commonalities at the physical level to have a reduction, Mendelian genetics is an autonomous discipline, irreducible to chemistry and physics.

If so, a physical explanation of heredity is impossible. Mendelian genetics is independent of physical realization beyond whatever degree of physical complexity is necessary for something to be an organism at all. It matters no more to Mendelian genetics what genes are made of and how they work than it matters to arithmetic or computer science what adding machines are made of and how they work. Genetics merely describes whatever commonalities obtain at some high functional level of abstraction appropriate to the taxonomy that fits the Mendelian laws. Genes may be token-identical to segments of DNA (or ABC or . . .) molecules, but their behavior cannot be explained in molecular terms. If we take this route, whatever it was they did, Watson and Crick did not discover anything of explanatory interest about "the molecular biology of the gene," to use the title of Watson's great textbook (Watson, 1977). Nor did they offer a program for investigating what is normally called the mechanics of heredity, for heredity is an autonomous functional notion in Mendelian genetics. Their work may be viewed as contribution to chemistry, perhaps, but not to biology.

The obverse of autonomy is elimination. If we accept irreducibility and reject autonomy, we might say that Mendelian genetics is not explained but eliminated in favor of molecular biology. What Watson and Crick showed was not that genes are segments of DNA molecules, but that there are no such things as genes. There are just segments of DNA molecules. Heredity, as an object of Mendelian genetics, simply disappears. We have elimination on the "better explanation" pattern articulated by Kemeny and Oppenheim (1970). If we go this way, though, it is unclear why a similar story would not apply to the phenotypic characteristics Mendelian genetics explains, such as eye color or biological sex. Do we want to deny that there are eyes with particular colors or that there are organisms with particular sexual characteristics? Strictly the issue is whether these characteristics are phenotypes. We might not have to give up eye color or sex, but we would have to give them up as phenotypes. But this would be giving up quite a lot. It would give us at least a start on the full-fledged elimination of the manifest world of macroscopic objects advocated by Churchland (1979). We may end up with nothing but point masses in space-time.

6. CONSTITUTION AND IDENTITY IN GENETICS

Neither of these alternatives are attractive or accord with ordinary scientific judgment uncontaminated by philosophy. Some, like Churchland, may revel in elimination. Others bite the biological bullet on autonomy (e.g., Rosenberg, 1985). But more plausibly, molecular biology does reduce Mendelian genetics. If Watson and Crick did not show how to give physical explanations of heredity, what did they show? We need not leave the issue with a rhetorical question. It seems that the physical properties of DNA described by molecular biology explain features of transmission genetics, for instance, why inherited characteristics show up in the ratios they do in descendent generations; how it is that some characteristics are recessive and others dominant, and so forth. The realization or implementation of genetics in DNA is explanatory if anything is. If we accept that molecular biology provided a reduction of or a guide to producing reductions in transmission genetics, there seem to be two possibilities. Either

(a) reduction to different physical bases shows that we do not have the same functional state,

or

(b) whether we have a physical reduction of a kind of functional state cannot depend on whether it is always to the same physical basis.

In the first option we have parallel classic type-type identities holding between similar but distinct functional states and their various reduction bases. In the second we have reduction of what is in some sense the *same* functional state to multiple reduction bases.

Call the sort of explanation involved in cases like the genetic one *provincial*. Such explanation typically involves cases where the specific mechanisms that constitute the macrophenomena which interest us differ across classes of individuals. The claim that provincial explanation is explanation is at least that it is explanatory to appeal to the particular mechanisms that are sufficient but not necessary for that phenomenon to occur.[12] To have an explanation, reductive or other, it is enough to state the mechanism by which some phenomenon is produced or constituted. It is not necessary that this be the only mechanism by which that phenomenon could be produced or constituted, or even that it be related in interesting ways to all the other such mechanisms. Reduction here is not bound to the empiricist sense of the term. It is rather a matter of explicating the mechanisms that produce or constitute some state, process, or entity, an enterprise that may or may not be deductive or nomological.[13]

Whether either of the two options, (a) or (b), hold in any case depends largely on the facts of the matter in the particular instance. Suppose Martian hereditary material is made of ABC, functionally identical but structurally distinct from DNA. If we insist that genes are *type-identical* to segments of DNA, having just the properties of DNA, Martians will not have genes. No matter: they will have *schmenes,* which are just as good as genes for the purpose (the explanation of inherited characteristics). Schmenes obey the laws of Mendelian genetics, except that when we wish to be pedantic we replace the expression *gene* with *schmene* throughout. Generally, the difference can be ignored, and we can say that Martians have genes which are governed by Mendelian genetics.

If, on the other hand, schmenes are triple-helixed EFG (a genetic material both physically and functionally distinct from DNA), giving different ratios of inherited characteristics in descendent populations, schmenetics will not be Mendelian: the transmission laws will be different. Here we cannot ignore the difference between genes and schmenes for practical purposes because it shows up on the functional level. (Note that there is a physical explanation for this fact.) In either case, holding the DNA-gene identity constant, biology will be provincial, in that we will have a set of class-specific biologies that vary, roughly, with the sort of conditions under which various kind or classes of organisms evolved.

Alternatively, we might give up the troublesome premise that genes are strictly identical to DNA in the sense of sharing all properties, including physical ones. Here, humans and Martians would have genes (the same sorts of things), and genes would be the same as DNA in humans but the same as (ABC or EFG) in Martians. Call the relation of sameness that applies here *constitution:* the same thing may be constituted or made up from different materials. Identity is a limit

---

[12]I am not offering an "account" of explanation as the provision of a sufficient but unnecessary condition, or indeed a general account of explanation at all, although were I to attempt such an account it would be a mechanical one; that is, I think that explanation is elucidation of causal mechanisms. Here I am offering a very partial (though I hope adequate for the purpose) characterization of the provincial aspect of a certain sort of reductive explanation.

[13]For this notion of explanation, applied to probabilistic rather than reductive contexts, see Railton (1981) and Salmon (1984, 1989). Railton attempts to revive a sophisticated version of the D-N model in this scientific realistic context; I think laws are nice if you can get them but their absence does not deprive an account of a mechanism that produces or constitutes some phenomenon of explanatory power.

case of constitution in which a thing or property can be constituted only one way. For other cases we give up Leibniz's law (that identical things share all properties) and allow that the same thing may have different microstructural properties. Which way it might turn out is an empirical question, and because all the genes we know are DNA, highly speculative.

How we go in a particular case, once the facts are specified, depends on the theoretical advantages of choosing one rather than the other approach. Course (b), opting for constitution, has the advantage of ontological simplicity: we don't multiply kinds of hereditary material at the functional level. If hereditary material is functionally identical to DNA or ABC, this course seems attractive. On the other hand, constitution might seem a more obscure and less familiar notion than identity—although hardly less puzzling (see Hirsch, 1982). So if hereditary material is functionally distinct DNA or EFG, we might prefer to mark the double difference (functional and physical) by choosing option (a), insisting on identity. I'm not sure that a great deal rests on the choice once we know the facts. It would be up to the scientists to decide what to say.

Either way, the possibility that genes may be differently constituted does not block explanatory appeal to a particular constitution in a particular case, such as human eye color or biological sex. That is, we can say it explains why someone has blue eyes and is biologically female that they have the genes (or, technically, cistrons) for blue eyes and have XX chromosomes, even if that explanation doesn't work for blue-eyed *Martian* women. Insofar as such appeal counts as explanation of the phenomenon at a more basic level, we have a reduction or at least a reduction program. This is so even if (nonidentificatory) constitution blocks nice type-type connections or multiple parallel identities block a universal genetics.[14]

7. GENETICS AND PSYCHOLOGY

If "multiple realizability" does not show that genetics is independent of physical realization, it does not show that psychology is either. It might rather show that the functional character of mental states permits reduction, at least in the sense that genetics is reducible. Suppose there were good type-type connections be-

---

[14]A reduction program is a research program for finding reductive explanations based on the use of certain techniques (e.g., those of molecular biology or cognitive neuroscience) and based on exemplary explanations already achieved in the domain. All real examples of reduced sciences are reduction programs based on clusters of promising reductive explanations of certain phenomena. There is not—nor will there be—a single case in which we attain the positivist ideal of a complete reduced science, all of the laws and predicates of which are derived via bridge-laws from a more basic science, and the whole expressed in nice axiomatic form. To deny that a science is in fact reduced because what one has is a reduction program instead of a philosopher's fantasy is to legislate to science, which is not the philosopher's mandate.

tween human mental and physical states, and likewise with Martians, but no nice cross-species fit. Should we conclude psychology is irreducible or just that it has different reduction bases? Should we search only for an abstract functional psychology that describes whatever humans and Martians have in common, or do we (also) look for psychological generalizations that apply to each species, and for the physical basis of these in the particular cases?

The classic type identity thesis can be preserved, then, at the cost of the claim that beings of different physical constitutions could share identical mental states. This is option (a): physical difference is sufficient for denial of functional sameness. The mental state that correlates with human C-fiber firings is identical to pain; that which correlates with Martian Z-fiber firings is identical to *schmain*, and so forth, giving parallel reductions of the provincial psychologies of various sorts of cognizers to the particular reduction base that realizes them. Mental states would not be multiply realized at all. They would be uniquely realized in particular types of physical states. Neurophysiology and psychology would co-vary among classes of cognizers.

We would of course be interested in functional commonalities or similarities as corollary (not an alternative) to a reductive project. To say that Martians had a different psychology is not to say that they have no psychology, any more than to say that they have a different biology is to say that they have no biology. The proposal, then, is not chauvinist. On option (a) we need not even give up a universal psychology to predict, explain, and otherwise interact with nonhuman cognizers. We may abstract from or ignore the differences for certain purposes— say, moral ones. What Martians feel when they are burned or stabbed is technically schmain, not pain, but since schmain is aversive and horrible, we can treat schmain as the moral equivalent of pain, and say that it is wrong to cause needless pain to people, including Martians.

As in the biological case the plausibility of this move depends in part on the facts. Option (a) is most plausible for the mental if Martian psychology is quite different from ours functionally as well as physically, as with the EFG heredity case. If Martian biology differs radically from ours in the right ways, Martian psychology probably would as well. Imagine that Martian sensory modalities, and thus the character of their experience, is quite alien. They directly perceive magnetic fields or magnetic variations as we do light and are "visually" sensitive to electromagnetic radiation only in the FM band. They have three sexes to go along with their triple-helixed schmenes and so the generalizations that describe their sexual impulses are very different from the ones that describe ours. Here we might give up the idea that they have the same mental states as humans—thus keeping the classic identity thesis, although this might not matter for many purposes, for instance communication of scientific results, negotiation about politics, arranging tours of Martian "artists" (as we would call them), and the like.

If, however, Martian psychology was functionally just like ours (although realized in silicon-based neural tissue), we might choose option (b): that functional sameness admits of reduction to different physical bases. This would involve giving up type-identities for relations of constitution, the classical identity thesis for *constitutive* materialism. On this view, differently constituted beings could share the same mental states in a nonidentificatory sense of *same*. This allows multiple realizability, in a sense, but it allows reductive explanation too. Types of mental states would not be type-identical to types of physical ones, but neither would the former be merely token-identical to the latter. Rather mental types would be constituted variously but systematically by different sorts of physical types, allowing us to explain a psychological state or process in physical terms within each class of beings, although not universally. In either case, psychology would be universal; reduction, provincial.

Either approach allows us to preserve reductionism for psychology in the same sense that we have it for genetics. If a Watson and Crick of the mind tomorrow publish the *psychological code,* revealing the kind of physical mechanisms that constitute most human thought, it would be a reduction even if there are large areas of thought and behavior to which the psychological code has no direct application, as there are large areas even of genetics (e.g., population genetics) where molecular genetics has no direct application, and even if most of the phenomena in the domain of the psychological code theory are too complex to produce explanations in its terms, as is the case with genetics.

The same considerations apply to connectionism as an implementation of GOFAI or indeed of commonsense psychology. At present it would be premature, to say the least, to claim that connectionism is the psychological code or to propose Rumelhart and McClelland as psychology's Watson and Crick. Unsurprisingly, given the recency of the revival of connectionist models, we do not have a connectionist theory nearly as well articulated as classical computational theory. What we have instead are exciting and suggestive connectionist models of specific processes, like Rumelhart and McClelland's (1986, Vol. 2, pp. 216–271) model for learning the past tense of English verbs, which appears to simulate the kinds of errors and progress humans make in this sort of syntactic learning. (Pinker & Prince, 1988, criticize the adequacy of the model.)

Suppose, though, that Fodor and Pylyshyn are right that such models merely implement, in human brains, cognitive processes correctly described by GOFAI models. That is no reason to deny that connectionism explains cognition in humans, or to assert that connectionism isn't psychology. It may be only human psychology, but what's wrong with that? In any particular case, say one involving nonconnectionist Martians, we would be faced with a choice structurally similar to the one previously discussed. We can say either that human psychology is connectionist but Martian psychology isn't (option [b]) or that humans have psychology, since our cognition is connectionist, but Martians have *schmychology,* since theirs isn't (option [a]). Which we might wish to say depends in part on whether the implementation makes a difference at the functional level. Similar reasoning applies, *mutatis mutandis,* if radical connectionists (see Cummins & Schwarz, 1988) are right that connectionism should displace GOFAI as our account of cognition and be construed instead as a direct implementation of or explanation for commonsense psychology.

8.   UNFAIR TO ALIENS?

The biological argument shows that there may be no universal transmission genetics. It will be objected that this conclusion is to be resisted for psychology. One can argue that because of its subject matter (intentional behavior), psychology is universal in a way that biology is not. Provincialism misses out just what it is we and the aliens have in common, namely our mental states. Fodor (1981) writes:

> We could, if we liked, *require* the taxonomies of the special sciences to correspond to the taxonomy of physics by insisting on distinctions between the kinds posited by the former whenever they correspond to distinct kinds in the latter. That would *make* the laws of the special sciences exceptionless if the laws of the basic science are. But it would also likely lose us precisely the generalizations we want to express. (p. 143)

The generalizations of psychology apply universally because beings of various constitutions can be in the same states governed by the same psychological generalizations. Exceptions can be explained away nonpsychologically by appeal to more basic sciences.

A good deal turns on what counts as *the same* mental state. Any functionalist will individuate a mental state by its causal role in mediating sensory input and behavioral output, such that same role, same state. If difference in reduction bases makes no difference in role, then human and alien mental states are the same in the relevant sense of *same,* that is, they play the same functional role. This is option (b), holding that functional sameness is enough for sameness, whatever implementation explains the operation of the function in a given case. *Pace* Fodor, it explains why a particular cognizer has a given mental state to advert to its parochial physical constitution, although such an explanation may not be to the point in a particular pragmatic explanatory context. But we retain whatever functionally expressed generalizations we want the special (here, intentional) sciences to give us.

Suppose, though, that psychology initially fails to reflect functional differences that show up under physical description, but the physical theories that cover the behavior of the correlates of a state "shared" by humans and aliens produce different predictions about or explanations of their respective behavior.[15] Fodor suggests that we treat the psychological failure as an anomaly to be physically explained: psychology is immune from revision in the face of physical evidence. This is not a contradiction: in explaining away the physically induced deviations, we cease to do psychology.[16] But if the "generalizations we want to express" fail to capture important differences in behavior or its causes, they are false, in which case we may not want to express them. The alternative—option (a)—is to say that we have different mental states because their implementation is physically different. For some purposes, strict falsity may not matter and we can treat the generalizations as idealizations. In that case we do not lose them.

9. SAMENESS OF CONTENT

The objection may be sharpened as follows. Provincialism, it might be said, requires us to abandon the intuitively plausible claim that beings of varying physical constitution can share intentional states *of the same content*. In 1974, Cornell astronomers at Arecibo Observatory in Puerto Rico sent a radio telescope message to star cluster M13, which says—has as its content—among other things, the proposition (call it p) that "there are about four billion intelligent creatures whose genetic basis is DNA on the third planet from a given star" (Sagan, 1979, p. 321). The point was to produce in the aliens in M13 the same belief that we had. On my account, though, if Martians are silicon-based, it appears that they cannot entertain our belief that p. But surely our intuition that they can share our belief that p is far stronger than our intuition that beliefs are identical to some type of neural structure! If one of the intuitions has to go, it is the reductionist one that backs provincialism.[17]

The relevant disanalogy with biology is in the reliance of psychology on the notion of *content*. This (it is said) has no biological parallel. The universality of

---

[15]It is not unusual for a reduced theory to differ from its original formulation. Classical thermodynamics was anomalous because unlike the rest of classical physics it was not time-reversal invariant. Under statistical mechanical reduction, the anomaly vanished. Finding such improvements, often inaccessible at the level of the special science, is a motivation for seeking reduction.

[16]Here Fodor sounds more like Davidson than he might like. Fodor insists that his irreducibility claim is empirical, while Davidson (1980) purports to have an in-principle argument for his anomalous monism. I suspect that Fodor's attachment to a universal psychology is as a priori as Davidson's to the universality of decision theory.

[17]This objection depends on accepting (as Fodor and I do) that psychological explanations may advert to content. I don't think, though, that Fodor can maintain both this and his methodological solipsism (see footnote 2). The objection is not open to Stich, who maintains that psychological explanations must be purely syntactic and content-free—a thesis, popular among cognitive scientists, sometimes called "the formality constraint."

psychology implies that if the aliens are intentional agents they must be able to instantiate the same intentional contents as humans. This a charitable reading of Fodor's (1981) claim, quoted above, that reduction "would lose us precisely the generalizations which we want the special sciences to express" (p. 143), that is, generalizations framed in terms of sameness of propositional content.[18]

One reply derives from a naturalized account of content like that defended by Dretske (1988). We can preserve identity of content by making content depend not on the particular internal physical state that realizes an intentional attitude, but on the complex sort of causal covariation that, if some suitably intricate causal theory of content is right, counts as representing that p. Two intentional states will have the same content if they are causally related in the right way to whatever they represent. Thus we and the aliens may be said to have the same belief that p in virtue of the fact that both of our internal states adjust in appropriately similar ways in response to a causal input from the same source. That the physical realizations of the functional states may differ qualitatively would be either irrelevant, if what matters is that they play the same functional role in adjusting in response to input, or no more relevant than the fact that each instantiate numerically different instances of the representation.

Another answer (explored in Schwartz, in press) presupposes no controversial theory of naturalized representation. It is controversial in another way. Here we bite the bullet and allow that humans and differently constituted aliens would not share content. This need not be a costly concession. For most purposes we could ignore the differences and proceed as if the content were the same, that is, ascribe the same contents *ideal typically*. The expression is due to Max Weber (1949), who proposed that rational actor explanations in sociology ought to be made in this way. People's motivations often deviate considerably from economic rationality, as Weber knew, but he suggested that for sociological purposes the best methodology was to *abstract* from the various heterogeneous and irrational motivations and, where possible, to use the ideal type of the rational actor as the basis for explanation of action.[19] I suggest that we may abstract similarly from fine differences in content.[20]

---

[18]The uncharitable reading is that the same intentional generalizations should be valid for all intentional agents.

[19]Weber (1949) writes: "An ideal type is formed by the *one-sided accentuation* of one or more points of view and by the synthesis of a great many diffuse, discrete, more or less present and occasionally absent *concrete individual phenomena,* which are arranged according to those one-sidedly emphasized viewpoints into a unified *analytical* construct. In its conceptual purity, this (analytical) construct cannot be found anywhere in reality" (p. 90).

[20]The idea is similar to (and inspired by) the Putnam-Burge thesis that "meanings ain't in the head," where that means at least that content ascription depends on factors external to the agent's internal states. See Schwartz (in press, section 10.4) for discussion and development of this thesis. As Burge's (1979) variation on the idea shows, the proposal does not require, although it is not inconsistent with, either a causal or a naturalized theory of content.

This may be what we in fact do in ascribing propositional attitudes to humans. A growing body of evidence suggests that the propositionalist "language of thought" model that, as Fodor argues persuasively, is embedded in our common-sense psychology, is false as an account of human cognition.[21] According to propositionalism, thought is structured like a natural language, a notion that is articulated in GOFAI models of cognition. Connectionism is one way of providing a systematic alternative to the idea that cognition is a structure of propositions, seeking insight from neural structure in a way that Fodor (for one) thinks is impossible. Rather than crunching structured symbols according to rules, connectionists claim, in thinking we are "processing activation vectors through artfully weighted networks" (Churchland, 1989, p. 195). The case for connectionism—its superior performance on a number of dimensions and in a number of areas where GOFAI is weak—supports the anti-propositionalist orientation. The results of Kahneman, Slovik, and Tversky (1982) or Nisbet and Ross (1980) can be interpreted as showing that people do not think in logic or work with mental sentences at all. Johnson-Laird (1983) has proposed that people operate functionally not on propositions but on *mental models* which may be thought of as three dimensional quasi-images. It may be possible to integrate these cognitive ideas into the brainlike artificial intelligence models of connectionism.

Our actual mode of representation "in the head" probably diverges from the language of thought model on several dimensions (syntactic and inferential, as I argue in Schwartz (in press)). No matter. It is good enough for the purposes for which we use it to serve us well. Failing a Churchlandian conversion to self-ascription terms of neurophysiology (which might not serve our purposes), we abstract from whatever may actually be in the head and use our current and evolving psychology. As among ourselves, so with nonhuman cognizers. Communication, explanation of behavior, and so forth, is possible as long as we and they ascribe to each other propositional attitudes. We might learn each other's neurophysiology and try to communicate in those terms, but why make life difficult? Reference to propositions is pragmatically convenient, and good enough for most purposes—speaking with one's spouse, persuading the electorate, discussing mathematics with aliens.

This suggests a different construal of the universality of psychology. Psychology is universal insofar as it is ideal-typical. As soon as we cash out (i.e., reduce) the ideal-typical ascriptions we make in terms of the actual mechanisms that produce behavior, it goes provincial. The sense in which we may hope for a universal psychology is just that for many purposes, the differences won't matter much. We could then safely abstract from them. So, although perhaps philosophically drastic, the revision would be practically minimal. For some scientific purposes we would have a better understanding of the psychologies of various

---

[21]It's controversial whether a language-of-thought thesis correctly captures or commonsense psychological ascriptions. Stich (1983) and Fodor (1975) offer strong cases that it does.

sorts of beings, and that would make about as much difference in our ordinary lives, or in scientific work that is peripheral to cognitive psychology, that deep scientific theory usually does—not necessarily very much.

10. NIHIL HUMANUM

The multiple realizability argument for autonomous functionalism owes most of its power not to the technical details of its mistaken empiricist model of reduction but to the antichauvinist appeal of the universality of psychology. The deep presupposition is that anything that deserves to be called psychology must apply in some sense in the same way to any cognizer whomsoever, however different physically such a being might be from us. A similar idea motivates the dismissal of connectionism as "mere" implementation of GOFAI as a universal model of cognition. We should resist the Siren call of such "antichauvinism." After all, it is human beings we are interested in when we do psychology and social science. We are especially interested in understanding, explaining, and predicting human behavior because it is our behavior, and what we do matters a great deal to us. If theories developed for these purposes happen to fit aliens or computers, that's all to the good. But we should not hobble our development of such theories, including their development through reduction, by insisting that they must do so.

Although the view urged here is not chauvinist in that it does not deny mentality to the differently-constituted, it is provincial in that it sets the primary task to hand of the intentional sciences to be the explanation of human behavior. This sort of provincialism does not "lose us precisely the generalizations which we want the special sciences to express" (Fodor, 1981, p. 143), I have pursued an analogy with biology; taking a cue from Fodor, I turn to an analogy with economics.

If an economic theory that applies to our own society fails to be adequate to all societies in all times and places, do we reject it as insufficiently general? If a good candidate for an absolutely general economic theory came along we would jump at it. But we do not insist that any economic theory meet such standards, or we'd be rather short on economic theory. Likewise, a good human psychology might not be all we want, but it would be nice to have one. If human psychology, as reduced to its provincial physical basis, turns out not to apply to Martians because their provincial physical basis is different, this no more casts doubt on the explanatory force of human psychology than the failure of neoclassical economics to describe feudal economies casts doubt on its explanatory force for capitalist ones.[22]

---

[22]Other things may cast doubt on the explanatory force of neoclassical economics: Institutionalist economists like Thorsten Veblen and Marxist political economists object that its abstractions leave out too much that is important and relevant to the understanding of economic phenomena, such as class relations and aspects of the organization of the production process. But this is a quite different

Given this interest in human beings, the demand of absolute generality raises the following question. The antichauvinist intuition suggests that *intentional agent,* where that includes the class of entities that could have a psychology, is a kind larger than that of human beings. If we make their commonalities constitutive of psychology, could it turn out that psychology doesn't apply to homo sapiens? The point is not that the demand for absolute generality makes an autonomous psychology a priori, but that the a priori demand for generality makes it an issue about how well such a psychology will do for humans. Similarly, an absolutely general biology that fits any possible form of life (carbon- and silicon-based, etc.) might fail to describe much of what interests us about any particular biology.

On the economic analogy, the possibility that an abstract universal psychology might fail to fit humans is far from implausible. According to one view, held in different ways by von Mises (1979) and Friedman (1979), economics is the logical deduction from certain a priori axioms of conclusions about the behavior of highly abstractly described rational actors.[23] Now economics, so regarded, may not have much to do with what goes on in banks and factories. But if what goes on in banks and factories is what interests us, we should keep far from economics and study what goes on in banks and factories.[24] Or we might say that economics should study just this. Such a response turns on a different set of interests and a different—a scientific realist—conception of science from Friedman's or von Mises's. These concerns may be related. We may reject instrumentalism (Friedman, 1979) and a priorism (von Mises, 1979) because we think that it is part of the job of science to describe the actual mechanisms that produce or constitute the phenomena that interest us and because we think that more accurate knowledge of these mechanisms, among other things, will lead to better predictions.

---

objection from the one that economics may not be universal; rather the problem is supposed to be that it is bad in the particular case. Fodor and Pylyshyn's objection that connectionism is misleading and impoverished, failing to explain too much that matters, is an objection of this sort, quite distinct from their a priori and universalist claim that implementation is irrelevant. If the former objection can be made to stick (something I don't consider), connectionism is doomed—but because it is misleading and impoverished, not because it is merely an implementation.

[23]See von Mises (1979, p. 64); Friedman construes economic theory (and scientific theory generally) in an austerely instrumentalist way, as a "set of tautologies" to be evaluated by the criteria appropriate to judging a "filing system" (Friedman, p. 21). An important difference is that Friedman thinks that empirical adequacy matters to economics, while von Mises does not. Economic science is a "mental experiment . . . involv[ing] thinking through the implications of a proposition in the light of its compatibility with other propositions we accept as true [whether or not these] make reference to experience" (von Mises, p. 61).

[24]This is precisely what Marxists and Institutionalists say about neoclassical economics. Interestingly a common neoclassical economist's reaction is to reply that the research done by Marxists and Institutionalists isn't economics—at best it's sociology. "Real" economics, neoclassicists say, is mostly abstract mathematics describing the behavior of idealized rational actors under constraints.

If psychology, as understood by autonomous functionalists, isn't about humans, let's study what is about humans and see how it fits with physics, neurophysiology, and the other sciences. Or we might call the study of human behavior psychology and say that the abstract theory (GOFAI? propositional attitude psychology?) which applies to the broader kind—all cognizers—may deserve the name, but this enterprise, human psychology, certainly does. And here the implementation or particular realization of human psychology in physical brains and (perhaps) connectionist networks may matter a lot, both in suggesting new avenues for research and in solving puzzling problems that resist approaches at a higher level of abstraction. No matter if this emphasis on the particular undermines universality because it may not apply to Martians. Let's not take anti-chauvinism so far that we deny what is important to us on behalf of beings who may not even exist!

We may be able to do better than a provincial psychology. It is possible that there is a universal psychology, and perhaps it is a propositional attitude psychology best modeled by GOFAI. I have suggested that we could construe such universality as a function of idealization. It is even possible that there is, perhaps as a matter of physical fact, a unique realization or implementation for anything that might count as being a full-fledged psychology. These are empirical questions. My plea is a conditional one for the legitimacy of provincialism. Given our interests and general desiderata about what can count as a psychological explanation, or a physical reduction thereof, provincial explanations and reductions are fine if they are all we can get. Moreover: it is a constraint on any more general such explanations that they be reasonably close approximations to the provincial ones. What is human had better not be alien to us.

The prospect for reduction is open. Materialism need not be stripped down to the mere token identity theory. The truth of the classic identity theory or of constitutive materialism would depend on empirical results, but multiple realizability defeats neither of them. Neither does multiple realizability deprive connectionist models of explanatory interest with regard to GOFAI or commonsense psychology, supposing that connectionism can avoid the objections of misleadingness and impoverishment. The multiple realizability argument is the main case for autonomous functionalism and the irrelevance of implementation, so the orthodoxy should be rejected—the autonomy claim, that is, and not the functionalism. As a theory of mind and as research program in psychology, functionalism has nothing to do with multiple realizability.

ACKNOWLEDGMENTS

Thanks are due for helpful comments to John Dinsmore, Alan Gibbard, Don Herzog, David Hills, Peter King, Robert McCauley, Diana Raffman, Peter Railton, and Laurie Stowe.

REFERENCES

Armstrong, D. M. (1968). *A materialist theory of the mind*. London: Routledge & Kegan Paul.

Bechtel, W. (1988). Connectionism and the philosophy of mind: an overview. In T. Horgan and J. Tienson (eds.), Connectionism and the philosophy of mind: Spindel conference 1987 [Special issue]. *Southern Journal of Philosophy XXVI*, 17–42.

Block, N. (1980). Troubles With Functionalism. In N. Block (Ed.) *Readings in philosophy of psychology* (Vol. 1, pp. 268–305). Cambridge MA: Harvard University Press.

Burge, Tyler. (1979). Individualism and the mental. In P. A. French, T. Uehling, Jr., & H. Wettstein (Eds.), *Midwest studies in philosophy IV. Studies in metaphysics* (pp. 73–122). Minneapolis: University of Minnesota Press.

Churchland, P. M. (1979). *Scientific realism and the plasticity of mind*. Cambridge: Cambridge University Press.

Churchland, P. M. (1989). *A neurocomputational perspective*. Cambridge MA: MIT Press.

Cummins, R. & Schwarz, G. (1988). Radical connectionism. In T. Horgan & J. Tienson (Eds.), Connectionism and the philosophy of mind: Spindel conference 1987 [Special issue]. *Southern Journal of Philosophy XXVI*, 43–62.

Davidson, D. (1980). *Essays on actions and events*. Oxford: Clarendon Press.

Dretske, F. (1988). *Explaining behavior: Reasons in a world of causes*. Cambridge MA: MIT Press.

Fodor, J. (1975). *The language of thought*. New York: Thomas Crowell.

Fodor, J. (1981). *Representations: Philosophical essays on the foundations of cognitive science*. Cambridge MA: MIT Press.

Fodor, J. & Pylyshyn, Z. (1988). Connectionism and cognitive architecture: A critical analysis. In S. Pinker & J. Meler (Eds.), *Connections and symbols* (pp. 3–72). Cambridge MA: MIT Press.

Friedman, M. (1979). The methodology of positive economics. In F. Hahn and M. Hollis (Eds.). *Philosophy and economic theory* (pp. 18–35). Oxford: Oxford University Press.

Haugeland, J. (1985). *Artificial intelligence: The very idea*. Cambridge MA: MIT Press.

Hirsch, E. (1982). *The concept of identity*. Oxford: Oxford University Press.

Hull, D. (1974). *Philosophy of biological science*. Englewood Cliffs, NJ: Prentice-Hall.

Johnson-Laird, P. N. (1983). *Mental models*. Cambridge, UK: Cambridge University Press.

Kahneman, D., Slovic, P., & Tversky, A. (Eds.). (1982). *Judgment under uncertainty: Heuristics and biases*. Cambridge, UK: Cambridge University Press.

Kemeny, J. G. & Oppenheim, P. (1970). On reduction. In B. A. Brody (Ed.), *Readings in the philosophy of science*, (1st ed., pp. 307–318). Englewood Cliffs NJ: Prentice-Hall.

Kim, J. (1980). Physicalism and the multiple realizability of mental states. In N. Block (Ed.), *Readings in philosophy of psychology* (Vol. 1, pp. 234–236). Cambridge, MA: Harvard University Press.

Nagel, E. (1961). *The structure of science*. New York: Harcourt, Brace, & World.

Nisbett, R. & Ross, L. (1980). *Human inference: Strategies and shortcomings of social judgment*. Englewood Cliffs, NJ: Prentice-Hall.

Pinker, S. & Prince, A. (1988). On language and connectionism: Analysis of a parallel distributed processing model of language acquisition. In S. Pinker & J. Meler (Eds.), *Connections and symbols* (pp. 73–194). Cambridge MA: MIT Press.

Putnam, H. (1975). *Mind, language, and reality: Philosophical papers* (Vol. 2). Cambridge, UK: Cambridge University Press.

Railton, P. (1981). Probability, explanation, and information. *Synthese, 48*, 233–256.

Richardson, R. (1979). Functionalism and reductionism. *Philosophy of Science, 46*, 533–558.

Rosenberg, A. (1985). *The structure of biological science*. Cambridge, UK: Cambridge University Press.

Rumelhart, D. E., McLelland, J. L., & the PDP Research Group. (1986). *Parallel distributed processing: Explorations in the microstructure of cognition*. (Vols. 1 & 2) Cambridge MA: MIT Press.

Sagan, C. (1979). The quest for extraterrestrial intelligence. In *Broca's brain: Reflections on the romance of science* (pp. 314–325). New York: Ballentine Books.

Salmon, W. C. (1984). *Scientific explanation and the causal structure of the world*. Princeton, NJ: Princeton University Press.

Salmon, W. C. (1989). Four Decades of Scientific Explanation. *In* P. Kitcher & W. Salmon (Eds.) *Scientific explanation: Minnesota studies in the philosophy of science XIII* (pp. 3–219). Minneapolis: University of Minnesota Press.

Schwartz, J. (in press). Propositional attitude psychology as an ideal type. *Topoi*.

Schwartz, J. (1991). Reduction, elimination, and the mental. *Philosophy of Science, 58*, 203–220.

Smart, J. C. C. (1968). *Between science and philosophy: An introduction to the philosophy of science*. New York: Random House.

Smart, J. C. C. (1971). Sensations and brain processes. In D. M. Rosenthal (Ed.) *Materialism and the mind-body problem* (pp. 53–66). Englewood Cliffs, NJ: Prentice Hall.

Stich, S. (1983). *From folk psychology to cognitive science: The case against belief*. Cambridge, MA: MIT Press.

Tienson, J. (1988). Introduction to connectionism. In T. Horgan & J. Tienson (Eds.), Connectionism and the philosophy of mind: Spindel conference 1987 [Special issue]. *Southern Journal of Philosophy XXVI*, 1–16.

von Mises, L. (1979). The science of human action. In F. Hahn & M. Hollis (Eds.), *Philosophy and economic theory* (pp. 57–64). Oxford: Oxford University Press.

Watson, J. (1977). *The molecular biology of the gene* (3rd ed.). New York: Benjamin.

Weber, M. (1949). *The methodology of the social sciences* (E. A. Shils & H. A. Finch, Ed. & Trans.). New York: Free Press.

6

Exploring the Symbolic/Subsymbolic Continuum: A Case Study of RAAM

Douglas S. Blank
Lisa A. Meeden
James B. Marshall
Indiana University

1. INTRODUCTION

It is difficult to clearly define the symbolic and subsymbolic paradigms; each is usually described by its tendencies rather than any one definitive property. Symbolic processing is generally characterized by hard-coded, explicit rules operating on discrete, static tokens, whereas subsymbolic processing is associated with learned, fuzzy constraints affecting continuous, distributed representations. In addition, programming languages such as LISP and mechanisms such as Turing machines are typically associated with the symbolic paradigm, whereas connectionism is frequently associated with the subsymbolic paradigm. Debates contrasting the two paradigms sometimes center on these mechanisms, for example comparing the capabilities of Turing machines with those of connectionist networks (see Adams, Aizawa, & Fuller chap. 3 in this volume). However, connectionist networks can be proven to be computationally equivalent to the abstract notion of Turing machines (Franklin & Garzon, 1990). Therefore the computational mechanism is not the crucial issue in separating the symbolic and subsymbolic paradigms. What then is the crucial issue?

We believe there are three major issues that distinguish the symbolic paradigm from the subsymbolic paradigm: (a) the type of representations; (b) the style of composition; and (c) the functional characteristics. We have summarized the key elements of these differences between the two paradigms in Table 6.1. However, most cognitive science and classical Artificial Intelligence (AI) models cannot be completely characterized as either purely symbolic or purely subsymbolic using these criteria. Instead, most models fall somewhere in between the two extremes, or in the so-called *Gap*. For this reason, it seems appropriate to view the para-

TABLE 6.1
Comparison of the Subsymbolic and Symbolic Paradigms

	Subsymbolic	Symbolic
Representation	distributed	atomic
	continuous	discrete
	emergent	static
	use affects form	arbitrary
Composition	superimposed	concatenated
	context-sensitive	systematic
Functionality	microsemantic	macrosemantic
	holistic	atomistic

digms as defining two opposite corners of a three-dimensional continuum as shown in Fig. 6.1.[1] In the following introductory sections we examine each of the issues from Table 6.1 in detail and then discuss where to place some existing models within this symbolic/subsymbolic continuum.

1.1. Representation

As Smolensky (1988) noted, the term *subsymbolic paradigm* is intended to suggest symbolic representations that are built out of many smaller constituents: "Entities that are typically represented in the symbolic paradigm by symbols are typically represented in the subsymbolic paradigm by a large number of subsymbols" (p. 3). Smolensky suggested that for the purposes of relating these two paradigms, it is often important to analyze subsymbolic models at a higher level: "to amalgamate, so to speak, the subsymbols into symbols" (p. 3). There is a problem with this type of analysis because a conglomerate of subsymbols does not form a traditional symbol. Classically, symbols have been *arbitrary* labels, such as strings of letters, which are *atomic, discrete,* and *static.* In contrast, a symbol in the subsymbolic paradigm is *distributed* over a collection of subsymbols, and each subsymbol may be associated with *continuous* numerical values. In addition, the subsymbolic paradigm is strongly committed to learning at the subsymbolic level. Through learning, an amalgamated symbol gradually emerges in such a way that its form reflects its function, or use, in the training tasks. We see examples of this in the experiments described in section 5.

Typical symbols in a symbolic model might be the letter strings *waiter* or

---

[1]Table 6.1 and Fig. 6.1 were inspired by Robert Port and Timothy van Gelder. They conceived of viewing classical and connectionist models as varying along a number of abstract dimensions that define a space of possible representation schemes. They were specifically interested in representations for natural language (Port & van Gelder, 1991). We have extended these ideas by contrasting paradigms in general rather than focusing solely on representational issues.

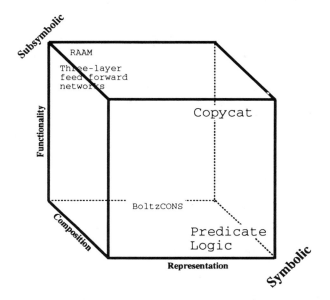

FIG. 6.1. Subsymbolic/symbolic continuum. This figure illustrates the three-dimensional space of paradigms defined by the three characteristics from Table 6.1: representation (across the bottom), composition (extending out), and functionality (up the side). The Gap between the symbolic (front, lower, right corner) and subsymbolic (back, upper, left corner) paradigms can be viewed as the central region of the cube. Five models are shown in their approximate position in the space. Font size reflects distance from the front of the box.

customer. These symbols may be placed into structured relationships with other symbols, and may be bound to a variety of values during the course of processing, but the forms of the symbols themselves never change. The symbolic model would work equally well if *waiter* were replaced by *xyz* throughout the model's data structures, because *waiter* is simply an atomic label possessing no internal structure of its own. In contrast, a typical symbol in a subsymbolic model might be the pattern of continuous values [$+0.562$ -0.891 -0.143 -0.382 $+0.966$]. During processing, this might evolve to the slightly different but similar pattern [$+0.589$ -0.900 -0.139 -0.412 $+0.999$], which, although distinct from the original symbol, still behaves in a closely related way. However, the subsymbolic model would produce very different results if this symbol were replaced by some other completely arbitrary pattern.

These fundamental differences in representation between the two paradigms directly influence the functional capacities and compositional styles exhibited by each.

1.2. Composition

One of the main criticisms that has been leveled against the subsymbolic approach is that the representations developed by subsymbolic models are unable to exhibit useful compositional structure (Fodor & Pylyshyn, 1988). It is claimed that the representations operated on by subsymbolic computation cannot be combined into higher-order composite representations that preserve the integrity of the constituent parts out of which they are assembled. This capability is clearly present in symbolic models. One need only imagine a model that operates on representations encoded as symbols organized into structured trees or lists. These representations can be easily decomposed into their constituent parts by using standard destructuring operations, such as the *car* or *cdr* operators in LISP, and then re-assembled into new representations using standard *concatenative* operations, such as the *cons* operator in LISP.[2]

Pollack (1988) developed a subsymbolic model, called Recursive Auto-Associative Memory (RAAM), that provides a direct counterexample to the claims that subsymbolic models cannot exhibit useful compositional structure (see also Chalmers, 1990b; van Gelder, 1990). This chapter focuses on the RAAM model as an exemplar of the subsymbolic paradigm. However, we do not wish to claim that RAAM is an accurate model of human cognition; we simply feel that it provides a clear illustration of the characteristics of the subsymbolic region of the continuum.

The basic purpose of RAAM is to allow familiar recursive data structures such as trees and lists to be encoded into distributed representations suitable for processing by connectionist networks. However, the result of subsymbolic composition is very different from the explicit concatenative compositional structures created in the symbolic paradigm. A RAAM produces fixed-length distributed patterns of continuous numerical values that encode compositional structure implicitly. The length of the distributed patterns cannot expand or contract to match the size and depth of the compositional structures to be represented (like a LISP list does as elements are *cons*ed onto it), so the structure must be superimposed across the fixed subsymbols. In this way, a composite of symbols in RAAM is itself a symbol, and has the same general form and functionality as the original symbols it was constructed from. The details of how a RAAM constructs and decomposes compositional structures is a major focus of this chapter and is examined extensively in subsequent sections.

When symbols are composed in a symbolic style, they form well-defined structures with a *systematic* organization. This explicit structuring allows for precise relationships between symbolic symbols. For instance, the form of *waiter* in a symbol structure will not be altered by using that symbol in two slightly

---

[2]Given that *x* is bound to the list (1 2 3) in LISP, (*car x*) returns 1, (*cdr x*) returns (2 3), and (*cons 4 x*) returns (4 1 2 3).

different ways, such as (*he gave it to the waiter*) and (*she handed it to a waiter*). On the other hand, the subsymbolic paradigm allows for context to play a role in a compositional representation. In a subsymbolic system, the same symbol used in slightly different contexts may reflect that difference in its form. Although some systematicity is useful, too much can make a system inflexible. This *context-sensitivity* may allow for the functionality of a subsymbolic system to take advantage of information that has been abstracted out of the symbols in a symbolic system.

1.3. Functionality

The functionality of the two paradigms depends directly on their style of representations. Subsymbolic representations reflect the tasks encountered in the training process, in that the generalizations needed to successfully perform the tasks tend to be captured within the internal structure of the representations themselves. In this way, symbols used similarly will develop similar representations. This gives subsymbolic symbols internal relationships to one another, or a *microsemantics*. In contrast, symbolic symbols are arbitrary and atomic, and have no internal semantics. The complete functionality of symbolic systems rests on the structured relationships existing between the arbitrary symbols, or a *macrosemantics* (Dyer, 1990). In effect, a microsemantics is internal to symbols and a macrosemantics is external to symbols.

Probably the most important difference in the functionality of the two paradigms lies in the methods by which symbols can be operated on. If a composite structure in a symbolic system, say a LISP list, were to have its fourth element tested for some criterion, one must first remove the first three elements of the list to get to the fourth. In fact, to do anything to the list involving the elements of that list, one must first decompose it. Thus, symbolic list structures can only be operated on *atomistically*. Many AI practitioners have exclusively used concatenative data structures, thus the need for this initial deconstruction step seems to be a natural consequence of building data structures. In the subsymbolic paradigm, however, an operation can act *holistically* on an entire symbol structure (Blank, 1990; Chalmers, 1990a). In this way, a subsymbolic operation can, in one step, perform a complex function without decomposing the representation of a symbol structure into its constituent parts. A number of examples of holistic operations on composite RAAM representations are described later in this chapter.

1.4. The Symbolic/Subsymbolic Continuum

Figure 6.1. depicts the symbolic/subsymbolic continuum as a three-dimensional space delineated by the three main issues given in Table 6.1. Positioned within this continuum are several representative models selected to illustrate different aspects of the continuum: formal logical inference systems that use predicate calculus; three-layer feed-forward connectionist networks; Boltz-CONS, a constraint-satisfaction memory system; Copycat, an analogy-making system; and the RAAM model to be discussed in this chapter. This next subsections briefly discuss these systems and their positions within this continuum.

1.4.1. Predicate Logic.   In the predicate calculus, abstract atomic objects are called *tokens* and can be concatenated together in recursively defined ways to form arbitrarily complicated logical expressions. These tokens and structured collections of tokens can be used to represent knowledge by assigning to them some type of semantic interpretation, and specifying transformation rules that manipulate them in ways consistent with this interpretation. These expressions and transformation rules can be said to model particular aspects of the world to the extent that the causal relationships that exist among concepts and information in the outside world are captured by the causal interaction of the tokens and logical expressions as governed by the rules.

Certain tokens are assigned unique interpretations, perhaps as variables or logical operators such as *And, ForAll,* or → (implication). We could perhaps represent the fact that all dogs are mammals by the expression:

$$[ForAll(x) \ [Dog(x) \rightarrow Mammal(x)]]$$

and the fact that Fido is a dog by the expression *Dog(Fido)*. These representations can then be manipulated by transformation rules in order to extract useful information from them. Given the fact *Dog(Fido)* and the previous implication expression, an inference system might deduce the fact *Mammal(Fido)* by first breaking these expressions up into their constituent tokens and then recombining them using logical transformation rules such as unification and resolution.

The inference process is atomistic and based entirely on the macrosemantics of the tokens. The database facts are represented concatenatively and the inference rules are applied systematically to these facts. The tokens are static, discrete, and arbitrary. Therefore standard inference systems based on predicate calculus, are prototypical examples of the symbolic paradigm and have been positioned in the symbolic corner of the continuum in Fig. 6.1.

1.4.2. Three-layer Feed-forward Networks.   An example of a connectionist subsymbolic architecture is a network of processing units arranged into hierarchical layers. These layers are usually shown with input coming in from the bottom and output exiting from the top (see Fig. 6.2). Each unit in any given layer (except the output layer) is connected by weighted connections to each unit in the layer above it. Various amounts of activation are applied to each of the units in the bottom layer, representing some particular pattern being presented as input to the network. This activation then flows across the connections to higher

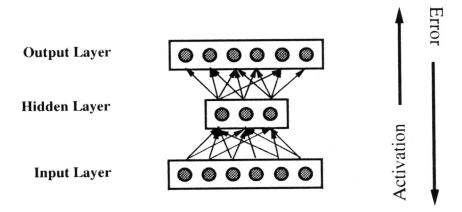

FIG. 6.2. Basic connectionist network. This schematic diagram of a simple network depicts layers as rectangles, units as shaded circles, and weights as arrows. In this standard feed-forward three-layer network, activation begins at the bottom in the Input Layer, proceeds upward through the Hidden Layer, and ends in the Output Layer. Learning is accomplished by propagating errors from the Output Layer back through the network to the Input Layer.

layers of the network, with the weights on the connections mediating the amount of activation that is passed on to successive units. The final pattern of activation present on the topmost layer is considered to be the output pattern produced by the network from the given input pattern.

A learning algorithm such as back-propagation (Rumelhart, Hinton, & Williams, 1986) can be repeatedly applied to the network, enabling it to learn to associate arbitrary pairs of input and output patterns by gradually adjusting the weights on the connections between units. These input–output patterns can be interpreted as representing information received from and sent to the network's surrounding environment. As a result of this training process, the network learns to recode each of the input patterns into different patterns of activation at each successive intermediate layer of units (called hidden layers), so that the appropriate output pattern may be successfully generated at the output layer. This process of learning to recode input patterns into intermediate patterns of activation spread across the hidden layers amounts to the development of distributed internal representations of the input information by the network itself.

The ability of connectionist models to develop their own distributed internal representations—or *hidden representations*—is an extremely important property of this class of models, and provides the basis for placing them in the subsymbolic corner of Fig. 6.1. Individual hidden units participate in the simultaneous creation of many different hidden representations, which are superimposed on top of each other in the network, because different hidden representations are activated across the same set of hidden units depending on the current input to the network. In this way individual units can be viewed as playing different roles, depending on which hidden representation is currently active.

1.4.3. BoltzCONS. BoltzCONS (Touretzky, 1990) is a system that stores and processes traditional symbolic data structures such as lists and trees in a nontraditional fashion (see also Barnden chap. 7, in this volume). The central component of BoltzCONS is a distributed memory that allows LISP-like data structures to be stored and retrieved. After storing a complex nested list structure (i.e., a tree) in memory, the tree may be traversed by performing associative retrieval on the distributed memory. The memory is implemented as a constraint-satisfaction connectionist network containing a large number of units, each of which is configured to respond to a randomly specified subset of all possible trees. The presence or absence of a specific tree in memory is determined by how many of the tree's associated units are activated. Storing a tree in memory is accomplished by activating all of the tree's associated units; similarly, deleting a tree is accomplished by turning off all of the units. Over time, due to the distributed nature of the representations, storing and deleting from the memory causes a gradual degradation of the memory's contents.

In terms of Table 6.1, BoltzCONS' representations could be considered sub-symbolic. The symbol for a tree is distributed across many units in the memory and may be superimposed over other symbols, as in many connectionist models. At any given moment, trees are present in memory to some degree, depending on the total activation across their associated units, rather than always being either completely present or absent. Thus, symbols in BoltzCONS are more continuous than they are discrete and the ability to accurately retrieve them depends on the current contents of the memory. On the other hand, these representations contain no microsemantics; they are arbitrary and static. The nodes in the memory that will respond to a given set of trees are fixed initially and remain bound to the same trees throughout the processing. As in many symbolic systems, the representations in BoltzCONS rely on the macrosemantics between the symbols for their functionality.

BoltzCONS combines aspects of both symbolic and subsymbolic paradigms, but does not seem to be completely characterizable as either. Its representations are continuous and distributed but are also static and arbitrary. For this reason it has been positioned in the middle of the representation dimension of the continuum. Its composition is context-sensitive and superimposed, positioning it on the subsymbolic end of the composition dimension of the continuum. Finally its functionality depends on macrosemantics and therefore it has been positioned at the symbolic end of the functionality dimension.

1.4.4. Copycat. Another system that lies in the Gap is Copycat, a program designed to solve idealized analogy problems (Hofstadter, 1984; Hofstadter & Mitchell, in press). These analogies are stated in terms of letter strings: Given that *letter-string1* changes into *letter-string2*, what does *letter-string3* change into? A typical problem might be: If *abc* → *abd* then *ijk* → ?

When presented with a particular analogy problem, Copycat gradually builds an internal representation of the problem in terms of a set of basic concepts intrinsic to the program. Constructing this representation entails building a mapping between corresponding pieces of the problem, which then serves as a guide for producing a reasonably analogous answer. Building the mapping is accomplished over time by the collective efforts of a large number of independent, small, locally acting processes known as *codelets* executing in parallel. Individual codelets are responsible for building only small pieces of the overall mapping structure. At any given time there may be several incompatible pieces of structure competing for inclusion in the final mapping, in which case the winner is generally chosen according to the degree to which it strengthens the consistency of the context in the already existing structures. The quality of the final answer produced by Copycat directly depends on the construction of a strong final mapping, and the central task of the program is essentially to search for such a mapping through a vast space of possibilities.

However, there is no overarching executive process monitoring the construction of the mapping, or controlling the activity of the codelets. The global course of the processing—the search for a good characterization of the problem through the space of all possible mappings—emerges at a higher level, out of the sustained activities of many hundreds of codelets. Thus, Copycat has a strong subsymbolic flavor, at least along the functional dimension.

On another dimension, the representations developed by Copycat, namely the mappings between letter strings constructed by the codelets, retain many of the qualities of traditional symbolic representations. Structural components included in the final mapping are either present or absent, although it is possible for representational structures to be only tentatively present during the course of building the mapping. These virtual structures may eventually acquire a permanent status in the final mapping, or they may be replaced by stronger structures. The notion of partially present representational components exists in Copycat despite the symbolic nature of its representations, although to a lesser degree than in BoltzCONS. Therefore Copycat has been placed in the upper, front, right corner in Fig. 6.1.

In this section, we have positioned several models within the symbolic/subsymbolic continuum. In the remainder of the chapter we examine the RAAM model in terms of the three dimensions in Fig. 6.1 and demonstrate that it belongs in the subsymbolic corner of the continuum.

2. RECURSIVE AUTO-ASSOCIATIVE MEMORY

Recall that RAAM is designed to allow traditional symbolic data structures such as trees to be represented subsymbolically as distributed patterns of activation.

The general architecture of RAAM is a three-layer feed-forward network of processing units, in which the input and output layers contain equal numbers of units to allow for *auto-association* of the patterns presented to the network. That is, given some pattern on the input layer, the network must reproduce that same pattern on the output layer by first *encoding* the input into some internal representation distributed across the hidden layer, and then *decoding* this hidden representation back to the original pattern on the output layer. The back-propagation learning algorithm is used to perform the auto-association. Furthermore, the hidden layer must be smaller than the input and output layers in order to force the network to accomplish the auto-associative mapping by creating compressed hidden representations. The set of connections from the input layer to the hidden layer serve as the encoding (or composing) mechanism, and the set of connections from the hidden layer to the output layer serve as the decoding (or decomposing) mechanism.

Using the auto-association technique, a RAAM can encode general tree structures of variable depth and fixed branching size into fixed-length distributed representations. The depth may be arbitrary in that no specific upper bound is placed on the depth of the trees encoded, just as there is no specific upper bound on the number of trees that may be stored in a single RAAM network. Of course, as with any connectionist model, the number of patterns that may be stored and retrieved accurately by any particular RAAM depends on the network's size and the number of training patterns involved. But in principle, the RAAM model is capable of encoding arbitrarily large recursive data structures into distributed, compositional representations, and then recovering the underlying constituent structures out of which these representations are composed.

Consider a tree to be represented in a RAAM as being structured in the following manner: The leaves of the tree correspond to individual elements stored in the tree, and the internal branching nodes specify the way these elements are related in the tree. Suppose we represent each of the leaf elements by some unique pattern of activation of length n. The particular encoding we choose for the elements is arbitrary, but the chosen patterns must all be distinct. A RAAM for encoding a set of trees with fixed branching size k will consist of input and output layers that both contain k groups of units—one group of each possible branch of a tree node—with n units in each group, for a total of $k \times n$ units in each layer. The hidden layer consists of a single group of n units (see Fig. 6.3).

Starting with the representations for the leaves, we recursively construct representations for each intermediate branching node by compressing the representations for each of its k child nodes into a single representation for the branching node, of length n. The encodings created for the internal branching nodes are saved and placed in the appropriate input slots when creating the encoding for their internal parent node. We continue this process up the tree until we have a compressed representation for the root node, which corresponds to a single, encoded representation for the entire tree structure. We can encode a number of

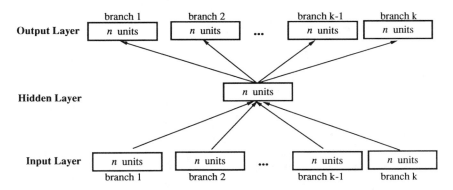

FIG. 6.3. General RAAM architecture. This general RAAM architecture is defined for encoding and decoding trees of arbitrary branching factors. Here k branches, each of n units, are compressed into n units.

trees using the same RAAM by simply performing this process for every tree we would like to encode.

Once we have an encoded representation of a tree, we may reconstruct the entire tree by utilizing the trained connections from the hidden layer to the output layer in the RAAM, which effectively serve as a decoding mechanism. The representation for the root node is first placed on the hidden layer, and the representations for each of the root node's children are recovered by propagating the root node pattern through the hidden/output layer connections. The rest of the tree is then recovered by recursively performing this operation on each of the resulting child node representations, until the leaves are recovered. A decision procedure must be specified to determine when leaves have been recovered. The representations for the leaves were chosen a priori, so the decision procedure merely specifies the allowable range of continuous numerical values that will designate one of the original representations. Concrete examples of the encoding and decoding procedures are presented in the next section.

The encoding produced by a RAAM do not explicitly reflect the structure they represent. Understanding the implicit structure in the representations often requires the use of analytical techniques such as cluster analysis and principal component analysis. In the next section we describe a very simple experiment in which the RAAM encodings are small enough to be dissected and examined without resorting to these more complicated analytical tools.

3. ANALYSIS OF
A SIMPLE SEQUENTIAL RAAM MODEL

In the experiments described in this chapter, we use a slightly restricted version of the general RAAM model discussed above, called a *sequential RAAM*. The sequential model is just like the general version, except that the data structures that are stored and retrieved are ordered lists or *sequences* of elements, rather than general trees. Any sequence of elements can be represented as a simple left-branching or right-branching binary tree, so the sequential model is really just a special case of the more general model. However, in the general model, the size of the hidden layer representations must be exactly the same as that of the representations chosen for the leaf elements, because for arbitrary trees it is impossible to know beforehand whether a particular branch out of a branching node will contain the representation for a leaf, or the representation for some other branching node. This is not the case for a binary tree representation of a sequence of elements, because the left (or right) branch always contains the representation for some leaf, and the other branch always contains the representation for some other branching node. Thus, the representations chosen for our sequence elements, and the compressed representations created by the network for the sequences themselves, can differ in length. One advantage of employing the sequential model is that it allows us to use a larger number of processing units for the compressed hidden representations, in order to improve the information storage and retrieval capacity without having to change the representational scheme chosen for the sequence elements. There is also no need to arbitrarily decide how the subtrees will be grouped; the sequential model will always branch to the side.

It is useful to consider how a sequential RAAM is analogous to a stack data structure.[3] The compression step is like the stack *push* operation and the decoding step is like the stack *pop* operation. When a sequence of elements (represented as a left or right branching tree) is compressed, the next element to be pushed and the current stack are given to the RAAM as input. It then creates an updated version of the stack, containing the new element, on its hidden layer. When a sequence is decoded, the representation of a stack is placed on the hidden layer. The topmost element and the remainder of the stack are produced as output.

To gain some intuition into the types of representations formed by a sequential RAAM, we devised the following very simple experiment. We trained a RAAM to encode sequences of two symbols, *A* and *B*. The symbols were represented by a single *bit*, a binary digit, either 0 or 1. The training sequences consisted of all the possible combinations of length three of the two symbols (see Table 6.2). The input and output layers contained three units each—one to represent the symbol (either *A* or *B*) and two to represent the encoded internal tree nodes. The hidden layer contained two units. This architecture is referred to as a *3-2-3 RAAM* and is pictured in Fig. 6.4.

---

[3]A stack is a data structure similar to a plate dispenser at a cafeteria. You may push a plate onto the top of the stack, or you may remove (pop) a plate from the top. This is also known as last-in-first-out processing.

TABLE 6.2
Sequences in the Training Corpus of the
3-2-3 RAAM

Number	Sequence
1	AAA
2	BAA
3	ABB
4	BBB
5	AAB
6	BBA
7	ABA
8	BAB

After many learning trials with the training corpus, the RAAM's representational accuracy was tested by first encoding one of the sequences into a compressed representation and then immediately decoding that representation back into its constituent elements. If the decoded constituents match the original sequence elements, then the RAAM has learned to adequately represent that particular sequence.

Figure 6.5 depicts the steps required to encode and decode one of the sequences, *ABB*, in the 3-2-3 RAAM. To encode it, the representation for an *A*, a 0, was placed in the input symbol slot (unit *i1* in Fig. 6.4), and the representation

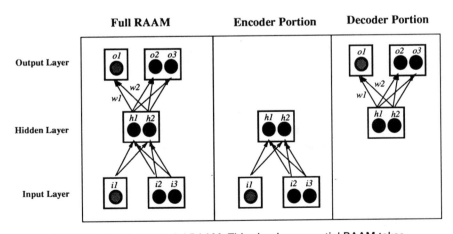

FIG. 6.4. 3-2-3 sequential RAAM. This simple sequential RAAM takes in one symbol at a time on the *i1* unit. Units *i2* and *i3* take in the previous hidden layer activations (from units *h1* and *h2*). The leftmost diagram shows the entire RAAM network; the middle diagram shows the encoder portion of the network; and the rightmost diagram shows the decoder portion of the network.

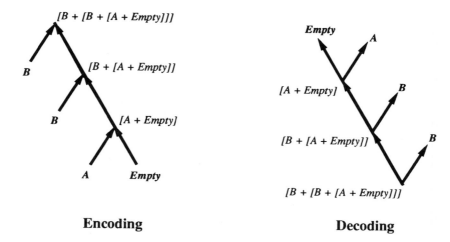

Encoding   **Decoding**

FIG. 6.5.   Encoding and decoding in 3-2-3 RAAM. The left half of this figure depicts the encoding of the sequence *ABB,* and the right half depicts the decoding of the same sequence. Notice that the decoding removes the symbols in the reverse order from that of the encoding.

for the empty stack, (0.25, 0.25), was placed in the previous hidden layer slot (units *i2* and *i3* in Fig. 6.4). Propagating these activations forward produced a compressed representation of [*A + Empty*] on the hidden layer. Next, the representation for *B,* a 1, was placed on unit *i1,* and the representation of [*A + Empty*] created in the previous step was placed on units *i2* and *i3*. Propagating these activations forward produced a compressed representation of [*B + [A + Empty]*] on the hidden layer. Finally in the third encoding step, a compressed representation of the entire sequence is obtained. To decode, this compressed representation [*B + [B + [A + Empty]]*] is placed on the hidden layer and activations are propagated forward to produce activations on the output layer. Decoding the entire sequence also requires three steps, as shown on the right of Fig. 6.5.

The testing revealed that the RAAM was unable to learn all eight sequences perfectly. It produced decoding errors on the first element of sequences 4 and 8. This difficulty in mastering the training corpus was due to the very restricted size of the hidden layer. However, because the hidden layer was limited to two units, we could examine the RAAM's encoding directly by plotting them in a two-dimensional graph, as follows.

First, a graph was constructed in which the y-axis represented the value of hidden unit *h2* and the x-axis represented the value of the hidden unit *h1*.[4] Both

---

[4]This area is often called the *representational space* of a connectionist network. For every unit in the hidden layer, there is a dimension in representational space. This example, containing two hidden units, can be mapped in two dimensions.

of these values ranged between 0.0 and 1.0. Next, the RAAM's encoding of an entire sequence was plotted as the first point. Then the RAAM was allowed to decode the last item in a sequence.[5] After decoding the last item, the encoding of the remainder of the sequence appeared on the two rightmost output units (*o2* and *o3* in Fig. 6.4). This was plotted as the second point. Then the middle item of the sequence was decoded. Again the encoding of the remaining sequence was plotted. This process was continued until the entire sequence had been decoded. Thus each plot contains four points: (a) the encoding of the tree that represents the entire sequence; (b) the encoding of the tree that represents the first two elements; (c) the encoding of the tree that represents the first element; (d) the encoding of the empty tree.

Figure 6.6 shows the decoding plots formed by all eight sequences trained in the 3-2-3 RAAM. The numbered boxes mark the beginning and the arrowheads indicate the end of each plot. Notice that each plot moves in a clockwise progression though the space. Let us examine sequence 3, *ABB,* more closely. The point at the box represents the entire sequence, in reverse order as on a stack— *BBA.* The next point represents the encoding of the remainder of the tree after the final element has been decoded or popped off the stack—*BA.* The third point represents the tree after the middle element has been decoded—*A.* The final point represents the empty tree.

How has the RAAM partitioned the hidden layer space to represent these sequences? One way to determine this is to examine the activations of unit *o1* in the output layer of the RAAM. When the activation of *o1* is less than 0.5, an *A* has been decoded (because an *A* is designated by a 0), and when the activation is greater than 0.5 a *B* has been decoded (because a *B* is designated by a 1). If we could determine when unit *o1*'s activation is 0.5, we could see how the RAAM has used the hidden layer activations to encode the sequences. Referring to Fig. 6.4, *o1*'s activation is given by the equation:

$$act(o1) = sigmoid((act(h1) \times w1) + (act(h2) \times w2) + bias(o1)$$

where $act(x)$is the activation of unit, x, $bias(x)$ is the internal threshold of unit x, and $sigmoid\ (y) = \dfrac{1}{1 + e^{-y}}.$ By setting $act(o1)$ to 0.5 and substituting in the known values for $w1$, $w2$, and $bias\ (o1)$, the following equation is found, representing a line in the space of hidden unit activations:

$$act(h2) = (1.78 \times act(h1)) - 0.801$$

---

[5]Recall that the RAAM builds up its representation of a sequence from left to right, but when it decodes the sequence it must reverse the process. So the elements of the sequence are returned in reverse order.

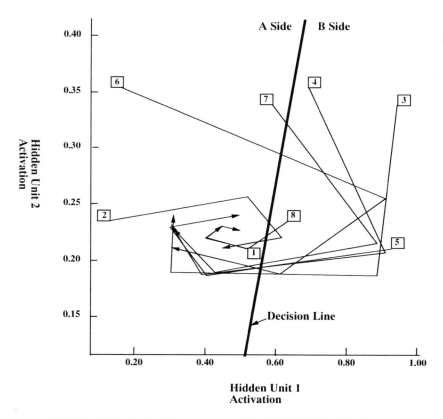

FIG. 6.6.   Plot of all eight sequences of the 3-2-3 RAAM. This diagram shows the decoding plots of each of the sequences from Table 6.2. Each plot begins with its sequence number in a small box, travels in a clockwise motion, and ends at an arrowhead. The decision line defines where the activation of unit *o1* (see Fig. 6.4) is 0.5.

This line has been plotted in Fig. 6.6 and labeled as the *decision line*, because it divides the representational space into an *A side* and a *B side*.

So we can now see that the RAAM has clustered all of the encodings according to whether the topmost element in the stack is an *A* or a *B*. All points to the right of the diagonal line designate encodings containing a *B* as the next element to be decoded, whereas all points to the left of the diagonal designate encodings containing an *A* as the next element to be decoded. The two sequences that were decoded incorrectly, 4:*BBB* and 8:*BAB*, both returned an *A* as the first element rather than a *B*. This is reflected in the fact that the third point in each of their plots is to the left of the diagonal, instead of to the right, as it should be.

The RAAM has also partitioned the hidden layer space in at least one other way: All plots that begin above the horizontal line $act(h2) = 0.30$ (this line is not shown in the figure), represent sequences whose middle element is a B (sequences 3, 4, 6, and 7). Similarly, all plots that begin below this horizontal line represent sequences whose middle element is an A (sequences 1, 2, 5, and 8).

Even in this very simple experiment, the richness of subsymbolic representations is evident. Hidden unit $h2$ can be viewed as a subsymbol that encodes the middle element in the sequence. The combination of both hidden units can be viewed as a symbol encoding the current top-most element in the sequence. Additionally, the two hidden units can be seen as a symbol for the entire composed sequence structure. All of this information is simultaneously represented in the continuous numerical values of two simple units with respect to the RAAM's weighted connections.

It is interesting to note that the values we chose to represent the empty tree had a dramatic effect on how the RAAM partitioned the hidden unit space, and on its ability to accurately represent all eight sequences. Recall that the empty tree values are the initial values placed on units $i2$ and $i3$ in the first step of encoding a sequence. For the results discussed earlier, the values 0.25 and 0.25 were used to represent the empty tree. Figure 6.6 shows that all eight sequence plots do, in fact, end in the vicinity of this point. We ran other experiments in which both of the empty tree values were 0.0, 0.5, 0.75, and 1.0. In the 0.0 case, the RAAM could learn only four of the sequences correctly, and the decision line was much closer to horizontal (rather than vertical as in the 0.25 case). When we tried the same experiments with a 4-3-4 RAAM, these effects were not found, suggesting that if given enough hidden units for a given task, a RAAM can adequately represent the sequences without regard to the particular empty tree values chosen.

4. GENERALIZATION

One of the most useful qualities of connectionist models such as RAAM is their ability to learn a set of training examples and then to generalize from this training corpus to produce appropriate output for novel inputs. Connectionist models are often evaluated on their generalization performance. If a model can respond suitably to the majority of novel inputs (typically a performance of 75% or greater is considered good), then it must have developed a veridical representation of the entire task environment and not simply of the trained portion. More importantly, even when a connectionist model makes mistakes on novel inputs, this mistakes often reflect generalizations of the training task.

Several factors affect a network's ability to produce useful generalizations: the complexity of the environment to be modeled, the contents and size of the training corpus, the number of exposures to the training corpus, and the size of the hidden layer (in three-layer feed-forward networks). If the training corpus does not contain a diverse enough sampling of the possible inputs, the network will only be able to respond reasonably well to novel inputs that are closely related to the training examples. If the network is trained until it responds perfectly to all of the training examples, or if the hidden layer is very large, it may succeed at the training task by simply memorizing every example, rather than forming useful generalizations. Finally, as we have already seen with the 3-2-3 RAAM, if the hidden layer size is too restricted, the network may not be able to learn the training examples adequately, although it may still form useful generalizations about the examples it does learn.

Consider the 3-2-3 RAAM once more. It was trained on all of the possible sequences of length three, so there were no remaining novel sequences with which to test its generalization abilities. Instead, we devised a different kind of generalization test. We again represented the hidden layer activation space as a two-dimensional graph, just as in Fig. 6.6. Then we selected a sample point from this activation space, placed it on the hidden layer of the trained RAAM, and decoded it for a single step. This produced another point in the hidden layer activation space on the output units $o2$ and $o3$. We plotted the original point and its decoded result as a vector with the arrowhead ending at the decoded result. Figure 6.7 shows how a large number of these sample points decoded to produce the next point in sequence. Although most of these sample points did not correspond to any of the trained sequences, the RAAM's outputs all followed the same trends observed for the trained sequences. The vector field moves in a counterclockwise direction through the space; vectors originating near the edges of the space are typically long, often crossing the decision line; and the overall tendency of the field is to converge toward the vicinity of the empty tree point (0.25, 0.25). The 3-2-3 RAAM's responses to novel inputs closely follow its responses to trained inputs. It has formed generalizations of the training data in a way that allows it to make reasonable responses to novel data.

In the remainder of the experiments to be described, we use generalization tests as one method for evaluating: (a) whether the RAAM itself has developed useful representations, and (b) whether additional networks that take these RAAM representations as input can generalize over them in an interesting way.

5. RAAM-ENCODED SIMPLE SENTENCES

The simple sequence experiments performed on the 3-2-3 RAAM reveal some of the potential offered by subsymbolic representations. To explore this potential more fully we devised a similar but more complicated set of experiments where sentences were represented as sequences of words. A corpus of two- and three-word sentences was created using a small grammar, a *tarzan grammar* if you will, and then encoded by a sequential RAAM. Here we describe the generation of the sentences from the grammar, specify the RAAM architecture used, and perform an analysis of the RAAM's encodings of the sentences.

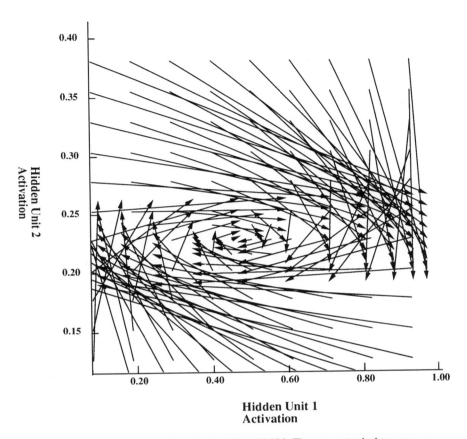

FIG. 6.7.   Generalization in the 3-2-3 RAAM. The same technique as shown in Fig. 6.6 was used, except that the decoding was begun at points all over the plane and was followed for only one step. This illustrates the generalization ability of the network.

We chose natural language as the domain for these experiments because it requires complex, structure-sensitive operations that have traditionally been modeled in the symbolic paradigm. These RAAM experiments are presented to illustrate the contrasting styles of representation, composition, and functionality available in subsymbolic models, and should not be construed as a linguistic model.

5.1.   Creation of Simple Sentences

A trivial program to generate English-like sentences was written to produce two- and three-word sentences from a set of 26 words (15 nouns and 11 verbs). An additional word, *stop*, was used to indicate the end of a sentence. The words

TABLE 6.3
Categories of Lexical Items Used in Sentence Generator

Category	Members
NOUN-ANIMATE	*tarzan jane boy cheetah chimp rhino bigfoot junglebeast*
NOUN-AGGRESSIVE	*cheetah rhino bigfoot junglebeast*
NOUN EDIBLE	*coconut banana berries meat*
NOUN-SQUISH	*banana berries*
NOUN-MOBILE	NOUN-ANIMATE + *jeep*
NOUN-SWINGER	*tarzan chimp*
NOUN-HUNTER	*jane*
NOUN	NOUN-ANIMATE + NOUN-EDIBLE + (*jeep tree rock*)
NOUN-REAL	NOUN-(*bigfoot junglebeast*)
VERB-FLEE	*flee*
VERB-HUNT	*hunt*
VERB-AGGRESS	*kill chase*
VERB SQUISH	*squish*
VERB-MOVE	*move*
VERB-EAT	*eat*
VERB PERCEIVE	*see smell*
VERB-INTRANS	*see smell*
VERB-EXIST	*exist*
VERB-SWING	*swing*

were described by the lexical categories given in Table 6.3. Note that one word may belong to several different categories. For instance, *cheetah* is a member of the following categories: NOUN-ANIMATE, NOUN-AGGRESSIVE, NOUN-MOBILE, NOUN-REAL, and NOUN. The sentence templates given in Table 6.4 specified the ways that the lexical categories could be combined to form sentences. All of the sentences were either of the form NOUN VERB or NOUN VERB NOUN. There are 26^2 possible two-word sequences and 26^3 possible three-word sequences for a total of 18,252 possible sequences; the grammar

TABLE 6.4
Templates Used in Sentence Generator

Template	Word1	Word2	Word3
1	NOUN-ANIMATE	VERB-FLEE	NOUN-AGGRESSIVE
2	NOUN-AGGRESSIVE	VERB-AGGRESS	NOUN-ANIMATE
3	NOUN-ANIMATE	VERB-SQUISH	NOUN-SQUISH
4	NOUN-ANIMATE	VERB-EAT	NOUN-EDIBLE
5	NOUN-ANIMATE	VERB-PERCEIVE	NOUN
6	NOUN-MOBILE	VERB-MOVE	
7	NOUN-ANIMATE	VERB-INTRANS	
8	NOUN-REAL	VERB-EXIST	
9	NOUN-SWINGER	VERB-SWING	
10	NOUN-HUNTER	VERB-HUNT	
11	NOUN-AGGRESSIVE	VERB-HUNT	

restricted this to a very small subset of 341 valid sentences. This grammar was inspired by one used by Elman (1990) in his experiments on sentences for his simple recurrent network architecture (see also Lee and Gasser, chap. 8 in this volume). Table 6.5 gives some examples of typical sentences produced by the generation program.

To represent these words as input to a RAAM, each word was randomly assigned an individual code. The code consisted of 27 bits. We used a *localist* representation; for each word one bit was on, and the other 26 were off. Each input symbol was orthogonal to all of the others and had no microsemantics. For the majority of the experiments described later, the corpus consisted of 100 unique sentences to be used for training and another 100 to be used for generalization tests.

5.2. RAAM Processing of Sentences

The structure of the RAAM used is shown in Fig. 6.8. The input is divided into a set of 27 word units and a set of 30 encoded units (from the previous hidden layer activations). The words were given a localist representation, so only one of the word units was on at a time. The number of words used determined the number of word units needed. Determining an appropriate number of encoding units was not as straightforward; the number should be large enough to allow the RAAM ample space to successfully compress and reconstruct trees of the required depth, but small enough to allow useful generalizations to develop. The number of encoding units was chosen by sampling the RAAM's performance over a small number of tests with the hidden layer size ranging from 20 to 50. By this trial-and-error process, the hidden layer size was set to 30 units.

Recall that this is not a general RAAM, but a sequential RAAM (the left set of units always encodes a single element and the right set of units encodes the rest

TABLE 6.5
Sentences Generated from the
Categories and Templates

Template	Example Sentence
1	*jane flee junglebeast*
2	*cheetah kill chimp*
3	*boy squish banana*
4	*rhino eat meat*
5	*bigfoot see jeep*
6	*tarzan move*
7	*chimp smell*
8	*tree exist*
9	*tarzan swing*
10	*jane hunt*
11	*junglebeast hunt*

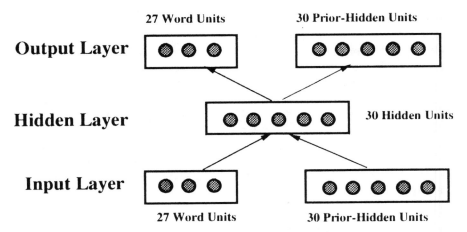

FIG. 6.8. RAAM architecture used for simple sentence experiments. Sentences from the *tarzan grammar* were encoded using this network architecture.

of the binary tree). The primary reason we chose to use the sequential model rather than the general model was that we didn't want to make any prior commitment to a particular syntactic structuring. With the general model, it would be necessary to structure the input as some form of parse tree, with the internal units representing syntactic groupings such as noun phrases or verb phrases. We wanted to make as few assumptions as possible about the form of the input, and so the simpler sequential version was more appropriate.

Treating each sentence as a sequence of words, we trained a 57-30-57 RAAM network to read in one word at a time, from left to right, as in the simple RAAM experiment described earlier. The 100 training sentences were presented in a random order. The hidden units were cleared between sentences. After approximately 21,000 presentations of each sentence, training was halted.

To test the accuracy of the RAAM's performance, the sentences were encoded into a distributed representation and decoded back into their localist representation. A decoding was considered an error when the activation of the correct word unit did not exceed 0.5, or if another word was more strongly active than the correct word unit. The 100 trained sentences and 80% of the 100 new sentences were decoded perfectly. In 15 of the new sentences that caused errors, all of the correct word units were activated, but the activation was not above 0.5 for at least one of the words in each sentence. These errors could probably be alleviated if the RAAM were to be trained for a longer time. In each of the other five sentences that produced decoding errors, one word was decoded as another word. This is a much more serious error. Some of these severe errors can be explained by examining the training corpus more closely. The average frequency of the 11 verbs in the 100 trained sentences was 9%. The average frequency of the 15 nouns was 12.3%. In two of the five errors, the RAAM decoded *jane* rather than the correct word *jeep*. In another, it decoded *flee* instead of *swing*. The frequency of *jeep* (1%) was well below the average for nouns. The RAAM may not have had enough examples over which to generalize a representation of *jeep*. In the *swing* case, the random sentence generator did not generate a single sentence containing that particular word for the training corpus. Therefore it is not surprising that the RAAM was unable to decode it correctly when it was presented with it for the very first time.

It is interesting to note that even when the RAAM made a serious mistake such as decoding the incorrect word, the word it usually returned was of the same grammatical type. For instance, a noun was often substituted for another noun (i.e., *jane* for *jeep*). Thus it appears that the RAAM is making useful generalizations in its encodings.

One final set of generalization tests reveals the context-sensitive quality of the RAAM's compositions. We created 20 ungrammatical sentences and tested whether they could be decoded correctly. Some of these sentences were ungrammatical in very subtle ways. For example *tarzan chase bigfoot* is ungrammatical because *tarzan* is not a member of the NOUN-AGGRESSIVE category, and *bigfoot exist* is ungrammatical because *bigfoot* is not a member of the NOUN-REAL category. This majority of the test sentences were ungrammatical in more obvious ways. For instance *berries chase meat* is ungrammatical because *chase* requires a subject from the NOUN-AGGRESSIVE category and an object from the NOUN-ANIMATE category, while *eat tree eat* does not even follow the (NOUN VERB NOUN) sentence structure. The RAAM could only decode 35% of the novel ungrammatical sentences correctly as opposed to the 80% reported earlier for the novel grammatical sentences. Of the ungrammatical sentences decoded correctly, 86% were only subtly ungrammatical. The RAAM had difficulty encoding and decoding ungrammatical sentences, so it appears that it has taken advantage of the regularities in the grammatical training corpus to form its hidden representations. Clearly in these experiments, the RAAM's ability to accurately represent novel sentences was context-sensitive. However, RAAMs can exhibit systematicity within the training context and on novel inputs that mirror the training environment (Chalmers, 1990a).

5.3. Analysis of Sentence Encodings

To examine the RAAM's development of generalizations more directly, a cluster analysis, based on Euclidean distance, was performed on the encoded representations of the 100 trained sentences. This procedure clusters similar patterns together for comparison, collapsing a 30-dimensional space into a compact tree structure. Figure 6.9 shows the general structure of the entire clustering, and one subcluster of 26 sentences in detail.

At first glance, the clustering seems to be based mostly on the last word of the

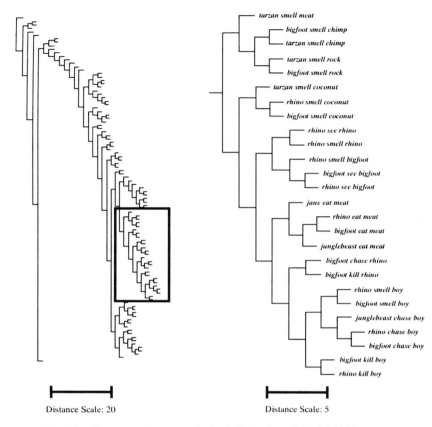

tarzan smell meat
bigfoot smell chimp
tarzan smell chimp
tarzan smell rock
bigfoot smell rock
tarzan smell coconut
rhino smell coconut
bigfoot smell coconut
rhino see rhino
rhino smell rhino
rhino smell bigfoot
bigfoot see bigfoot
rhino see bigfoot
jane eat meat
rhino eat meat
bigfoot eat meat
junglebeast eat meat
bigfoot chase rhino
bigfoot kill rhino
rhino smell boy
bigfoot smell boy
junglebeast chase boy
rhino chase boy
bigfoot chase boy
bigfoot kill boy
rhino kill boy

Distance Scale: 20   Distance Scale: 5

FIG. 6.9.   Sentence cluster analysis. A clustering of the RAAM's representations of the sentences of the grammar is shown. The left tree shows the entire cluster of the 100-sentence training corpus, while the right tree is an enlarged view of the boxed area.

sentence. For example, there is a large cluster of sentences near the bottom of Fig. 6.9, all of which end in *boy*. Although this is sometimes the case, it is not the whole story. For instance, the middle cluster, which includes *rhino see rhino*, contains sentences of the form: Aggressive nouns perceiving aggressive nouns. Some of these sentences end with *rhino* and some with *bigfoot*. Two other sentences ending with *rhino* (*bigfoot chase rhino* and *bigfoot kill rhino*) have been clustered separately. These two separate sentences contain aggressive verbs, rather than perceiving verbs as in the middle cluster. Sentences ending with the word *meat* have also not all been clustered together; the smelling of meat has been separated from the eating of it.

On the portion of the cluster analysis not shown in detail, all sentences ending with the words *berries* and *banana* have been clustered together. This cluster is quite far away from the one shown on the right side of the figure. The other two edible nouns were *coconut* and *meat*. The only difference in the ways these two sets of nouns were used was that *berries* and *banana* were squishable while *coconut* and *meat* were not. Clearly the RAAM's representations of these words are sensitive to the context in which they are used.

Another indication of the RAAM's attention to context is evident in its representations of sentences of the form NOUN-ANIMATE *eat meat* and NOUN-ANIMATE *smell coconut*. In both of these clusters, the sentences in which NOUN-ANIMATE is also aggressive are closer together than those sentences in which NOUN-ANIMATE is nonaggressive. So in sentences where the last two words are identical, the RAAM is using both the actual first word and its context to disambiguate the sentences.

In summary, the cluster analysis of the sentence encodings provides some evidence that the RAAM has developed generalizations of aggressive animates, squishable edibles, and aggressive verbs. However, using the clustering of the sentence representations to make inferences about the word representations is somewhat indirect. Elman (1990) designed a more direct method to examine his simple recurrent network's internal representations of words. We also applied this method to the RAAM.

For this method, the 100 sentences in the training corpus were again passed through the encoder portion of the RAAM after the completion of training. The hidden layer activations created by each word combined with the context of the current sentence were saved. For the 286 words in the 100 sentences, we obtained 286 numerical vectors of length 30 (the size of the hidden layer). All of the vectors produced by a particular word were then averaged together to create one composite vector for each of the 26 unique words. Each composite vector reflects all of the contexts in which a word has been used in the 100 training sentences. These composite vectors are shown schematically in Fig. 6.10. Some similarities between these composite vectors stand out quite clearly; the activation of the sixth hidden unit (shown in the sixth column in Fig. 6.10) seems to encode whether the word is a verb or a noun. For all of the verbs, the activation is quite high, and for all of the nouns (with the exception of *jeep*), the activation is quite low. As noted previously, *jeep* only appeared once in the training corpus, so the RAAM did not have an adequate number of examples to form an appropriate representation for this word.

To further examine the similarities between these composite word vectors, another cluster analysis was done (see Fig. 6.11). Again it is clear that the RAAM has made a distinction between verbs and nouns, although there are eight exceptions. Some of these exceptions (*hunt*, *jeep*, and *tree*) appeared infrequently in the training corpus and can be explained in this way. However, the other exceptions appeared more frequently than the average for verbs and nouns. There are several possible explanations for these anomalies: (a) perhaps the small size of the training set combined with the relatively large size of the hidden layer allowed the RAAM to develop special representations for some of the words, and (b) perhaps the 100 sentences randomly selected for the training corpus were not

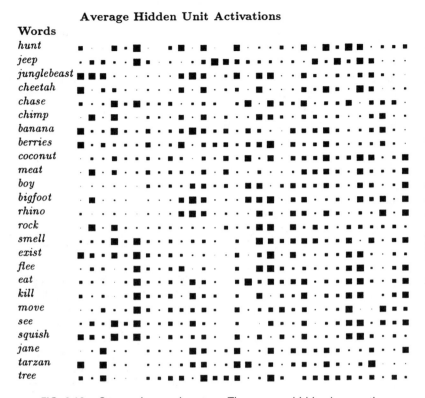

FIG. 6.10. Composite word vectors. The average hidden layer activations associated with each word in its various contexts are depicted. One column of rectangles is shown for each of the 30 units in the hidden layer. All activations fall in the range from 0 to 1. The area of a rectangle encodes the magnitude of the average activation.

representative of the grammar. In either case, increasing the size of the training corpus should eliminate or decrease the anomalous cases.

We tested this hypothesis by creating a new training corpus containing 300 randomly selected sentences (from the 341 possible sentences) and training a new RAAM. As was expected, the clustering of the composite word vectors for the RAAM trained on the larger corpus had fewer exceptions (five as opposed to eight). In addition, only two of these exceptions, *jane* and *cheetah*, were the same. The size and contents of the training corpus clearly affected the RAAM's ability to generalize. In Elman's (1990) experiments in which he used a similar grammar, the training corpus contained 10,000 sentences, and all of the network's composite representations of nouns and verbs appeared in separate clusters. Unfortunately, the simple *tarzan grammar* we devised restricted the number of valid sentences drastically, so such an extensive test was not possible.

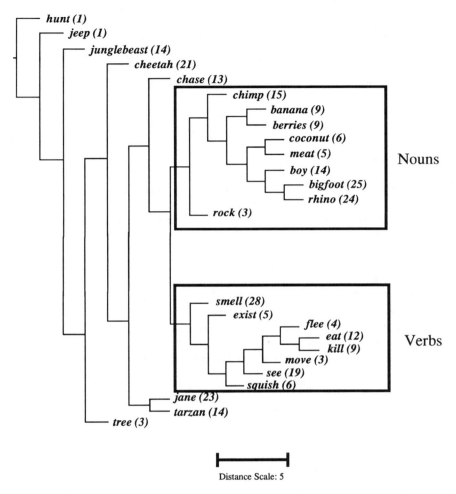

FIG. 6.11. Composite word vector cluster analysis. The clustering of the average hidden layer activations associated with each word in its various contexts is shown. The number in parentheses following each word indicates the number of times it appeared in the 100-sentence training corpus. This is another method of visualizing the information in Fig. 6.10.

Further examination of Fig. 6.11 reveals that the RAAM has made more than just a noun/verb distinction; within the noun cluster there are additional discriminations. The squishable foods, *banana* and *berries,* have been clustered together, as have the nonsquishable foods *coconut* and *meat.* The aggressive nouns within the noun cluster, *bigfoot* and *rhino,* are also clustered together.

Although the RAAM was never given any explicit information about the tarzan grammar, the cluster analyses reveal that its representations of the sentences and words do reflect the grammar's rules to a certain extent. How the words were used (their context) in the example sentences directly affected the form of the RAAM's representations. Furthermore, the cluster analyses shows that the representations do possess a microsemantics.

6. HOLISTIC OPERATIONS

To explore the unique functional capabilities resulting from the accessible microsemantics in RAAM representations, we designed experiments that take RAAM-encoded sentences as input and operate holistically on these representations to produce output. Three types of experiments are described: detectors, decoders, and transformers. Each experiment was accomplished with a feed-forward network.

6.1. Detectors

All of the detection experiments followed the same basic outline: Train a new feed-forward network to take an encoded sentence representation from the RAAM and produce a simple YES or NO as output if the presence or absence of some feature (or combination of features) is detected in the input. This was accomplished by having a single output unit that is trained to produce a 1 in a positive instance and a 0 in a negative instance. Figure 6.12 shows the basic architecture of each detector network.

  6.1.1. Aggressive-Animal Detector.   The premise for this experiment is straightforward: Given a sentence, is a member of the NOUN-AGGRESSIVE

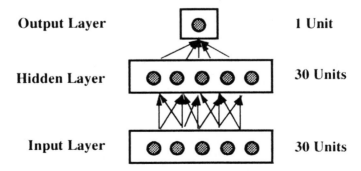

FIG. 6.12.   Feed-forward network architecture for detectors. The single output unit was trained to produce a 1 for positive instances of the detection tasks and a 0 for negative instances.

category present? For example, *tarzan eat banana* should produce a NO, whereas *junglebeast kill chimp* should produce a YES. Note that this is not a detector for an aggressive animal acting in an aggressive manner; the syntactic presence or absence of an aggressive noun is all that matters. So the sentence *bigfoot smell banana* is also a positive example for this detector.

The composed representation of a sentence was placed on the input units. Then the original sentence was examined to see if one of the aggressive nouns appeared in the sentence, and the output target was set accordingly. This feed-forward network was trained on 50 of the sentences from the training corpus for approximately 300 trials.

The other 50 sentences from the original training corpus were then tested in the network to see if it had generalized the task. The network made six errors getting 88% of these novel sentences correct. Four of the errors were false NOs, and two were false YESs. No single characteristic seems to satisfactorily account for all of the errors.

Following this test of generalization, the 100 sentences not trained in the RAAM where encoded via the RAAM and tested in this network. This is a double test of generalization: first in the RAAM, and second in the feed-forward network. Surprisingly, the network performed just slightly less accurately than in the previous test, scoring 85% correct over the 100 sentences.

6.1.2. Aggressive-Animal-and-Human Detector. This detector is similar to the previous one with an additional constraint: Is there a member of the NOUN-AGGRESSIVE category and a HUMAN in the sentence? This could be viewed as the logical AND of two smaller detectors where both must be positive for the entire detector to be positive. However, the network will of course build its own representation of the problem. The HUMAN category includes the nouns: *tarzan, jane,* and *boy* and was not explicitly part of the grammar.

The training proceeded exactly as described earlier with the added constraints mentioned. The network was trained for approximately 300 trials and performance was nearly identical. Again, the network was tested on 50 RAAM-trained composite representations this time missing 8, for 84% correct. The network performed nearly the same on the 100 generalized RAAM sentences missing 15 of 100 for 85% correct.

It is not surprising that five of the six representations that caused errors in the aggressive-animal detector were also missed by the aggressive-animal-and-human detector.

It is interesting to note that the RAAM had trouble decoding some of the sentences that the detectors processed correctly. In fact, of the 15 errors that the RAAM decoder made, only two of those were ones that a detector had problems with also.

6.1.3. Reflexive Detector. Although both of the previous detectors trained easily and generalized quite well, the following experiment proved to be a tougher problem. A feed-forward detector was trained to produce a YES if the subject and object of the encoded sentence were the same. To ensure that the corpus had adequate examples of these types of sentences (e.g., *junglebeast smell junglebeast*) and to remove two-word sentences, a new data set was created. The following five verbs were considered reflexive: *flee, chase, kill, smell,* and *see,* and only the eight animate nouns could be used reflexively. These requirements combined with the restrictions imposed by the grammar, resulted in only 28 reflexive sentences (2 for each of the 4 non-aggressive animates, and 5 for each of the 4 aggressive animates). To increase the number of reflexive sentences *chimp* and *boy* were treated as aggressive nouns for this experiment only. This created 6 more reflexive sentences for a total of 34. The training corpus consisted of 28 of the 34 reflexive sentences and 40 randomly chosen non-reflexive sentences. Finally, the architecture of the detector network was slightly modified. The hidden layer was decreased to 15 units, in an attempt to force the network to make useful generalizations.

A new version of the sentence encoding RAAM from Fig. 6.8 was trained on the 68-sentence corpus. These encoded sentences were then used to train the new detector network for 600 trials. After this training, two types of generalizations were tested: (a) generalizations over the verb, and (b) generalizations over the noun (or the reflexive word).

In the first case, the network was trained on the representation for sentences such as *bigfoot see bigfoot,* and then given the novel representation for *bigfoot smell bigfoot.* All of these types of encoded sentences were correctly detected as being reflexive. The network also correctly detected nonreflexive encoded sentences over a verb, and therefore generalized 100% correctly.

In the second case, the network was unable to master generalization over the noun. In the training corpus, *tarzan* and *jane* never appeared in the same sentence together, nor did either appear in the same sentence twice. The network was then given encoded representations for sentences of the form *tarzan VERB tarzan* and *jane VERB jane* where *VERB* was one of the possible reflexive verbs. The network did not respond positively to any of these generalization tests. When the network was given *jane VERB tarzan* and vice versa, it correctly responded with a negative. However, it responded negatively in all cases indicating that it was not performing the task satisfactorily.

After examining the network and the method of encoding, it seems that the network was not easily finding a strong relationship between the representation of a word used in the first position and the representation of the same word used in the third position. If a general relationship existed between these representations a straightforward method of deciding if the words were the same would exist. However, the network failed to make this generalization. We believe that this might have been caused by the fact that the grammar was too constrained. By developing a more complex grammar, and allowing for deeper trees, the network would have to conserve the representational space of each symbol. This might force it to develop generalized representations so that representations of the same word used in two positions would be more similar.

The three detector experiments show that a feed-forward network can detect the presence and absence of particular features in the composed sentence representations produced by a RAAM without decomposing the sentence into its constituent words. The question remains: Is it only generalized features of the composed structures that are directly accessible in subsymbolic representations, or are the actual constituents themselves accessible as well?

6.2. Parallel Decoding

We have seen that when a RAAM is trained, an encoder and a decoder are naturally created as a by-product of auto-associating through a compressed hidden layer. By using these trained connections, we are able to treat the hidden representation developed by a sequential RAAM as a *stack,* so that the last symbol encoded into the stack is the first one decoded. But is this sequential peeling-off of one symbol at a time the only method to retrieve information from the composite representation?

To address this question, we designed a feed-forward network to decode all of the words in composed sentence representation in parallel (see Fig. 6.13). The architecture of this network is very similar to the detectors, however instead of having a single unit on the output layer, each word of the sentence is represented on the output layer from left to right. The first word of the sentence is trained to appear in the far left of the output, followed by the second word, and third (if one exists).

The encoded representations of the first 50 sentences from the original RAAM corpus were trained for approximately 7,200 trials. Attempting to decode the

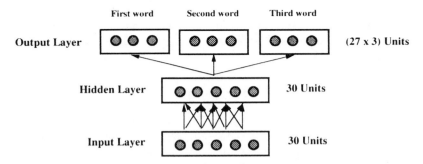

FIG. 6.13.   Feed-forward network architecture for parallel decoding. This shows the architecture for decoding composed sentences in one step. The words of each sentence were trained to appear on the Output Layer, from left to right. If only two words were in a sentence then the rightmost output slot was trained to give no activation.

remaining 50 sentences could result in a possible 150 mistakes: for each of the three-word sentences the decoder had to correctly produce all three words and for each of the two-word sentences the decoder had to correctly produce the two words and fill the third output slot with no activation. The network successfully decoded all but 29 of the words for an overall score of 81% correct. When the network made a mistake, it again consistently selected a noun for a noun and a verb for a verb, much like the original RAAM.

The parallel decoder experiment demonstrates that the actual constituents of composed structures in the subsymbolic paradigm are readily accessible.

6.3. Syntactic Transformations

So far the experiments employing the RAAM representations have been *detectors* and *decoders,* but it is also possible to build *transformers* that directly convert RAAM encoded sentence representations into modified RAAM encoded representations (Chalmers, 1990a). Again, it must be emphasized that these transformations act directly on the subsymbolic forms—no decoding is done to accomplish the task. Decoding is performed afterward only to test the accuracy of the transformation. The transformation task chosen for this experiment was to convert encoded representations of the form *NOUN1 chase NOUN2* directly into encoded representations of the form *NOUN2 flee NOUN1*. This transformation is considered syntactic because a symbolic system need only apply syntactic rules to accomplish the task; no outside information about the words or their relationships is needed.

For these experiments it was necessary to train a new RAAM with a new data set that included sentences of the appropriate type. A new corpus was created with 20 sentences containing the verb *chase,* the 20 corresponding sentences containing the verb *flee,* and 110 miscellaneous sentences. The RAAM architecture from Fig. 6.8 was used. The RAAM was trained for 3,700 trials on the new 150 sentences. Then every compositional representation containing the word *chase* or *flee* was separated from the rest. In addition, four new *chase* sentences and the corresponding *flee* sentences were also encoded in the RAAM and saved.

Sixteen of the RAAM-trained patterns that were formed by encoding the *chase* sentences were then trained to be associated via the feed-forward network (shown in Fig. 6.14) to the sixteen corresponding *flee* encoded patterns. The feed-forward network quickly mastered the task in approximately 75 trials.

After training, the feed-forward network was presented with eight novel sentences, four of which had been trained in the RAAM and four of which had not. The transformation network successfully generalized the correct *flee* sentence representations 100% of the time for the RAAM-trained input and 75% of the time for the doubly novel input (novel to the RAAM and to the transformer). The one error made by the network was only on a single word; it transformed *junglebeast chase chimp* into *chimp flee cheetah*. The accuracy of the transfor-

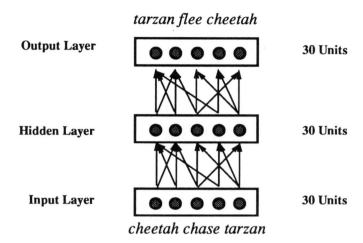

FIG. 6.14. Feed-forward network architecture for transformations. The network was trained to take an encoded *chase* sentences as input and to produce the corresponding encoded *flee* sentence as output.

mation was checked by taking the resulting output from the feed-forward network and decoding it in the trained RAAM. Figure 6.15 shows the various steps that were necessary to accomplish this experiment. First the sentence to be transformed was encoded with the trained RAAM. Then the composed representation of the entire sentence was given as input to the transformation network and the network converted this composed structure directly into another composed sentence structure. Finally this output from the transformation network was decoded with the trained RAAM.

The transformation experiment further demonstrates that subsymbolic representations of symbol structures can be operated on in a holistic fashion that is not possible in traditional symbolic systems.

7. CONCLUSIONS

In this chapter we have characterized the symbolic and subsymbolic paradigms as two opposing corners of an abstract space of paradigms. This space, we propose, has at least three dimensions: representation, composition, and functionality. By defining the differences in these terms, we are able to place actual models in the paradigm space, and compare and contrast these models on somewhat common terms.

RAAM lies in the symbolic portion of the space. We have examined in detail the RAAM architecture, representations, compositional mechanisms, and func-

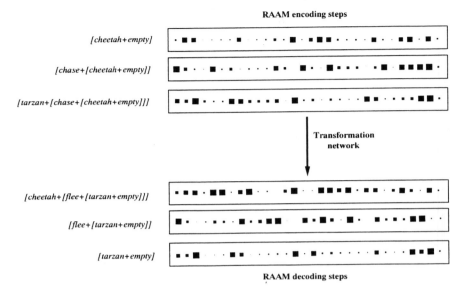

FIG. 6.15. Holistic transformation process. This diagram shows each of the steps in the transformation process: encoding a *chase* sentence, holistically transforming the *chase* sentence into the corresponding *flee* sentence, and decoding the *flee* sentence.

tionality. In conjunction with other simple feed-forward networks, we have exhibited detectors, decoders, and transformers that act holistically on the composed, distributed, continuous subsymbolic symbols created by RAAM. These tasks are accomplished without the need to decode composite structures into their constituent parts, as symbolic systems must do.

The RAAM model, developed quite recently, has extended the functionality of the subsymbolic paradigm a great deal. Pollack (1989), the inventor of RAAM, compares RAAM's representations to those of classical symbolism:

> Like feature-vectors, they are fixed-width, similarity-based, and their content is easily accessible. Like symbols, they combine only in syntactically well-formed ways. Like symbol-structures, they have constituency and compositionality. And like pointers, they refer to larger symbol structures which can be efficiently retrieved. But, unlike feature-vectors, they compose. Unlike symbols, they can be compared. Unlike symbol structures, they are fixed in size. And, unlike pointers, they have content. (pp. 529–530)

In order to achieve the ultimate goal of computationally stimulating human cognition, a complex architecture seems warranted that takes advantage of the characteristics of both extremes of the continuum—from the systematic macrosemantics of the symbolic paradigm to the holistic operations and microsemantics of the subsymbolic paradigm. However, many current models reside near the periphery of this paradigm space, staying close to one paradigm in all aspects, or taking advantage of the other paradigm primarily along only one dimension. Recently, there has been an increased interest in building hybrid models in order to explore the power achieved by combining the two paradigms (Dyer, 1990) (see also Kwasny & Faisal, chap. 9 in this volume and Lange, chap. 10 in this volume). It is our expectation that in the future, as systems become more complex and ambitious, the Gap in the center will gradually be filled with systems that blend the capabilities of both paradigms in an effective way.

ACKNOWLEDGMENTS

We would like to thank Michael Gasser, Robert Port, John Dinsmore, David Chalmers, John Nienart, Jon Rossie, and Ken Aizawa for their comments on drafts of this chapter.

REFERENCES

Blank, D. S. (1990). Differences between representational schemas in connectionism and classical artificial intelligence; or why a rose by a symbolic name might not smell as sweet. In J. Dinsmore & T. Koschmann, (eds.), *Proceedings of the Second Midwest Artificial Intelligence and Cognitive Science Society* (pp. 8–14). Huntsville, AL: Intergraph Corporation.

Chalmers, D. J. (1990a). Syntactic transformations on distributed representations. *Connection Science, 2*, 53–62.

Chalmers, D. J. (1990b). Why Fodor and Pylyshyn were wrong: The simplest refutation. In *Proceedings of the 12th Annual Conference of the Cognitive Science Society* (pp. 340–347). Hillsdale, NJ: Lawrence Erlbaum Associates.

Dyer, M. G. (1990). Distributed symbol formation and processing in connectionist networks. *Journal of Experimental and Theoretical Artificial Intelligence, 2*, 215–239.

Elman, J. L. (1990). Finding structure in time. *Cognitive Science, 14*, 179–212.

Fodor, J. A., & Pylyshyn, Z. (1988). Connectionism and cognitive architecture: A critical analysis. *Cognition, 28*, 3–71.

Franklin, S., & Garzon, M. (1990). Neural computability. In O. Omidvar (ed.), *Progress in neural networks* (Vol. 1). Norwood, NJ: Ablex.

Hofstadter, D. R. (1984). The Copycat project: An experiment in nondeterminism and creative analogies (AI Memo No. 755). Cambridge, MA: Artificial Intelligence Laboratory, MIT.

Hofstadter, D. R., & Mitchell, M. (in press). An overview of the Copycat project. In Holyoak and Barnden (eds.), *Connectionist approaches to analogy, metaphor and case-based reasoning.* Norwood, NJ: Ablex.

Pollack, J. B. (1988). Recursive auto-associative memory: Devising compositional distributed representations. In *Proceedings of the 10th Annual Conference of the Cognitive Science Society* (pp. 33–39). Hillsdale, NJ: Lawrence Erlbaum Associates.

Pollack, J. B. (1989). Implications of recursive distributed representations. In D. S. Touretzky (ed.), *Advances in neural information processing systems I* (pp. 527–536). San Mateo, CA: Morgan Kaufmann.

Port, R. & van Gelder, T. (1991). Representing aspects of language. In *Proceedings of the Thirteenth Annual Conference of the Cognitive Science Society* (pp. 487–492). Hillsdale, NJ: Lawrence Erlbaum Associates.

Rumelhart, D., Hinton, G., & Williams, R. (1986). Learning internal representations by error propagation. In J. McClelland & D. Rumelhart (eds.), *Parallel distributed processing* (Vol. I, pp. 318–362). Cambridge, MA: MIT Press.

Smolensky, P. (1988). On the proper treatment of connectionism. *Behavioral and Brain Sciences, 11,* 1–74.

Touretzky, D. S. (1990). BoltzCONS: Dynamic symbol structures in a connectionist network. *Artificial Intelligence, 46,* 5–46.

van Gelder, T. (1990). Compositionality: A connectionist variation on a classical theme. *Cognitive Science, 14.*

7

Connectionism, Generalization, and Propositional Attitudes: A Catalogue of Challenging Issues

John A. Barnden
New Mexico State University

1. INTRODUCTION

1.1. Refining the Debate

My goal is to bring up some neglected issues involved in the business of applying connectionism (mainly of the distributed variety) to the high-level cognitive tasks that symbolic artificial intelligence (AI) has been applied to, such as reasoning and natural language processing. Most of the points I raise present something of a problem to (certain styles of) connectionism, although one or two are about opportunities for connectionism to contribute something distinctive to the achievement of those tasks.

Therefore, I present neither a condemnation of connectionism nor a championing of it. Connectionists may well be able at some stage to produce systems that overcome the problems I present. My claim is merely that the problems are important, their solution may require mechanisms beyond those that are currently being entertained, and there is more to certain central notions such as *systematicity* and *structure sensitivity* (explained later) than is currently being given credit for in the connectionist literature. On the other hand, connectionists may well encounter difficulties in trying to exploit the opportunities I mention. Thus, both the problems and opportunities are potentially rich issues for further research. It would be a mistake to think that the lack of championing of either symbolicism or connectionism in this chapter means that the discussion does not advance the symbolicism/connectionism debate. On the contrary, in seeking to achieve genuine advances in the debate it is valuable to look carefully at the true variety, subtlety and complexity of the issues involved, rather than to assume that the primary goal is to prove that connectionism is better than symbolicism or the other way round.

As I aim only at cataloguing and clarifying some issues, I do not present much in the way of detailed suggestions about how to overcome/exploit the problems/opportunities, let alone present a specific system. This is despite my own work on developing a structured connectionist system aimed precisely at "closing the gap" (Barnden 1988, 1989c, 1991; Barnden & Srinivas, in press). Although I make occasional reference to this system, the chapter is not aimed at establishing that Conposit has special leverage on the problems and opportunities (which is not to say that I think it does not!).

1.2. Generality, Systematicity, and Structure-Sensitivity

The issues I discuss deal in one way or another with *generalizations*. One of the central advantages claimed for connectionism is that it supports automatic generalization, by virtue of activation pattern similarity effects, away from the specific situations it has seen in the past. I do not impugn this claim, but present some types of generalization that are not catered for in the current connectionist literature and that present interesting challenges. These types are summarized in section 1.5.

The generalization issues are bound up with the notions of *systematicity* and *structure-sensitivity*, which are of great topical importance, notably in regard to the gap between symbolicism and connectionism. Fodor and Pylyshyn (1988: pp. 46ff) cast systematicity of *inference* as a matter of a system being able to do all inferences of a particular logical type, not just some of them (unless the deficiencies are just a matter of resource bounds being exceeded). A system would fail to be systematic if, for instance, it could infer from $P \wedge Q \wedge R$ to P but could not infer from $P \wedge Q$ to P, or vice versa. In fact, it is reasonable and useful to extend the notion to apply to inferences that are not just a matter of content-free logical deduction. For instance, the inference that people can hear from the premise that they can speak is systematic if it applies to anyone under any description. Systematicity of inference is actually just a special case of the more general notion of systematicity of *processing*. This more general notion is implicit in Fodor and Pylyshyn (1988, especially pp. 37ff).

Systematicity of *representation* (Fodor & Pylyshyn, 1988, pp. 39–41) is, broadly speaking, the ability of a system just to be able to *represent* proposition P given (a) that it can represent proposition Q and (b) that P and Q are sufficiently similar in some defined sense. For example, under systematicity of representation we would require that if the system can represent *John loves Mary* then it should also be able to represent *Mary loves John*. A more complex case is that if the system can represent *John loves Mary* and can also represent definite descriptions like *the man with the red hat and a long nose* then it should automatically be equipped to represent *The man with the red hat and long nose loves Mary.*

Both systematicity of inference (or processing in general) and systematicity of representation are qualities of *generality* in a system. In learning systems they can also be qualities of *generalization.*

Structure-sensitivity is the ability of a system to process encodings in accordance with the structure of the items they encode. For instance, the conversion of an internal encoding of an active sentence into the corresponding passive sentence is an operation that must be sensitive to the structure of the active sentence. The types of systematicity currently being focused on in the high-level connectionist literature generally rest on structure-sensitivity, as they are to do with the encoding and inference of items with significant internal structure.

1.3. Propositional Attitudes

A special purpose of the chapter is to point out how various issues that are more or less strongly bound up with *propositional attitudes*—beliefs, intentions, hopes, desires, and the like—pose problems for connectionism. I must declare a special interest here. In previous research I have been much concerned with propositional attitudes (see, e.g., Ballim, Wilks, & Barnden, 1990, 1991; Barnden 1983, 1986, 1989a,b). However, until now I have not brought this work into any significant contact with my concern with high-level connectionism. The interaction has led to the issues discussed in this chapter. They are general issues extending beyond the particular concerns of propositional attitudes, but they take on important special forms in the propositional attitude arena, and some of my arguments appeal to special points about propositional attitudes.

The main focus in propositional attitude research is on the semantics, and use in inference, of natural-language *attitude reports.* A typical example of such a report is the *belief report:*

John believes that all of Susan's brothers are stupid.

The portions of this chapter that address propositional attitude issues are concerned primarily with how a cognitive agent X is to interpret incoming attitude reports and to represent and reason about other agents' mental states. The chapter does not address the formal semantics of attitude reports or the philosophical question of clarifying the nature of attitudes.

The propositional attitude area is one of the most central and troublesome *within* the traditional symbolic paradigm. Propositional attitudes are central in the semantic/pragmatic theory of natural language—see Barwise and Perry (1983), Cresswell (1985), Fauconnier (1985), and Mates (1950) for just a few pieces of evidence for this. As for their importance for AI and connectionism (localist or distributed), it is obvious that propositional attitudes are important even in mundane multiagent interaction scenarios, and are often explicitly reported in perfectly mundane natural language discourse. They are also held to play a central implicit role in the communicative acts effected by natural language discourse (see, e.g., Allen, 1983; Cohen & Levesque, 1985; Grosz & Sidner, 1986; Sperber & Wilson, 1986; Wilks & Bien, 1983).

Given the central importance of propositional attitudes and natural language reports of them, it should be an important objective for high-level connectionism to represent them and reason about them. This is especially so because of the high degree of sublety and intricacy that has characterized technical attempts, within the traditional symbolic sectors of philosophy, linguistics, and AI, to address propositional attitude representation and reasoning. See Barwise and Perry (1983), Creary (1979), Cresswell (1985), Hobbs (1985), Maida (1988), Perlis (1985), and Zalta (1988) for a small sample of complex representational/notational proposals.

It is surprising, therefore, that so far the symbolicism/connectionism debate has given very little detailed, technical consideration to the question of how to represent or reason with propositional attitudes. See, however, Gasser (1989) for a connectionist system that deals to some extent with the goals, intentions, and purposes of various classes of agent; and see Rey (1988) for some claims that propositional attitudes present problems for connectionism. Connectionism and similar techniques have been used to handle belief maintenance (truth maintenance, belief revision) and degrees of belief (see, e.g., Craddock & Browse 1986; Pearl 1986). However, such work has been concerned with maintenance/degrees of belief within only the artificial cognitive agent X that one is designing, rather than X's interpretation of belief reports about other agents.

1.4. Beliefs Eliminated?

Connectionism has also been used by eliminative materialists in philosophy as a basis for claims that the notions of belief and so on, which are often dubbed as folk-psychological, should not be part of a mature philosophy and scientific psychology, and may even disappear from our language and thought ultimately (see, e.g., Churchland, 1986). However, this point, even if justified, has very little impact on the concerns in the present article. Consider a cognitive agent Xavier (person, artificial system, or whatever). Let us grant for the sake of argument that it is not philosophically/scientifically accurate or useful to characterize Xavier as operating on the basis of beliefs and so on. However, Xavier is still faced with interpreting sentences uttered by other agents, and these utterances are replete with explicit mention of agents' attitudes. Furthermore, a human speaker Susan of such an utterance has *folk-psychological* views of any agent Yolanda she is talking about; and it is important for Xavier to be able to think in Susan's terms about Yolanda in order to achieve a coherent understanding of what Susan is saying. This is so no matter how philosophical-ly/scientifically ill-conceived Susan's folk-psychological views are.[1] Therefore, the scientifically respectable characterization of an agent's mental states, be that agent Xavier, Susan, or Yolanda, has little if anything to do with how Xavier himself should represent his interpretations of the utterances of Susan about the mental states of Yolanda. Those utterances do not, even implicitly, have anything to do with scientifically respectable characterizations of mental states, except perhaps if Susan happens to be a thorough-going eliminative materialist.

At risk of belaboring the point, we should note that the argument in the previous paragraph has a more mundane analogy that may make matters clearer. If Xavier had to interpret Susan's utterances about the tourist attractions of New Mexico, it would be entirely inappropriate for Xavier to interpret a statement Susan makes about desert thunderstorms in terms of some scientifically accurate theory of thunderstorms. Such a theory would be irrelevant to Xavier's under-standing of what Susan is saying, except in the special case of Xavier taking Susan to be knowledgeable about the theory.

1.5. Plan of the Chapter

Section 2 argues that connectionist systems must be able to construct *explicit generalizations*, not just to generalize their responses, which is what current connectionist learning theories are aimed at. The argument rests in part on propositional attitude considerations.

Sections 3, 4 and 5 highlight three forms of generalization that have been given inadequate attention in connectionism. The first is rapid generalization from recent examples, by analogical matching. This rests on an ability to find matches between two or more complex *short-term* representations.[2] This con-trasts with the implicit matching to *long-term* information structures in most localist or distributed connectionist studies.

Section 4 discusses the second type of troublesome generalization. This is generalization of a connectionist system's representation and reasoning to cope with *anomalous combinations* of concepts, departing markedly from combina-tions it has been trained on. Propositional attitude contexts are among the more important types of context in which anomalous combinations arise.

---

[1]This point is at the heart of the metaphor-based treatment of propositional attitudes in Barnden (1989b, 1990), because most folk-psychological ways of looking at mental states are infused with metaphor.

[2]A *short-term representation* is a representation sitting in the short-term memory of some cog-nitive agent (whether a person or an AI system). Typically the representation will only be *temporary* in that it will only recently have been created and will be lost or destroyed after a short time. A short-term representation might, for instance, encode the agent's interpretation of some sentence that it has just heard, or a conclusion recently inferred from other short-term or long-term knowledge.

Section 5 points out that reasoning must often be *embedded* within one or another type of context. A primary special case is that of reasoning within the context of a given agent's beliefs. Embedded structure-sensitive processing presents problems for the so-called *nonconcatenative* representations used in some connectionist systems. The embedding of a particular sort of reasoning can be regarded as a result of *generalizing* the processing involved.

Section 6 concludes by summarizing the various issues raised.

2. EXPLICIT GENERALIZATION

Current work on generalization and learning within connectionist systems is concerned almost exclusively with *implicit* generalizations, in a sense to be made clear. In contrast, I argue for the need for connectionist systems to construct *explicit* generalizations. The argument depends partly on an appeal to propositional attitude representation.

2.1. Implicit and Explicit Generalization

Imagine a typical sort of generalizing connectionist system, such as a feed-forward back-propagation network, trained to output the conclusion "atheist" on examples of specific communists living in the town. Let us suppose that it succeeds in generalizing to all or most communists living in the town. Then it can make the right inference about each individual member of that class: When given a description of some individual member, the system can be viewed as coming out with an activity pattern representing an assertion that that person is an atheist. This assertion can then be passed to other processes; in particular, it might cause the system to output the sentence *That person is an atheist.* However, what the system has not done is to construct (or develop the means of constructing) an activity pattern representing the *generalization* (that all or most communists living in the town are atheists) as such.

In short, a typical generalizing connectionist system is able to cope with specific new cases individually, but is not able to come up with an explicit generalization.

Why should it be desirable for systems to construct explicit generalizations? One reason is as follows: Surely one can imagine wanting to ask the trained system what it knows about communists, and expecting it to answer that all (or most) communists living in the town are atheists if in fact this is a generalization that has been trained into it. But also, and perhaps more importantly, the explicit generalization might be needed in order to feed into other inference processes. For instance, suppose the system is in some sense able to apply, or behave as if it is applying, the rule:

If all (or most) communists living in a town are atheists then the town is eligible for a grant from the Fundie Fund.

The crucial point here is that the system must recognize that there is a generalization over a class; mere conclusions that particular members of the class are atheists are simply not enough for the rule to be applied. If, on the other hand, as a result of its training the system were able to produce an activity pattern representing the explicit generalization in question, then some subnetwork that embodies the rule could take that generalization as input.

However, we must be careful to avoid a hasty conclusion that the explicit generalizations are certainly needed. Suppose, as a result of training, some module G of the system maps the communist/living-in-the-town combination to an atheism assertion. More precisely, suppose that there is a *communist* feature unit, a *living in the town* feature unit, and an *atheist* feature unit, among many others. (This localist encoding assumption is made simply for ease of illustration.) Module G includes those three specific feature units, and is such that *yes* activation on the first two (with *don't-care* activation on all others) causes *yes* activation to appear on the *atheist* unit. The grant eligibility rule could then be respected in roughly the following way. The system would try to satisfy the condition of the rule by deliberately putting the yes value at the communist and living-in-the-town units—even though the system is not currently perceiving or otherwise considering any specific communist, so in effect the system is *deliberately imagining* an indefinite communist-living-in-the-town. Then, if the atheism conclusion pops out, the system causes the eligible-for-grant conclusion to appear. Thus, module G has been used in place of an explicit generalization.[3]

Lest we appear to have saved the day for the typical connectionist system, note carefully that we have assumed several abilities that go beyond what is typically entertained for connectionist systems:

1. The ability to deliberately imagine an indefinite individual (as opposed to merely processing an individual handed to it as input).

2. A procedural control capability for manipulating module G in the appropriate way as a sort of subroutine in the course of doing the grant-eligibility inference.

In sum, getting a connectionist system to use a rule like the one discussed, whose condition part appeals to a generalization, requires either (a) the production of an

---

[3]Note however that the representation is less powerful than a typical symbolic representation would be: Without further elaboration the connectionist system is not able to infer that people are not communists living in the town if they are not atheists. However, this lack is not exploited in our argument.

activity pattern *A* explicitly representing the generalization in question or (b) the use of control facilities that go beyond those put forward in most connectionist proposals. If (a) is the case, and the system has learned the generalization from training, then that learning must have the effect not only of enabling the system to conclude the atheism of any individual communist living in the town that is handed to it, but also of constructing activity pattern *A* (or of developing the means of generating *A* on demand).

2.2. General Sentences and Beliefs

In fact, there is an obvious consideration that advances the case for option (a). The system needs also to be able to understand general natural language sentences such as *All the communists in the town are atheists,* and to feed the fruits of such understanding through, say, the grant-eligibility rule (even though the system itself has not been trained to believe that all communists in the town are atheists). It is natural to suggest that the system constructs an explicit generalization from the sentence. It is much more difficult now to suggest that this construction could be avoided by the *G*-based method. Even assuming that it would be simple and quick to construct or develop *G* as a direct result of processing the sentence, we have the point that *G* is not something that the system necessarily wants to maintain outside of the context of the sentence. It may well be that the system should merely take the sentence to convey something the speaker believes, rather than to convey a truth. Module *G* must not be allowed to infect the system's own reasoning about the world, even momentarily; that is, we have to devise machinery for stopping the system using *G* to conclude for itself that the town is eligible for the grant. Also, it is very possible that there is no need for the system to remember later on that the speaker believes all the communists in the town are atheists. So, *G* would have to be dismantled in some way (unless we were prepared to tolerate the system developing an indefinite number of useless modules like *G*).

In sum, a generalization communicated in natural language to the system may well need to be recorded as merely being a speaker belief, and therefore barred from affecting the system's reasoning from its own beliefs, and, moreover, may well not need to be given a long-term representation by the system. Both of these points militate against reliance on a *G* module and in favor of production of an activity pattern representing the generalization. If this is accepted, then for the sake of uniformity in the system, if the system *learns* the generalization from individual instances it should also develop (a means of generating on demand) an activity pattern that represents the generalization. That is, option (a) is to be preferred over option (b). This requires a major extension of the capabilities of current connectionist learning systems.

2.3. Vague Quantification

Connectionism has benefits because it emphasizes the importance of *incomplete* generalizations—using *most* rather than *all*—and the practicality of reasoning under their influence. This is because of the inherent fuzziness of many types of connectionist systems. A typical generalizing connectionist system need never get to the stage where literally all communists living in the town are inferred to be atheists. Rather, exceptional features, or lack of enough input features, could lead to the inference not being made. The ability to handle exceptions to otherwise emergent rules gracefully is one claimed strength of connectionism (cf. Rumelhart & McClelland, 1986). Of course, much work has gone into default rules and exceptions to them in the plausible-reasoning area of traditional AI, and most AI people probably subscribe to the view that quasi-universals are more important for most of AI than are true universals. But at least connectionism reinforces this view and gives it some alternative flesh.

Nevertheless, the current ability of connectionist systems to embody incomplete generalizations does not go very far toward coping with the general issue of incomplete generalization and other forms of vague quantification (manifested by words such as *several* and *few* in English). Consider the following sentence, spoken by John to the system:

Most communists living in the town are atheists.

Let us presume that the system decides to record this as a belief of John's, not as a new fact in the system's own long-term knowledge. Even if the *G*-module method had been suitable for complete generalizations, it would in any case be inappropriate here. Consider what a *G*-module would have to be like. It would have to produce less certain atheism conclusions than was the case in section 2.2. This would presumably mean either that atheism conclusions would only be produced stochastically, with high probability less than 1, on the setting of the communist and living-in-the-town feature units to *yes,* or that an atheism conclusion is always produced but the *atheist* unit has a degraded activation value. But in either case a particular number (a probability or degraded activation value) would have to be adopted. Such a number might be forthcoming in the case of a *system* belief that most communists living in the town are atheists, particularly if that belief arose from training on individual communists living in the town. The number could reflect the proportion of the training set that are atheists. However, it is inappropriate in the case of the system representing *John's* belief in that generalization. This is for two reasons.

First, we cannot assume (without considerable extra argument and evidence) that people's incomplete generalizations are encoded with the aid of any sort of numerical measure of majority. After all, it seems reasonable to entertain the possibility that a person's belief in *most X are Y* is encoded in that person's mind by means of representation that uses a vague-quantification device analogous to the English word *most*.

Second, even if the connectionist system could assume that John is indeed using a numerical measure of majority in his belief, it is illegitimate (without extra argument and evidence) for us to allow the system to assume a particular value for that measure. It appears very likely that different people have different numerical criteria for using the word *most*.

The sentences we have looked at in this subsection have not been attitude reports, although the implicit layer of speaker belief has been important to our argument. Of course, the considerations arise even more centrally in the case of attitude reports, such as *Mike believes that most communists living in the town are atheists.* As an aside, it is worth noting that the interpretation of vague quantification in belief reports has been largely pushed aside in propositional attitude research. This is especially surprising in view of the fact that the strict quantifiers have been very extensively studied in that research, and yet are far less important for practical, and even philosophical, purposes. When one studies belief reports one should be concerned, *even as a philosopher*, with the sorts of belief people really have, not with over-idealized sorts of belief.[4]

3. SHORT-TERM STRUCTURE MATCHING

This section deals with the first of three types of generalization that a cognitive system needs to be able to perform but that have not been shown to be well catered for by current connectionist systems, whether localist or distributed. The type considered in this section is to do with *analogies* between two or more novel propositions conveyed by discourse. This brings in the problem of *short-term structure matching,* which has not been studied enough within either localist or distributed connectionism.

The issues also argue for an extension of the usual notion of *systematicity of inference* (Fodor & Pylyshyn, 1988, pp. 46ff). As treated in the connectionist literature, systematicity of inference and the closely related issue of structure-sensitivity have exclusively been a long-term matter in a certain sense. For instance, the inference from speaking to hearing is naturally taken to be a matter of long-term knowledge. Hence, it is natural in connectionism to assume that the systematicity is immanent in some weight settings that implicitly capture the system's long-term knowledge, whether this results from training or from

---

[4]Of course, this concern takes us into the field of psychology, and a consequent psychologicalization of propositional attitude research. See Barnden (1989a, 1989b) for further discussion of the need for psychologicalization.

the hand-coding of rules. In the former case, it is assumed that systematicity is to do with similarity of current inputs to large numbers of past training instances.

However, there is a type of generalization involving systematicity and structure-sensitivity that is to do with *short-term similarity*—similarity between two individual inputs arriving close together in time—and that involves *on-the-fly associations* as opposed to learned associations. Suppose the system inputs:

Micky hates his sister for being taller. He's always being mean to her.

Then suppose that soon afterward the system inputs:

Billy hates his brother for being taller.

Surely it is reasonable to expect the system to infer at least tentatively that Billy is always being mean to his brother.[5] And, this should happen even if the system has never before encountered the idea of someone being mean to someone as a result of hating the latter, and even if the system is too ignorant to come up with an explanation of the hater's behavior.

Part of the issue being addressed is the question of how to establish an approximate structural match between two short-term representations, namely the representation of Micky hating his sister and the representation of Billy hating his brother. This question has largely been ignored in connectionism because of the concentration on using a short-term structure to retrieve approximately matching structures from *long*-term memory.[6] This focus exists even in work on applying connectionism to high-level cognitive processing. Indeed, virtually the whole field of analogical processing, connectionist or not, seems to be focused on matching target structures to source structures retrieved from long-term memory.

Nevertheless, besides the argument from sibling hatred, there are strong reasons for wanting short-term matching (short-term similarity). We may take three well-known types of example from the pragmatics of natural language understanding.

Consider the reasoning involved in tying together what is being said by two natural language sentences that are saying the same thing at different levels of detail, as in: *Go along this street for a while. Go for three blocks and turn right.* This example, adapted from one in Hobbs (1985), requires an understanding that just one going-along is being advocated—the speaker is not telling the listener to go along the street for a while and *then* go for three blocks. The listener must,

---

[5]This can all be wrapped within a speaker belief context, but I omit this for simplicity.

[6]The studies of Bienenstock and von der Malsburg (1987) and Gasser and Smith (1991) are exceptions.

among other things, detect the approximate match between going along the street for a while and going along the street for three blocks.

For the second example, consider the task of understanding the sentence: *Just as John hates his brother for being taller, Sally hates her sister for being thinner.* The system should presumably represent the fact that a correspondence is being set up between John and Sally, between brother-of and sister-of, and between taller and thinner. Third, syntactic and semantic parallelism between two nearby parts of a discourse has also been exploited in the resolution of pronoun references (Carbonell & Brown, 1988).

Of course, what might in principle be immanent in a connectionist system's weights is a *mechanism* for assessing the similarity of two working-memory structures, and such a mechanism may conceivably be learnable. However, the difficulty lies not just in the learning, but also in how to do the structure comparison at all. I have been addressing the short-term-structure-comparison problem in extending the aforementioned Conposit system to a case-based reasoning or analogy-based reasoning version (Barnden & Srinivas, in press).

In summary, I claim that the notion of systematicity should be broadened to include reasoning by analogy, even when the analogy holds between two short-term structures rather than involving analogical sources in long-term memory.

4. ANOMALOUS COMBINATIONS

This section addresses another type of potentially troublesome generalization. The issue concerns *anomalous combinations of ideas* in sentences. The issues raised connect with the notions in Fodor and Pylyshyn (1988) of *systematicity of representation* (pp. 39–41) and *systematicity of inference* (pp. 46ff). The discussion also briefly touches on metaphor.

The reader should bear in mind that I am not seeking to show that the mentioned type of connectionist system will definitely not be able to handle the type of generalization in question. Rather, I try only to show that the requirements of systematicity are more onerous than is made apparent by the connectionist literature. I touch on one or two suggestions as to how the connectionist systems in question might in the future discharge the onus.

4.1. Speaking Bananas: An Anomalous Combination

The fundamental problem to be addressed here is the sheer arbitrariness and novelty of the way concepts can be combined in natural language sentences. Consider for instance the clause *the banana can speak*. Ridiculous at first sight, it could well appear as a sentence in a joke or a children's story (or some other type of fantasy), and be a literal truth within the framework of the joke or story.

Variants of it could also be intended as metaphorical statements, a matter I go into later on in this section. The anomalous clause *The banana asked for a glass of water* could be taken metonymically in, say, a restaurant context, as conveying that *the person who ordered* the banana asked for a glass of water. A counterfactual can contain anomalous combinations—consider for instance the sentence, *If bananas could speak, peaches probably could too.* Negation provides another sort of context for anomalous combinations: indeed, the sentence *Bananas cannot speak* or *It is not the case that bananas can speak* is weird but literally true.

For my own purposes the most important way the clause *the banana can speak* could appear is as a description of someone's belief. This could arise because of an explicit attitude report, such as

Micky believes that the banana can speak.

This sentence could be true because of Micky being, say, a tiny tot or a grown-up lunatic. But the utterance of merely *The banana can speak* by a speaker Susan is *implicitly* embedded in an attitude context. The simplest possibility is for the hearer to take the utterance to be a sincere act of assertion and infer that Susan *believes* that the banana can speak. For illustrative clarity, however, I use belief reports like the one just displayed and ignore the speaker.

We have thus mentioned seven types of context in which an anomalous combination of ideas such as *banana* and *speaking* could plausibly appear—jokes, children's stories, metaphor, metonymy, counterfactuals, negation, and attitude contexts. We can sum up by means of the aphorism that *it is not anomalous for mundane discourse to contain anomalous combinations of ideas.*

Before going on I should stress that anomaly is a matter of degree, and I am concerned not just with extremely anomalous combinations, as in the banana example, but also with less extreme examples. I use an extreme example for the sake of illustrative vividness.

4.2. Systematicity of Processing

The problem I wish to present is that anomalous idea-combinations may cause a connectionist system to fail to perform systematic structure-sensitive processing that we would surely want it to perform. This problem may arise in a class of connectionist systems that has been recently advanced as a way of performing structure-sensitive inferencing. The systems supposedly learn to perform structure-sensitive processing of statements[7] by virtue of being trained on input–output pairs that exemplify the required processing. The class includes the sys-

---

[7]For simplicity, we use the term *statement* to cover both propositions and natural-language sentences.

tems of Blank, Meeden, and Marshall (chap. 6 in this volume) and Chalmers (1990). To fix ideas, let us consider the system presented in Chalmers (1990). It consists of two three-layer backpropagation subnetworks:

1, A Recursive Autoassociative Memory (RAAM) network (Pollack 1988, 1990).
2. A transformation network.

The RAAM takes what I call an *external* encoding of three-word active-voice sentences, such as *John loves Michael,* on the bottom layer, produces an *internal* distributed encoding on the middle (hidden) layer, and can furthermore decode the latter encoding into (a close approximation to) the original external encoding on the top layer. The representation vectors on the bottom and top layers are split up into three segments, one for each word; but the representation vector on the hidden layer is nonconcatenative (monolithic or holistic) in that it cannot be broken down into parts corresponding to the parts of the sentence. Also, by an iterative use of the same network, passive-voice sentences like *Michael is loved by John* can be given an internal encoding on the middle layer. Notice carefully that the RAAM is a backpropagation network, and is *trained* to be able to do the external-to-internal encoding and internal-to-external decoding on a specific corpus of sentences.

The transformation network is *trained* to take *internal* encodings of active sentences and produce *internal* encodings of the corresponding passive sentences. These internal encodings are taken from the hidden layer of the RAAM. Chalmers makes the interesting observation that, even when the transformation network is trained on only half of the sentence corpus used to train the RAAM network, the transformation network generalizes correctly to the remaining half.

According to the claim, the transformation network learns to be sensitive to the structure of sentences, without needing to decode the internal representations into representations of the parts of the sentences. Thus, the processing in the transformation network is *holistic* or *direct*—it does not need to proceed via the *external* representations of the sentences.

I worry that networks of this sort may not generalize to sentences whose concept-combinations are sufficiently different from the combinations appearing in the training corpus. Notice that in the Chalmers experiment mentioned earlier, the testing corpus for the transformation network was a randomly selected half of all the sentences in the RAAM's training set. What is of more interest, and of direct relevance to the speaking-banana problem, is the transformation net's performance on sentences different from those in the RAAM's training set. In fact, one of Chalmer's experiments involved training the RAAM encoder/decoder only on a random 40 of the 125 possible active sentences and the corresponding 40 of the possible passive sentences. The 40 active/passive pairs in the RAAM training set were used to train the transformation net as well. The

RAAM correctly generalized to *only* about 84% of a test set consisting of a further 40 active and 40 passive sentences (Chalmers 1990, p. 58). Chalmers claims that this generalization rate is "remarkably good," but it is not clear what this value judgment is based on, given that the system is only a toy one, no evidence is given that the generalization rate will not drop lower in a bigger system, and no evidence is given that an 84% ability to encode novel propositions is adequate for cognition. Moreover, and not surprisingly, the imperfections in the RAAM encoding led to errors in the transformation net, which only generalized to 65% of the test set. (The figure went up to about 70% in a different training regime for the transformation net.) In the experiment previously discussed, the RAAM was trained on *all* the possible sentences and the transformation net did generalize perfectly. But the significance of this is unclear, in that in general we surely want cognitive systems to be able to perform structure sensitive inference on structures other than those the system has specifically been trained to represent.

In sum, Chalmers's results, though certainly interesting and giving us cause for hope, are hardly sufficient to justify a firm conclusion at the present time that his style of network is powerful enough to cope with the full problem of systematic structure sensitivity. In particular, his results do not provide any particular reason to think that his sort of system will cope well with the speaking banana issue.

We should also note that his results do not cover the case where the agent or patient phrase of a sentence is a complex description such as *the man with the red trousers and blue hat*. With regard to this sort of example, the structure sensitivity and systematicity we want are coupled with an ability to *ignore* structure—that is, to be able to handle the agent and patient phrases without any regard whatsoever to their internal structure.

Blank, Meeden and Marshall (chap. 6 in this volume) present a very similar approach for applying simple transformations to statements. In one of their systems, the transformations network was trained to directly convert internal representations of statements of the form *X chase Y* to the internal representations of corresponding statements of the form *Y flee X*. Training on 16 chase statements allowed it to generalize moderately well to 8 chase statements not in that training corpus. (The transformation is reported as being successful 87.5% of the time on the latter 8 statements. Presumably this means it performed correctly on 7 of the statements.) Another of the Blank *et al.* systems is meant to detect *reflexive* statements like *junglebeast smell junglebeast*. However, it was found that the net failed to see that statements of the form *tarzan V tarzan* and *jane V jane* were reflexive, even when *V* was a verb that appeared in reflexive statements in the training corpus. The authors suggest that the failure results because neither *tarzan* nor *jane* appeared reflexively in the statements in the training corpus. Indeed, the authors say, "it seems that the network wasn't easily finding a strong relationship between words that it hadn't seen together before." In short, a double appearance of *tarzan* in a statement was an *anomalous combination* as far as the net was concerned, and caused it to fail.

To return to the example of speaking bananas, suppose a connectionist system of the sort in question has been trained to make the plausible inference that if someone can speak then they can also understand language. That is, the proposition *X can speak* for many different people *X* has been paired with *X can understand language* in the training set. There is the danger that the internal representation of *The banana can speak* may be sufficiently different from that of *X can speak* for any person *X* that the desired output, *The banana can understand language,* may simply not be generated (or may only be generated with very low confidence, or with a greatly corrupted activity pattern, etc.). After all, the representations of all the *X*s may involve high activity of a *person* feature or pattern, which would be lacking in the representation of *the banana*.

Now, in some systems the representation of the individual people, actions, and so forth themselves would be learned during the course of processing statements (Lee, Flowers, & Dyer 1989; Miikkulainen & Dyer 1989). Then, entities get similar representations to the extent that they appear in similar contexts in statements. With the types of training ordinarily used, banana representations and people representations are not likely to end up being very similar. Again, in systems where the entity representations are fixed in advance by the system designer, the representations are likely to be (micro)feature based: Then, if bananas and persons do not share many features, their representations may be insufficiently similar for the desired generalization to bananas to occur. Of course, bananas and people are indeed similar to the extent of being organic physical objects of a medium sort of size. Hence, we should remember that instead of bananas in our examples we could use types of entity that were even more distant from people—molecules, clouds, the wind, for instance.

4.3. Systematicity of Representation

Quite apart from systematicity of inference, an even more radical difficulty raised by speaking bananas is systematicity of *representation* (Fodor & Pylyshyn, 1988, pp. 39–41). It needs to be shown that connectionist systems that learn a mapping from an external representation to an internal representation exhibit sufficient systematicity of representation, let alone systematicity of inference. (The systems at issue now include simple recurrent sentence-processing networks such as those of Elman, 1988, 1989, and Harris and Elman, 1989, as well as the RAAM-based systems mentioned earlier.) It is crucial to note that the mapping from external to internal representations rests on similarity to training instances. Thus, we are led to wonder whether the statement *the banana can speak* can even be represented internally in an adequate manner (given training only on people as speakers), let alone subjected to inferencing.

The potential connectionist difficulty with systematicity of representation is an important point, because it holds good even if one were to deny the desirability of the aforementioned type of systematicity of *inference* (X-can-speak → X-can-understand-language). The system should at least be able to respond to the sentence *Bananas can speak* with something like *But that's stupid—bananas can't speak*. The point is, the ability to form the response on the basis of the input sentence itself requires significant systematicity of representation (and processing). The sentence has to be noticed as being stupid and the negation of it has to be formed; moreover, the fact that the proposition that bananas can speak is (let us assume) a belief of the speaker's has to be represented. We should demand that the system be able to make responses like *But that's stupid—bananas can't speak* even if we allowed the system to get away with not being able to perform deeper types of processing, such as inferring that Micky probably also believes that bananas can understand language.

A similar question of systematicity of representation is also brought up by the sentence *It is not the case that bananas can speak*. It seems reasonable to require the system to be able to respond to this sentence appropriately, even when there has so far been no mention of bananas or speaking in the current discourse. Even if the reasonable response is *I knew that!* the system must have some way of representing the content of the sentence, and part of this task is to deal with the combination of the banana idea with the speaking idea.

To sum up, a system should be able to represent, notice, and analyze weirdness, not pretend it isn't there.

A symbolic system would at least not have any serious problem on sheer representation, because it would have the ability to form essentially arbitrary combinations of symbols. Of course, it might be that the system, when it encounters *bananas can speak* for the first time, embodies a selectional restriction to the effect that only people are allowed to be put in the agent position of a can-speak predication inside the system, whether that predication is couched as a logic expression, semantic network fragment, frame instance, or whatever. However, this prohibition would reside in some particular rule or data structure, which could now be explicitly noticed, and then thrown away or weakened.

We see here an advantage of the symbolic system's *separation of representation of structure from representation of components:* arbitrary combinations can be formed because that formation process is (or can easily be made to be) independent of the nature of the items combined. Thus, for example, the conventional data structuring techniques of pointers, sequential allocation, and associative addressing can be used to link together any sort of information one likes. This is in contrast to the relevant connectionist systems, where the encoding of associations among parts of a statement is inextricably linked with the encoding of what is associated.

An advantage of connectionist systems that merely implement standard symbolic processing is of course that they maintain the separation of structure from components. A pure example of such a system is provided by the Conposit system (Barnden 1988, 1989c, 1991). Here there is a working memory consisting of a two-dimensional array of (active) registers into which any symbols (from the set of symbols embodied in the system) can be placed. This arbitrariness of symbols sitting in registers at any given movement is parallel to the arbitrariness of bit-strings in computer memory cells, and confers on Conposit the systematicity of representation required to deal with anomalous combinations.

4.4. Some Possible Retorts

Here I look at some suggestions for how the speaking-banana challenge might be met by the type of connectionist system under discussion. The suggestions are all of some interest and promise, but would require a substantial amount of work to be turned into convincing demonstrations that the problem can be avoided.

One might try to deal with the speaking-banana problem by suggesting a dual system in which there was a similarity-based connectionist subsystem of the sort already portrayed, for coping with nonanomalous cases, and another system that coped with anomalous cases and worked on different principles. One might claim that the latter worked in a more cautious mode, and perhaps would be more likely to involve conscious deliberation and puzzlement. However, I maintain that this suggestion should be put aside until other alternatives have been investigated and rejected, so as to avoid getting into the position of having to duplicate large parts of the inference-making apparatus as well.

In addition, it is conceivable that if a connectionist system were trained with examples of the form *Xs can speak* where the *X*s included a wide variety of things (people, cars, walls, clouds, etc.), but *excluded* the particular case of bananas, the system might learn to ignore totally the specific nature of the *X* in the way it forms its internal representations and process them. It would then be able to deal with the *X* = banana case even though bananas were very dissimilar to all the training *X*s. Similarly, one might wish to claim, if one is interested in connectionist models of mind, that children do get enough of the right sort of practice with strange combinations of concepts. However, such a claim would need to be backed up by firm empirical evidence.

It has also been suggested that even if the author of the connectionist system were to grant that it should be able to deal with speaking bananas, there is no reason for that author to agree that it should be able to handle much more abstract agents of speaking, as in *Monday speaks*. (Assume for the sake of argument that it is known that *Monday* is the day name, not a person's name.) Thus, there are reasonable limits to the semantic anomaly of combination that we should expect a system to handle. However, notice that a joke or riddle, say, might start as follows:

Monday said to Tuesday, "I'm more important than you because I'm earlier in the week."

Notice that this immediately leads to presumptions in the hearer that Tuesday can hear, can understand language, and can speak. We would not be at all surprised, for instance, to hear now that Tuesday replied, *No, it is I who is more important because* . . . So, despite the (putatively) much greater anomaly of *Monday said* as compared to *The banana said* the possible and desirable inferences are very much the same in both cases—and, incidentally, very much the same as when a person is reported as saying something. That is, there is a priori evidence to suppose that the degree of plausibility/desirability of inferences made by humans is not well correlated with the degree of anomaly in the statements on which the inferences are based.

Moreover, the Monday example also shows that the speaking-banana problem cannot be dismissed by claiming that bananas and people are sufficiently similar, despite my previous comments, for the connectionist systems to be able to generalize sufficiently well to speaking bananas. For instance, Jay McClelland [personal communication] has made a claim on the following lines. Bananas and people, both being organic physical objects of a medium sort of size, enter into enough similar interactions (e.g., both can be kicked) for a connectionist system of *realistic* size to have similar enough representations of bananas and people to be able to cope with speaking bananas. I do not deny that this may be so—but it is something that still remains to be established. And, even if it turns out to be true, it does not readily extend to the Monday example.

Furthermore, McClelland [personal communication] has also suggested that a connectionist system with a very rapid learning algorithm could train its RAAM or whatever on the spot to handle new combinations of concepts. This is an interesting possibility, but it is not clear that the system would not also have to apply more training to its other subnetworks (such as the transformation net in the Chalmers case). It is then not clear how the system is to know which particular subnetworks to apply further training to.

Finally, one might claim that no learning system, connectionist or otherwise, human or otherwise, could be expected to make the desired inferences in the banana case, for example the inference that the banana can think and hear, if it had only ever seen the person cases. Certainly, the problem I am pointing out does generalize to some extent beyond connectionism. However, it is easier to see how a nonconnectionist system using standard symbolic representations could make the generalization to bananas even though only trained on human speakers. Suppose a symbolic system has constructed the following explicit rules as a result of its training:

1. If X is a person and X can speak then X can understand language.
2. If X is not a person then X cannot speak.
3. If X is not a person then X cannot understand language.

Let us suppose that the proposed system is able to tolerate a merely partial match of a rule condition part. Then, because of the first rule, it is plausible to suggest the system could come out with *the banana can understand language* with some moderate degree of confidence, when presented with *the banana can speak*. The second rule would apply but could be discounted in the present reasoning context as a result of producing a conclusion that contradicts the premise that the banana can speak. Now, it is reasonable to propose that a rule with the same condition part as an already discounted rule itself becomes discounted or at least suspect. This is on the heuristic that if one predication about a certain type of situation turns out to be faulty, other predictions about that type of situation also become dubious. On this proposal, the third rule becomes suspect, and is therefore not able to defeat the tentative conclusion from the first rule.

The central point is that the system can easily tolerate a merely partial match of a compound condition part, such as that of the first rule. On the other hand, connectionist systems of the sort in question have internal representations that do not manifest the syntax of the represented statements. That is, those activity patterns do not have a structure of subpatterns corresponding to the structure of the statement. (See also van Gelder 1989, 1990 on this *nonconcatenative* type of system.) The representing of structure is only implicit in some way in an internal representation, so that the representation of the structure is intimately mixed in with the representation of the individual parts. Therefore, it is not easy to see how the connectionist system could emulate the symbolic system's partial-match reasoning without also generating nonsensical inferences. Certainly, it might be that the internal representation of *the banana can speak* is sufficiently similar to internal representations of statements like *X is a person and X can speak* for the system to be able to produce the desired conclusion, *the banana can understand language*. However, if the notion of "sufficiently similar" is loose enough for that to be the case, might it not be that the internal representation of some totally irrelevant statement like *Blurg is a horse and Blurg can neigh* also just happened to be similar enough to *X is a person and X can speak* for the conclusion *Blurg can understand language* to pop out? That is, a representation scheme in which *structural* aspects of a statement are intimately mixed in with the representation of the *components* of a statement makes for difficulty in providing a notion of *sufficiently similar* between two statements S and T that simultaneously satisfies the following requirements: (a) it is allowable for S to match only a part of T (or vice versa); and (b) but the parts of S and T that do match must match pretty exactly. By contrast, a standard symbolic representation separates structure from components and therefore has no problem in simultaneously satisfying the requirements.

4.5. Personification and Metaphor

Elman [personal communication] has suggested that the system should personify Monday or the banana in the earlier examples. But what might this involve? Confining attention for brevity to the Monday example, I mention three representative possibilities (though no doubt there are others).

1. Monday and Tuesday are viewed *metaphorically* as people. The metaphor is cashed out in terms of a traditional analogical mapping between part of the days-of-the-week domain and part of the human being domain. The individual item correspondences involved in this mapping are then treated as connectionistically implemented bindings.

2. Monday and Tuesday are again reviewed metaphorically as people. However, no bindings are involved. Rather—and this is Elman's version of the suggestion[8]—the connectionist representation of Monday is "deformed" by being made more like the representation of a person. (In the simplest case this might involve turning on the *person* feature unit or, say, *has-mind* and *has-mouth* feature units. These units would of course normally be off in the representation of a day.) The representation of speaking might also be deformed temporarily to make it more like something that could be attributed to bananas. For instance, speaking could be relieved of the normal attribute of being produced by an animal mouth.

3. It has been further suggested to me that the system forms a representation of a person wearing a placard on which the name *Monday* is written, and similarly another person with *Tuesday*. These people are the participants in the discourse reported in the example. This suggestion is a *metonymic* approach, in contrast to the metaphorical approach of the other two suggestions.

The first possibility is circular because it assumes the ability to represent bindings between arbitrary types of things—that is, it assumes that arbitrary combinations of concepts can be formed. This is the problem we started with. The third possibility appears viable, although it implies a major amount of machinery over and above the sort typically entertained in connectionist systems currently. There is a specific worry about the method because it may go too far in the personification, in that we may need specific properties of days still to be operative in the example. The carry-over of day properties to the two imagined people is not a necessary consequence of the third possibility as stated, so that extra assumptions must be made. One would be to regard the two people metaphorically as days, but then we are back with some variant of the first or second possibility.

The second possibility may be viable, and is certainly worth investigating further. Indeed, Elman (1988) reported a recurrent connectionist network that forms distributed representations of simple sentences on its hidden layer and in a sense performs deformations of the sort under discussion. More precisely, the system was trained on a certain corpus of sentences involving strong constraints on verb-noun relationships. Then, the weights were frozen and the corpus was fed through a final time with the modification that the totally novel pseudo-word *zog* was substituted for every occurrence of the word *man*. Under a certain way Elman presented of estimating the prototypical representations of individual

---

[8]See also the cup-of-coffee example in Smolensky (1988).

words on the hidden layer, it turned out that the representation of *zog* bore the same hierarchical clustering relationship to the other words as the word *man* did. (This does not quite amount to saying, though, that the *zog* representation was closely similar to the *man* representation.) Thus, there is a sense in which the expectations of the system for seeing *man* in certain contexts cause *zog* to be treated much as if it had been *man*. This effect is certainly promising from the point of view of this section, but one should realize that there is a lot left to be demonstrated. It must be shown that the internal representations of the *zog* sentences are actually similar enough to the corresponding *man* sentences to be able to support similar inferences.

Possibility (2) is interesting not least because it is an important opportunity for connectionism to contribute something distinctive to high-level cognition. We need to exercise caution about it, though. I conjecture that when we interpret the sentence *Micky believes that bananas can speak* we do not necessarily commit ourselves to making proper sense of the complement (the clause following the *believes that*). That is, all we do, unless we decide to think about the sentence carefully, is to assume that *there exists a way in which* Micky sees bananas as able to speak, without committing ourselves to any particular way, and therefore without needing to effect the distortions just discussed. It is conceivable, then, that what we need in a good connectionist model of human cognition, and also perhaps in a good connectionist artificial intelligence, is a way for the system to turn off the mutual sensitivity of concepts that are being combined. That is, the mutual sensitivity had better not be too automatic. If this is so, then the system should be able to form a straight combination of incompatible concepts, a trivial task for a traditional symbolic system.

Here we see a way in which hearers' processing of just *Bananas can speak* might differ, at least in degree, from their processing of that same anomalous combination when it is embedded in an attitude report, such as *Micky believes that bananas can speak* or *Susan wants Micky to believe that bananas can speak*. The more explicit layers of attitude context there are, the less the pressure to make full sense out of the idea of bananas speaking. Unless the hearer has some particular motive for thinking in some depth about Micky's belief state or Susan's desire state, the hearer can refrain from delving into the idea of bananas speaking. There could indeed be such a motive: one that is independent of the discourse, or one that is introduced by the exigencies of coherently linking the sentence to other sentences in the discourse. Notice, however, that it might be that the speaker's only intention in reporting Micky's belief was to emphasize the weirdness of Micky's beliefs, in which case no deep understanding of the belief would be necessary. Of course, the attitude-free sentence *Bananas can speak* is embedded in an implicit speaker-attitude context, but in this case it is more likely that the statement will link up in some meaningful way with other speaker statements. The speaker might go on to say, *So I'll get that banana over there to tell my wife I've gone to El Paso*. The hearer would need to reason that the speaker also believes that bananas can understand language and have memories.

A further complication is that variants of the banana example can have mundane metaphorical interpretations. For instance, the sentence *The bananas spoke to John of luxury* could mean that the presence of the bananas in a certain household indicated to John that the household was luxurious, in a context in which bananas were luxury items. To worsen the complication, however, one might claim that metonymy is involved here rather than metaphor. The use of *spoke* could be viewed as a metonymic way of referring to the normal result of speaking, namely the implanting of information in the mind of the hearer. But if metaphor is indeed what is involved, it might be seen as requiring a deformation of the concept of banana and/or the concept of speaking. These deformations would be favorably looked on in an interactionist theory of metaphor (see Waggoner, 1990, for a review).

5. EMBEDDED
STRUCTURE-SENSITIVE PROCESSING

The idea of nonconcatenative versus concatenative representations was used in the previous section. A nonconcatenative representation, like that in the middle layer of a RAAM, is in a sense holistic, not having any natural structural similarity to whatever is represented. Rather, we only assume that there are well-defined mechanisms *of some sort* for transforming a nonconcatenative representation of an item X into representations of the parts of X, and for creating the representation of X out of the representations of its parts. Let us call these two types of transformation the *analysis* transformations and the *synthesis* transformations respectively. In the nonconcatenative case, these transformations are not just a matter of breaking the X representation down into its parts or of bunching the representations of X's parts together, respectively.

A large part of the current interest in the internal representations in systems like those addressed in the previous section is based on their being not only (a) nonconcatenative but also (b) susceptible to being processed *directly,* that is, without first being unpacked into the corresponding external representations by means of the analysis transformations. With regard to (b), if the internal representations could be used in inference or other processing *only* indirectly, then they would lose much of their point, even in the eyes of their proponents. And, it is certainly of great interest and importance to see whether useful forms of processing can be done directly on the nonconcatenative representations.

However, there are various modes of reasoning that are not readily catered for by direct processing of nonconcatenative representations. These modes are various forms of *embedded* reasoning. A particular form of embedded reasoning is important in the propositional attitude arena. I discuss that type first, and then briefly mention others.

In reasoning about the beliefs of another agent a system must often make inferences embedded within the context of that agent's beliefs, so to speak. Thus, if John believes both that Sally is a chess champion and that all chess champions are clever, the system may need to make the (plausible) inference that John has concluded (and therefore believes) that Sally is clever. Now, such inferences about John on the system's part could be performed by means of reasoning schemata of the following form:

A believes that X is a P
A believes that all P are Q

A believes that X is Q

However, this involves a style of reasoning where the A *believes that* layer is explicitly carried through all steps, resulting in extra complexity in the necessary matching—for example, in the matching of the premise *John believes that Sally is a chess-champion* to the first line of the displayed schema. Therefore, propositional attitude theorists have often proposed (e.g., Creary 1979; Haas 1986; see also Dinsmore, 1991) that *simulative reasoning* be used. In our example, this would involve steps such as the following. First, the system records the fact that it is reasoning within the context of John's beliefs. Next, it perceives that the statements *Sally is a chess-champion* and *All chess-champions are clever* match the premises of the schema

X is a P
All P are Q

X is Q

The system then draws the conclusion that Sally is clever. It now backs up out of the John belief environment, and is able to report that *John believes that Sally is clever*. (The backing-up can be accompanied by a reduction of confidence in the conclusion, given that people do not always draw conclusions from their beliefs.)

The point, of course, is that this simulative reasoning procedure involves simpler reasoning schemata and simpler matching. Another important point is that the $X/P/Q$ reasoning schema used is the very same one that the system would itself use to conclude that Sally was clever if it believed her to be a chess-champion and believed all chess-champions to be clever. There is no need for the system to have the more complex schema displayed earlier. The extra simplicity is bought at the minor expense of the system's having to keep track of the context it is reasoning within, and to strip off and restore *John believes that* layers.

Now consider a system that has a nonconcatenative internal representation I1 of *John believes that Sally is a chess-champion* and a nonconcatenative internal representation I2 of *John believes that all chess-champions are clever*. One could make a variety of suggestions as to how the internal representation I3 of the (plausible) conclusion that *John believes that Sally is clever* could be produced:

1. The system produces I3 directly from I1 and I2 purely by virtue of having had the training sufficient to enable it to produce the conclusion *Sally is clever* from *Sally is a chess-champion* and *All chess-champions are clever*. That is, there is automatic generalization to the case of that inference being embedded within a belief context.

2. The system has had training as in (1) but goes through the simulative reasoning procedure described earlier: It uses an analysis transformation to produce internal representations for *Sally is a chess-champion* and *All chess-champions are clever* from I1 and I2 respectively, produces *Sally is clever* from these new internal representations, by generalization from its training, and then uses a synthesis transformation to construct I3.

3. The system has been trained on structurally similar examples of embedded inference (e.g., on the inference from *Mike believes that Susan is a musician* and *Mike believes that all musicians are refined* to *Mike believes that Susan is refined*), and this is sufficient for generalization to occur to our John/Sally example.

Now, the third method is undesirable because it introduces a scale up problem. Not only must analogous training be done in the case of (some) other types of attitude, rather than belief, but it must also be done for nonattitude forms of embedded reasoning. Perhaps worse, separate training would have to be done for each extra layer of attitude that is added. Thus, it is reasonable to draw the plausible conclusion that *John intends George to believe that Sally is clever* from *John intends George to believe that Sally is a chess-champion* and *John intends George to believe that all chess-champions are clever*.

It would be very nice if the first method was feasible. But, until it (and the corresponding approaches to other types of embedded reasoning problem) is shown to be feasible, we cannot rely on it. The problem increases with the depth of embedding. Thus, a nonconcatenative internal representation of, say, *John intends George to believe that Sally is a chess-champion* is only going to be weakly similar as an activation pattern to a nonconcatenative internal representation of *Sally is a chess-champion*. Therefore, the chances of direct processing of the latter representation generalizing to correct direct processing of the former are questionable.

The second method is antithetical to the spirit of nonconcatenative representations, as implied earlier. One might as well use a concatenative representation in the first place (or at least a hybrid representation, whereby, in representing *A believes that Z*, the combination of *A*, belief and *Z* is done concatenatively but *Z* is represented nonconcatenatively).

Within-attitude reasoning is an especially important form of embedded reasoning, but there are others. For instance, counterfactual reasoning raises similar issues. In making the argument *If Sally were a chess-champion she would be clever* (using a background assumption that chess-champions are clever) we need to reason within a counterfactual context in which Sally is a chess-champion. (See Fauconnier, 1985, and Dinsmore, 1987, 1991, for a general framework in which belief spaces, counterfactual spaces, fictional spaces, and several other types of space are unified.) Another important case of embedded reasoning arises from the observation that, in ordinary propositional logic, if S is a subformula of F and S is logically equivalent to a formula T, then F is logically equivalent to the formula G obtained from it by replacing some or all occurrences of S in F by T. For example, F and G might be

$$p \rightarrow (q \wedge (u \rightarrow v))$$

$$p \rightarrow (q \wedge (\neg v \rightarrow \neg u))$$

respectively, with S being $u \rightarrow v$ and T being $\neg v \rightarrow \neg u$. Notice that S can be a small and/or deeply embedded component of F, making approaches similar to the first and third methods even more questionable. Furthermore, the structure of non-S parts of F is completely arbitrary.

The Conposit implementational-connectionist system (Barnden 1988, 1989c, 1991) uses concatenative representations throughout, and could therefore cope with embedded reasoning in a relatively straightforward way. For instance, the John/Sally belief context example would be handled in outline as follows. Each statement of the form *A believes that Z* is broken up into two subrepresentations within Conposit's working memory: one part that can be thought of as *A believes that x* for a variable *x*, the other part being Z together with a binding of it to *x*. Reasoning can proceed directly on the Zs; and this does not even require the Z parts to be broken out first, as they are already separate from the *A believes that x* parts. Thus, simulative reasoning presents no special problems. (And it is straightforward to keep track of the contexts.)

This section carries the moral that structure-sensitivity (Fodor & Pylyshyn, 1988) of processing, which is a primary challenge to systems using nonconcatenative representations, is not just a matter of the *whole* structure of a represented item. Thus, with reference to the propositional logic example just mentioned, the structure-sensitivity involved in mapping from S ($u \rightarrow v$) to T ($\neg v \rightarrow \neg u$) is more than a matter of transforming S as a free-standing structure to T. Rather, the structure-sensitivity involves the ability to map any F containing S *as a part* to the corresponding G. Similar observations hold for other sorts of embedding, such as belief contexts. To go back to Chalmers's sentence passivization network (see section 4.2), what is needed is for the system to be able to do not just passivization but also embedded passivization, such as transforming *John believes that Michael loves Bill* to *John believes that Bill is loved by Michael,* and so on at deeper levels of embedding.

Hence, direct processing of nonconcatenative representations of structured objects is at a severe disadvantage. The particular object part that is to be subjected to structure-sensitive processing on a given occasion is intimately mixed in with the other parts, requiring the direct processing mechanism to somehow preserve those other parts while manipulating the part in question. The corresponding preservation in the case of concatenative representation is trivial.

6. CONCLUSION

We have looked at various challenging issues to do with getting connectionism to cope with high-level cognitive activities such as reasoning and natural language understanding. The issues are to do with various facets of generalization that are not commonly noted. We have been concerned in particular with the special forms these issues take in the arena of propositional attitude processing. The main problems we have looked at are:

1. The need to construct explicit representations of generalizations, not just generalize correctly to individual cases.
2. The need to be able to match two or more complex short-term information structures, to enable rapid generalization from recent examples rather than from long-term memories.
3. The need to represent and reason with anomalous combinations of concepts.
4. The need to perform embedded reasoning. This presents special problems for systems using nonconcatenative representations.

We also touched on vague quantification in attitude report complements. Neither this topic nor that of analogies between short-term structures has been adequately addressed in the symbolic framework, let alone in connectionism.

One opportunity we saw for connectionism to contribute something distinctive to the realization of high-level cognition lies in its support for the automatic distortion of the concepts involved in anomalous combinations, including those arising in metaphor, to make them fit together appropriately (assuming the combinations can be dealt with at all).

There are some other connections between connectionism and propositional attitude research that we have not discussed. As noted in section 1, one connection already studied by others is the possibility of connectionism accounting naturally for degrees of belief, desire, and so on. Another connection is the opportunity for connectionism to provide a way of handling intermediate types of attitude. The usual attitude types (belief, intention, hope, etc.) are almost always cast in AI, linguistics, and philosophy as being clearly distinguishable from each other. Nevertheless, there is reason to think that the distinctions are fuzzy, and that intermediate types are possible. What I have in mind here is, say, a state intermediate between believing something to be true and wishing it to be (cf. wishful thinking). Another example is provided by the sentence *He half hoped she would come and half dreaded it.*

The opportunities and problems covered are put forward as things worth being optimistic about or pessimistic about, respectively. They are not put forward as decisive arguments for or against connectionism. Hopefully this chapter contributes to a greater understanding of the connectionist/symbolist gap by presenting some unusual issues and by throwing new light on some well-known ones.

ACKNOWLEDGMENTS

This work was supported in part by grant AFOSR-88-0215 from the Air Force Office of Scientific Research and grant NAGW-1592 under the Innovative Research Program of the NASA Office of Space Science and Applications.

I am deeply indebted to John Dinsmore for creating the opportunity for me to develop the lines of thought in this chapter. I thank Jeff Elman, Tom Eskridge, David Farwell, Mike Gasser, Margarita Gonzalez, Rocio Guillen, Cathy Harris, Steve Helmreich, Trent Lange, Jay McClelland, Tim van Gelder, Jin Wang, Fuliang Weng, and Yorick Wilks, as well as John Dinsmore and anonymous reviewers, for useful questions, criticisms and suggestions.

REFERENCES

Allen, J. F. (1983). Recognizing intentions from natural language utterances. In M. Brady & R. C. Berwick (Eds.), *Computational models of discourse.* Cambridge, MA: MIT Press.

Ballim, A., Wilks, Y., & Barnden, J. A. (1990). Belief ascription, metaphor, and intensional identification. In S. L. Tsohadzidis (Ed.), *Meanings and prototypes: Studies in linguistic categorization* (pp. 91–131). London and New York: Routledge.

Ballim, A., Wilks, Y., & Barnden, J. A. (1991). Belief ascription, metaphor, and intensional identification. *Cognitive Science, 15* (1), 133–171.

Barnden, J. A. (1983). Intensions are such: An outline. *Proceedings of the Eight International Joint Conference on Artificial Intelligence* (pp. 280—286). Los Altos, CA: Morgan Kaufmann.

Barnden, J. A. (1986). Imputations and explications: Representational problems in treatments of propositional attitudes. *Cognitive Science, 10* (3), 319–364.

Barnden, J. A. (1988). Conposit, a neural net system for high-level symbolic processing: Overview of research and description of register-machine level. (Memoranda in Computer and Cognitive Science, No. MCCS-88-145). Computing Research Laboratory, New Mexico State University.

Barnden, J. A. (1989a). A misleading problem reduction in belief representation research: Some methodological considerations. *Journal of Experimental and Theoretical Artificial Intelligence, 1* (2), 4–30.

Barnden, J. A. (1989b, May). Belief, metaphorically speaking. *Proceedings of the First International Conference on Principles of Knowledge Representation and Reasoning* (pp. 21–32). San Mateo, CA: Morgan Kaufmann.

Barnden, J. A. (1989c, August). Neural-net implementation of complex symbol-processing in a mental model approach to syllogistic reasoning. *Proceedings of the Eleventh International Joint Conference on Artificial Intelligence* (pp. 568–573). San Mateo, CA: Morgan Kaufmann.

Barnden, J. A. (1990). Naive Metaphysics: A metaphor-based approach to propositional attitude representation. (Memoranda in Computer and Cognitive Science, No. MCCS-90-174). Computing Research Laboratory, New Mexico State University, NM 88003, USA.

Barnden, J. A. (1991). Encoding complex symbolic data structures with some unusual connectionist techniques. In J. A. Barnden & J. B. Pollack (Eds.), *Advances in connectionist and neural computation theory* (Vol. 1, pp. 180–240). Norwood, NJ: Ablex.

Barnden, J. A., & Srinivas, K. (in press). Overcoming rule-based rigidity and connectionist limitations through massively-parallel case-based reasoning. *International Journal of Man-Machine Studies*.

Barwise, J., & Perry, J. (1983). *Situations and attitudes.* Cambridge, MA: MIT Press.

Bienenstock, E., & von der Malsburg, C. (1987). A neural network for invariant pattern recognition. *Europhysics Letters, 4* (1), 121–126.

Carbonell, J. G., & Brown, R. D. (1988). Anaphora resolution: A multi-strategy approach. *Proceedings of the Twelfth International Conference on Computational Linguistics* (pp. 96–101).

Chalmers, D. J. (1990). Syntactic transformations on distributed representations. *Connection Science, 2* (1 & 2), 53–62.

Churchland, P. S. (1986). *Neurophilosophy.* Cambridge, MA: MIT Press.

Cohen, P., & Levesque, H. (1985, July). Speech acts and rationality. *Proceedings of the Meeting of the Twenty-Third Annual Meeting of the Association for Computational Linguistics.* (pp. 49–60). University of Chicago.

Craddock, A. J., & Browse, R. A. (1986, August). Belief maintenance with uncertainty. *Proceedings of the Eighth Conference of the Cognitive Science Society.* Hillsdale, NJ: Lawrence Erlbaum Associates.

Creary, L. G. (1979, August). Propositional attitudes: Fregean representation and simulative reasoning. *Proceedings of the Sixth International Joint Conference on Artificial Intelligence.* (pp. 176–181). Los Altos, CA: Morgan Kaufmann.

Cresswell, M. J. (1985). *Structured meanings: The semantics of propositional attitudes.* Cambridge, MA: MIT Press.

Dinsmore, J. (1987). Mental spaces from a functional perspective. *Cognitive Science, 11* (1), 1–21.

Dinsmore, J. (1991). *Partitioned representations: A study in mental representation, language processing and linguistic structure.* Dordrecht: Kluwer.

Elman, J. L. (1988). *Finding structure in time* (Tech. Rep. No. 8801). San Diego, CA: Center for Research in Language, University of California.

Elman, J. L. (1989, August). Structured representations and connectionist models. *Proceedings of the Eleventh Annual Conference of the Cognitive Science Society* (pp. 17–25). Hillsdale, NJ: Lawrence Erlbaum Associates.

Fauconnier, G. (1985). *Mental spaces: Aspects of meaning construction in natural language.* Cambridge, MA: MIT Press.

Fodor, J. A., & Pylyshyn, Z. W. (1988). Connectionism and cognitive architecture: A critical analysis. In S. Pinker & J. Mehler (Eds.), *Connections and symbols.* Cambridge, MA: MIT Press and Amsterdam: Elsevier.

Gasser, M. (1989, August). Robust lexical selection in parsing and generation. *Proceedings of the Eleventh Annual Conference of the Cognitive Science Society* (pp. 82–89). Hillsdale, NJ: Lawrence Erlbaum Associates.

Gasser, M., & Smith, L. B. (1991). *Comparison, categorization, and perceptual dimensions: A connectionist model of the development of the notion of sameness.* Unpublished Manuscript, Computer Science Department, Indiana University, Bloomington, IN.

Grosz, B. J., & Sidner, C. L. (1986). Attention, intentions, and the structure of discourse. *Computational Linguistics, 12* (3), 175–204.

Haas, A. R. (1986). A syntactic theory of belief and action. *Artificial Intelligence, 28,* 245–292.

Harris, C. L., & Elman, J. L. (1989, August). Representing variable information with simple recurrent networks. *Proceedings of the Eleventh Annual Conference of the Cognitive Science Society* (pp. 635–642). Hillsdale, NJ: Lawrence Erlbaum Associates.

Hobbs, J. R. (1985, July). Ontological promiscuity. *Proceedings of the Twenty-Third Annual Meeting of the Association for Computational Linguistics* (pp. 61–69). University of Chicago.

Lee, G., Flowers, M., & Dyer, M. G. (1989, August). A symbolic/connectionist script applier mechanism. *Proceedings of the Eleventh Annual Conference of the Cognitive Science Society* (pp. 714–721). Hillsdale, NJ: Lawrence Erlbaum Associates.

Maida, A. S. (1988). A syntactic approach to mental correspondence. *Proceedings of the Conference of the Canadian Society for Computational Studies of Artificial Intelligence,* Edmonton, Alberta.

Mates, B. (1950). Synonymity. *University of California Publications in Philosophy, 25,* 201–226.

Miikkulainen, R., & Dyer, M. G. (1989). Encoding input/output representations in connectionist cognitive systems. In D. Touretzky, G. Hinton, & T. Sejnowski (Eds.), *Proceedings of the 1988 Connectionist Models Summer School.* San Mateo, CA: Morgan Kaufmann.

Pearl, J. (1986). Fusion, propagation, and structuring in belief networks. *Artificial Intelligence, 29* (3), 241–288.

Perlis, D. (1985). Languages with self-reference I: Foundations. *Artificial Intelligence, 25* (3), 301–322.

Pollack, J. B. (1988, August). Recursive auto-associative memory: Devising compositional distributed representations. In *Proceedings of the Tenth Annual Conference of the Cognitive Science Society* (pp. 33–39). Hillsdale, NJ: Lawrence Erlbaum Associates.

Pollack, J. B. (1990). Recursive distributed representations. *Artificial Intelligence, 46* (1–2), 77–105.

Rey, G. (1988). Sanity surrounded by madness. *Behavioral and Brain Sciences, 11,* 48–50.

Rumelhart, D. E., & McClelland, J. L. (1986). On learning the past tenses of English verbs. In J. L. McClelland, D. E. Rumelhart, & the PDP Research Group (Eds.), *Parallel distributed processing* (Vol. 2). Cambridge, MA: MIT Press.

Smolensky, P. (1988). On the proper treatment of connectionism. *Behavioral and Brain Sciences, 11,* 1–74.

Sperber, D., & Wilson, D. (1986). *Relevance: Communication and cognition.* Oxford: Blackwell.

van Gelder, T. (1989, August). Compositionality and the explanation of cognitive processes. In *Proceedings of the Eleventh Annual Conference of the Cognitive Science Society* (pp. 34–41). Hillsdale, NJ: Lawrence Erlbaum Associates.

van Gelder, T. (1990). Compositionality: A connectionist variation on a classical theme. *Cognitive Science, 14* (3), 355–384.

Waggoner, J. E. (1990). Interaction theories of metaphor: Psychological perspectives. *Metaphor and Symbolic Activity, 5* (2), 91–108.

Wilks, Y., & Bien, J. (1983). Beliefs, points of view and multiple environments. *Cognitive Science, 7* (2), 95–119.

Zalta, E. N. (1988). *Intensional logic and the metaphysics of intentionality.* Cambridge, MA: MIT Press.

8

Where Do Underlying Representations Come From?: A Connectionist Approach to the Acquisition of Phonological Rules

Chan-Do Lee and Michael Gasser
Indiana University

1. INTRODUCTION

Over the last several years, there have been many discussions of the foundations of cognitive science. Is intelligence "the result of the manipulation of structured symbolic expressions"? Or is it "the result of the transmission of activation levels in large networks of densely interconnected simple units" (Pinker & Mehler, 1988, p. 1)? The subject of study here is representational mental states and the principles of organization of computational systems.

Although both classical symbolic and connectionist subsymbolic systems postulate mental representations, they differ in many ways. Fodor and Pylyshyn (1988) argued that only classical systems are committed to a *language of thought,* that is, to representational states that have combinatorial syntactic and semantic structure. These systems are based on the productivity of thought, the systematicity of cognitive representation, the compositionality of representations, and the systematicity of inference.

Even though these seem to be good reasons for the symbolic postulate, there are several compelling deficits of rule interpretation when taken literally as a model of mind (Pollack, 1990):

1. *New rules are not easily learned in symbolic systems.* In symbolic systems all rules are hard wired into the system, hence making changes in the rules is difficult. In most cases, whenever a new rule is introduced, it has to be added explicitly to the code of the system.

2. *Symbolic systems do not easily scale up to real problems.* Most symbolic systems are for the toy problems with less than a thousand rules. It may require more than a thousand rules to solve real problems.

179

3. *Symbolic systems do not exhibit plausible behavioral profile.* Symbolic systems exhibit no temporal behavior that is psychologically plausible. Being able to accommodate temporal processing is very important because language is inherently of a temporal nature. Language is not a static entity, but a dynamic one that must be processed continuously in real time. In symbolic systems this kind of temporal processing is very difficult.

4. *Symbolic systems are not generally capable of parallel processing.* Some decisions in human language processing are made by parallel constraint satisfaction. When a person hears an ambiguous word, he might use all the information he has, lexical, syntactic, semantic, and contextual, to decide on its meaning. There is no easy way to create distributed memory and process according to parallel constraints in symbolic models.

5. *Symbolic systems do not show biological plausibility.* Symbolic systems have not been evolutionarily or neurally justified.

Connectionism can be viewed as a systematic attack on these problems, although any single connectionist model today only addresses one or two of them at a time.

In this chapter we report on a connectionist approach to the acquisition of phonological rules. Phonology is the study of the systems underlying the selection and use of sounds in the languages of the world. It focuses on the internal representation of sound units and tries to explain the nature of phonological phenomena. Questions for a connectionist approach include the following: Are the internal representations worth studying? Why are there certain phonological phenomena? How is phonology related to cognition?

One example of a phonological process is the pronunciation of the English plural suffix. The English regular plural morpheme has three variants: /s/, /z/, and /ɪz/, depending on the final segment in the noun stem. For example, the plural of *hat* is pronounced /hæts/ and that of *zone* is /zonz/, whereas *page* has the plural form /peʤɪz/. To account for these variants in traditional phonology, one must posit an underlying abstract representation, and one or more rules have to be invoked that transform the underlying representation into either /s/, /z/, or /ɪz/. The derivation of a form like *hats* begins with the underlying representations of the morphemes *HAT* and *PLURAL,* and the rules turn these into the surface form /hæts/.

If we assume that phonological phenomena are related to some form of cognitive processing, then the representations best suited to deal with these phenomena, whether they be symbolic or subsymbolic, might lead to an initial hypothesis as to what mental representations in general are like.

Phonology is generally regarded as symbolic, rule-governed behavior. To account for this behavior using connectionist networks presents many challenges that have been noted by researchers who subscribe to classical symbolic tenets, including Pinker and Prince (1988) and Fodor and Pylyshyn (1988). In classical symbolic systems the acquisition of underlying representations has been difficult to account for, and this fact has in part motivated the idea of innate predispositions of certain linguistic structures. The very existence of underlying representations that can be manipulated by rules was one of the points Pinker and Prince (1988) and Fodor and Pylyshyn (1988) made against the adequacy of connectionist systems in explaining phonological processes. If we can overcome them by explaining some phonological rules without the benefit of any *explicit* rules,[1] or underlying representations, it will strongly support the appropriateness of connectionist networks to this task.

In this chapter, we describe the problem of learning phonology and how some phonological processes can be accounted for in a connectionist network where no underlying representations and no explicit rules are to be found. Our experiments examine English plural morpheme acquisition (*English-plural task*) and an artificial suffix rule that adds an /o/ after the voiced stem or an /s/ after the voiceless stem at the end of the words from an artificial language to form a *plural* (*non-assimilatory suffixation task*). We also analyze the hidden layer representations that the network builds, which are analogous to the underlying representations of symbolic models. The chapter concludes with a discussion of some limitations of the current model.

2. THE PROBLEM: LEARNING PHONOLOGY

There are various theories about how and why some observed phonological phenomena occur in the way they do. However, most traditional phonological theories presuppose abstract underlying representations and a set of rules to obtain the surface realization. Modern generative phonology is based on the notion of *deriving* forms through the application of rules, each of which takes a linguistic representation as input and yields one which is in some sense closer to the *surface*. The idea is that behind surface forms are underlying representations, abstractions within which each morpheme has an invariant form.

Consider again, as an example, the English plural. The regular plural morpheme takes three different forms, /s/, /z/, and /ɪz/. To account for them in traditional phonology, two rules are invoked:

1. Voicing Assimilation. Spread the value of voicing from one phoneme to the next in word final position.

---

[1]For the purpose of our discussion, a *rule* is a function that maps one representation onto another. By *without the benefit of explicit rules* we mean that in our system rules are not directly represented; they arise in a very natural way from the connectionist architecture we employ in the current study when presented with the task of relating form and meaning, as is demonstrated as we go along.

2. Vowel Insertion. Word-finally, separate with the vowel /ɪ/ adjacent conso-
nants that are too similar in place and manner of articulation.

The first rule is invoked to add /s/ to the nouns that end with voiceless conso-
nants, for example, *hat,* or /z/ to those with voiced final phoneme as with the
case of *zone,* whereas the plural suffix of *page* calls for the second rule due to the
similarity of /ʤ/ and /z/.

There are, however, a number of questions that have been raised regarding
this approach. Are surface forms really derived from underlying representations
with the application of rule(s)? Most classical symbolists believe so. Lachter and
Bever (1988) noted, "The generality of the application of such rules highlights
the fact that they apply to abstract subsets of features, not to actual phonetic or
acoustic objects" (p. 202). Pinker and Prince's (1988) critical analysis of the
Rumelhart and McClelland (henceforth, "RM") (1986) past-tense model is crucially based on the claim that the linguistic and developmental facts provide good
evidence for rules and underlying representations.

The RM model, together with later extensions by Marchman and Plunkett
(1989), is one of the most important earlier efforts to answer the question of how
rulelike behavior might emerge in connectionist networks. The model is a simple
two-layer pattern associator that exhibits the acquisition of the marking of past
tense in English. It maps representations of present-tense forms of English verbs
onto their past-tense versions, without any involvement of semantic characterization.

In spite of its success, the model has drawn harsh criticism, notably from
Pinker and Prince (1988). The points Pinker and Prince made include the following:

1. The model is incapable of representing certain kinds of words. The model
adopts a scheme proposed by Wickelgren (1969) to encode context sensitivity.
According to this scheme a string is represented as the set of the three-character-
sequences that it contains. Rumelhart and McClelland called such trigrams *Wick-
elphones.* Example, a word like *net* translates to $\{_{\#}n_e, _ne_t, _et_{\#}\}$. Here a
"word-boundary (#)" is a character, too. There is a serious problem with this
representation scheme because distinct lexical items may be associated with
identical representations (e.g., *algal* and *algalgal*).

2. It easily models many kinds of rules that are not found in any human
languages. It is as easy to represent and learn a quintessential unlinguistic map
such as mirror-reversal of phonetic strings (e.g., pit to tip) in the RM model as it
is to represent the identity map.

3. It fails to capture central generalizations about English sound patterns.
Elaboration tolerance (McCarthy, 1988) is the ability of a model to be extended
to additional problems. One example is the problem of knowledge transfer, how

a pattern of activity learned by one network becomes interpretable by another. The model cannot be elaborated to explain the commonality between the /t/-/d/-/ɪd/ alternations found in regular past-tense forms and the /s/-/z/-ɪz/ alternations found in the third-person singular, regular plural nouns, possessive, and so on.

4. It cannot handle the elementary problem of homophony. Distinct lexical items may share the same phonological composition, thus the notion of lexical representation distinguishes phonologically ambiguous words such as *wring* and *ring*. The model represents individual objects as sets of their features. Nothing, however, represents the fact that a collection of features corresponds to an existing individual.

Yet, contrary to what Pinker and Prince seemed to be arguing, these weaknesses turn out to be specific to the RM model, rather than inherent in any connectionist account. There are alternatives to the Wickelfeature approach to context that do not share its problems. In particular, simple recurrent networks, as becomes evident, give a system the required context sensitivity and allow all possible words to be distinguished. Furthermore, redefining the task to be one of production and recognition results in constraints on the kind of rules that can be learned, permits homophonous words to be distinguished, and makes possible generalizations across the sound system of the language.

In this chapter, we offer an alternative to the RM model that deals with two fundamental problems that are overlooked by classical accounts of phonological processes as well as the RM model. In doing so, we answer three of Pinker and Prince's criticisms, 1, 2, and 4 in the previous list. We have discussed generalization issues in Lee (1991). Experiments on knowledge transfer show how a network trained on one rule can go on to learn another similar rule.

First, how does knowledge about rules and underlying representations relate to the psycholinguistic processes of production and perception, which relate form and meaning, rather than associating form to form? The linguistic knowledge in rules and underlying representations is meant to belong to *competence* and should thus be shared by both production and perception. Production might to some extent parallel phonological derivations, but perception would be the reverse process. Thus we are confronted with the familiar problem of using rules in one direction when they were designed for another.

A more serious problem, however, occurs in imagining how knowledge about rules and underlying representations might ever be learned. That is, given only surface input forms together with meanings inferrable from context, how is a learner to figure out how the form-meaning relation gets mediated by abstract underlying representations? Where do underlying representations come from? How are rules found and related to each other?

It is customary to assume that a language learner is helped by having certain predispositions about language wired in; however, we begin with an approach that is far more constrained. We assume that the basic building blocks of language acquisition and processing are the simple, neuronlike processing units that connectionist models start out with. What gives such a system its intelligence is its architecture. First, we need some means of representing patterns that take place in time. An effective approach developed in the last 3 years is the *simple recurrent network* (SRN), to be described in detail in the next section. It has recurrent connections from the hidden layer that give the network the capacity to develop a kind of short-term memory. SRNs are usually trained on prediction tasks: Given an input event, the network is to say what it thinks the next event will be.

Second, we need a means of handling both meanings and forms. Throughout this chapter, by *form* we mean a series of phonemes, whereas by *meaning* we mean the lexical entry of the word in question, together with relevant grammatical features. For example, the word pronounced /hæts/ has the meaning *HAT + PLURAL*.[2] The networks that we use extend the basic SRN architecture to incorporate both *form* (a series of phonemes) and *meaning* units on input and output. The recurrent hidden layer combines meaning and form. A network like this may be provided with segments (one at a time) and/or meanings and be expected to predict the next segment or generate the appropriate meaning. In this way, the knowledge that is learned is potentially usable in both perception and production tasks.

What we are describing in this chapter is a rudimentary sort of *performance* phonology; its goals are different from the goals of generative phonology, which is *competence* phonology. We are arguing not against rules and underlying representations per se, but against generative/transformational competence rules and underlying representations; we are for the performance rules and underlying representations modeled in a connectionist architecture. For example, the fact that the plural of *top* is pronounced as /tɑps/ can be explained in competence phonology as:

/tɑpz/ Underlying representation[3]
/tɑps/ Rule 1 as stated earlier
[tɑps] Surface Form

In contrast, performance phonology does not require any explicit rules and underlying representations. They are to be learned in the process of generalizing

---

[2]Our concern is with the arbitrary relationship between form and meaning; hence we need not concern ourselves in this chapter with genuine semantics.

[3]Here the underlying representation of *plural* is assumed to be /z/.

over a set of training instances that exhibit the alternations between English singular and plural nouns, for example,

$$\text{TUB + SINGULAR} \rightarrow \text{/t}\Lambda\text{b/}$$

$$\text{TUB + PLURAL} \rightarrow \text{/t}\Lambda\text{bz/}$$

where the items in capitals represent meanings.

We think our approach is more psychologically plausible; and if such an approach can handle perception, production, and acquisition, then generative phonology would become superfluous. We do not think that each underlying segment goes through a derivation employing phonological rules to produce a *surface* segment. What counts is that for speakers meanings trigger the phonological/phonetic productions, whereas for listeners phonetic/phonological material directly evokes word meanings. Here the rules are built into the associations between forms and meanings and underlying representations are encoded as distributed representations somewhere in the associations.

Through experiments on the English-plural task and non-assimilatory suffixation task, we show that (a) rules in this system are determined by the connection weights between units that the network develops while trying to produce correct outputs and (b) underlying representations are learned as the pattern on the hidden layer that mediates the relationship between form and meaning. First let us describe our model in detail.

3. SYSTEM STRUCTURE

We use a relatively constrained three-layer network, one in which feedforward connections are supplemented by limited feedback connections. Figure 8.1 shows the network architecture we have started with.

The architecture shown in Fig. 8.1 is a slight modification of the SRN developed by Elman (Elman, 1989, 1990) as a modification of a related architecture by Jordan (1986). The basic structure of an SRN is shown in Fig. 8.2. An SRN is a simple feedforward network with limited feedback connections. In the figure, the solid arrows denote the learnable one-to-many connections between units on the lower level and those on the higher level; for example, one unit on the input layer connects to all units on the hidden layer. The dashed arrow denotes the fixed one-to-one connections, on which no learning takes place with only one connection from a given higher level unit to a single lower level unit. Phonological processes are temporal, that is, phonetic input/output occurs through time, so we need to have some kind of short-term memory (STM) to store the previous input. The system cannot know how to behave on the basis of only the current input; the context of preceding event is essential. The feedback connections from

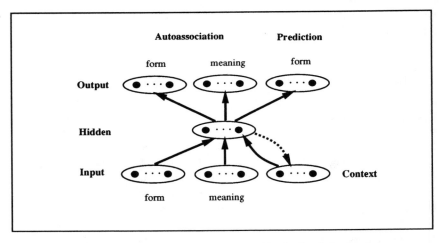

FIG. 8.1.   Architecture of the network used in the English-plural alternation study.

the hidden layer to the input layer serve this purpose. STM is held by *context units,* which are the copies of the hidden layer from the previous time step. Thus at any given time step, the network has not only the current input but also some memory of the previous inputs. But because the previous input was also a function of the previous STM pattern, the network has information from many previous time steps that has degraded in a continuous fashion.

SRNs have another advantage over simple feed-forward networks because they also avoid the difficulty of having fixed-length representations for variable-

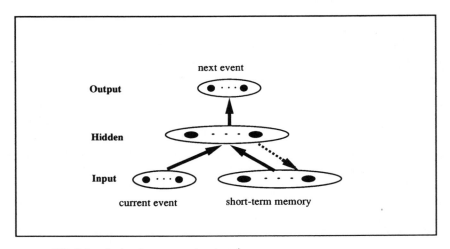

FIG. 8.2.   A simple recurrent network.

length patterns, because the length of the input patterns is not explicitly represented in the network architecture. In a *window representation,* the size of the input layer dictates the size of the window; but in a dynamic network one event is processed at a time, thus eliminating the difficulty of representing a variable-length input within a fixed-length input layer (see Port, 1990, for the issue of representation of temporal patterns).

Elman and others (e.g., Servan-Schreiber, Cleeremans, & McClelland, 1989) have used SRNs for various prediction tasks; given an input sequence, the goal of the network is to predict the next event. The standard back-propagation learning rule (Rumelhart, Hinton, & Williams, 1986) is used to train the network. Our model differs from other SRNs in that it is trained on auto-association as well as prediction. This is a way to force the network to distinguish the different input patterns on the hidden layer (Servan-Schreiber et al., 1989). Now let us consider the architecture used in the current work in more detail.

The *form and meaning cliques*[4] in the input layer receive input from the outside, whereas the context units receive a copy of activations on the hidden layer from the previous time step. The *hidden units* receive activations from the input layer and feed the output layer. The output layer receives activations from the hidden units. It produces outputs in accordance with the current form and meaning and predicts the next form. There are no intralevel connections in the units in any clique or between cliques.

This network has the capacity to associate form with meaning and meaning with form as well as form with form and meaning with meaning. Thus it can perform the task of the production of a sequence of segments given a meaning or the recognition of a meaning given a sequence of segments. It also has the potential to make a generalization across phonologically related words.

4. EXPERIMENTS

In a series of experiments, we trained networks with the architecture described in the previous section on the English-plural task[5] and non-assimilatory suffixation task.

Our results indicate that a network like this is capable of learning phonological rules by encoding underlying representations on the hidden layer and using them in recognition and production tasks. That is, given training on the singular, but not the plural of *hat,* we are later able to ask the network to generate the appropriate plural suffix following the stem or to tell us the number of /hæts/, a form it has never seen.

---

[4]A clique is a collection of units that have common functionality.

[5]See Gasser and Lee (1990) for more details about experiments on the acquisition of English plural morphemes.

For example, we would like to train the network on pairs like the following:

$$\text{CHIP} + \text{SINGULAR} \rightarrow \text{/t}\int\!\text{ıp/} \qquad (1)$$

$$\text{CHIP} + \text{PLURAL} \rightarrow \text{/t}\int\!\text{ıps/} \qquad (2)$$

$$\text{LIP} + \text{SINGULAR} \rightarrow \text{/lıp/} \qquad (3)$$

and then test it on pairs like the following to see if it yields correct phonological realizations:

$$\text{LIP} + \text{PLURAL} \rightarrow \text{??.} \qquad (4)$$

where the items in capitals represent meanings and expressions with phonetic symbols and slashes refer to forms.

A somewhat simpler test task, which would still offer evidence of generalization, is the following:

$$\text{LIP} + \text{PLURAL} \rightarrow \text{/lıp/} + \text{??.} \qquad (4')$$

However, this solves the problem in only the production direction. Our model should also predict meanings given forms. That is, we would like the model trained on Equations 5, 6, and 7 to be able to get the correct meaning in Equation 8 or just the correct grammatical number in Equation 8'.

$$\text{/t}\int\!\text{ıp/} \rightarrow \text{CHIP} + \text{SINGULAR} \qquad (5)$$

$$\text{/t}\int\!\text{ıps/} \rightarrow \text{CHIP} + \text{PLURAL} \qquad (6)$$

$$\text{/lıp/} \rightarrow \text{LIP} + \text{SINGULAR} \qquad (7)$$

$$\text{/lıps/} \rightarrow \text{??.} \qquad (8)$$

$$\text{/lıps/} \rightarrow \text{LIP} + \text{??.} \qquad (8')$$

4.1. Stimuli

Input words were composed of sequences of segments. We employed modified Chomsky–Halle phonetic features (Chomsky & Halle, 1968) and represented a segment with a vector of binary numbers: 1 for the presence of a particular feature and 0 for its absence. Traditional *generative phonology* (for an introduction, see Kenstowicz & Kisseberth, 1979) is based on the kind of phonological analyses that require the feature matrices that define the phonological inventory of the language in question, such as voicing, tenseness of vowels, tongue position, and so on. The distinctive features included are as shown in Table 8.1. Each segment type was uniquely specified as a binary vector of 13 or of 8 features depending on the tasks.

There were 20 words for each stimulation. Twelve of them were designated *training* words, eight *test* words. For each of these basic words, there was an

TABLE 8.1
Chomsky–Halle Distinctive
Feature Matrix

---

1. vocalic
2. consonantal
3. high
4. back
5. low
6. anterior
7. coronal
8. round
9. tense
10. voiced
11. continuant
12. nasal
13. strident

---

associated plural form. The network was trained on both the singular and plural forms of the training words and only on the singular forms of the test words. Words were presented one phonological segment at a time. Each word ended in a word boundary pattern consisting of all zeroes.

Stem meanings (hereafter referred to as *s-meaning*) were represented by arbitrary patterns consisting of 3 units on within the group of 6 s-meaning units.[6] A single unit represented grammatical number (hereafter *g-number*) of the word: 1 for plural and 0 singular.

4.2. Training Regimen

The input and target meaning patterns in the output layer were held constant throughout the presentation of a word (except in the simulation involving *uncertainty* described later).

Initially the network was trained on the *basic* autoassociation and prediction task: The network was always given noise-free segments and meanings as input; the desired outputs were the same segment plus meaning, as well as the next segment. This resulted in the desired learning in the prediction direction, but not in the perception direction: The network could predict the correct plural morpheme given the stem and the meaning, but it failed to come up with the correct g-number given the word and the s-meaning. To help the network learn in this direction, uncertainty was introduced in the input and the network was retrained: On four out of every five words, the network was given complete words and meanings as before. On one out of every five words, the input g-number was

---

[6]With six units to represent these in which exactly three units are turned on, we get $C(6, 3) = 20$ possible words.

TABLE 8.2
Inputs for the Word Chip for the "Unknown Number" Case

Segment		S-meaning	G-number
tʃ	CHIP	0.5	(target = 0)
ɪ	CHIP	previous NUMBER output	(target = 0)
p	CHIP	previous NUMBER output	(target = 0)

treated as unknown. That is, the g-number unit was set to an intermediate value of 0.5 word-initially and in the subsequent segments to the value that it took on the previous time step. For example, the inputs for the word *chip* for the "unknown number" case are given in Table 8.2.

Why did training with uncertainty improve the performance? First, the noise that resulted from having the g-number unit copy its activation value from the output layer effectively expanded the data set. Even though the network had to learn longer, it ultimately helped the network recognize better when it was given novel words. Second, the introduction of noise helped the network defer its decision on grammatical number until it saw any conclusive input data. Third, this training procedure was closer to the actual testing procedure, and it is assured that the trajectory of weight space moved along the desired paths.

Training continued until the network performed correctly on the training set, that is, until the error for every output was less than 0.05. The weights were then frozen and the network was tested for generalization.

4.3.   Experiment 1: English-Plural Task

4.3.1.   Method.   The overall structure of the network is as shown in Fig. 8.1. The *form clique* in the input and output layers consists of 13 units, which represent a phonological segment. Each *meaning clique* consists of 7 units: 6 for an s-meaning and 1 for the g-number. The network has 32 hidden units and 32 context units.[7]

The input corpus for this simulation consisted of 20 one-syllable English nouns as shown in Table 8.3. Twelve of these (*top, lip, ache, hat, Tom, saw, job, zone, judge, dish, page, catch*) were designated *training* words, whereas the other eight (*chip, bat, cake, mom, tub, tone, match, age*) were *test* words. Note that both the training and test words include nouns taking all three of the plural morpheme allophones. The network was trained until the error for every output was less than 0.05: 270 epochs for the first run; 160 for the second.[8]

---

[7]Pilot studies were performed to estimate the optimum size of the hidden layer. Smaller hidden layers might give us a better picture of the underlying representation at the cost of performance. Our primary concern was our model's performance.

[8]The backpropagation learning algorithm is sensitive to initial weights (Kolen & Pollack, 1990), so we ran two separate simulations.

TABLE 8.3
List of Words and their Representations Used in the English Plural Acquisition Task

Words	ASCII Transcript	IPA Transcript	Training	Testing
top	tap	tɑp	x	
lip	llp	lɪp	x	
ache	ek	eɪk	x	
hat	hAt	hæt	x	
Tom	tam	tɑm	x	
saw	s)	sɔ	x	
job	j ˆb*	ʤɑb	x	
zone	zon	zon	x	
judge	j ˆj	ʤʌʤ	x	
dish	dlS	dɪʃ	x	
page	pej	peɪʤ	x	
catch	kAC	kætʃ	x	
chip	Clp	tʃɪp		x
bat	bAt	bæt		x
cake	kek	keɪk		x
mom	mam	mɑm		x
tub	t ˆb	tʌb		x
tone	ton	ton		x
match	mAC	mætʃ		x
age	ej	eɪʤ		x

*This should be *jab*. Unfortunately the error was discovered in the last minute; yet we do not think it would have affected the results of our experiments.

4.3.2. Results. Two separate simulations were run with different random initial weights. The results are stated in terms of the two separate runs.

To test the network's performance on the production task, we gave the network the appropriate segments for the stem successively, along with the meaning of that stem and the g-number unit on for plural. We then examined the prediction output units at the point where the plural morpheme should appear. Thus the network was pushed along the right path through *teacher forcing;*[9] the task is that of Equation 4' in the beginning of section 4 rather than Equation 4. Based on Euclidian distance, we converted each output pattern to the nearest phoneme. The network predicted the correct segments for all but 2 of the stem segments and 14 of the 16 suffixes in the two runs. The two suffix errors involved substituting /tʃ/ for /s/ in *bats* and /f/ for /z/ in *tones*.

To test the perception performance, we gave the network the sequence of input segments of a word, set the stem meaning units to the appropriate pattern, and set the g-number unit initially to 0.5, that is, to unknown. At the presentation of each new segment, the g-number unit was copied from the output on the previous

---

[9]On each time step, the correct segment was provided as input rather than the one the network predicted.

time step. We then examined the output g-number unit after the appearance of either the appropriate plural form or the word boundary. Thus, with respect to stem meaning, teacher forcing was again used, and the network's task was that of Equation 8' rather than Equation 8 as shown in the beginning of section 4. For the training words, the output g-number unit fluctuated around 0.5 until the relevant information was given. Then it correctly turned on or off according to whether the word boundary or plural ending appeared. For the test words, the network consistently output 0 before the appearance of the relevant information. This is not surprising because the network only saw singular forms during training. When the word boundary appeared in the input, the output unit correctly turned off. When the plural morpheme appeared, the output of the g-number unit was correct for 15 of the 16 test items. In the only error, the network treated the novel plural pattern chips as singular. Results are summarized in Table 8.4.

We have also been able to train the network to generate entire phonological words given only their meanings and produce complete stem meanings given only the phonological words, but this has not been possible with novel combinations, that is, for the plural forms of the test words (Equations 4 and 8).

4.3.3.   *Analysis.*   Where does this leave underlying representations? In the connectionist network already described, it is the pattern on the hidden layer that mediates the relation between form and meaning; therefore, these patterns are the analogue of underlying representations in our networks. We employed teacher forcing in training, so the hidden representation of the stem for a given word is naturally similar during the perception and the production tasks; thus, it is not possible to draw a conclusion about underlying representations for the stems.

The question that needs to be asked is: Is there a single hidden-layer pattern shared by different realizations of the plural morpheme? This chapter points out that analysis of the hidden layers of the network indicates that certain units there are dedicated to representing the plural morpheme, independent of its surface form. Thus it appears that our network has the capacity to learn distributed underlying representations.

Initially, we analyzed the hidden unit representations that the network developed during the first run of the English-plural task. Figure 8.3 shows a box plot of the hidden unit activations of 18 randomly picked words (test words as well as

TABLE 8.4
Results of English Plural Acquisition Experiment

	Perception (%)		Production (%)		
	Sg	Pl	Sg	Pl	n
Training	100	100	100	100	24
Testing	100	93.8	100	87.5	16

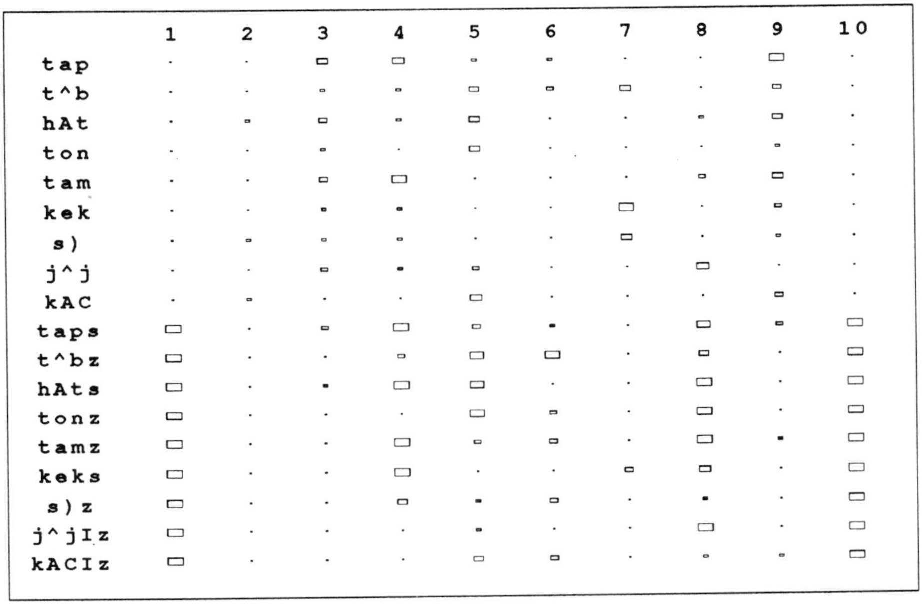

	1	2	3	4	5	6	7	8	9	10
t a p	·	·	□	□	▫	▪	·	·	□	·
t ^ b	·	·	▫	▫	□	▫	□	·	▫	·
h A t	·	▫	□	▫	□	·	·	▫	□	·
t o n	·	·	▫	·	□	·	·	·	▫	·
t a m	·	·	□	□	·	·	·	▫	□	·
k e k	·	·	▫	▪	·	·	□	·	▫	·
s)	·	▫	▫	▫	·	·	□	·	▫	·
j ^ j	·	·	▫	▪	▫	·	·	□	·	·
k A C	·	▫	·	·	□	·	·	·	▫	·
t a p s	□	·	▫	□	▫	▪	·	□	▫	□
t ^ b z	□	·	·	▫	□	□	·	▫	·	□
h A t s	□	·	▪	□	□	·	·	□	·	□
t o n z	□	·	·	·	□	▫	·	□	·	□
t a m z	□	·	·	□	▫	▫	·	□	▪	□
k e k s	□	·	·	□	·	·	▫	▫	·	□
s) z	□	·	·	▫	▪	▫	·	▪	·	□
j ^ j I z	□	·	·	·	▪	·	·	□	·	□
k A C I z	□	·	·	·	□	▫	·	▫	·	□

FIG. 8.3.   Box plot of hidden layer activations before recognizing plurality during the perception task in the first English-plural run.

training words) at the segment before it recognizes the plurality (perception task), that is, just after the appropriate plural form was input for plural or after the word boundary for singular words. Only 10 selected units are shown in the figure. Big boxes represent activation values close to 1.0 and dots denote values close to 0.0. From the figure it appears that unit 1 and unit 10 distinguish plurality. But further analysis shows that unit 1 always responds to the sibilant phonemes, such as /s/, /z/, and /ʤ/ regardless of their positions (see Fig. 8.4).

Figure 8.4 shows the hidden unit activations for the words *judge, saws, zones,* and *chips* after each segment is presented during the perception task. In the figure "#" denotes a word boundary. Let us examine unit 10 more closely. For *judge* it is always off, yet for *saws* and *zones,* it correctly turns on after /z/ is input, signaling that it is a plural. For *chips* it turns on after /p/ is presented, making a spurious prediction (and quickly turns off when the word boundary is available, which is not shown in the figure) and stays on when /s/ is given at the next time step. In a word, unit 10 is not turned on until it has enough information to decide the number of the word in question.

Now what happens when the network is given the production task? In this case we found that unit 11 is responsible for producing plural morphemes; the unit is on for the singular words and off for the plural words.

Figure 8.5 shows a plot of hidden unit activations for the production task after

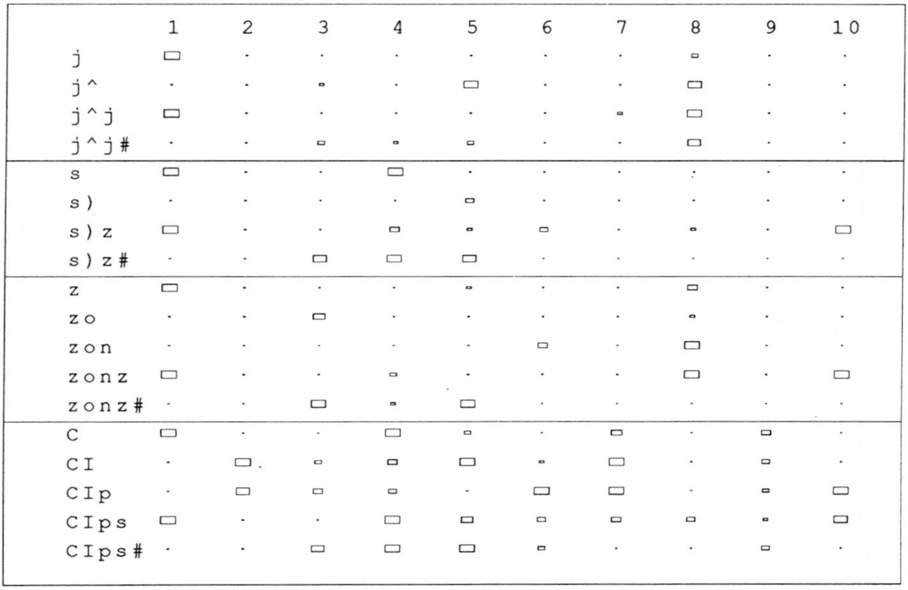

	1	2	3	4	5	6	7	8	9	10
j	□	·	·	·	·	·	·	▫	·	·
j ^	·	·	▫	·	□	·	·	□	·	·
j ^ j	□	·	·	·	·	·	▫	□	·	·
j ^ j #	·	·	▫	▫	▫	·	·	□	·	·
s	□	·	·	□	·	·	·	⁚	·	·
s)	·	·	·	·	□	·	·	·	·	·
s) z	□	·	·	▫	▫	▫	·	▫	·	□
s) z #	·	·	□	□	□	·	·	·	·	·
z	□	·	·	·	▫	·	·	□	·	·
z o	·	·	□	·	·	·	·	▫	·	·
z o n	·	·	·	·	·	▫	·	□	·	·
z o n z	□	·	·	▫	·	·	·	□	·	□
z o n z #	·	·	□	▫	□	·	·	·	·	·
C	□	·	·	□	▫	·	□	·	▫	·
C I	·	□ .	▫	▫	□	▫	□	·	▫	·
C I p	·	□	▫	▫	·	□	□	·	▫	□
C I p s	□	·	·	□	□	▫	▫	▫	▫	□
C I p s #	·	·	□	□	□	▫	·	·	▫	·

FIG. 8.4. Box plot of hidden layer activations for some of the words showing that unit 1 is responsive to the sibilant phoneme and unit 10 encodes plurality during the perception task in the first English-plural run.

	11	12	13	14	15	16	17	18	19	20
t a p	□	·	·	▫	·	□	·	▫	□	□
t ^ b	□	·	·	▫	▫	·	·	·	·	□
h A t	□	·	·	·	▫	▫	·	□	·	▫
t o n	□	·	□	·	▫	▫	·	·	·	▫
t a m	□	·	▫	▫	·	·	·	▫	·	▫
k e k	□	▪	·	·	·	□	·	·	□	▫
s)	·	·	▫	□	▫	□	□	·	□	□
j ^ j	▪	·	□	·	▫	□	·	·	·	·
k A C	□	▫	□	□	▫	▫	·	□	·	·
t a p s	·	·	·	▫	·	·	·	▫	□	·
t ^ b z	·	·	·	□	▫	·	·	·	·	·
h A t s	·	·	·	·	▪	·	·	□	·	·
t o n z	▫	·	□	·	▫	·	·	·	·	·
t a m z	·	·	▪	□	·	·	·	▪	·	·
k e k s	·	·	·	·	·	·	·	·	□	·
s) z	·	·	·	□	▪	·	□	·	□	·
j ^ j I z	·	·	□	·	▫	·	·	·	·	·
k A C I z	·	·	□	□	▫	·	·	□	·	·

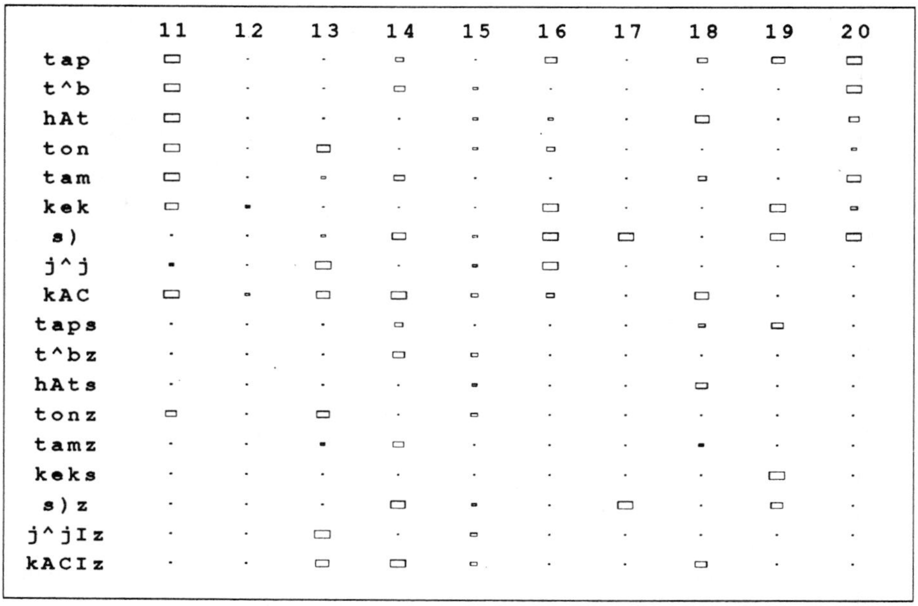

FIG. 8.5. Box plot of hidden layer activations after the stems are input during the production task in the first English-plural run.

the stems were presented. In the figure, 10 different units are shown selected from the same 32 hidden units.[10] Unit 11 for *saw* is off. Even though it correctly predicts the word boundary with the current threshold of 0.5, if we were to use the lower threshold, it predicts /z/, which is the plural for the word. The activation value of unit 11 for *judge* is very small. Again it is close to predicting /ɪ/, which would come next if it were a plural. The activation of unit 11 for *tons* is high; it predicts /f/ instead of /z/. One might argue that because number is presented in the input layer the unit can easily represent it by simply copying the value. But this is not the case. The unit turns on only after the stem for singular words.

Figure 8.6 shows the hidden unit activations for the words *hat* and *Tom* after each segment is presented during the production task. If unit 11 were simply copying the value of the number unit in the input layer, it would be on all the time for the singular words. But it is not. It is turned on only after the stem, where the singular occurs. Table 8.5 shows the mean values of unit 11's activations across all the input words at before-stem-end, at-stem-end, and after-stem-end in the word.[11] This clearly shows that only after the stems were presented did the unit turn on for the singular words, signaling the word boundary. For plural words, it remained off, producing plural morphemes.

So far we have examined the behavior of the hidden units during the first run to see if they encode an underlying representation for plurality and have shown that unit 10 acts as a detector for the g-number during the perception task whereas unit 11 is responsible for producing the plural morpheme. At this point, some questions arise: Was it just a fortunate coincidence that we were able to find some units that encode plurality? Or is it really safe to say that our network developed an underlying representation? To answer these questions we analyzed the other run.

In the second run, it turned out that unit 6 acts as a detector for the g-number for both perception and production tasks. Figure 8.7 shows a box plot for 18 randomly picked words during the perception task in the second run. Only the first 10 units are shown. From the figure we can easily see that unit 6 is responsible for the g-number. The activation value of unit 6 for *chips* is very small, around 0.2. This is the word for which the network made a wrong prediction: It predicts singular. We can safely say that the activation value of unit 6 is consistent with the results of the prediction task. By looking at Fig. 8.7, we might be able to say that unit 10 is also sensitive to the g-number. But further analysis shows that this is not the case. In Fig. 8.8 we can see that unit 10 is on with the singular as well as plural nouns.

Figure 8.8 shows the hidden unit activations for the words *hat* and *Tom* after

---

[10]The numbers 11 to 20 were used to distinguish them from the previous 10 units.

[11]The numbers were obtained from the integer rounded activation values; even though some of the numbers shown in the figure are 0.000, they are in fact a little bigger than zero.

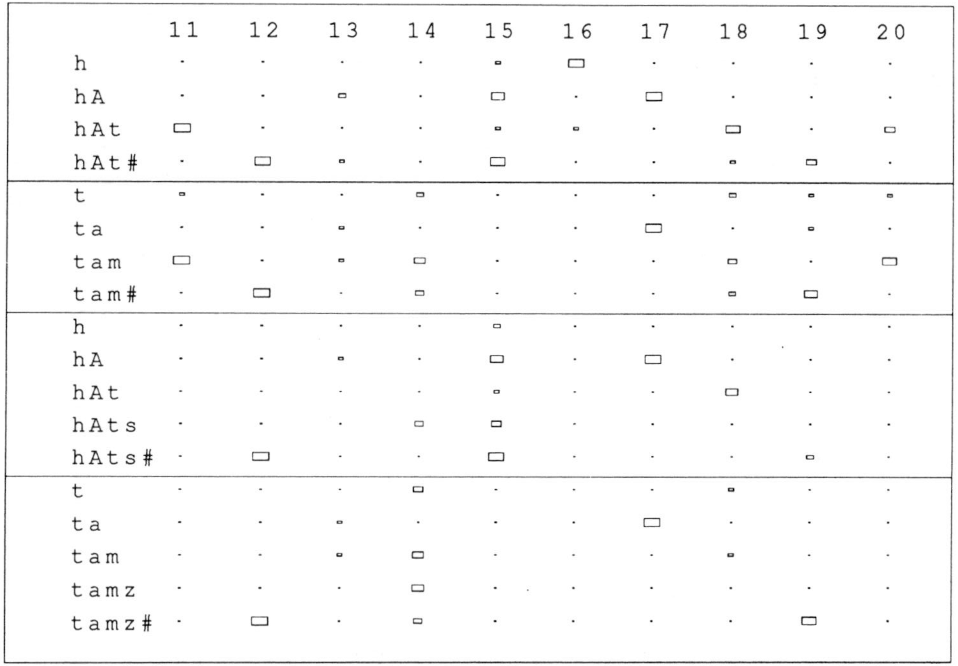

FIG. 8.6. Box plot of hidden layer activations for *hat* and *Tom* after each segment is presented during a production task in the first English-plural run (including word boundary).

TABLE 8.5
Mean Values of Unit 11 Activations Across the Input Words
During a Production Task in the First English-Plural Run

	Training		Test	
	Sg	Pl	Sg	Pl
Before Stem	0.033	0.000	0.206	0.000
At Stem	0.642	0.000	0.813	0.075
After Stem	0.008	0.000	0.038	0.000

each segment is presented during the perception task. Again, let us examine unit 6 more closely. For *Tom* it is always off, yet for *Toms,* it correctly turns on after /z/ is input, signaling that it is a plural. For *hat* it turns on after /t/ is presented, making a false prediction, and quickly turns off when additional information (the word boundary) is available. For *hats* it correctly predicts that the word is plural.

Now what happens when the network is given the production task? Figure 8.9 shows another plot of hidden unit activations for the production task, that is, after the stems were presented. Again unit 6 tells us if the next segment should be a plural or a singular. As with the case of the first run, it changes its value only

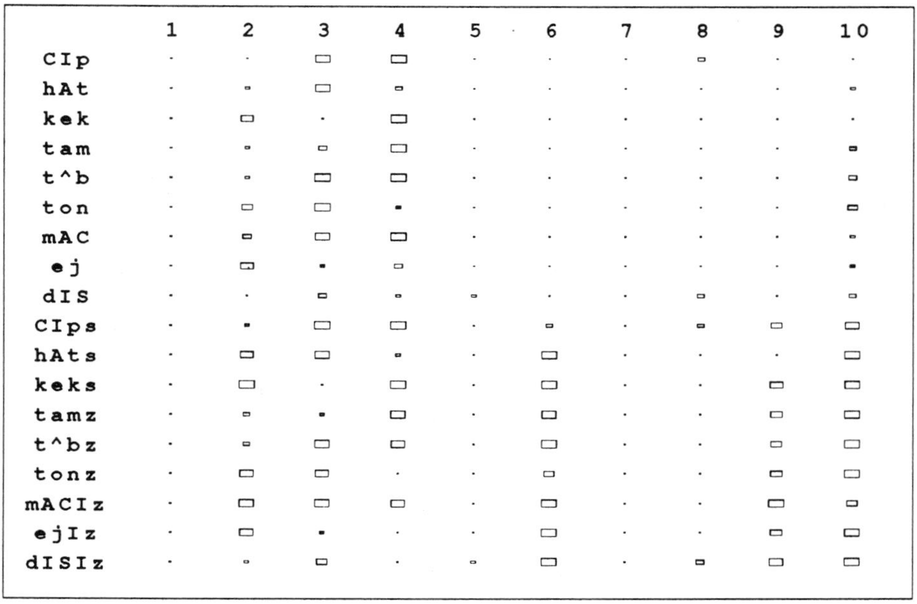

	1	2	3	4	5	6	7	8	9	10
C I p	.	.	□	□	.	.	.	▫	.	.
h A t	.	▫	□	▫	.	.	.	.	.	▫
k e k	.	□	.	□	.	.	.	.	.	.
t a m	.	▫	▫	□	.	.	.	.	.	▫
t ^ b	.	▫	□	□	.	.	.	.	.	▫
t o n	.	□	□	▪	.	.	.	.	.	▪
m A C	.	▫	□	□	.	.	.	.	.	▫
e j	.	□	▪	▫	.	.	.	.	.	▪
d I S	.	.	▫	▫	▫	.	.	▫	.	▫
C I p s	.	▪	□	□	.	▫	.	▫	□	□
h A t s	.	□	□	▪	.	□	.	.	.	□
k e k s	.	□	.	□	.	□	.	.	□	□
t a m z	.	▫	▪	□	.	□	.	.	□	□
t ^ b z	.	▫	□	□	.	□	.	.	□	□
t o n z	.	□	□	.	.	▫	.	.	□	□
m A C I z	.	□	□	□	.	□	.	.	□	▫
e j I z	.	□	▪	.	.	□	.	.	□	□
d I S I z	.	▫	□	.	▫	□	.	▫	□	□

FIG. 8.7. Box plot of hidden layer activations before recognizing the plurality during perception task in the second English-plural run.

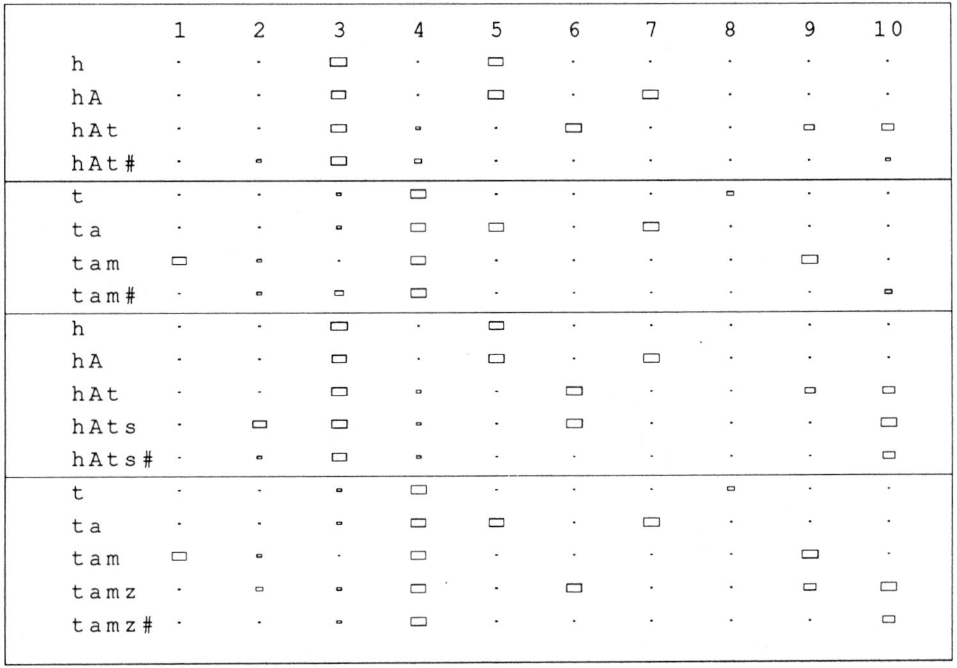

FIG. 8.8. Box plot of hidden layer activations for *hat* and *Tom* after each segment is presented during a perception task (including word boundary) in the second run.

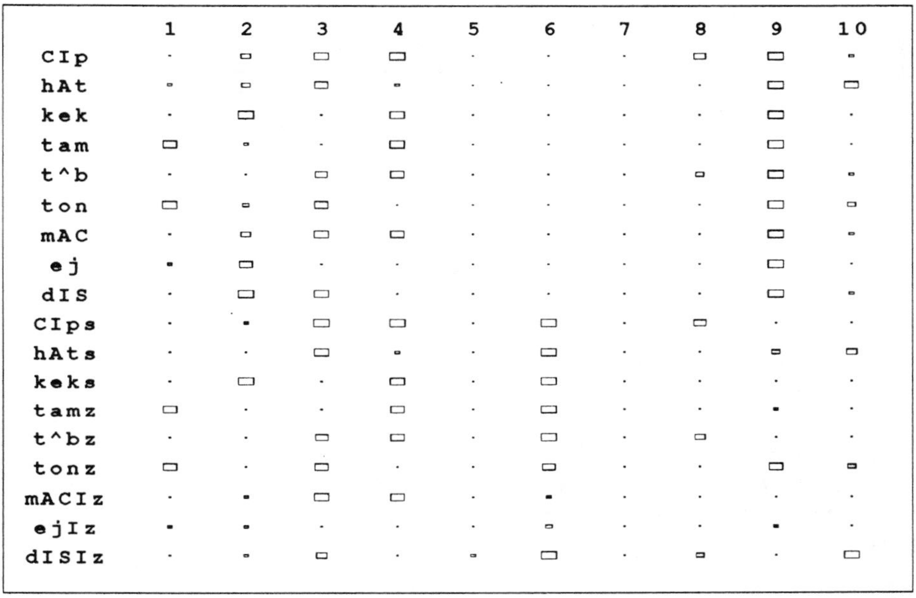

	1	2	3	4	5	6	7	8	9	10
C I p	·	▫	□	□	·	·	·	▫	□	▪
h A t	▪	▫	□	▪	·	·	·	·	□	□
k e k	·	□	·	□	·	·	·	·	□	·
t a m	□	▪	·	□	·	·	·	·	□	·
t ^ b	·	·	▫	□	·	·	·	▫	□	▪
t o n	□	▫	□	·	·	·	·	·	□	▫
m A C	·	▫	□	□	·	·	·	·	□	▪
e j	▪	□	·	·	·	·	·	·	□	·
d I S	·	□	□	·	·	·	·	·	□	▪
C I p s	·	▪	□	□	·	□	·	□	·	·
h A t s	·	·	□	▪	·	□	·	·	▫	□
k e k s	·	□	·	□	·	□	·	·	·	·
t a m z	□	·	·	□	·	□	·	·	▪	·
t ^ b z	·	·	□	□	·	□	·	▫	·	·
t o n z	□	·	□	·	·	□	·	·	□	▫
m A C I z	·	▪	□	□	·	▪	·	·	·	·
e j I z	▪	▪	·	·	·	▫	·	·	▪	·
d I S I z	·	▪	□	·	▫	□	·	▫	·	□

FIG. 8.9. Box plot of hidden layer activations after the stems are input during production task in the second English-plural run.

after the stem. For the cases of *matches* and *ages,* the values are small, 0.1 and 0.2 respectively. This seems to be because of the insertion of the vowel /ɪ/.

4.4. Experiment 2: Non-Assimilatory Suffixation Task

After the English-plural runs, we asked this question: Does the network really encode the notion of plurality, or does it just encode the rule that adds a sibilant, /s/ or /z/, at the end of the nouns taking advantage of the phonetic cue that points to the right suffix by way of assimilation? In other words, can the network produce correct results and encode g-number even when there is no phonetic relationship between the suffixes? If the answer is yes, it might give us stronger grounds for our claim that our model indeed represents underlying plural on the hidden layer. To answer this question we ran the non-assimilatory suffixation task.

4.4.1. Method and Results. For this run we used a smaller network by representing a segment with only 8 binary features[12]: The input layer had 15

[12]Only *vocalic, high, back, anterior, coronal, voice, strident,* and *round* were used.

TABLE 8.6
Results of Non-Assimilatory Suffixation Task

	Perception		Production		
	Sg	Pl	Sg	Pl	n
Training	100	100	100	100	12
Testing	100	75.0	100	75.0	8

units, the hidden layer 21, and the output layer 23. The input corpus consisted of 20 CVC[13] randomly generated words from an artificial language. The plurals of the words were constructed by adding either an /o/ after the voiced stem or /s/ after the voiceless stem.

The network was trained according to the schedule as described in the section on training regimen. After the model responded perfectly to the training data, the network predicted the correct segments for all of the training words and six of eight test words. The output g-number unit was correct for all training words and six test words. The results are summarized in Table 8.6.

4.4.2. Analysis.   Are there really some units on the hidden layer that are dedicated to representing the plural morpheme, not just the sibilant phoneme? To answer this question, we analyzed the hidden unit representations that the network developed during the non-assimilatory suffixation run.

Figure 8.10 shows a box plot of hidden unit activations of 18 randomly picked words at the segment before it recognizes plurality during the perception task in the non-assimilatory suffixation run. From the figure we can see that unit 3 clearly distinguishes singular words from plural ones.

Now what happens when the network is given the production task? Figure 8.11 shows another plot of hidden unit activations for the production task in the non-assimilatory suffixation run. From the figure we can see that the box sizes for unit 2 and unit 5 are quite different for singular nouns than for plural nouns. Further analysis (see Fig. 8.12) shows that unit 2 turns on only after the stems are given, indicating that what comes next should be a singular morpheme. In Fig. 8.12 only four words are shown. In fact, we used the same kind of analysis as shown in Table 8.5 for the production task in the non-assimilatory suffixation run, obtaining the same results.

4.5. Summary of the Results

Though the analysis of hidden unit representations during the English plural morpheme acquisition task and the non-assimilatory suffixation task, we have

---

[13]C stands for consonant, and V for vowel.

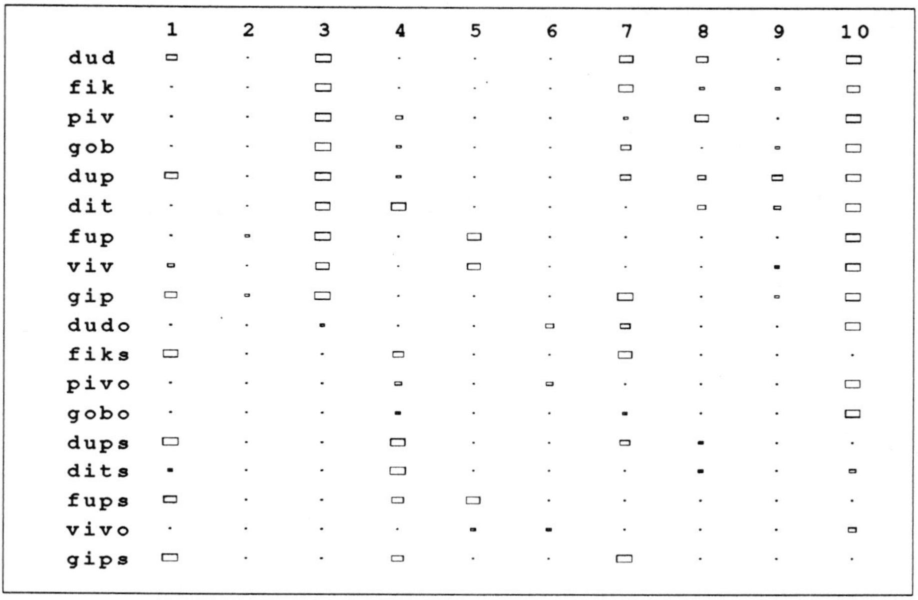

	1	2	3	4	5	6	7	8	9	10
dud	□	·	□	·	·	·	□	□	·	□
fik	·	·	□	·	·	·	□	□	□	□
piv	·	·	□	□	·	·	□	□	·	□
gob	·	·	□	□	·	·	□	·	□	□
dup	□	·	□	□	·	·	□	□	□	□
dit	·	·	□	□	·	·	·	□	□	□
fup	·	□	□	·	□	·	·	·	·	□
viv	□	·	□	·	□	·	·	·	□	□
gip	□	□	□	·	·	·	□	·	□	□
dudo	·	·	□	·	·	□	□	·	·	□
fiks	□	·	·	□	·	·	□	·	·	·
pivo	·	·	·	□	·	□	·	·	·	□
gobo	·	·	·	□	·	·	□	·	·	□
dups	□	·	·	□	·	·	□	□	·	·
dits	□	·	·	□	·	·	·	□	·	□
fups	□	·	·	□	□	·	·	·	·	·
vivo	·	·	·	·	□	□	·	·	·	□
gips	□	·	·	□	·	·	□	·	·	·

FIG. 8.10. Box plot of hidden layer activations before recognizing the plurality during perception task in the non-assimilatory suffixation run.

	1	2	3	4	5	6	7	8	9	10
dud	□	□	·	·	□	·	·	·	·	·
fik	·	□	·	·	□	·	·	□	□	·
piv	·	□	·	·	□	·	·	·	·	·
gob	·	□	·	·	□	·	·	·	·	·
dup	□	□	·	·	□	·	·	□	□	·
dit	□	□	·	□	□	·	·	□	■	·
fup	·	□	·	·	□	·	·	·	·	□
viv	·	□	·	·	□	·	·	·	·	·
gip	□	□	·	·	□	·	□	□	□	□
dudo	□	·	·	·	·	·	·	·	·	·
fiks	□	·	·	·	□	□	·	□	□	·
pivo	·	·	·	·	·	·	·	·	·	·
gobo	·	·	·	·	·	·	·	·	■	·
dups	□	·	·	·	·	·	·	□	□	■
dits	□	·	·	□	·	·	·	□	■	·
fups	·	·	·	·	·	·	·	□	·	□
vivo	■	·	·	·	·	·	·	·	■	·
gips	□	□	·	·	·	·	□	□	□	□

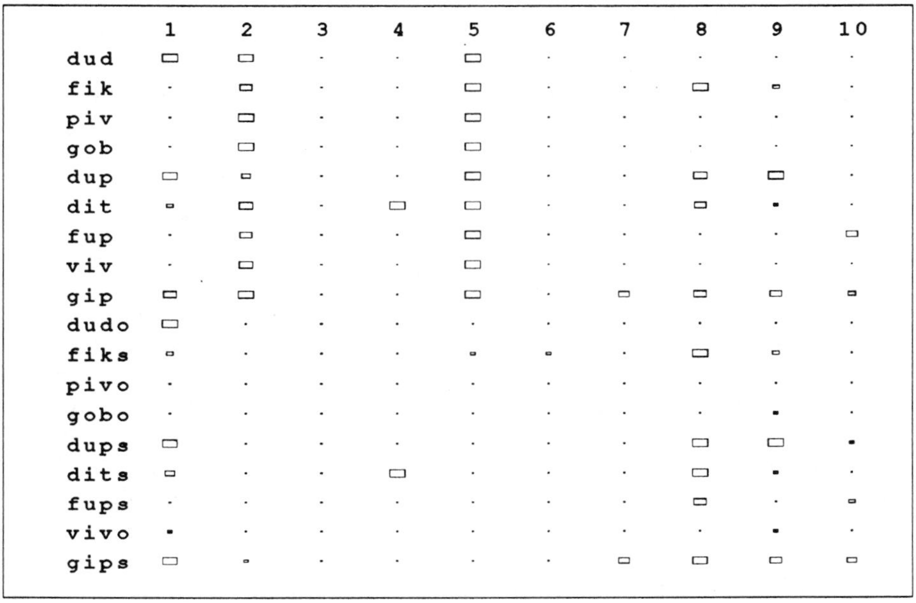

FIG. 8.11. Box plot of hidden layer activations after the stems are input during production task in the non-assimilatory suffixation run.

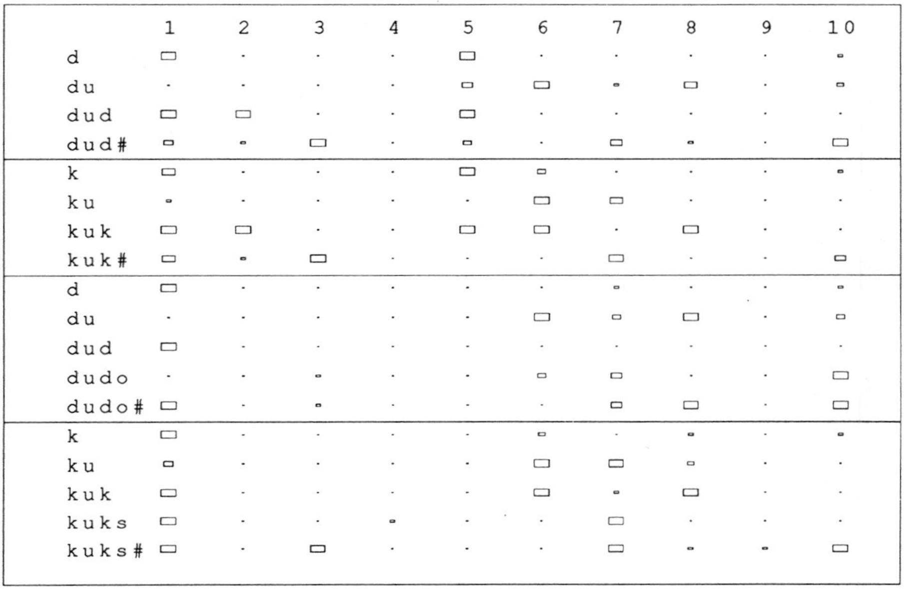

	1	2	3	4	5	6	7	8	9	10
d	□	·	·	·	□	·	·	·	·	▫
d u	·	·	·	·	▫	□	▫	□	·	▫
d u d	□	□	·	·	□	·	·	·	·	·
d u d #	▫	▫	□	·	▫	·	□	▫	·	□
k	□	·	·	·	□	▫	·	·	·	▫
k u	▫	·	·	·	·	□	□	·	·	·
k u k	□	□	·	·	□	□	·	□	·	·
k u k #	□	▫	□	·	·	·	□	·	·	▫
d	□	·	·	·	·	·	▫	·	·	▫
d u	·	·	·	·	·	□	▫	□	·	▫
d u d	□	·	·	·	·	·	·	·	·	·
d u d o	·	·	▫	·	·	▫	□	·	·	□
d u d o #	□	·	▫	·	·	·	▫	□	·	□
k	□	·	·	·	·	▫	·	▫	·	▫
k u	▫	·	·	·	·	□	□	▫	·	·
k u k	□	·	·	·	·	□	▫	□	·	·
k u k s	□	·	□	▫	·	·	□	·	·	·
k u k s #	□	·	□	□	·	·	□	▫	▫	□

FIG. 8.12. Box plot of hidden layer activations for *dud* and *kuk* after each segment is presented during a production task in the non-assimilatory suffixation run.

shown that the network indeed encodes underlying plural as a distributed representation. In the analysis of hidden representations during the first English-plural run and the non-assimilatory suffixation run, we were not able to find a single unit responsible for plurality; rather two units were involved, one for perception and the other for production. Also the encodings were found to be different in three runs. In the first English-plural run the g-number unit was on for plural in the perception task, whereas the other unit was on for the singular nouns in the production task. The g-number unit was on for plural nouns during both perception and production tasks in the second English-plural run. The units responsible for g-number in the non-assimilatory suffixation run were on for singular nouns during both perception and production tasks. Despite the differences among these runs, we can safely say that there are certain units that are responsible for detecting the g-number. For a given morpheme, English plural or an artificial plural, there is a commonality among the hidden layer patterns for all realizations of the morpheme. And in one case, the network chose to dedicate the same unit to representing plurality for both tasks. (This may not have been a coincidence; the probability of choosing the same unit twice is around 0.11, considerably smaller than the 0.33 we got.) This is what is required for an underlying representation to be part of competence.

5. DISCUSSION

Our model successfully learned a phonological rule by making generalizations from the exemplars on the connection weights during the process of learning. The set of weights the model developed in producing the desired plural morphemes constrained the model's outputs to follow the desired patterns, and what looks like a rule is in fact embodied in these weights. Even though the network does not yet achieve all that we would like, the results indicate that it has the ability to learn apparent rule-governed phonological processes in a manner that makes use of associations between forms and meanings.

The analogues of underlying representations are encoded as a distributed representation on the hidden layer that the network develops. As has been clearly shown in this chapter, this underlying representation is phonological and not simply the encoding of the meaning feature PLURAL in the hidden layer.

Despite its successes, the RM model suffers from many deficiencies. Our model responds to some of the problems raised by Pinker and Prince (1988). First, because this model makes use of the association between forms and meanings, it is readily available to distinguish phonologically ambiguous words such as *son* and *sun* unlike other models that do not employ meanings as input at all.

Second, the kind of *dynamic* representation employed in our model, together with the more realistic tasks of production and perception, results in constraints on what can be learned. In particular, the system has difficulty learning several processes that are not found in any human languages and the RM model was capable of doing. This result is extensively discussed in Gasser and Lee (1991).

Third, our model has the capacity to distinguish all words. The Wickelfeatures employed by RM are a very ad hoc way of acquiring context sensitivity; this scheme has the problem that distinct lexical items may be associated with identical representations. An SRN avoids this problem by utilizing a STM, achieving the context sensitivity in a more natural and constrained way, a way that Pinker and Prince did not envision.

An important question for future investigation concerns what happens in cases where the traditional analysis posits a sequence of rules operating on intermediate representations at different levels of abstraction. Ordered-rule interaction is a necessary foundation for conventional generative phonology. For example, consider the pronunciation of *writing* /raytiŋ/ and *riding* /raydiŋ/. In some dialects of English, they differ phonetically just in that the stressed vowel of the former is shorter than the stressed vowel of the latter, the medial consonant in both cases being a voiced flap /ɾ/. To account for this phenomenon, two rules should be applied in the order specified here:

1. *Vowel Lengthening*. Make vowel long before voiced consonant.
2. *Flapping*. Change /t/ or /d/ to flap /ɾ/ between vowel, if the first vowel is stressed.

If we apply rule 2 before rule 1, we have the same pronunciation /ray:riŋ/ for both *writing* and *riding,* which is wrong.

In an effort to eliminate the need for rule orderings, Touretzky and Wheeler (see Touretzky & Wheeler, 1990, among others) developed a model with three different layers based on the ideas of Lakoff (Lakoff, 1988, 1989). In Lakoff's theory, and also in Touretzky and Wheeler's implementation, there are three distinct levels of representation: the morphemic (M), the phonemic (P), and the phonetic (F). Phonological processes expressed as rules in standard theories are instead treated as *constructions* of two types:

1. Cross-level M-P and P-F constructions, which state allowable correlations between levels.
2. Intralevel P and F constructions, which state well-formedness constraints within a level.

There are no explicit rule orderings; all constructions at a given level apply simultaneously. However, by allowing both inter- and intralevel constructions, the theory achieves the effect of an extrinsic rule ordering.

Is our network as it is powerful enough to produce correct outputs when there are some alleged rule interactions? Do we need to make some modifications to our model to incorporate rule interactions? Will changing some of the parameters affect the behavior of the networks enough to accommodate the seemingly more difficult problems? We have not tried more difficult problems involving rule interactions, so we are not able to answer these questions. Modifying the training regimen to learning in stages might be enough: The network learns the easier rules first and then is gradually introduced to more difficult tasks. But at the moment we speculate that our model should have more hidden layers to correctly encode several rules and underlying representations: The network might need inherent rule orderings. For example, our network might be able to learn the rule-interactions shown earlier with two hidden layers: One hidden layer encodes the rules and underlying representations and the other controls the order of rule applications. But precisely how this might work is still unclear.

We employed the teacher forcing training technique in the experiments reported in this chapter. We have also been able to train the network to generate entire words given only their meanings and to produce complete stem meanings given only words. However, this has not been possible with novel combinations, that is, for the plural forms of the test words (Equations 4 and 8 in the beginning of section 4). When and if we are successful on this task, we will need to examine the hidden representations of the stems to see if any commonality can be found that could be analogous to underlying representations for those stems.

The experiment reported here was carried out on only a small number of inputs in the corpus. To be able to claim the plausibility of this model as an adequate system for modeling phonological phenomena, we need to expand our study to include more data and to cover different types of phonological processes. For example, the model should handle irregular plural as well as the regular plural morpheme alternations.

The representation scheme used in this study, that is, phonetic feature representation, is borrowed from standard generative theory. Feature bundle representations do not in themselves fully reconstruct the systematic nature of the actual phonological phenomena. There are other kinds of representational schemes. For example, a more recent theory, *nonlinear phonology,* departs from the feature matrix type of representation and posits a different kind of representation: a nonlinear representation, where features are organized in tiers (cf. Goldsmith, 1990). Of course, it would be even more desirable if inputs were raw speech data. However, given the scope of the task here, the decision was to utilize a generative-type feature matrix; the use of a feature matrix seems unproblematic for the current study, and the decision to borrow it from standard generative phonology does not bear on the model's performance.

6. CONCLUSION

In this chapter, we have discussed the problem of learning phonology and showed how a recurrent connectionist network can learn the English plural morpheme and an artificial plural morpheme without explicit rules or underlying representations. The model successfully learns phonological rules by abstracting the generalization from the exemplars on the connection weights in the process of learning. The set of weights the model developed in the process of producing desired plural morphemes constrains the model's outputs to follow the desired patterns, and what looks like a rule is in fact the generalization embodied in these weights. The results indicate that it has the ability to learn apparent rule-governed phonological processes in a manner that makes use of associations between forms and meanings, thus eliminating the need for presupposing abstract underlying representations and rules, which constitute the major part of generative phonology. This model answers many of the questions raised by Pinker and Prince (1988) on RM's past-tense model by employing a different type of architecture and input representations. For instance, it easily distinguishes homophonous words. Also, the nature of the training task constrains the system in such a way that certain rules that are nonoccurring in natural language cannot be learned.

As far as we know, the study reported here is one of the first attempts to train a single recurrent network on both production and perception tasks. Finally, the network avoids problems with using windowed input; it uses more psychologically plausible continuous input.

We believe our study has shed some light on how a particular type of cognitive phenomenon can be accounted for without reference to explicit symbols or rules.

It remains to be seen how much of a gap is still to be bridged between our approach to the relatively trivial processes dealt with here and the elaborate mechanisms posited by traditional phonology or by their connectionist descendants (Touretzky & Wheeler, 1990) for handling complex processes.

REFERENCES

Chomsky, N., & Halle, M. (1968). *The sound pattern of English*. New York: Harper & Row.

Elman, J. (1989). *Representation and structure in connectionist models*. (Tech. Rep. No. 8903). La Jolla: University of California, Center for Research in Language.

Elman, J. (1990). Finding structure in time. *Cognitive Science, 14*, 179–211.

Fodor, J., & Pylyshyn, Z. (1988). Connectionism and cognitive architecture: A critical analysis. In S. Pinker & J. Mehler (Eds.), *Connections and symbols* (pp. 3–71). Cambridge, MA: MIT Press.

Gasser, M., & Lee, C.-D. (1990). Networks that learn about phonological feature persistence. *Connection Science, 2*, 265–278.

Gasser, M., & Lee, C.-D. (1991). A short-term memory architecture for the learning of morphophonemic rules. In R. Lippman, J. Moody, & D. Touretzky (Eds.), *Advances in neural information processing systems 3*. (pp. 605–611). San Mateo: CA: Morgan Kaufmann.

Goldsmith, J. (1990). *Autosegmental and metrical phonology*. Cambridge, England: Basil Blackwell.

Jordan, M. (1986). Attractor dynamics and parallelism in a connectionist sequential machine. In *Proceedings of the Eighth Annual Conference of the Cognitive Science Society* (pp. 531–546). Hillsdale, NJ: Lawrence Erlbaum Associates.

Kenstowicz, M., & Kisseberth, C. (1979). *Generative phonology*. New York: Academic Press.

Kolen, J., & Pollack, J. (1990). Back propagation is sensitive to initial conditions. *Complex Systems, 4*, 269–280.

Lachter, J., & Bever, T. (1988). The relationship between linguistic structure and associative theories of language learning: A constructive critique of some connectionist learning models. In S. Pinker & J. Mehler (Eds.), *Connections and symbols* (pp. 195–247). Cambridge, MA: MIT Press.

Lakoff, G. (1988). A suggestion for a linguistics with connectionist foundations. In *Proceedings of the 1988 Connectionist Models Summer School* (pp. 301–314). San Mateo, CA: Morgan Kaufmann.

Lakoff, G. (1989, May). Cognitive Phonology. Paper presented at the Constraints Versus Rules Workshop. University of California, Berkely.

Lee, C. D. (1991). Learning to perceive and produce words in connectionist networks. (Report No. 334) Bloomington, IN: Indiana University.

Marchman, V., & Plunkett, K. (1989). Token frequency and phonological predictability in a pattern association network: Implications for child language acquisition. In *Proceedings of the 11th Annual Conference of the Cognitive Science Society* (pp. 179–187). Hillsdale, NJ: Lawrence Erlbaum Associates.

McCarthy, J. (1988). Epistemological challenges for connectionism. *The Behavioral and Brain Sciences, 11*, 44.

Pinker, S., & Mehler, J. (Eds.). (1988). *Connections and symbols*. Cambridge, MA: MIT Press.

Pinker, S., & Prince, A. (1988). On language and connectionism: Analysis of a parallel distributed processing model of language acquisition. In S. Pinker & J. Mehler (Eds.), *Connections and symbols* (pp. 73–193). Cambridge, MA: MIT Press.

Pollack, J. (1990). Electronic discussion on *Connectionist mailing list*, December 20, 1990.

Port, R. (1990). Representation and recognition of temporal patterns. *Connection Science, 2*, 151–176.

Rumelhart, D., & McClelland, J. (1986). On learning the past tense of English verbs. In J. McClelland, & D. Rumelhart (Eds.), *Parallel distributed processing* (Vol. 2, pp. 216–271). Cambridge, MA: MIT Press.

Rumelhart, D., Hinton, G., & Williams, R. (1986). Learning internal representations by error propagation. In D. Rumelhart & J. McClelland (Eds.), *Parallel distributed processing* (Vol. 1, pp. 319–362). Cambridge, MA: MIT Press.

Servan-Schreiber, D., Cleeremans, A., & McClelland, J. (1989). Learning sequential structure in simple recurrent networks. In D. Touretzky (Ed.), *Advances in neural information processing systems 1* (pp. 643–652). San Mateo, CA: Morgan Kaufmann.

Touretzky, D., & Wheeler, D. (1990). A computational basis for phonology. In D. Touretzky (Ed.), *Advances in neural information processing systems 2* (pp. 372–379). San Mateo, CA: Morgan Kaufmann.

Wickelgren, W. (1969). Context-sensitive coding, associative memory, and serial order in (speech) behavior. *Psychological Review, 76*, 1–15.

9 Symbolic Parsing Via Subsymbolic Rules

Stan C. Kwasny
Washington University

Kanaan A. Faisal
King Fahd University of Petroleum and Minerals
Dhahran, Saudi Arabia

1. INTRODUCTION

How can native English speakers process and generate English so adeptly while computational and other models that look so promising in theory yield such limited results? The task of Natural Language Processing (NLP) by computer is very complex and elusive. It should be obvious, therefore, that solutions, even partial solutions, must be capable of addressing that complexity through the proper abstraction mechanisms. The task must necessarily be divided into smaller pieces in order to have any hope of making progress, but dividing up the task incorrectly will not generally lead to progress with any lasting character. And yet some simplification is necessary because no single theory yet proposed encompasses all of human thought. Such a theory would be necessary if a single, complete account of the English language is to be provided. However, in the process of simplifying, care must be taken not to oversimplify, nor to trivialize important components. The results should scale to further dimensions as more of the solution unfolds. Many promising approaches have had difficulty generalizing to new domains and scaling to larger problems.

Connectionism provides a perspective on the decomposition of large tasks into smaller ones. Similar to the blackboard architectures (Engelmore & Morgan, 1988) that grew out of research on speech, various modules (called *knowledge sources* in blackboard systems) can often provide a degree of expertise, but are unable to fully address the larger task alone. Distributed representations, supported through connectionism, provide a means by which partial solutions can be encoded as activation patterns leaving other aspects of the solution to be addressed by other components. Here, the notion of competition is fundamental.

While a particular part of the solution is unknown, possible solutions compete based on corroborating evidence from relevant sources.

Connectionist approaches to Natural Language Processing, although by most accounts not yet as successful as symbolic approaches, stand as an important counterpoint to them. In connectionism, there is the promise of robust decision making, generalization, and other benefits of a style of programming based on the explicit presentation of input–output patterns (sometimes called *extensional programming*). Symbolic approaches enjoy the perspective of years of linguistic study, the application of well-understood methods, and a certain security that only comes from computing symbolic intermediate structures to reassure that processing is proceeding according to design.

However, symbolic approaches require engineering—often in areas where the principles to guide that engineering are poorly understood or nonexistent. One cannot open up the brain of an adult language speaker and identify the competence rules of a grammar (or, for that matter, any similar structure) among the neural cells. The guiding principles must be inferred by very indirect means. Here, connectionism can provide insights into the organization of such systems. Studies can be performed that permit the examination of a self-organized system to see what structure emerges as relevant to a task. Although often crude in their approximation to brain function, such studies can offer insights useful in the creation of intelligent systems.

Many other intelligent tasks might be examined under a connectionist approach, but none can really match the task of language understanding that we, as humans, uniquely possess to a greater degree than any other entity. It can be taken as the hallmark of intelligence. Pinker and Prince (1988) saw language as the crucial test case for connectionism:

> Language has been the domain most demanding of articulated symbol structures governed by rules and principles and it is also the domain where such structures have been explored in the greatest depth and sophistication, within a range of theoretical frameworks and architectures, attaining a wide variety of significant empirical results. Any alternative model that either eschews symbolic mechanisms altogether, or that is strongly shaped by the restrictive nature of available elementary information processes and unresponsive to the demands of the high-level functions being computed, starts off at a seeming disadvantage. Many observers thus feel that connectionism, as a radical restructuring of cognitive theory, will stand or fall depending on its ability to account for human language. (p. 78)

Certainly the importance of language cannot be refuted, but Pinker and Prince have the story backward: The radical restructuring of cognitive theory is what has happened under a strong symbolic influence. The subsymbolic, connectionist view builds on the natural association between cognition and brain and espouses to make cognitive theory more brain-based, more bottom-up.

Language can be viewed from a subsymbolic perspective just as validly as from a symbolic one. As Pinker and Prince pointed out, the symbolic viewpoint has predominated because in many respects symbols play critical roles. Certainly this is true in traditional methods of analysis. Written language, as an example, relies on discrete, symbolic alphabets to convey thought. Language is also subsymbolic as evidenced by the nature of speech, the fuzziness of concepts, and the high degree of parallelism that is difficult to explain as a purely symbolic phenomenon. Thus, the gap is very apparent in language. It follows that the task of building a processor of natural language lends itself to a hybrid approach that combines symbolic with subsymbolic processing.

Our proposal in this chapter is an attempt to take advantage of the strongest features of connectionism while using symbolic data structures for what at this point seems difficult to do any other way. Clearly, this is an evolutionary process. We have chosen to explore the gap starting with conservative steps from the symbolic end. Our objectives are to investigate ways of maintaining the benefits of both approaches as much as possible while minimizing their disadvantages. Linguistically the work described in this chapter is organized around syntax, but our view is not limited exclusively to it. Our ongoing efforts have begun to consider additional components. In the process, our goal is to attain a clearer idea of which components are best accomplished symbolically and which ones subsymbolically. Our research agenda aims at progressing toward a more fully connectionist realization, but not until several of the intermediate alternatives are understood. The primary issue is how to draw the line between the two processing approaches and how to build the bridges that connect them.

2. MOTIVATION

Whereas humans handle language almost without thinking, computer systems are not yet able to process natural language with any kind of facility. Systems built in the laboratory have resisted attempts to scale them up to larger systems. In our view, connectionism has a much better chance of succeeding in this regard than previous methodologies. In this section, we discuss why we are motivated to explore the gap between symbolic and subsymbolic approaches and how a deterministic view of language processing is consistent with that motivation.

2.1. Language Studies

Studies have shown that a computer system equipped with a grammar of English, no matter how detailed, can still expect to encounter novel (ill-formed or ambiguous) sentences that will be difficult to handle properly.

For example, Thompson (1980) conducted an extensive set of experiments studying natural language queries to a database system. She analyzed 1,615 sentences of which only 1,093 were parsable. A total of 446 (27.6%) contained some kind of error due to ungrammaticality, fragmentary response, vocabulary, punctuation, or spelling.

In another set of experiments, Eastman and Mclean (1981) analyzed 693 English queries to a data base system. They found that as high as 32.8% of the queries were ungrammatical in some way. Co-occurrence violations (e.g., subject-verb disagreement), errors in tense, and errors in case occurred in 12.3% of the inputs, whereas incomplete or elliptical sentences, omitted or extraneous words or phrases, and similar problems occurred in 14.0% of the sentences analyzed.

In another set of experiments that involved inputs by managers to an English-language management-support system, Malhotra (1975) found that 105 (21.2%) out of 496 sentences were unparsable and contained some kind of problem for the language processor.

Although the results vary due to differences in what is counted, each of the studies mentioned concluded that in order to fully address the processing of language, mechanisms capable of handling what are considered to be ill-formed or ungrammatical inputs are required.

Computational linguists have long recognized the need to extend their language processors beyond the boundaries fixed by the rules. Wilks (1976) was perhaps the first to write about this need. Weischedel (1977) also recognized the need and constructed an intelligent German tutoring system (Weischedel, Voge, & James, 1978) to demonstrate what could be accomplished. Extensive work by Kwasny (1980), Sondheimer (Kwasny & Sondheimer, 1981), Weischedel (Weischedel & Sondheimer, 1983), and others led to the notion of rule-based ill-formedness, which argues that the rules of language processing could be relaxed or violated according to another set of (meta-) rules. But the meta-rules embodied in that work suffer from the same sharp boundaries and brittleness as the rules they are meant to manipulate. Thus, progress along that line slowed for want of better paradigms.

Recently, McRoy, and Hirst (1990) used timing to examine issues related specifically to syntactic disambiguation and as a major criterion for building and attaching structure. The approach is innovative and may suggest new ways to think about parallelism in NLP.

Connectionism provides an alternative in which both regularities and exceptions can exist in one system. The most famous example of this is a system that learns the past tense of English verbs (Rumelhart & McClelland, 1986). Furthermore, generalization enables a system to possess more processing capability than originally designed into it.

2.2. Deterministic Processing View of Language

In our work, we assume the validity of the determination hypothesis (Marcus, 1980) that Marcus put forth in his work on PARSIFAL. It states, in its revised form, that "there is enough information in the structure of natural language in general, and in English in particular to allow left-to-right deterministic parsing of those sentences which a native speaker can analyze without conscious effort" (p. 204). With the development of PARSIFAL, the determinism hypothesis became a viable theory of language processing. PARSIFAL showed that a rule-based system could be developed to syntactically process a large subset of English without backtracking and without building unnecessary structure. Furthermore, it suggested a correspondence between the language subset that could be processed in this manner and the language processing humans perform below the level of conscious effort. It thereby omits those "garden-path" sentences that apparently require some amount of reanalysis at a conscious level by humans.

Formally, parsing is a mapping that maps an input sentence into its parse tree. For example, Fig. 9.1 is the parse tree for the sentence *John did hit Jack.* In this figure we see how the constituents of a sentence are placed under the proper tree node. *John* is the subject noun-phrase (Subj-NP). *Did* is an auxiliary (AUX) and *hit* is the main verb (MVB). *Jack* is the object (Obj-NP) and a constituent, along with the MVB, within the verb-phrase (VP). The sentence (S) contains Subj-NP, AUX, and VP.

Although grammaticality judgments can be made by humans, they are very difficult to explain. For our purposes, we assume an operational definition of grammaticality. Whether a sentence is grammatical or not in this sense is dictated by whether it can be derived from a particular set of symbolic grammar rules. Note that in this sense all rule-based parsing systems parse grammatical sentences. In particular, all deterministic rule-based natural language parsing systems parse grammatical sentences deterministically. They fail sharply however when presented with even slightly unexpected forms. Although it is possible to modify systems of this type to perform correctly on some types of these forms, such changes involve adding these anticipated forms to the rules. Usually, the rules or rule interpreters require extensive modification and perhaps invention of new mechanisms. Obviously this merely extends the boundaries of grammaticalness and does nothing to smooth them out. Still, the revised system can be faced with unexpected forms that it cannot parse.

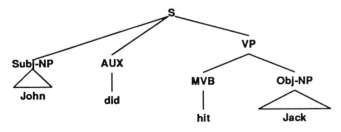

FIG. 9.1. Parse tree of *John did hit Jack.*

For example a sentence like *John did hit Jack* is grammatical and can be parsed successfully to produce the parse tree of Fig. 9.1 with a simple set of rules. However, if presented with *John did hitting Jack,* or similar ungrammatical sentence form, a parser can get stuck and produce no structure. PARAGRAM (Charniak, 1983) is a deterministic parser that has been extended specifically to parse ungrammatical sentences, but fails to parse this sentence form correctly because the example is reported to be beyond its capabilities. Our goal is to smooth out these boundaries and permit reasonable structures to be constructed in such situations. Figure 9.2 shows what our hybrid system produces for this sentence.

The system is developed and tested with grammar rules derived from several different deterministic rule-based grammars. Examples are drawn from published work on deterministic parsing. Data is presented, based on two complementary training techniques, which is explained in section 3.2, to demonstrate the superiority of the method. Grammatical sentences are tested to establish that training has succeeded. Ill-formed sentences, including ungrammatical and lexically ambiguous sentences, are tested to demonstrate generalization from the rules. In testing with sentence forms such as those shown in Figs. 9.1 and 9.2, our parser matches and exceeds the capabilities of comparable symbolic systems.

3.   DETERMINISM AND CONNECTIONISM

McClelland and Kawamoto (1986) were the first to discuss the idea of investigating a connectionist approach to language processing based on a deterministic parser. In this section, a brief overview of deterministic parsing is presented and our specific architecture for introducing connectionism is summarized.

3.1.   Deterministic Parsing of Language and its Mechanisms

The starting point for the hybrid parser is simply the deterministic syntactic parser used in PARSIFAL (Marcus, 1980). An overview of that parser is given in

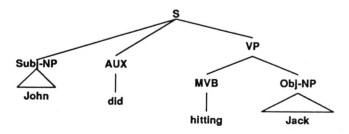

FIG. 9.2.   Parse tree of *John did* hitting *Jack.*

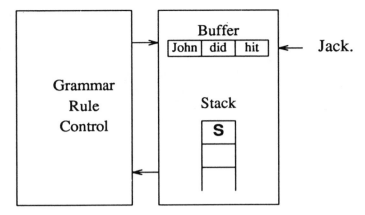

FIG. 9.3.   Basic mechanisms of deterministic parsing.

Fig. 9.3. This framework provides a buffer that holds a fixed number of constituents, typically three, and a stack for manipulating embedded structures. Grammatical expertise is stored as condition-action rules. These rules control the building of structure and the manipulation of the stack and buffer through a limited set of actions. Typically, these actions may create new constituent nodes in the structure, attach one constituent as a piece of the structure of another, switch the order of constituents in the buffer, insert a missing constituent into the buffer, pop a constituent off the stack placing it into the buffer, or stop the processing.

Initially, a starting constituent node (S) may be placed on the stack and the initial portion of the sentence moved into sequential locations in the buffer. From here, rules are matched to the buffer and stack to determine which rule can apply. In PARSIFAL, conflicting rules are mediated through their presence in rule packets (which are activated and deactivated under rule control), through a static priority rating within a packet, and through special diagnostic rules. One rule is uniquely determined and executed on each step of the parse. A single processing step consists of selecting a rule, firing the rule, and performing its actions. Rule packets are usually associated with the current (top-level) node of the structure being built. Actions effect changes to the stack and buffer. After a series of processing steps, a termination rule fires and processing is halted leaving the final structure on top of the stack.

Deterministic parsers process input sentences primarily left-to-right and never build any structure that will later be discarded due to backtracking or pseudo-parallel processing. Determinism is accomplished by permitting a lookahead of up to a fixed number of constituents with the constituent buffer designated for that purpose. Once a decision about structure has been made, however, it cannot be undone. Deterministic parsers are known to be context free in their computational power (Nozohoor-Farshi, 1987).

In its original form, PARSIFAL has certain limitations. As shown in Fig. 9.4, several researchers are investigating extensions to PARSIFAL aimed at overcoming some of these limitations. These have been independently proposed for parsing of ungrammatical sentences (PARAGRAM; Charniak, 1983), resolving lexical ambiguities (ROBIE; Milne, 1986), acquiring syntactic rules from examples (LPARSIFAL; Berwick, 1979, 1982, 1985), and acquiring rules dealing with lexical ambiguity (FIDDITCH; Hindle, 1989). But each of these systems has its own limitations and no single symbolic system exists, to our knowledge, that incorporates all of these capabilities. The integration of their processing capabilities is one specific goal of our work. The bulk of our examples and grammar rules, therefore, are derived from descriptions of these systems.

3.2. Other Work
on Connectionist Natural Language Parsing

Although many aspects of NLP are being actively pursued under a connectionist, hybrid approach (see Lange, chap. this volume, for example), we have chosen to focus on the task of building a syntactic processor. Indeed, several researchers have attempted to process natural language using connectionism. In many of these parsers (e.g., Cottrell, 1989; Fanty, 1985; Waltz & Pollack, 1985), gram-

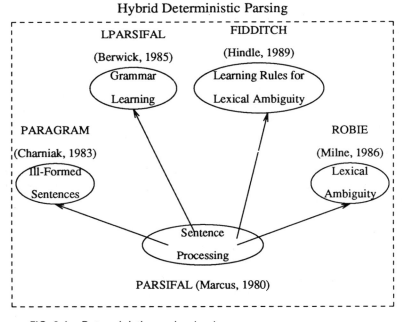

FIG. 9.4. Deterministic parsing landscape.

mar rules are processed into a network of units connected with excitatory and inhibitory links. The number of units required to realize a given grammar is a function of the maximum input sentence length and the complexity of the grammar. But this introduces a limitation on the number of elements that can be present in the input. Sentences are processed within such a framework by presenting them, possibly in a simulated left-to-right fashion, at the input side of the network and activations are permitted to spread through the network. Other approaches such as simulated annealing (Selman & Hirst, 1985) have also been attempted with limited success.

Any plausible model of language processing should permit alternative linguistic structures to compete (in the same sense as the TRACE models; Mc-Clelland & Elman, 1986) while inputs arrive in a left-to-right manner. Computer models based on backtracking—for example, Augmented Transition Networks (ATNs) or Definite Clause Grammars (DCGs)—do not adequately capture the competitive nature of sentence processing because there is no evidence from human experiments that any conscious reprocessing of inputs is routinely performed. Garden path sentences are perhaps an exception to this.

Connectionist methods for constructing parsers that process language naturally on an element-by-element basis have been investigated by Elman (Elman, 1988, 1989). In his architecture, recurrent connections are permitted that link the hidden layer of the network to context units in the input layer. When compared to networks studied by Jordan (1986), whose recurrent links originate from the output layer, these networks are thought to be more powerful (Cottrell & Tsung, 1989). The recurrent links provide information from the previous state of the process. It is important that this information be available at the current decision-making point so that parsing decisions can depend on what has been seen previously. These networks are not designed to represent structure explicitly. Next-word predictions are used to demonstrate the nature of grammatical knowledge learned. Similarly, Gigley's HOPE system (Gigley, 1988) has proven effective in achieving predictive capabilities and in modeling certain aspects of aphasia.

Wermter and Lehnert (Wermter, 1990; Wermter & Lehnert, 1990) are investigating the analysis of nouns phrases based on a hybrid architecture. He is utilizing noun phrases from a collected corpus of titles and queries of scientific references in the literature. Plausible relationships between noun phrases, as manifested in prepositional connectives, are learned by a system. The system design itself is built on three levels: connectionist-localist, connectionist-distributed, and symbolic. The result is a system that can make accurate assessments of how prepositional phrases should be associated with other constituents in an utterance based on plausibility measures of the noun phrases involved. This is an important proposal for the solution of an important problem.

Most of these attempts jump too quickly into a fully connectionist realization of their parser. Our strategy is to proceed cautiously and demonstrate capabilities for each form of hybrid.

3.3. The Hybrid Deterministic Parser

A temporary solution to bridging the gap is to construct a hybrid system, as pointed out by Dinsmore (chap. this volume). Work reported here takes that view in order to demonstrate the potential for building such systems and to examine their properties. In the long run, as mentioned earlier, our hope is to explore methods for performing more of the task on the connectionist side of the gap without degrading previously demonstrated capabilities.

Classically, NLP is performed under the direction of a set of grammar rules. Symbolic rules are an essential part of most linguistic accounts at virtually all levels of processing, from speech signal to semantics. But systems based too literally on rules tend to be brittle because, as mentioned before, there is no direct way to process linguistic forms that have not been anticipated by the rules. No complete set of rules for English exists, nor does it seem possible to construct a complete set, so this is unsatisfactory.

Our hybrid parser (Kwasny & Faisal, 1990) replaces the rules of the deterministic parser with a single, feedforward network (see Fig. 9.5). The network is trained through backpropagation (Werbos, 1974; Rummelhart, Hinton, & Williams, 1986) and conjugate-gradient methods (Polak, 1971; Press, Flannery, Teukolsky, & Vettering, 1988) from rule templates or sentence traces derived from a deterministic grammar. Actions in the hybrid parser are performed symbolically on traditional data structures, which are also maintained symbolically. The symbolic component manages the input sentence and the flow of constitu-

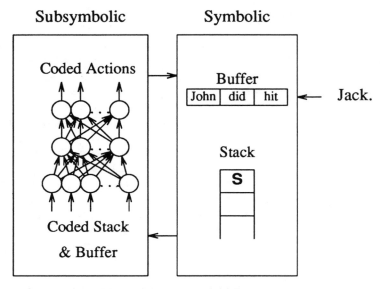

FIG. 9.5. Hybrid deterministic parser initialized.

ents into the lookahead buffer, coding them as required for the input level of the network in the subsymbolic component. On the output side, it evaluates the activations of the output units, decides which action to perform, and performs that action, potentially modifying the stack and buffer in the process. After several iterations, a step action is performed yielding the configuration shown in Fig. 9.6.

The responsibility of the subsymbolic component, therefore, is to examine the contents of the buffer and stack and yield a preference for a specific action. In recent versions of our system, we have also tried networks whose output specifies a particular rule template, thus providing the potential to explain from where the decisions may have come.

3.3.1. Training the Network. Learning itself occurs off-line and can be time consuming, but the processing times for sentences only depend on one feed-forward pass through the network for each processing step, which is very fast. Computations need only flow in one direction in the network during parsing. The feed-forward multiplication of weights and computation of activation levels for individual units produce the pattern of activation on the output layer. Activation of output units is interpreted in a winner-take-all manner, so that the unit with the highest activation determines the action to be taken.

During training, patterns are presented to the layered network and the appropriate action is reinforced. The training patterns represent encodings of the buffer positions and the top of the stack from the deterministic parser. Note that the size of this is fixed, which makes it easy to present to a fixed-size network. The output of the network contains a series of units, each representing an action to be

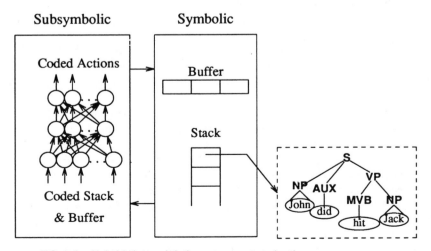

FIG. 9.6. Hybrid deterministic parser on termination.

performed during processing. Network convergence is observed once the network can produce the correct output on all the training patterns themselves and the error measure has decreased to an acceptable level, determined experimentally. The weights derived from training provide the syntactic knowledge of the parser. The network is sufficiently trained if it can make the correct decision for every step of every grammatical sentence. If a grammatical sentence fails due to an incorrect action, then the weights must be recalculated. In practice, we train the network to an error value that guarantees the rules have been learned.

3.3.2.   Types of Training.   In Faisal and Kwasny (1990), we examine two distinct approaches to training a network to parse sentence forms. Each of these training strategies results in a slightly different version of the hybrid parser. One approach uses rule templates, training patterns derived from the rules. This type of learning is deductive in the sense that a very general form of each rule is learned from which the parser must derive actions specific to individual cases. The second approach uses training data derived from sentence processing traces. This form of training is inductive in the sense that the parser must arrive at general patterns of performance from the specific instances presented. The goal of both deductive and inductive training is to produce a network capable of mimicking the rules or sentence forms on which its training is based and to do so in a way that generalizes to many additional cases. One initial learning has been accomplished, simulation experiments can be performed to examine the generalization capabilities of the resulting networks.

In deductive training, each grammar rule is encoded as a training template, which is a list of feature values, but templates are not grouped into rule packets. In general, the top of the stack and each component of the symbolic buffer are represented by an ordered vector of values representing the features in which a vector position is ON($+1$) if the feature must be present, OFF(-1) if the feature must not be present, and DON'T CARE (?) if the feature is irrelevant to the rule. A rule template is instantiated by randomly changing ? to $+1$ or -1. Thus, for deductive training, each template represents many training patterns and each training epoch is slightly different. Figure 9.7a illustrates the process of extracting training patterns from the grammar rules.

In inductive training, the primary difference is in the origin of the training patterns. Sentences are manually taken through the steps of parsing with decisions about what action to take on each step left to the discretion of the human trainer and his concept of the grammar rules. (These may or may not be actually written down.) These sentence traces differ from rule templates primarily in the absence of DON'T CARE (?) elements because they are derived directly from sentence forms with real features. The traces are collected and merged together to eliminate duplicates. One such collection forms an epoch for training purposes. In both training modes, the network learns the inputs on which it can rely in constructing its answers and which inputs it can ignore. Figure 9.7b illustrates the process of extracting training patterns from traces of sentence processing.

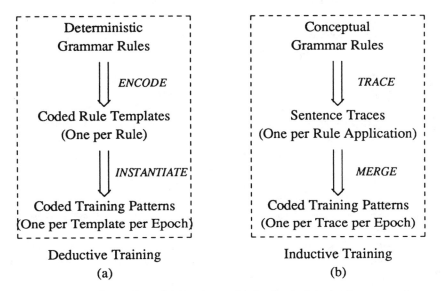

FIG. 9.7.   Extraction of deductive and inductive training patterns.

3.3.3.   Treatment of Don't Care Conditions.   The probability of a ? becoming a $+1$ or -1 during instantiation of a rule template varies according to the training that we are conducting. Each rule template containing n ?s can generate up to 2^n unique training cases. Some rule templates have over 30 ?s, which means they represent approximately 10^9 training cases. It is obviously impossible to test the performance of all these cases, so the expected value (average) of the feature is substituted for each ? in the rule template to provide testing patterns. Although in actual processing this value may not be encountered, it represents the mean of the range of values seen during training and as such provides an unintrusive component useful for such testing.

Each grammar rule takes the following form:

$$\{ \ \langle \text{Stack} \rangle \ \langle \text{1st Item} \rangle \ \langle \text{2nd Item} \rangle \ \langle \text{3rd Item} \rangle \ \rightarrow \ \text{Action} \ \}$$

Grammar rules are encoded into rule templates by concatenating the feature vectors of the component constituents from the stack and buffer. For example, a rule for Yes/No questions, modeled after PARSIFAL, could be written:

$$\{ \ \langle \text{S node} \rangle \ \langle \text{"have"} \rangle \ \langle \text{NP} \rangle \ \langle \text{VERB, -en} \rangle \ \rightarrow \ \text{Switch 1st and 2nd items} \ \},$$

whereas a rule for imperative sentences could be written:

$$\{ \ \langle \text{S node} \rangle \ \langle \text{"have"} \rangle \ \langle \text{NP} \rangle \ \langle \text{VERB, inf} \rangle \ \rightarrow \ \text{Insert YOU} \ \}.$$

By replacing each constituent with its coding, a rule template is created. In the two aforementioned rules, rule templates are created with a ? value for many of the specific verb features of the initial form "have" in each rule, but are coded to show the differences in the third buffer position. Different actions are required, so these are also coded to have different target values during training.

3.3.4. *Mixing Deductive and Inductive Training.*

The hybrid parser, therefore, can exhibit different properties depending on the patterns used in training. Inductive learning requires much more data than deductive training and this must be collected through sentence traces. Deductive training, on the other hand, requires a solid set of rules, which is tedious in itself to collect. Inductively trained networks depend greatly on the completeness of the examples presented for the range of sentence types handled. Deductive training imposes an ordering on the training patterns that assures a completeness that is difficult to achieve with inductive training, but inductive training patterns reflect the frequency of rule occurrences seen in actual sentence processing. It is not clear, therefore, which training method is the best.

A third method of training combines both deductive and inductive patterns. This mixed training provides the best of both methods. Networks trained in this way exhibit good generalization characteristics, as expected from deductive training, as well as excellent performance on specific sentences, as expected from inductive training.

Deductive training can be thought of as analogous to textbook learning in which general rules and principles are enunciated. Someone wishing to learn the subject matter can quickly read and understand these abstracted notions from the textbook. On the other hand, inductive training can be considered analogous to learning from experience. Actual cases or instances are presented for analysis and by studying what decisions arise under what circumstances, one can derive their own rules and principles. We claim that neither type of learning by itself is adequate in learning a complex domain, such as language. Our hybrid parser supports the combination of these two different learning strategies in a convenient and direct way.

For training purposes, the distinction between deductive and inductive training patterns is useful in constructing a training set of deductive patterns and a test set of inductive patterns. In this way, training must occur from the general, deductive patterns and yet the measure of convergence comes from the inductive patterns.

4. RESULTS

In this section, we report on the performance of the parser on several sentence forms. There are several dimensions to consider when measuring performance of our system.

4.1. Performance Measures

The first question should be whether the structure built by the parser is considered acceptable. When presented with a fully grammatical sentence form, our criteria is simply the same as it would be for the symbolic system based on the same grammar rules. When presented with a form that is not fully grammatical, we attempt to relate the form to one that is fully grammatical or otherwise exercise our judgment as to its acceptability. In all of the examples shown in this chapter, the parser constructs a parse tree, which on examination is considered reasonable and acceptable.

A second dimension for consideration relates to the convergence criteria used in training. It is well known that tight training—training that produces very small errors in the training set—can be at odds with the ability of the network to generalize. The reason for this is not fully understood, but it seems that in the final stages of training, the general patterns of the data have been learned and all that is left are the idiosyncrasies of the training data. These, of course, do not help the network to generalize. We have conducted numerous training runs, but we do not have any perfect strategy. The examples shown in this chapter are chosen from one particular training run. Similar results can be obtained from a wide variety of training strategies.

There are several other factors that affect the performance during parsing. The frequency of occurrence of any particular pattern during training may affect the amount of error present when such a pattern occurs during parsing. It may also affect the extent to which that pattern will seem appropriate when an unexpected form is presented, as during tests with ungrammatical and other poorly formed sentences. Certain limitations inherent in the grammar are inherited by the hybrid parser. If the grammar is not written to produce appropriate structure for embedded sentence forms, for example, then by using it in training a network for the hybrid parser will not somehow create that capability.

In reporting performance, we have chosen to report simply the error encountered during each parsing step. This can be taken as an indication of how expected or unexpected the particular situation is relative to the patterns seen during training. We calculate the error by first noting which output unit has the most activation then calculating the sum of squares (Euclidean) distance from the actual vector of output unit activations to an idealized vector having a $+1$ in the winning position and -1 everywhere else. The idealized vector represents a particular type of corner in the hypercube of activation values and our measure is just the distance between our computed point and the corner in the hypercube. Note that this error is exactly the same as the error being minimized during the training process itself. Therefore, grammatical sentences are expected to encounter low error values during the entire course of processing whereas nongrammatical sentences are expected to encounter higher error values at those points where unusual patterns arise.

4.2. Summary of Grammars

As mentioned earlier, we have enjoyed some success in building a syntactic parser, composed of symbolic and subsymbolic parts, for processing inputs that are not always well-formed according to the grammar rules. Development of symbolic rules is still necessary, thus we have constructed our system to be both a hybrid parser as well as a testbed for grammars. By loading a set of weights for the network, our system becomes a hybrid parser ready to be tested with a variety of sentence forms. By loading a set of templates, the system becomes a symbolic parser with capabilities identical to that of other deterministic parsers.

Although we have developed several distinct grammars, we make no claims about the completeness of any of them. Table 9.1 summarizes those grammars. Our experimentation has ranged from a small demonstration grammar to a very large grammar. Several medium grammars have been constructed, each with slightly different capabilities and architectures. The largest grammar is comparable to the most complete deterministic grammars published and is based on the largest grammar given by Marcus (1980). Grammar construction and development can be a tedious process. In fact, some researchers devote years of their professional lives to such activities. Our goal at this point in the research is to produce grammars similar to the ones already done, but aimed at demonstrating specific features of our work.

Table 9.1 classifies each grammar as small, medium, or large. The small grammar, used in a prototype version of the hybrid parser, is based on an example shown in the popular Artificial Intelligence textbook by Winston (1984). Both medium and large grammars are taken from appendices in Marcus (1980) and demonstrate the range of capabilities of deterministic parsing. Most of our experimentation has centered on the medium grammars because these are quickly trained and yet embody nontrivial capabilities. They vary slightly along

TABLE 9.1
Summary of Grammars Used in Hybrid Parser

Size of Grammar	No. of Buffers	No. of Rules	No. of Actions	Lexical Features	Network Size		Grammar Based On
					Units	Weights	
Small	3	13	5	6	44-15-5	755	Example (Winston, 1984)
Medium	2	22	20	11	35-20-20	1140	
	3	24	21	11	52-30-24	2334	Appendix C
	3	24	21	11	53-30-24	2364	(Marcus, 1980)
	3	22	19	11	53-30-22	2302	
Large	2	73	40	21	66-40-40	4292	Appendix D
	2	75	39	21	66-40-75	5755	(Marcus, 1980)

the dimensions indicated, as well as slightly in complexity of grammatical structures processed.

In PARSIFAL, Marcus argued that three buffer positions are sufficient for this type of language processing. Others have used two. The size of the buffer is important in determining the range of sentence forms acceptable. We agree with Marcus that probably three is required, but often use two simply to reduce the size of our network.

Table 9.1 also shows the size of each grammar measured in terms of the number of rules, the number of actions, the number of lexical features required to represent a word, and the size of the networks required. Network size is measured both as a count of the number of weights and as a count and arrangement of units. The number of output units matches either the number of actions or the number of rules depending on which method is used. As mentioned earlier, requiring the network to produce a rule number helps in determining the reason for performing an action.

We have experience in performing both deductive and inductive training with our grammars. We lack experience in combining deductive with inductive into mixed training sequences, although preliminary data shows this to potentially be the most powerful technique. Such experimentation is ongoing.

How input items are coded depends on the way in which the grammar is written. We have chosen encodings based primarily on syntactic features (e.g., noun, prep, aux-verb-attached, etc.). Others (McClelland & Kawamoto, 1986) have chosen to use semantic microfeatures. Clearly the choice of features limits the range of information available about each item. We are experimenting with several schemes for this encodement.

As a particular case, what can be done with novel or unknown words (i.e., words not in the lexicon) based on their syntactic context? For example, a newly invented word (e.g., *scud*) or a person's name is not likely to be in a lexicon, unless it is ambiguous as a common English word (e.g., *bill, bob, carol*). If the parser performs in a manner analogous to how it processes a lexically ambiguous item, we should find some ability for the parser to treat the item as appropriate to its context. This is indeed the case (Kwasny & Kalman, 1991). Furthermore, we are investigating a method for back-propagating error values to unknown items so that lexical entries can be developed for unknown items and they can be transformed in time to their proper entry. This method of representation is based on work by Miikkulainen and Dyer (1988).

4.3. Samples of Processing Capability

For expository reasons, our examples are taken from the 53-30-24 medium grammar. Figure 9.8 shows examples of sentence forms that the grammar is capable of successfully processing into parse trees. These are divided into gram-

Grammatical Sentence Forms

1. John did hit Mary.
2. They can(v) fish.
3. Can(aux) they hit?
4. The meeting should have been scheduled on Tuesday.
5. John did hit Mary on the head.
6. Did John hit Mary on the head?
7. John was kissing Mary.
8. Schedule the meeting!
9. Have you scheduled the meeting?
10. The meetings have been scheduled.
11. John should have scheduled the meeting.

Ungrammatical Sentence Forms

12. John have should scheduled the meeting.
13. The meeting have should been scheduled on Tuesday.

Lexical Omissions

14. John did *clobber* Mary.

FIG. 9.8.   Sentence forms.

matical and ungrammatical sentence forms. A sentence form containing a word omitted from the lexicon (*clobber*) is also shown. These are discussed later.

4.3.1.   Grammatical Sentence Forms.   The grammatical sentence forms in Fig. 9.8 parse successfully in both the symbolic as well as the hybrid parser. During parsing, an error value is computed for each step leading to the parse. Every grammatical sentence, by definition, parses normally with negligible error during the course of parsing. As an example, sentence 11 in Fig. 9.8 is correctly parsed by the hybrid. A graph showing the progression of error values for that sentence is presented in Fig. 9.9. As expected, the sentence shows little error across all 14 steps.

4.3.2.   Ungrammatical Sentence Forms.   One important capability demonstrated by our hybrid is the automatic extension of the grammar rules to parse limited ungrammatical forms. With a simple set of grammar rules, it is difficult to show very much capability, but the medium grammars seem to be just large enough to provide some results.

Figure 9.8 shows examples of sentence forms that are syntactically ill-formed. Sentence 11 is the grammatical counterpart to the ungrammatical sentence 12. Processing in both sentences results in the same structure except for the ordering

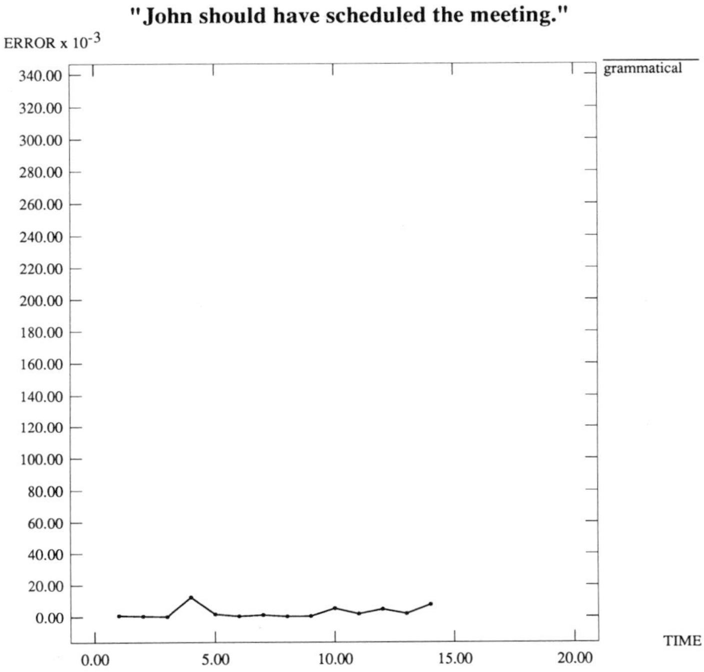

FIG. 9.9.   Plot of the processing of grammatical sentence form.

of the constituents have and should in the auxiliary component of the structure. Figure 9.10 shows a plot of the error during processing for both sentences 11 and 12.

The most noticeable feature is the large spike at the point in processing where the word order has been reversed in the auxiliary. Just prior to the spike, only a portion of the sentence (*John have*) has been processed. At that point, the parser is working on the auxiliary node in the parse tree. The first two elements of the buffer are *have* and *should*. The hybrid parser decides to attach *have* as a perfect tense to the auxiliary. Note that this action would not have been performed in the symbolic implementation because the conditions for the attachment are not strictly met. These conditions ask for a form of *have* in the first buffer position followed by a past participle verb in the second. In this example, the second location is filled with the modal, *should*. After the attachment of *have*, the buffer contains *should* followed by *scheduled*. A perfective is already attached to the auxiliary, so this situation is also not anticipated by the rules and consequently does not occur during training. The hybrid parser does produce a correct, though less definitive decision to attach the modal to the auxiliary node. Processing continues from that point and the final parse structure is produced.

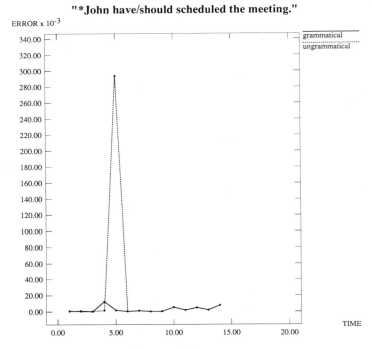

FIG. 9.10. Plot of the processing of ungrammatical sentence form.

The graph in Fig. 9.10 is typical of the behavior of the hybrid parser on ungrammatical sentences. As expected, error values rise at the point where unanticipated inputs are encountered, but remain low for all other situations.

4.3.3. Lexical Omissions and Ambiguity. Sentence forms often contain words that appear in the lexicon multiple times or perhaps not at all. We treat these cases similarly in the sense that such items are coded using an ambiguous coding. In the case of multiple lexical entries, the word is coded according to multiple syntactic categories. Likewise, omitted words are coded ambiguously across all possible categories distinguished in the grammar.

In sentence 14 in Fig. 9.8, we assume that the word *clobber* is not in the lexicon. The lexical access mechanism discovers the word is absent and codes it for presentation to the network according to a globally defined activation pattern that is selected to place equal emphasis on each categorical choice represented in the lexicon. During parsing, the particular choice appropriate to the context is made by the hybrid parser. Figure 9.11 plots the error for sentence 14 comparing processing when the verb *clobber* is contained in the lexicon with processing when it is not. In both cases, the word is attached as the main verb of the sentence and appropriate structure is built.

"John did *clobber* Mary."

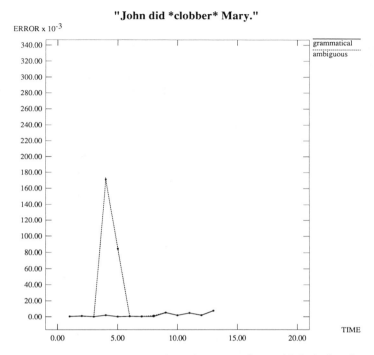

FIG. 9.11.   Plot of the processing of sentence form with lexical omission.

Note that the corresponding symbolic parser again requires buffer items to be matched by a single rule according to symbolic features. Although a more forgiving mechanism could be constructed for the symbolic case, multiple rules would have to be considered. The hybrid parser combines the matching and decision making into one network.

5.   IS THE GAP ANY NARROWER?

Has the gap between symbolic and subsymbolic approaches been reduced as a result of this work? Whereas the gap most certainly exists in our domain of syntactic parsing, we have provided just one method of traversing it. We are attempting to better understand the gap so that the answers are more likely to be made of enduring substance. We advocate a *causeway* strategy over a *bridge* strategy: Bridges are suspended over sparse underpinnings and can be fragile whereas causeways are well grounded from basic support along the entire span.

Each of the four symbolic deterministic parsing systems described earlier (LPARSIFAL, PARAGRAM, ROBIE, and FIDDITCH) provide improvements and enhancements to the PARSIFAL system. These improvements are complementary, so it is a desirable goal to combine their features into one system. Although we have chosen to pursue this goal on the subsymbolic side of the gap, could this be accomplished symbolically?

Attempting to combine these systems symbolically would require that several issues be addressed. ROBIE adds rules for dealing with lexical ambiguity, consequently it is somewhat overshadowed by FIDDITCH, which learns many of these rules. PARAGRAM handles ungrammatical sentences by changing some of the rules and introducing a scoring mechanism. Rules that are learned would have to be examined and made compatible with the scoring facility of PARAGRAM—certainly no easy feat. Furthermore, rule-learning in LPARSIFAL or FIDDITCH would have to be extended to provide the capability of learning the rules that the other system learns in addition to learning the rules and scoring mechanism added by PARAGRAM. At present, LPARSIFAL is only capable of learning a percentage of the existing rules in PARSIFAL and FIDDITCH does not attempt to learn any of these rules. Thus, for the symbolic approach to yield one system with all of these capabilities, the combinatorial interplay among the parts must be addressed. Although not impossible, the building of such a system would certainly be difficult.

The hybrid parser solves these problems in its hybrid architecture. The connectionist approach has several important advantages in unifying these five systems. Much of the capability is derived directly from properties of connectionist networks and therefore no special mechanisms are required for each. Learning, in the form of network training, is a fundamental feature of the approach. Ungrammatical sentences, comparable to and beyond those of PARAGRAM, are processed as a direct consequence of the generalization properties of the network. These same properties also aid in the disambiguation of lexical items and in the handling of lexical omissions.

Experimentation with grammatical sentences demonstrates the ability of the hybrid parser to perform as PARSIFAL. In the hybrid, the error value computed for each step of sentence processing is relatively low. This shows that the hybrid is accurately processing the sentence forms processed by PARSIFAL.

No explicit mechanism exists specifically for dealing with ungrammatical sentences in the hybrid parser. The mechanism used to process ungrammatical inputs employed by our parser is quite different from PARAGRAM. The behavior of the rules is represented by the network as a layered set of weights. In our parser, the training process develops weights that determine the mapping from stack and buffer to action or rule number. Unlike PARAGRAM, we do not engineer these scores manually. Such a process is susceptible to human error. PARAGRAM scores each test (sequentially) while the hybrid parser classifies an input pattern derived from the stack and buffer. We let the training process decide how to weight each input and consequently which action to execute. In the hybrid parser the network exhibits the behavior of all rules just as if all the rules are considered concurrently. The rule that wins is the rule node on the output layer with the highest activation.

Selected ungrammatical sentences are properly processed as a direct result of the generalization properties of the network. When presented an ungrammatical sentence, that is one for which the rules of the grammar would fail to find a parse, the network automatically relates the situations arising during parsing to similar situations on which it has been trained. The hybrid parser should not be expected to work well with drastically ungrammatical sentence forms, (i.e., sentence forms that bear little resemblance to the grammar on which the network has been trained), but the tendency is for the network to select the closest situation. Very often, this generates precisely the response required to accept the deviant form and construct an appropriate structure. Furthermore, as more varieties of forms are included in the grammar, we predict that the hybrid will succeed in greatly enhancing the overall coverage of the grammar. In fact, there is evidence for this already in our work in scaling up from the medium grammars to the large.

The problem of syntactic disambiguation in the hybrid parser is similar to that in ROBIE. All syntactic features for an ambiguous lexical item are presented simultaneously and the network is left to choose which syntactic sense is correct in this context. The parser utilizes syntactic context to resolve ambiguities and automatically relates these novel situations to training cases through the generalization capability of the network. As expected, the error values are high until the ambiguity is resolved.

Although the gap may not be narrowing, some navigation through the gap has taken place in our work. Answers have not come easily and much more work is necessary.

6. FUTURE

Bridges can be developed across the gap, but a closer integration of the two sides is required. It is difficult to know if our view of how to integrate symbolic and subsymbolic is correct. There are several directions in which our work is progressing that should lead to better answers to these concerns.

Some of the recent work on recurrent networks is being examined with the hope of improving the iteration properties of our system. Ultimately, it should be sufficient to present a final encoded structure as teaching data for a sentence form and permit the system to organize itself into the appropriate number and kind of processing steps necessary to build it. Although achieving such a completely extensional system will not happen soon, this work is expected to move away from the present (very strong) dependence on the organization associated with symbolic deterministic parsing.

Representation is a major issue. Methods of representation need to be further developed for unbounded structures that correspond to the resultant structures of language processing. Pollack's (1990) RAAM structures look promising as a means of representing arbitrary stacks and trees (see Blank, Meeden, & Marshall, chap. 6 in this volume). Further work is required to determine if these ideas will bear fruit.

Language processing may turn out to be best viewed in its relation to more behaviorally defined outputs. However, it is easy to show that what is commonly viewed as syntax is undoubtedly an important component of language processing and, therefore, should be investigated. As mentioned in the last section, we agree with Birnbaum (1989) that autonomous syntactic processing can not be completely successful in isolation from other components of the system, such as semantic, contextual, or lexical components. However, our parser should work successfully if incorporated with these other components. Our work has progressed beyond previous symbolic deterministic parsers in the way the hybrid parser provides competition among actions, and therefore structures, at any one point of parsing. These structures could be influenced by other components (semantic or contextual) to produce a correct structure when faced with syntactically ambiguous sentences. We are in the process of expanding the parser to incorporate some of these additional necessary components.

It follows that the issues at the semantic and lexical levels still need to be investigated. When a word appears in the buffer, our feature vectors capture the patterns of activation that that lexical component would produce. A model more consistent with ours would be one that produced distributed patterns of features that characterized the word. An unknown word would still have some biases based on its similarity to other known words and therefore some features would be similar.

The determinism hypothesis applies to only some forms of sentence processing. A great deal of English can be considered under this hypothesis, but there is certainly more happening when sentences are processed than it alone can explain. For deterministic parsing, garden path sentences are problematic due to the limit imposed by the size of the buffer. Garden path sentences, by definition, contain ambiguities that lure the hearer into structuring the sentence in one way only to discover later (beyond the buffer) that the structure is quite different. These sentences required some degree of conscious reprocessing. Symbolic deterministic parsing provides little means for recognizing when a garden path situation has been encountered and no means for reprocessing.

In the hybrid parser, an error value is measured for each parsing step. This value is constructed so that expected situations produce low values while unexpected or ambiguous situations produce high values. A high error value means there are actions competing with the action designated as the winner. In preliminary experiments with our software, we are attempting to specify criteria under which actions other than the winning action should be saved. These alternatives can then be restarted when the error value gets too high for processing to continue with any degree of reliability. Early results have been encouraging, but more work is needed to determine if global or relative thresholds are necessary to exert the proper control. In future versions of our parser, measures are expected to incorporate values from components other than syntax alone.

Crain and Steedman (1985) seemed to be correct in their assessment that weak interactions between syntax and semantics are necessary and must take place in parallel to enable proper influences to be exerted in reducing ambiguity. We are considering a form of beam search (Erman, Hayes-Roth, Lesser, & Reddy, 1980) with error measures, derived from all components working together, forming the basis for setting the beam. In this processing model, what is noticed consciously is the progression occurring due to search. Parsing can thus be considered a search process, albeit a very constrained one. Most states in the search yield exactly one successor and are little noticed. Where ambiguity cannot be totally filtered, more conscious effort is exerted to understand the sentence. Those cases are points of diversion where the beam search can legitimately consider more than one choice. If each choice leads to a good structure, then the sentence form is ambiguous. If one choice leads to a dead end whereas the other does not, then the sentence form is of the garden path variety.

Much of this future work is currently being pursued. Although early encouraging results have been obtained, we expect many more exciting developments before the gap is fully understood.

ACKNOWLEDGMENTS

The authors gratefully acknowledge the support and help from many sources. We thank the Center for Intelligent Computer Systems at Washington University and its sponsors, McDonnell Douglas Corporation and Southwestern Bell Telephone Company, for their earnest support and interest in our work. King Fahd University of Petroleum and Minerals has graciously supported the second author. We also thank the following people: Bill Ball, Anne Johnstone, Barry Kalman, Dan Kimura, Ron Loui, Gadi Pinkas, and the CICS research group at Washington University.

REFERENCES

Berwick, R. C. (1979). Learning structural descriptions of grammar rules from examples. In *Proceedings of the Sixth International Joint Conference on Artificial Intelligence* (pp. 56–58). Tokyo, Japan.

Berwick, R. C. (1982). *Locality principles and the acquisition of syntactic knowledge*. Unpublished doctoral dissertation, MIT, Cambridge, MA.

Berwick, R. C. (1985). *The acquisition of syntactic knowledge*. Cambridge, MA: MIT Press.

Birnbaum, L. L. (1989, August). A critical look at the foundations of autonomous syntactic analysis. In *Proceedings of the 11th Annual Conference of the Cognitive Science Society* (pp. 99–106). Hillsdale, NJ: Lawrence Erlbaum Associates.

Charniak, E. (1983). A parser with something for everyone. In M. King (Ed.), *Parsing natural language* (pp. 117–150). New York: Academic Press.

Cottrell, G. W. (1989). *A connectionist approach to word sense disambiguation*. London: Pitman.

Cottrell, G. W., & Tsung, F-S. (1989, August). Learning simple arithmetic procedures. In *Proceedings of the 11th Annual Conference of the Cognitive Science Society* (pp. 58–65). Hillsdale, NJ: Lawrence Erlbaum Associates.

Crain, S., & Steedman, M. (1985). On not being led up the garden path: The use of context by the psychological parser. In D. Dowty, L. Karttunen, & A. Zwicky (Eds.), *Natural language parsing: Psychological, computational, and theoretical perspectives* (pp. 320–358). Cambridge, England: Cambridge University Press.

Eastman, C. M., & McLean, D. S. (1981). On the need for parsing ill-formed input. *American Journal of Computational Linguistics, 7*, 257.

Elman, J. L. (1988). *Finding structure in time* (Tech. Rep. No. 8801). La Jolla, CA: University of California, San Diego, Center for Research in Language.

Elman, J. L. (1989, August). Structured representations and connectionist models. In *Proceedings of the 11th Annual Conference of the Cognitive Science Society* (pp. 17–25). Hillsdale, NJ: Lawrence Erlbaum Associates.

Engelmore, R., & Morgan, T. (Eds.). (1988). *Blackboard systems*. Reading, MA: Addison-Wesley.

Erman, L. D., Hayes-Roth, F., Lesser, V. R., & Reddy, D. R. (1980, June). The Hearsay-II speech-understanding system: Integrating knowledge to resolve uncertainty. *ACM Computing Surveys, 12*, 213–253.

Faisal, K. A., & Kwasny, S. C. (1990, January). Deductive and inductive learning in a connectionist deterministic parser. In *Proceedings of the International Joint Conference on Neural Networks* (pp. 471–474). Washington, DC.

Fanty, M. (1985). *Context-free parsing in connectionist networks* (Tech. Rep. No. 174). Rochester, NY: University of Rochester, Computer Science Department.

Gigley, H. (1988). Process synchronization, lexical ambiguity resolution, and aphasia. In S. Small, G. Cottrell, & M. Tanenhaus (Eds.), *Lexical ambiguity resolution* (pp. 229–267). San Mateo, CA: Morgan Kauffman.

Hindle, D. (1989). Acquiring disambiguation rules from text. In *Proceedings of the 27th Annual Meeting of the Association for Computational Linguistics* (pp. 118–125). Vancouver, British Columbia.

Jordan, M. (1986). *Serial order: A parallel distributed processing approach* (Tech. Rep. No. 8604). La Jolla, CA: University of California, San Diego, Institute for Cognitive Science.

Kwasny, S. C. (1980, November). *Treatment of ungrammatical and extra-grammatical phenomena in natural language understanding systems*. Bloomington, IN: Indiana University Linguistics Club.

Kwasny, S. C., & Sondheimer, N. K. (1981). Relaxation techniques for parsing ill-formed input. *American Journal of Computational Linguistics, 7*, 99–108.

Kwasny, S. C., & Faisal, K. A. (1990). Connectionism and determinism in a syntactic parser. *Connection Science, 2*, 63–82.

Kwasny, S. C., & Kalman, B. L. (1991, April). The case of the unknown word: Imposing syntactic constraints on words. In *Proceedings of the Third Midwest Artificial Intelligence and Cognitive Science Society Conference* (pp. 46–50). Carbondale, IL.

Malhotra, A. (1975, February). *Design criteria for a knowledge-based English language system for management* (Tech. Rep. No. MAC TR-146). Cambridge, MA: MIT Press.

Marcus, M. P. (1980). *A theory of syntactic recognition for natural language*. Cambridge, MA: MIT Press.

McClelland, J. L., & Elman, J. L. (1986). The TRACE model of speech perception. *Cognitive Psychology, 18*, 1–86.

McClelland, J. L., & Kawamoto, A. H. (1986). Mechanisms of sentence processing: Assigning roles to constituents of sentences. In D. E. Rumelhart & J. L. McClelland (Eds.), *Parallel distributed processing* (Vol. 2, pp. 272–325). Cambridge, MA: MIT Press.

McRoy, S. W., & Hirst, G. (1990). Race-based parsing and syntactic disambiguation. *Cognitive Science, 14*, 313–353.

Miikkulainen, R., & Dyer, M. G. (1988). Forming global representations with extended back-propagation. In *Proceedings of the IEEE Second Annual Conference on Neural Networks.* San Diego, CA.

Milne, R. (1986). Resolving lexical ambiguity in a deterministic parser. *Computational Linguistics, 12*, 1–12.

Nozohoor-Farshi, R. (1987). Context-freeness of the language accepted by Marcus' parser. In *Proceedings of the 25th Annual Meeting of the Association for Computational Linguistics* (pp. 117–122). Stanford, California.

Pinker, S., & Prince, A. (1988). On language and connectionism: Analysis of a parallel distributed processing model of language acquisition. In S. Pinker & J. Mehler (Eds.), *Connections and symbols* (pp. 73–193). Cambridge, MA: MIT Press.

Polak, E. (1971). *Computational methods in optimization: A unified approach.* New York: Academic Press.

Pollack, J. B. (1990). Recursive distributed representations. *Artificial Intelligence, 46*, 77–105.

Press, W. H., Flannery, B. P., Teukolsky, S. A., & Vettering, W. T. (1988). *Numerical recipes in C.* Cambridge, England: Cambridge University Press.

Rumelhart, D. E., Hinton, G., & Williams, R. J. (1986). Learning internal representations by error propagation. In D. E. Rumelhart & J. L. McClelland (Eds.), *Parallel distributed processing* (Vol. 2, pp. 318–364). Cambridge, MA: MIT Press.

Rumelhart, D. E., & McClelland, J. L. (1986). On learning the past tenses of English verbs. In D. E. Rumelhart & J. L. McClelland (Eds.), *Parallel distributed processing* (Vol. 2, pp. 216–271). Cambridge, MA: MIT Press.

Selman, B., & Hirst, G. (1985). A rule-based connectionist parsing system. In *Proceedings of the Seventh Annual Conference of the Cognitive Science Society* (pp. 212–221). Hillsdale, NJ: Lawrence Erlbaum Associates.

Thompson, B. (1980). Linguistic analysis of natural language communication with computers. In *Proceedings of the Eighth International Conference on Computational Linguistics* (pp. 190–201). Tokyo, Japan.

Waltz, D. L., & Pollack, J. B. (1985). Massively parallel parsing: A strongly interactive model of natural language interpretation. *Cognitive Science, 9*, 51–74.

Weischedel, R. M. (1977, February). Please re-phrase. (Tech. Rep. No. 77/1). Newark, DE: University of Delaware, Department of Statistics and Computer Science.

Weischedel, R. M., Voge, W. M., & James, M. (1978). An artificial intelligence approach to language instruction. *Artificial Intelligence, 10*, 225–240.

Weischedel, R. M., & Sondheimer, N. K. (1983). Meta-rules as a basis for processing ill-formed input. *American Journal of Computational Linguistics, 9*, 161–177.

Werbos, P. (1974). *Beyond regression: New tools for prediction and analysis in behavioral science.* Unpublished doctoral dissertation, Harvard University.

Wermter, S., & Lehnert, W. G. (1990). A hybrid symbolic/connectionist model for noun phrase understanding. *Connection Science, 1.*

Wermter, S. (1990). Combining symbolic and connectionist techniques for coordination in natural language. In H. Marburger (Ed.), *Proceedings of the 14th German Workshop on Artificial Intelligence.* Berlin: Springer-Verlag.

Wilks, Y. (1976). Natural language systems within the A.I. paradigm: A survey. *American Journal of Computational Linguistics.* Microfiche #40.

Winston, P. H. (1984). *Artificial intelligence* (2nd ed.). Reading, MA: Addison-Wesley.

10
Hybrid Connectionist Models:
Temporary Bridges Over the
Gap Between the Symbolic
and the Subsymbolic

Trent E. Lange
University of California, Los Angeles

1. INTRODUCTION AND MOTIVATION

Connectionist networks, often known as neural networks or spreading-activation networks, have recently been the subject of a tremendous rebirth of interest, as researchers have begun to explore their advantages for cognitive models ranging from low-level sensory abilities to high-level reasoning. Connectionist models employ *massively parallel* networks of relatively simple processing elements that draw their inspiration from neurons and neurobiology, as opposed to traditional symbolic artificial intelligence (AI) models, which are generally based on serial Von Neumann architectures. This chapter will explore the benefits of building models that combine three major levels of network architectures that can be considered connectionist in a very broad sense: *distributed connectionist networks* and *localist connectionist networks,* which fall under the strict definition of connectionism assumed elsewhere in this book, and *marker-passing networks,* the most connectionist of the symbolic architectures. Each has different types of cognitive models for which they are best suited.

Distributed connectionist networks, sometimes known as *Parallel Distributed Processing* or *subsymbolic* models, are networks which represent knowledge as *distributed* patterns of activation across their units (see Dinsmore, chap. 1, this volume). Most distributed network models have learning rules (such as back-propagation (Rumelhart, Hinton, & McClelland, 1986), to *train* their connections' weights to generate desired input/output behavior. With such training rules, distributed networks are able to perform statistical category generalization, perform noise-resistant associative retrieval, and exhibit robustness to damage. They have been successfully employed for low-level tasks such as visual pattern recognition (Fukushima, Miyake, & Ito, 1983), speech consonant recognition

(Waibel, 1989), and assigning roles to constituents of sentences (McClelland & Kawamoto, 1986). On the other hand, distributed networks have had difficulty with both dynamic variable bindings and the representation of structure needed to handle complex conceptual relationships, and so are not currently well-suited for high-level cognitive tasks such as natural language understanding and planning.

Localist connectionist networks, sometimes known as *structured* or *spreading-activation* networks, also use units with simple numeric activation and output functions (see Dinsmore, chap. 1 this volume), but instead represent knowledge using *semantic networks* in which concepts are represented by individual units and their labeled interconnections. Unlike distributed networks, localist networks are parallel at the knowledge level and have structural relationships between concepts built into the connectivity of the network. As a result, localist networks are especially well-suited for cognitive tasks such as word-sense disambiguation (Waltz & Pollack, 1985), limited inference (Shastri, 1988), and language generation (Gasser, 1988). Unfortunately, localist networks lack the powerful learning and generalization capabilities of distributed networks and also have had difficulty with dynamic variable bindings and other capabilities of symbolic models.

Marker-passing networks are unlike distributed networks and localist networks in that their units do not use numeric activation functions, but instead use built-in symbolic capabilities. Like localist networks, they also represent knowledge in semantic networks and retain parallelism at the knowledge level. However, instead of spreading numeric activation values, marker-passing networks propagate symbolic markers, and so support the variable binding necessary for rule application while retaining the power of symbolic systems. Thus, they have been able to approach high-level areas such as planning (Hendler, 1988) and natural language understanding (Charniak, 1986). On the downside, marker-passing networks' units are more complex than those of distributed networks and localist networks, they do not possess the learning capabilities of distributed networks, and they do not exhibit the constraint-satisfaction capabilities of localist networks.

Most connectionist researchers have explored and built models within a single connectionist level. However, although staying true to one connectionist approach has its appeal, the current limitations of each level often restricts the tasks one is able to perform. For researchers interested in modelling a particular human capability, it is therefore sometimes necessary to build *hybrid* models using elements from more than one level of connectionist modelling.[1] This chapter argues that building such hybrid models supports the long-term goal of explain-

---

[1]The term *hybrid model* is sometimes used to refer to networks that attempt to explicitly duplicate symbolic processing abilities. Marker-passing models are often called hybrid or symbolic models because of their explicit propagation of symbolic markers. The term is also occasionally used to refer to normal localist networks because their units have symbolic labels (though the labels generally do not affect network processing). In this chapter, however, the term *hybrid model* is used only to describe models that combine elements from more than one level (distributed, localist, marker-passing) of connectionist processing.

ing high-level cognitive behavior in terms of the actual structure of the brain by allowing progress on levels that might otherwise be stymied and highlighting areas that need more extensive research.

To illustrate the benefits of this approach, this chapter describes three models: (a) a localist connectionist network that illustrates that the abilities of hybrid models can often eventually be built into a single network level, (b) a hybrid network that is able to model an integration of cognitive functions not easily plausible in a single network level, and (c) a distributed connectionist network that is a step toward removing one of the hidden hybrid mechanisms found in most connectionist models.

1.1. Connectionist and Symbolic Models

To understand the need to build hybrid models, it is important to know the abilities and limitations of each connectionist level. Although it is possible that a single type of connectionist model (such as distributed connectionist networks) will eventually be able to model all levels of human cognition, this is certainly far from the case now. However, models from all levels of connectionist networks taken together currently span a wide range of human abilities (if only to a limited depth), ranging from low-level perceptual tasks to high-level reasoning.

On area that has been approached by all types of connectionist and symbolic models is that of semantic natural language understanding. Natural language understanding is a good area to illustrate the benefits and drawbacks of each connectionist level because it requires a whole range of abilities ranging from low-level pattern matching (such as retrieval of word meanings and simple case-role filling), to high-level manipulation of complex symbolic representations (such as for comprehending intricate stories or editorials), to working with noisy and incomplete data (requiring disambiguation and reinterpretation), to learning and generalization.

1.1.1. Symbolic Rule-Based Models.   Symbolic artificial intelligence (AI) systems have so far been the types of models best able to perform high-level reasoning and natural language understanding. A good example is BORIS (Dyer, 1983), a natural language understanding program for modelling in-depth understanding of relatively long and complex stories. BORIS had a hand-coded symbolic knowledge base containing knowledge structures representing various actions, plans, goals, emotional affects, and methods for avoiding planning failures. When reading in a story, BORIS would fire rules from its knowledge base to perform inferencing and form an internal representation of the story, about which it could then answer questions. Other models that have successfully approached complex parts of the language understanding process have all had similar types of knowledge representation and rule-firing capabilities.

Connectionist networks, however, have significant potential advantages over traditional symbolic approaches to the interpretation process. Their conceptual knowledge is stored entirely in an interconnected network of units whose states are computed in parallel, calculated solely by local update functions that are based on their previous state and that of the units to which they are connected. As a result, a major portion of the understanding process could potentially be controlled by a relatively simple and local spreading-activation mechanism, instead of by large collections of brittle and sometimes ad hoc rules.

1.1.2. Distributed Connectionist Networks.
Distributed connectionist models have had a great deal of success modelling low-level natural language understanding tasks, especially those requiring similarity-based learning. A number of researchers have argued that this new subsymbolic paradigm will completely subsume the symbolic paradigm, as the explicit rules used in symbolic models are replaced by the more robust interactions of distributed representations and connection weights learned from experience (Rumelhart & McClelland, 1986). Although some of the severest criticisms of this stand (Fodor & Pylyshyn, 1988; Pinker & Prince, 1988) have been partially rebutted by recent models showing that distributed models can represent some limited variable bindings and constituent structure (e.g., Pollack, 1990; Touretzky & Hinton, 1988), current distributed models are still quite limited in comparison to symbolic models in their abilities to perform high-level processing such as natural language understanding.

A good example of how distributed connectionist models have been used to approach language understanding is provided by the case-role assignment model of McClelland and Kawamoto (1986). The main task of their model is to learn to assign the proper semantic case roles for sentences. For example, given the syntactic surface form of the sentence *The boy broke the window,* their network is trained to place the semantic microfeature representation of the subject *Boy* into the units representing the Agent role on the output layer, whereas given *The rock broke the window,* it is trained to place the representation of the subject *Rock* into the Instrument role. Their network is also trained to perform lexical disambiguation, for example, mapping the pattern for the word *bat* to a *Baseball-Bat* for sentences such as *The boy hit the ball with the bat,* and to a *Flying-Bat* for sentences such as *The bat flew.* Once the input–output pairs have been learned, the network exhibits a certain amount of generalization by mapping the case roles and performing lexical disambiguation for novel inputs similar to the training sentences.

McClelland and Kawamoto's model for language understanding has the main limitation that its output can only handle direct, one-step mappings from the input to the output. This limits it to processing isolated sentences, and only those that can be understood and disambiguated based on the surface semantics of the input alone. Two distributed connectionist models that get around this limitation are the models of Miikkulainen and Dyer (1989) and St. John (1990). Both models use *recurrent networks* with a hidden layer of units whose activation pattern essentially stores the state (or *gestalt*) of the stories being understood. This allows them to learn to process more complex language based on scripts (such as going to a restaurant) and other script-like stories (Schank & Abelson,

1977). Both models have the lexical disambiguation abilities of McClelland and Kawamoto's model, but, more importantly, are able to infer unmentioned story events and role-fillers from the script that has been recognized by the hidden layer.

Unfortunately, there may be significant problems in scaling such *pattern-transformation* distributed connectionist models to handle more complex language. Both Miikkulainen and Dyer and St. John's models work by resolving constraints from input context to recognize one of their trained scripts and instantiate it with the bindings of the particular input story. However, much of language understanding involves the inference of causal relationships between events for completely novel stories in which no script or previously trained input/output pair can be recognized. This requires *dynamic inferencing*—a process of constructing chains of inferences over simple known rules, with each inference resulting in a potentially novel intermediate state (Touretzky, 1990). It remains to be seen whether a single blended activation pattern on the bank of hidden units in recurrent networks can simultaneously hold and make dynamic inferences from multiple, never-before encountered interpretation chains.

Other distributed models explicitly encode variables and rules, such as the models of Touretzky and Hinton (1988) and Dolan and Smolensky (1989). Consequently, such *rule-implementing* distributed models are able to perform some of the dynamic inferencing necessary for language understanding. Unfortunately, however, the types of rules they can currently encode are generally limited. More importantly, they are serial at the knowledge level because they can fire only one rule at a time. This is a serious drawback for natural language understanding, particularly for ambiguous text, in which the often large number of multiple alternative interpretations often requires that the inference paths be explored in parallel (Lange, in press).

1.1.3. Localist Connectionist Networks. Localist connectionist models represent knowledge in semantic networks in which concepts are represented by individual units and relations between concepts are encoded by weighted connections between those units. The numeric activation level on each conceptual unit generally represents the amount of evidence available for its concept in a given context. Knowledge is spread across the network (as opposed to the concentration of knowledge in the weights between the single input and output layer of most distributed models), thus localist models have the potential to pursue multiple candidate interpretations of a story in parallel as each interpretation is represented by activation in different local areas of the network. This makes them ideally suited to the disambiguation portion of the language understanding process, because it is achieved automatically as related concepts under consideration provide graded activation evidence and feedback to one another in a form of analog constraint relaxation.

As an example of how localist connectionist models process language and perform disambiguation, consider the sentence:

The astronomer married the star. (Star-Marriage)

The word *star* could be easily disambiguated to *Movie-Star* by a symbolic rule-based system having selectional restrictions (even astronomers cannot marry celestial bodies, except perhaps metaphorically). However, many readers report this and similar sentences as *cognitive doubletakes* because *astronomer* initially primes the *Celestial-Body* interpretation. Figure 10.1 shows an extended version of the semantic portion of the localist network Waltz and Pollack (1985) built to process Star-Marriage and illustrate this effect. After the input units for Star-Marriage are clamped to a high level of activation, the *Celestial-Body* interpretation of *star* initially acquires more activation than the *Movie-Star* interpretation because of priming from *Astronomer* through *Astronomy* (Fig. 10.2). However, *Movie-Star* eventually wins out because activation feedback over the semantic connections from the *Marry* unit to *Movie-Star* outweighs that spreading from the *Astronomer* unit to *Celestial-Body*.

Unfortunately, the applicability of localist connectionist models to natural language understanding has been severely hampered because of their difficulties representing dynamic role-bindings and performing inferencing.[2] Their lack of variable binding abilities leaves them prone to crosstalk even for simple sentences. For example, the network of Fig. 10.1 has no way to distinguish between the sentences *The astronomer saw the star* and *The star saw the astronomer,* despite the crucial difference that the role-bindings make in their interpretation. More importantly, without a mechanism to represent such dynamic bindings, they cannot propagate them to make the chains of inferences necessary for understanding more complex language. This has so far stopped them from going beyond simple language processing that can be resolved based solely on the surface semantics of the input.

1.1.4.   Marker-Passing Networks.   Marker-passing models operate by spreading symbolic markers in parallel across labelled semantic networks similar to those of localist connectionist networks. Interpretation of the input is achieved when propagation of markers finds a path of units connecting words and concepts from the input text. The symbolic information held in their markers and networks enables them to represent dynamic role-bindings to perform high-level inferencing for natural language understanding (cf. Charniak, 1986; Eiselt, 1987; Granger, Eiselt, & Holbrook, 1986; Norvig, 1989; Riesbeck & Martin, 1986).

As an example of how marker-passing networks process language and perform disambiguation, consider the following text (from Eiselt, 1987):

Fred asked Wilma to marry him. Wilma began to cry. (Marriage)

---

[2]Ajjanagadde and Shastri (1989), Barnden (1990), and Holldobler (1990) described structured models that can perform some variable-binding and inferencing, but that do not have the disambiguation abilities of normal structured spreading-activation models.

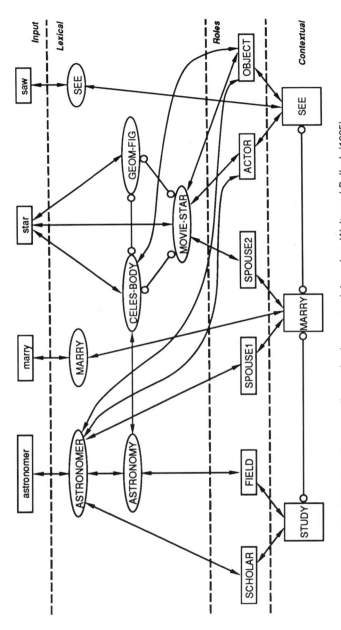

FIG. 10.1. Localist spreading-activation network based on Waltz and Pollack (1985). Lines with arrows are excitatory connections; lines with open circles are inhibitory.

243

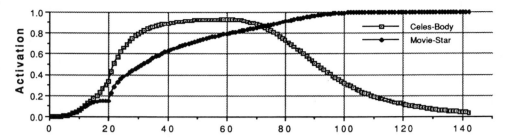

FIG. 10.2.   Activations of meaning of word *star* after *astronomer married star* is clamped for network in Fig. 10.1.

Interpreting this text requires that a causal relationship be inferred between Fred's proposal and Wilma's crying. One possible reason for her crying was that she was happy about his proposal and crying "tears of joy." To understand this sentence and resolve the ambiguity, ATLAST (Eiselt, 1987) uses the network shown in Fig. 10.3 by passing markers starting from the units for *Cry-Tears* and *Propose-Marriage*. This propagation of markers finds the path *Cry-Tears* ↔ *Happy-State* ↔ *Happy-Event* ↔ *Propose-Marriage*, returning the "tears of joy" interpretation. Besides finding the inference path representing the interpretation of the story, the symbolic pointers held in the markers also keep track of the role-bindings, so that the model can clearly resolve that it was Fred who did the *Propose-Marriage* and Wilma who did the *Cry-Tears,* and not the other way around.

Much text, of course, is ambiguous and has multiple possible interpretations, and the Marriage example is no exception. Another possible reason that Mary began to cry was that she was saddened or upset by Fred's proposal. The same propagation of markers that found the "tears of joy" path will therefore find a second path, *Cry-Tears* ↔ *Sad-State* ↔ *Sad-Event* ↔ *Propose-Marriage.* To resolve such ambiguities, marker-passing systems generally use a serial heuristic path evaluator separate from the marker-passing process to select the most relevant path from the many paths generated. Such path evaluators usually include rules that select shorter over longer paths, reject paths that do not include as much of the input as competing ones, and so forth. For example, to disambiguate between the "tears of joy" and "saddened" paths, ATLAST applies an evalua-

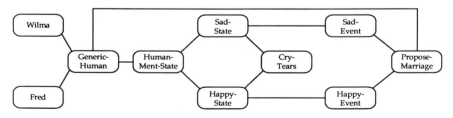

FIG. 10.3.   Marker-passing network from Eiselt (1987).

tion metric between two competing paths of equal length that selects the oldest path. The *Happy-State* path was discovered first (arbitrarily, in this example), and thus remains as the interpretation of the input.

As their use of heuristic path-evaluators indicate, marker-passing systems generally permit themselves the luxury of using traditional symbolic buffers and programs to complement the spreading-activation process of the network. This allows them to build up complex symbolic representations of stories outside the network (as done by Norvig, 1989) or hold rejected inference paths to allow reinterpretation if a path is rediscovered (as done by ATLAST when Marriage is followed by *Wilma was saddened by the proposal.*).

Marker-passing systems have the advantage that their parallel instantiation of inference paths makes them extremely efficient at generating different possible interpretations of the input. Unfortunately, the bottleneck for marker-passing systems is the separate path evaluation mechanisms used to select between generated interpretations (the heart of the disambiguation problem). The main problem is the extremely large number of spurious (i.e., nonimportant or logically impossible) paths that the marker-passing process generates, which the path evaluators must separately weed out. For even very small networks, these spurious paths often represent over 90% of the paths generated (Charniak, 1986). More importantly, as the size of the networks increase to represent more world knowledge, there is a corresponding explosion in the number of paths generated. These paths must be evaluated serially by a path evaluator, which negates marker-passing systems' main efficiency advantage.

1.2. Abilities and Limitations of Each Connectionist Level

As can be seen in the previous overview of how each connectionist level has been used for semantic language understanding, each level has a set of abilities and limitations that partially overlaps with the others. This is also true, of course, for their use in areas other than language understanding. A summary is presented in Table 10.1, which shows many of the processes necessary for cognitive modeling and how well each level of connectionist model performs them.[3]

1. *Self-Organization and Learning.* Distributed networks usually use learning algorithms such as backpropagation (Rumelhart et al., 1986) to train their weights to map inputs to desired outputs. Similarity-based generalization and categorization are natural side-effects of the learning process. No such learning algorithms exist to organize localist networks, which must have their knowledge hand-coded, though adding to an existing network by recruitment of new units has been demonstrated (Diederich, 1990). The knowledge in marker-passing

---

[3]A more detailed comparison between subsymbolic distributed network models and traditional symbolic models can be found in Dyer (1990).

TABLE 10.1
Relative Processing Abilities of Distributed Connectionist
Networks, Localist Connectionist Networks, Marker-Passing Networks,
and Traditional Symbolic Models.

Capability	Distributed Networks	Localist Networks	Marker-Passing Networks	Symbolic Models
Self-organization and Learning	+	(−)	(−)	(+)
Robustness to Noise and Damage	+	−	−	−
Memory Blending and Interference	+	(−)	(−)	(−)
Associative Retrieval	+	+	−	−
Simple Processing Elements	+	+	−	−
Smoothly Varying Commitment	+	+	−	−
Priming and Decay Effects	(−)	+	−	−
Complex Conceptual Relationships	(−)	+	+	+
Variable Bindings	(−)	(+)	+	+
Dynamic Constituent, Recursive Structure	−	(−)	+	+
Dynamic Inferencing	(−)	(+)	+	+
Knowledge-level Parallelism	(−)	+	+	−
Meta-Reasoning	−	−	+	+

+ indicates something the class of models does relatively well.
− indicates something the class of models does only with great difficulty, if at all.
(+) and (−) indicate an ability demonstrated only recently or in a subset of the models.

networks and symbolic models must generally be hand-coded also, though many symbolic models learn through one-shot explanation-based learning (e.g., Pazzani, Dyer, & Flowers, 1987) or case-based reasoning (e.g., Schank & Leake, 1989).

2. *Robustness to Noise and Damage.* Knowledge in distributed networks is distributed over a large set of units, so destruction or introduction of noise to a random subset of units, weights, or inputs has relatively little effect on input/output behavior (the models degrade gracefully). In contrast to this, destruction of random units or symbols in localist networks, marker-passing networks, and symbolic models causes permanent and localized damage to a specific piece of knowledge.

3. *Memory Blending and Interference.* Human memory is far from perfect, with similar memories often blending or interfering with each other. Such blending occurs naturally in distributed networks, because similar memories share similar weight interconnection values and output activation patterns. On the other hand, although some symbolic models are able to partially explain confusions by assuming that different knowledge structures point to shared substructures, it is generally difficult to explain memory blending in localist networks, marker-passing networks, or symbolic models, because individual units or symbols perfectly represent a given memory.

4. *Associative Retrieval*. Retrieving information in distributed networks and localist networks is generally done by clamping one or more of the network's inputs and allowing the network to settle into a state satisfying the largest number of constraints. Networks are often able to complete the pattern even when incomplete or noisy patterns are given as input, because the overall activation constraints from the partial pattern will likely be closest to those of the corresponding complete pattern. Retrieval in marker-passing networks is comparatively more brittle, because connections between units are generally all-or-none. Similarly, symbolic models generally retrieve only those items that match a set of explicit indices, so that any missing indices from partial input may rule-out retrieval. In general, it is more difficult for the binary nature of marker-passing networks and symbolic models to model the influence of contextual priming and varying influence of experience on retrieval.

5. *Simple Processing Elements*. Distributed networks and localist networks are made up entirely of relatively simple numeric processing units whose activations are based on their previous activations and the activations of their neighboring units (Feldman & Ballard, 1982). Marker-passing networks, on the other hand, use more complex units that can hold the symbolic backpointers and structured information of markers, and often use labeled connections that perform different actions depending on the type or contents of those markers. Marker-passing networks, however, are still simpler than most traditional symbolic models, which generally use specialized rules and procedures to operate on and between knowledge structures.

6. *Smoothly Varying Commitment*. The graded activation levels and weights in distributed and localist networks allow them to have smoothly varying levels of commitment to individual solutions, which can easily change given new biasing input. Marker-passing networks and symbolic models, on the other hand, generally use binary connections and rules so that a solution path can only be either active or inactive. Disambiguation and reinterpretation are thus more natural in distributed networks and localist networks, because each interpretation can have graded levels of activation, as opposed to marker-passing networks and symbolic models, in which disambiguation must be performed by separate (possibly conflicting) disambiguation heuristics.

7. *Priming and Decay Effects*. Activation on units in localist networks generally represents the amount of evidence available for concepts in a given context. Localist spreading-activation networks have therefore been able to model many human priming effects, such as how people respond more quickly when presented with inputs similar to what they've just seen. Such priming effects are impossible in standard feed-forward distributed networks, because they have no record of their immediately previous states. Recurrent distributed networks do provide some record of their previous states, so they do exhibit a form of priming, in that previous inputs influence future interpretations, but have no obvious way to model effects of priming on human reaction-times. Marker-passing networks and

symbolic models are very awkward at modelling priming effects because of their general difficulties with smoothly varying commitments.

8. *Complex Conceptual Relationships.* Complex relationships between concepts (such as planning relationships) can readily be represented in localist networks and marker-passing networks by structured connections between units in the network. Such relationship rules are similarly direct to represent with pointers and rules in symbolic models. This is not the case in distributed networks, which have until recently had difficulty representing complex structured relationships, one of their primary limitations (Fodor & Pylyshyn, 1988). These criticisms have been partially answered by recent rule-implementing distributed network models (cf. Touretzky & Hinton, 1988), and distributed models using recurrent networks and reduced descriptions (cf. Pollack, in 1990), but are still a problem.

9. *Variable Bindings.* Marker-passing networks and symbolic models use their built-in abilities to allow variables to be dynamically bound to symbols for any type of structure, and new symbols (or markers) can be created during program execution. Localist networks, having only numeric activation levels, have only recently become able to hold variable bindings (cf. Ajjanagadde & Shastri, 1989; Lange & Dyer, 1989), and are still limited with respect to symbolic models. Variable bindings have been even more problematic in distributed networks, but have also been shown to a limited degree in rule-implementing distributed networks. More traditional pattern-transformation distributed networks can also be trained to act as if they have variable bindings, but have the problem that bindings are often overridden by crosstalk from bindings that occurred often in the training set (St. John, 1990).

10. *Dynamic Constituent, Recursive Structure.* Marker-passing networks and symbolic models can form an unlimited number of bindings without crosstalk, so can easily represent constituency and recursive structures, such as *John told Bill that Fred told Mary that . . .* Because recent localist network bindings techniques are limited in their binding capacity, it is difficult for them to represent such dynamic recursive structures, though Barnden (1990) and Holldobler (1990) have shown that it can be done, at least in untraditional localist networks. Recurrent distributed networks can be trained to learn *static* recursive structures (e.g., Pollack, 1990), but have not yet been able to represent dynamic recursive structures that they have not been trained on.

11. *Dynamic Inferencing.* Symbolic models have the ability to perform dynamic inferencing from an initial set of bindings by applying their rules to infer novel intermediate states having new bindings. Further inferences can then follow repeatedly from the new intermediate states until the desired state is reached. This ability is crucial when a system cannot reach the desired state in a single step (Touretzky, 1990). Marker-passing networks and recent localist networks can hold variable bindings and propagate them in turn for inferencing, so they

can also perform dynamic inferencing, though their inference rules are generally limited in complexity relative to symbolic models. Traditional pattern-transformation distributed networks cannot perform dynamic inferencing, because they transform the input (or set of inputs) to the output in a single step. Rule-implementing distributed networks, on the other hand, are able to perform a limited amount of dynamic inferencing.

12. *Knowledge-Level Parallelism.* Marker-passing networks and localist networks are able to explore multiple solutions in parallel because alternative interpretations are represented by markers or activation patterns across different local areas of the network. This is crucial because with dynamic inferencing there are often a very large number of alternative solution paths, especially in language understanding and planning. In contrast, although distributed networks update their units in parallel, they are serial at the knowledge level because they represent all dynamic knowledge in a single set of units on the output or in a hidden layer, and so cannot make dynamic inferences from more than one potential solution at a time. Pattern transformation distributed networks can sometimes hold ambiguous solutions in a single blended activation pattern on their bank of hidden units, but it remains to be seen how far such blended activation patterns can be extended to simultaneously hold and make dynamic inferences from multiple, never-before encountered solution paths.

13. *Meta-Reasoning.* Symbolic models can reason and operate on knowledge from many different substructures of their program, so long as that knowledge is represented by globally interpretable symbolic structures. Marker-passing networks can do this also because they often employ a separate high-level symbolic program to interpret and work with the results from the network's marker-passing process. Pure distributed networks and localist networks, however, attempt to complete their tasks entirely within the network, and so cannot perform meta-reasoning by resorting to symbolic code.[4] In addition, the knowledge encoded in the weights of the network (especially in distributed networks) is generally meant to perform the network's given task, and is therefore not as readily interpretable by external mechanisms. It is theoretically possible for distributed or localist network models to perform meta-reasoning within the network or with other subnetworks, but this is an area of connectionist research that has remained relatively unexplored.

2. THE CASE FOR HYBRID MODELS

All other things being equal, it is always desirable to build models out of as simple and homogeneous building-blocks as possible. This is one of the attrac-

---

[4]For practical purposes, results of the network are almost always analyzed by symbolic code or the human modeler. However, this analysis is rarely considered an integral part of the model.

tions of connectionist models in general, and distributed and localist connectionist models in particular, because their entire knowledge and processing mechanisms are built up of simple numeric processing elements and their local connections. It is also a reason against building hybrid models, because by definition hybrid models are made up of heterogeneous building-blocks from different connectionist levels that may or may not integrate naturally.

However, as the previous section illustrated, it is often not possible to build a successful model of a given cognitive task with elements from a single connectionist level given their current limitations. One is then confronted with a choice: Abandon or scale back the task, attempt to extend the abilities of the connectionist level to handle the task, or utilize elements from another connectionist level to handle the task in a hybrid model. Obviously abandoning or scaling back the task is not always a desirable solution. Extending the abilities of the connectionist level to handle the task is perhaps ideally the best solution, and certainly a valuable long-term goal, but often requires theoretical breakthroughs that are not possible in a reasonable amount of time. Thus, if one is interested in building a model of human performance of a given task, then often the only possible approach is to build a hybrid model that combines elements and capabilities from multiple connectionist levels.

A number of researchers have recently argued that it is often desirable to build hybrid connectionist models (cf. Dyer, 1990; Hendler, 1989a; Holyoak, in press; Rose, 1990). One argument is from an engineering perspective—if one's goal is to build a certain application or model without regard to the solutions' simplicity or elegance, then building a hybrid system is often the simplest (if not only) solution. This is true for real-world applications that require both low-level pattern-matching abilities and high-level symbolic abilities, such as automated manufacturing or testing applications that need both low-level visual perception and expert reasoning (Hendler, 1989a). This is also true for researchers interested in modelling human performance, where matching psychological data is often more important than having a homogeneous model (Holyoak, in press).

Another reason for developing hybrid connectionist models is that they often turn out to be the most appropriate or useful level of description for complex systems. As Dinsmore (chap. 1 in this volume) points out, high-level symbolic models are often the best description of processes that may actually happen on a lower (i.e., connectionist) level. The high-level abstractions of symbolic models allow predictions of cognitive behavior that would otherwise be too complex to understand. On the other hand, some processes do not lend themselves to higher-level abstractions, and are best described at a lower connectionist level. For large cognitive models that combine multiple such types of processing, the best model for descriptive and predictive processes is therefore often a hybrid in which each component is described and processed at its most useful level of description.

Even when using a single connectionist level is a major consideration, and a theoretical breakthrough seems possible to extend its abilities to handle a certain task, there are often good reasons to build a hybrid model first. If it appears necessary to have a certain ability, and that ability is present in another kind of network, then building a hybrid model of the two networks can serve as a useful prototype to validate the approach. If the hybrid model solves the problem or comes close to solving it, then it verifies that finding a way to embed the missing ability within the original network level will indeed be a fruitful solution. However, if the hybrid model having the ability in question is not able to solve the problem, then it serves as strong evidence that either a different approach is needed or there are more facets to the problem than originally expected, and the desired ability is not enough. Depending on the answer to this question, the hybrid model can therefore either save substantial effort trying to give the original network an unnecessary ability, or can shed light on other abilities that are needed to model the task.

2.1. Previous Hybrid Connectionist Models

Most connectionist research in cognitive modelling has involved building models out of a single connectionist level. Only recently have researchers begun to explore hybrid connectionist models as the advantages and disadvantages of each level have begun to become more clear.

Most work on hybrid connectionist models has been on networks that integrate marker-passing and localist connectionist techniques. A good example of the development of such models is the transformation of Hendler's (1988) marker-passing planning model to a model that uses both marker-passing and localist connectionist techniques (Hendler, 1989b). In Hendler's original marker-passing planning system, a symbolic problem-solving program would assert known facts and desired goals by placing markers into its semantic network memory. The marker-passing system then propagated those markers in parallel throughout the network, with intersections between markers reported back to the symbolic problem-solving program. The program would then evaluate the paths of concepts meeting at those intersections with a set of path-evaluating heuristics to determine whether they proposed a solution to an existing problem, caused a conflict, or otherwise provided useful information to the planner.

One of the main problems for Hendler's original marker-passing system was the rigidity of the underlying symbolic representation scheme that it (and all marker-passing systems) depend on. As in all marker-passing systems, there must be a link between two concepts for the connection between them to be found and used—for example, a link classifying a knife as a weapon. However, in many cases a connection between two concepts needs to be found, but would not normally exist as an explicit connection—for example, an ornate Egyptian letter opener would not normally be classified as a weapon, but could be considered one in certain contexts (it is pointed, metallic, and sharp, like a knife). To more generally handle these kinds of cases, it is necessary to break the representation of concepts into the individual semantic features that describe them, something that causes problems in pure marker passing systems because of the all-or-none nature of marker-passing paths. Hendler (1989b) therefore expanded his networks to contain units representing needed semantic microfeatures and to include numeric *zorch* and threshold terms similar to the activation of localist connectionist networks. In the newer system, markers still propagate to find path intersections, but also hold numeric zorch terms representing their strength. Most importantly, these zorch amounts add up as activation on the individual units they reach, so that a unit that shares many features with another marked unit will receive a lot of activation and become part of the marker paths (e.g., a knife from a letter opener, because they are connected between the feature units for pointed, metallic, and sharp), but units that share only minimal features will not receive enough activation to support further marker propagation (e.g., a spoon from a letter opener, because it only shares the metallic feature). By including the analog evidence combination abilities of localist networks in his marker-passing system, Hendler was therefore able to solve a number of the representational problems of marker-passing systems and to approach a problem that neither level of modelling could perform well separately.

Kitano, Tomabechi, and Levin (1989) described a model for natural language parsing and disambiguation that integrates marker-passing and localist connectionist techniques for much the same reason. In their system, marker-passing with three different kinds of markers is used to generate inferences and different hypotheses of a text's interpretation. One of the types of markers in their system serves as an *activation marker* that holds a numeric *cost* of the interpretation that it is a part of. The activation markers' costs increase whenever they mark previously inactive (unprimed) concepts or do not satisfy constraints imposed on their interpretation path. The activation markers over the path of units whose interpretation best matches the context of the story therefore tend to have the lowest costs, and are selected to represent the winning interpretation. This numeric summation of costs allows their system to integrate priming information and constraints to perform disambiguation better than purely symbolic marker-passing systems. Like Hendler's (1989b) hybrid planning system, the integration of localist connectionist techniques with marker-passing into a hybrid model therefore enables processing that would be difficult in a purely marker-passing system.

Another hybrid marker-passing and localist connectionist network approach is to build localist networks that control their spread of activation using some of the symbolic techniques of marker-passing systems. Rose (1990) used this approach in SCALIR, a model that performs conceptual retrieval of legal documents from a large semantic network. SCALIR uses a localist network whose units and interconnections represent concepts and documents in the legal domain, but whose units hold hybrid vectors of activation rather than a single activation value. Like connections between units in marker-passing networks, SCALIR's connections have symbolic labels that have different effects on the spread of activation depending on their type. Connections with certain labels allow all components of the activity vector to be propagated through to the next unit after being multiplied by its weight, whereas connections with other labels let only a single specified component of the vector through. These different symbolic labels on SCALIR's connections allow the spreading-activation search process to be controlled symbolically, as in marker-passing systems, while retaining the associative retrieval and learning abilities of localist connectionist networks.

There have been fewer hybrid models that integrate localist connectionist and distributed connectionist networks. Sumida and Dyer (1989) proposed a potential solution to the problem of distributed connectionist networks' being serial at the knowledge-level by integrating subnetworks of distributed ensembles into a large network that globally resembles a localist semantic network. Each general concept is represented by a distributed ensemble of units, rather than the single unit they would be represented with in localist networks, so they can be trained to store actual long-term memory instances of those concepts using distributed learning techniques, giving them an advantage over pure localist networks. On the other hand, the fact that the network is structured globally like a localist network (with ensembles for related concepts being connected to each other) gives their networks the potential to retain knowledge-level parallelism, an advantage over pure distributed networks.

2.2. Hybrid Connectionist and Symbolic Models

The largest class of hybrid models are models that combine connectionist networks with traditional symbolic processing. Such hybrid symbolic/connectionist models allow exploration of cognitive abilities that could not otherwise be handled in purely connectionist or symbolic systems, while being guides to best courses of future research. Most such models are distributed connectionist models that utilize symbolic abilities to handle portions of the task that the distributed networks cannot yet handle, such as the use of symbolic buffers in Kwasny and Faisal's (chap. 9 in this volume) hybrid syntactic parser to store and manipulate the parse trees that their distributed networks are trained to operate on and build.

Hybrid symbolic/connectionist systems are especially valuable for functional approaches to model design, where a system is designed as a set of interconnected functional modules that are first implemented symbolically but are gradually replaced with connectionist modules. An example of this approach is DYNASTY (Lee, Flowers, & Dyer, 1990), a script-based story understander that uses multiple modules of recurrent distributed networks that access a symbolic dictionary. In their model, each distributed network is trained to serve as a module performing a separate processing subtask, such as parsing sequential input text into individual event representations, recognizing that a sequence of events fits into a particular script (e.g., going to a restaurant), and paraphrasing the recognized script. Many of these distributed modules were initially implemented symbolically to allow testing of the overall model's concept, and were replaced one-by-one as time and opportunity presented it. The remaining symbolic component of DYNASTY is a symbolic hash table used as a "global dictionary" to store the representations of concepts and events it has learned and the symbols that represent them. Different distributed network modules access and store values in this symbolic global dictionary when needed.

An example of a hybrid symbolic/connectionist model that uses localist networks is Kintsch's (1988) construction-integration model of the psychological time course of language comprehension. Kintsch's model uses a symbolic production system to build symbolic representations of the alternative interpretations of a text and to construct a localist network in which the different interpretations compete. The spreading-activation process of the constructed localist network then serves to integrate the constraints from context (in the form of the excitatory and inhibitory connections constructed by the production system) to disambiguate and choose the correct interpretation. The use of the symbolic production system allows Kintsch's model to perform the rule-firing and inferencing that is difficult for purely localist models, whereas the constraint satisfaction of the constructed localist network allows modeling of the time-course of disambiguation that is difficult for purely symbolic models.

Finally, hybrid connectionist/symbolic models occasionally make use of multiple levels of connectionist processing in addition to their symbolic components. An example of this is Wermter and Lehnert's (1989) hybrid localist, distributed, and symbolic model for interpreting noun phrases such as *Note on the cause of ionization in the F-region*. Their model uses a symbolic syntactic parser to construct a localist network that represents the different possible combinations of nouns and prepositions for the input noun phrase. The localist network thereby constructed integrates the semantic and syntactic constraints to disambiguate the noun phrase and compute a preferred structural interpretation. The distributed connectionist networks are trained on the relative plausibility of semantic relationships between nouns, and are used to initialize the activations of the localist network that does the actual disambiguation. By combining distributed networks, localist networks, and symbolic processing, their hybrid model allows for a combination of learning, integration of competing constraints, and symbolic extraction of concepts difficult for models that use only one of the three types of processing.

3. GOING FROM HYBRIDS TO A SINGLE LEVEL

If hybrid connectionist models are to be of value to researchers ultimately interested in building models on a single connectionist level, then it must eventually be possible to at least roughly recreate the hybrid capabilities in that level. Even a successful hybrid model can turn out to be little more than an engineering exercise for a researcher interested in pure connectionist models if it turns out to be impossible to implement the hybrid in the desired level. For example, a hybrid symbolic/connectionist model for playing chess that uses symbolic routines to perform brute-force search of the game tree and a distributed network as a pattern-matcher to evaluate the board positions might be a perfectly reasonable engineering approach to building a competitive chess-playing program. However, it would probably fail as a significant stepping-stone to a purely connectionist model of human chess playing because it seems unlikely that any connectionist mechanism will be able to perform the millions of individual search and evaluation steps needed to implement the hybrid's brute-force search with human response times.

On the other hand, if the elements and mechanisms borrowed from a foreign connectionist level in a hybrid model have things in common with the desired connectionist level, then it is more likely that the model will eventually be implementable in that level. If it is indeed implementable, then the hybrid model will have fulfilled its mission of confirming that those mechanisms will be useful to the task. When a mechanism is actually developed to allow the hybrid model to be implemented in a single level, it will likely have advantages over the hybrid model (besides its homogeneity), because the new mechanism within the level will likely integrate more smoothly with the rest of the level than the sometimes artificial interface between elements of different levels in hybrid models (such as between numeric activation and symbolic markers).

For example, suppose a researcher has built a hybrid localist connectionist and marker-passing model to test how well a localist connectionist network would work for language understanding if it had a marker-passing network's ability to hold variable bindings and perform inferencing. If the hybrid model works well, then it would confirm that it would be valuable to have a marker-passing network's variable binding abilities in localist connectionist networks. However, to complete the circle and make the whole effort worthwhile for a researcher mainly interested in localist connectionist networks, it must turn out to indeed be possible to implement the marker-passer's variable binding abilities within a purely localist connectionist network.

3.1. ROBIN: A Localist Connectionist Network with Hybrid Abilities

As described in section 1.1, semantic language understanding is such a large and difficult task that no level of connectionist or symbolic processing can currently perform many aspects of it particularly well. Localist connectionist networks seem best-suited to handling the ambiguity rife in language, but have had no way to represent the variable bindings and perform the inferencing necessary for comprehension. Marker-passing networks are well-suited for performing inferencing, but are awkward when it comes to resolving ambiguities.

An obvious solution to this dilemma is to build a hybrid marker-passing and localist connectionist network that propagates markers to generate alternative inference paths and uses the constraint-satisfaction of the localist network's activation to disambiguate between those inference paths. Such a hybrid model is relatively straightforward to build because of the similarity of the unit structure in marker-passing and localist networks. The two types of propagation can in fact proceed in parallel across a single set of hybrid units that can hold both activation and markers. Lange, Hodges, Fuenmayor, and Belyeav (1989) briefly described a simple such hybrid model that performs both inferencing and disambiguation within the network. Kitano, Tomabechi, and Levin (1989) also described a hybrid marker-passing and localist connectionist model that performs parsing and disambiguation.

Given that a hybrid marker-passing and localist connectionist model has many potential advantages for semantic language understanding, it would be desirable to build a purely localist connectionist model that has the variable binding and inferencing abilities of marker-passing networks while retaining its disambiguation abilities.

Role Binding and Inferencing Network (ROBIN) (Lange & Dyer, 1989) is a purely localist, nonhybrid connectionist model that has many of the variable binding and inferencing abilities of marker-passing networks. ROBIN also retains the disambiguation abilities of normal localist networks, so it is able to perform high-level inferencing that requires lexical and pragmatic disambiguation. As an example of the kinds of input ROBIN is able to understand, consider the phrase:

P1: *John put the pot inside the dishwasher*

To understand P1, ROBIN disambiguates the word *pot* to mean a *Cooking-Pot,* and infers that the most likely reason for John putting it inside the dishwasher was to get it clean. However, later context often shows the original inferences to be wrong, forcing reinterpretation of the input. This is the case if P1 is followed by:

P2: *because the police were coming.*

Suddenly, the best interpretation for *pot* in P1 changes to *Marijuana,* and John's *Transfer-Inside* action seems to be a plan for hiding the *Marijuana* from the police to avoid his arrest. This reinterpretation can only be made after generating a chain of inferences to find the causal relationship between the two phrases (collectively referred to as Hiding Pot). Table 10.2 shows the inferences ROBIN makes to dynamically create this interpretation.

TABLE 10.2
Inferences ROBIN Makes to Understand the Sentence *John Put
the Pot Inside the Dishwasher Because the Police Were Coming.*
(Hiding Pot)

I1: If the police see John's marijuana, then they will know that he possesses an illegal object (since marijuana is an illegal substance).

I2: If the police know that John is in possession of an illegal object, then they will arrest him, since possessing an illegal object is a crime.

I3: John does not want to get arrested.

I4: John has the goal of stopping the police from seeing his marijuana.

I5: The police coming results in them being in the proximity of John and his marijuana.

I6: The police being in the proximity of John's marijuana enables them to see it.

I7: John's putting the marijuana inside the dishwasher results in the marijuana being inside the dishwasher.

I8: The marijuana is inside an opaque object (the dishwasher).

I9: Since the marijuana is inside an opaque object, the police cannot see it, thus satisfying John's goal.

From Lange & Dyer, 1989, Connection Science, 1(2), p. 182.

3.1.1. Structure of ROBIN.   ROBIN's network consists entirely of connectionist units (Feldman & Ballard, 1982) that perform simple numeric computations on their inputs: summation, summation with thresholding and decay, or maximization. Connections between units are weighted, and either excitatory or inhibitory. These networks encode semantic networks of frames representing world knowledge. Each frame has one or more roles, with each role having expectations and selectional restrictions on its fillers. Every frame is related to one or more other frames, with pathways between corresponding roles (representing general knowledge rules) for inferencing. This section gives a short overview of ROBIN and how it performs inferencing, but Lange and Dyer (1989) provided a detailed description.

As in most localist connectionist models, there is a single unit in the network for each frame or role concept in the knowledge base, with relations between concepts being represented by weighted connections between the units. Activation on a conceptual unit is *evidential,* corresponding to the amount of evidence available for the concept (either a frame or role) and the likelihood that it is selected in the current context.

As described before, representing the amount of evidence available for a concept, however, is not sufficient for complex inferencing tasks. A solution to the variable binding problem requires that some means exist for identifying a concept that is being dynamically bound to a role, as marker-passing networks do with the symbolic backpointers on their markers. Furthermore, the network's structure must allow these role-bindings to propagate across unit pathways that encode the knowledge base's rules (as do markers), thus dynamically instantiating inference paths representing the input.

3.1.2. Variable Binding with Signatures in Localist Connectionist Networks.

Representing variables and role-bindings is handled in ROBIN by network structure holding *signatures*—activation patterns that uniquely identify the concept bound to a role (introduced in Lange & Dyer, 1988). Every concept in the network has a set of *signature* units that output its signature, a constant activation pattern different from all other signatures. A dynamic binding exists when a role or variable's *binding units* have an activation pattern matching the activation pattern of the bound concept's signature. For example, in Fig. 10.4, the *virtual binding* of the Actor role of action *Transfer-Inside* (representing somebody putting an object inside another, as in P1) to *John* is represented by the fact that its binding units have the same activation pattern as *John*'s signature. The same binding units could, at another time, hold a different virtual binding, simply by having the activation pattern of another concept's signature. The complete *Transfer-Inside* frame is represented in the network by the group of units that include the conceptual unit *Transfer-Inside,* a conceptual unit for each of its roles (the Object role not shown), and the binding units for each of its roles.

In general, signatures can be uniquely identifying activation patterns of any size. Ideally, signatures are distributed activation patterns (e.g., made up of semantic microfeatures) that are themselves partial representations of the concept for which they stand. This allows the signatures themselves to be used as inputs for distributed learning mechanisms after they have been propagated for inferenc-

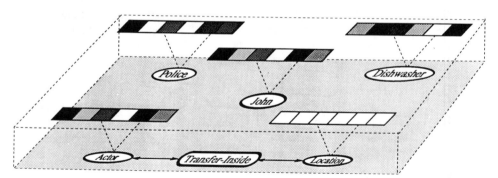

FIG. 10.4. Several concepts (ovals on lower plan) and their uniquely identifying signature patterns, along with the Actor and Location roles of the Transfer-Inside frame. Here each signature is a bank of six units, with increasing levels of activation represented by increasing darkness of shading (ranging from white = 0 to black = 1). The Actor role has a *virtual binding* to John because its binding units hold the same activation pattern as John's signature. The Location role shown here is currently unbound (binding banks have no activation).

ing. For simplicity, however, ROBIN's simulations are usually run with the signature patterns simply being arbitrarily generated scalar values that uniquely identify their concept.

3.1.3. Propagation of Signatures for Inferencing. The most important feature of signatures is that they can be propagated without change across long paths of binding units to dynamically instantiate candidate inference paths. Connections between binding units of frames' roles encode rules such as:

R1: [Actor X *Transfer-Inside* Object Y Location Z]
— results-in → [Object Y *Inside-Of* Location Z]
  (When an object is transferred inside of a location, then it is inside of that location)

Figures 10.5a and 10.5b illustrate how the network's structure automatically propagates signatures to fire rules such as R1. For simplicity, the signatures in the figure are uniquely identifying scalar values. Evidential activation for disambiguation is spread through the paths between conceptual units on the bottom plane (i.e., *Transfer-Inside* and its Object role), whereas signature activation for dynamic role-bindings is spread across the parallel paths of corresponding binding units (solid black circles) on the top plane. Units and connections for the Actor, Planner, and Location roles are not shown. As shown in Fig. 10.5, there are actually multiple binding units per role to allow simultaneous propagation of ambiguous bindings. In general, this requires that there be as many binding units per role as there are possible meanings of the most ambiguous word in the network.

Initially there is no activation on any of the conceptual or binding units in the network. When input for *John put the pot inside the dishwasher* (P1) is presented, the lexical concept units for each of the words in the phrase are clamped to a high level of evidential activation, directly providing activation for concepts *John, Transfer-Inside, Cooking-Pot, Marijuana,* and *Dishwasher.* To represent the role-bindings given by phrase P1, the binding units of each of *Transfer-Inside*'s roles are clamped to the signatures of the concepts bound to them.[5] For example, the binding units of *Transfer-Inside*'s Object are clamped to the activations (6.8 and 9.2) of the signatures for objects *Marijuana* and *Cooking-Pot,* representing the candidate bindings from the word *pot* (Fig. 10.5a).[6]

The activation of the network's conceptual units is equal to the weighted sum of their inputs plus their previous activation times a decay rate, similar to the

---

[5]ROBIN does not currently address the problem of deciding on the original syntactic bindings, that is, that *pot* is bound to the Object role of phrase P1. Rather, ROBIN's networks are given these initial bindings and use them for high-level inferencing.

[6]An alternative input, such as *George put the cake inside the oven,* would be done simply by clamping the signatures of its bindings (i.e., *George, Cake,* and *Oven*) instead. A completely different set of inferences would then ensue.

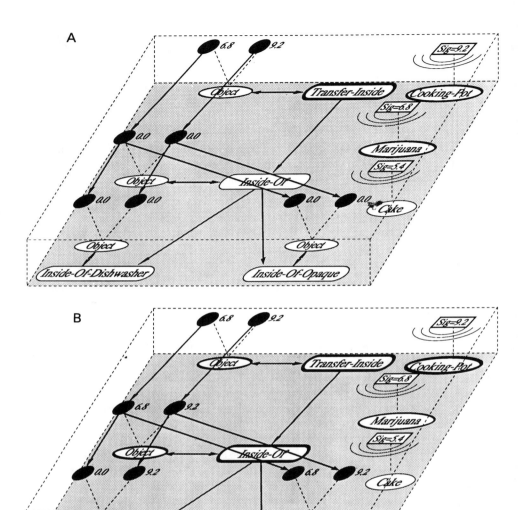

FIG. 10.5.   Simplified ROBIN network segment at two different cycles
during processing of P1 (*John put the pot inside the dishwasher*). Each
figure shows the parallel paths over which evidential activation (bottom plane) and signature activation (top plane) are spread for inferencing. Signature nodes (outlined rectangles) and binding nodes (solid
black circles) are in the top plane. Thickness of conceptual node
boundaries (ovals) represents their levels of evidential activation.
(Node names do not affect the spread of activation in any way. They
are simply used to initially set up the network's structure and to aid in
analysis.) From Lange & Dyer, 1989, *Connection Science, 1(2),* p. 192–
194. (a) Initial activation for P1. (b) Activation after quiescence has
been reached in processing for P1.

activation function of previous localist networks. The activation of the binding units, however, is equal to the maximum of their unit-weighted inputs, allowing signatures to be propagated without alteration. Binding units calculate their activation as the maximum of their inputs, because this preserves their signature input value even when the signature can be inferred from more than one direction. The actual relative signature activation values do not matter, because gated connections (not shown) ensure that two different signatures do not reach the same binding node (Lange & Dyer, 1989).

As activation starts to spread after the initial clamped activation values in Fig. 10.5a, *Inside-Of* receives evidential activation from *Transfer-Inside*, representing the strong evidence that something is now inside of something else. Concurrently, the signature activations on the binding units of *Transfer-Inside*'s Object propagate to the corresponding binding units of *Inside-Of*'s Object (Fig. 10.5b), because each of the binding units calculates its activation as the maximum of its inputs. For example, *Inside-Of*'s left Object binding unit has only one input connection, that from the corresponding left Object binding unit of *Transfer-Inside*. The connection has a unit weight and the left Object binding unit of *Transfer-Inside* has an activation of 6.8, thus *Inside-Of*'s left Object binding unit also becomes 6.8 (*Marijuana*'s signature), because 6.8 is its maximum (and in this case only) input. The potential binding of *Cooking-Pot* (signature 9.2) to *Inside-Of*'s right Object binding unit propagates at the same time, as do the bindings of *Inside-Of*'s Planner role to the signature of *John* and its Location role to the signature of *Dishwasher*.

The network has thus made the crucial inference of exactly which thing is inside of the other, by propagating signatures across binding paths encoding rule R1. Similarly, as time goes on, *Inside-Of-Dishwasher* (representing a kitchen utensil being inside of a dishwasher, a precondition for cleaning) and *Inside-Of-Opaque* (representing an object being inside of an opaque object, which blocks it from sight) receive evidential activation, with inferencing continuing by the propagation of signature activation to their corresponding binding units (Fig. 10.5b).[7]

Inferencing continues by propagation of signature and evidential activation. Figure 10.6 shows an overview of the signature bindings in a portion of the network after input for the rest of Hiding Pot (*because the police were coming*) is

---

[7]*Inside-Of-Dishwasher* and *Inside-Of-Opaque* are *concept refinements* (or specializations) of *Inside-Of*. Refinement frames here represent the *reason* for a particular action or state, and are useful because they allow more specific inferences to be made when role-bindings are known. For example, if the network has inferred that a dish is inside of a dishwasher (*Inside-Of-Dishwasher*), then it could infer that it is going to be cleaned. If the network has inferred that any object is inside of an opaque object (*Inside-Of-Opaque*), then the network could infer that what is important is that the object is blocked from sight. When more than one refinement of a frame can be inferred (as in Hiding Pot), one of them must be selected as the winning reason in the given context (e.g., is the object being cleaned or hidden?).

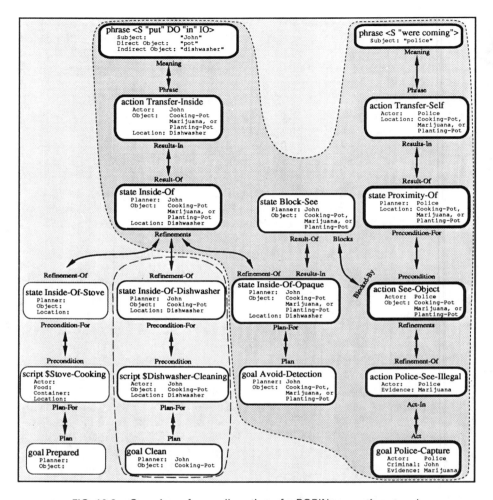

FIG. 10.6. Overview of a small portion of a ROBIN semantic network (actually embedded in network structure such as in Figs. 10.5a and 10.5b) showing inferences dynamically made after clamping of the inputs for phrases P1 and P2 of Hiding Pot. Thickness of frame boundaries shows the amount of *evidential* activation on the frames' conceptual nodes. Role fillers shown are the ones dynamically instantiated by propagation of *signature* activation over the role's binding nodes. Darkly shaded area indicates the most highly-activated path of frames representing the most probable plan/goal analysis of the input. Dashed area shows the discarded dishwasher-cleaning interpretation. Frames outside of both areas show a very small portion of the rest of the network. These frames received no evidential or signature activation from either phrase. From Lange & Dyer, 1989, *Connection Science, 1(2),* p. 199.

presented and the network eventually settles. The network has made inferences I1–I9 of Table 10.2, with most being shown in the figure. For example, I8 (the inference that the *Marijuana* is inside of an opaque object) is represented by the instantiation of state *Inside-Of-Opaque*. The role-bindings of the frames shown were instantiated dynamically with signature activation.

3.1.4.   Disambiguation and Reinterpretation.   As can be seen in Figs. 10.5 and 10.6, propagation of signature activations dynamically instantiates candidate inference paths in parallel in much the same way as marker-passing systems. If this were a marker-passing system, then an external symbolic path evaluator would have to be used to select between the dishwasher cleaning path and the longer hiding path connecting *John*'s *Transfer-Inside* to the *Police*'s *Transfer-Self*. The evaluation heuristics would also have to somehow recognize that at the end of processing, *Marijuana* should be selected over the *Cooking-Pot* and Planting-Pot bindings throughout the network.

However, in ROBIN, such disambiguation is performed entirely within the network, without the need to resort to a separate path-evaluation program. Deciding between the competing inference paths instantiated by signature activation is the function of the evidential portion of ROBIN's networks (such as the conceptual units on the bottom layer of Figs. 10.5a and 10.5b). The activations of the conceptual frame units are always approximately proportional to the amount of evidence available for them from their bindings and their related frames. The inference path selected as the interpretation at any given context is therefore simply *the most highly activated path of frame units* and their bindings.[8] Similarly, when there are multiple possible bindings for each role, the binding chosen at any given time is the one whose concept has the highest level of evidential activation.

ROBIN has been implemented in the DESCARTES connectionist simulator (Lange et al., 1989). Figures 10.7a and 10.7b show the evidential activations of the ambiguous meanings of the word *pot* and the competing *refinements* of *Inside-Of* as activation spreads through the network. Initially there is more evidence for the interpretation that John was trying to clean a cooking pot. This is shown by the fact that *Cooking-Pot* becomes more highly activated than *Marijuana* or *Planting-Plot* after *Inside-Of-Dishwasher* becomes activated (about cycle 60). However, after input for P2 is presented at cycles 51 through 61, the inferences about the police propagate through *Transfer-Self, Proximity-Of, See-Object,* and *Block-See,* until they reach *Inside-Of-Opaque* (about cycle 95), as in Fig. 10.6. Reinforcement from this hiding and police capture path eventually causes *Inside-Of-Opaque* to become more highly activated than *Inside-Of-Dishwasher* and *Marijuana* to become more highly activated than *Cooking-Pot* (by

---

[8]The network's *decision* or *selection* is actually simply the interpretation that the human modeler gives to the levels of activation present in it, as in all connectionist models.

A

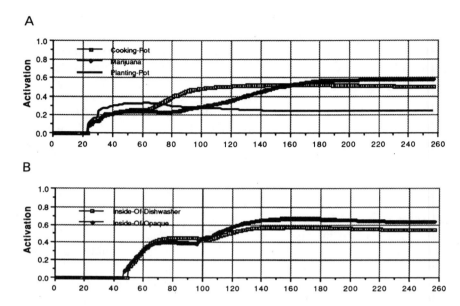

B

FIG. 10.7.   Time-course of evidential activations of meanings of word *pot* and competing refinements of *Inside-Of* after presentation of input for *John put the pot inside the dishwasher* (P1) at cycles 1 through 31 and presentation of input for *the police were coming* (P2) is presented at cycles 51 through 61.

cycle 160), so that the network's interpretation of the input changes to the hiding marijuana interpretation of the darkly shaded area in Fig. 10.6. Notice, however, that evidential activation remains on the units of the alternative paths, allowing another possible reinterpretation if the next sentence is *they were coming over for dinner in half an hour.*

3.1.5.   Elimination of Crosstalk: Interaction of Signature and Evidential Activation.   So far, signature and evidential activation have been described as propagating in parallel but along separate paths of units and connections. However, as described in (Lange, in press), the problem of *crosstalk* makes it crucial for the two paths of activation to interact so that the dynamic variable bindings in the network affect the spread of activation.

One way ROBIN controls crosstalk is by having units embedded within it that compute and enforce *selectional restrictions* on role-fillers to control the spread of activation when roles' binding constraints are violated. For example, the selectional restrictions on the Object role of *Inside-Of-Dishwasher* expect it to be filled only by objects that are cooking or eating utensils, and not objects like *Marijuana*. To enforce these selectional restrictions, each connection from one binding unit to another is actually a *multiplicative connection* (as in the sigma pi units described in Rumelhart, Hinton, and McClelland (1986) that is *gated* by another unit calculating whether the signature is a legal one. For example, the left gated link from the binding unit of *Inside-Of*'s Object to *Inside-Of-Dishwasher*'s Object in Fig. 10.5b is closed because the network recognizes that *Marijuana* (6.8) violates its selectional restrictions. Only the signature of *Cooking-Pot* (9.2) matches and is propagated to be considered as the Object of *Inside-Of-Dish-washer*.

In other cases, the role-filler's constraints on a frame are completely violated (e.g., *Inside-Of-Stove* and *Inside-Of-Restaurant* are impossible interpretations for P1). In these cases, the activations of the signature bindings interact with the activation on the evidential layer through gated connections that stop the violated frames from receiving activation, as can be seen in Fig. 10.6. These selection restrictions (or *logical binding constraints*) dramatically reduce the number of spurious inference paths generated by the propagation of signatures and thus eliminate a large potential source of crosstalk. The network structure imposing selectional restrictions is not important for the purposes of this chapter, but is described in Lange and Dyer (1989).

Another way in which the activation of the signature role-bindings and the activation of the evidential layer interact is by structure that assures that evidential activation is spread only between frames and their *actual* role-fillers. This is to solve localist connectionist networks' basic problem of not being able to distinguish between sentences such as *The astronomer saw the star* and *The star saw the astronomer* (sec. 1.1.3). Signatures partially solve this problem by allowing the network to differentially represent the bindings of the two different instances. However, if these bindings do not have an effect on the spread of evidential activation, then they might as well not be there in terms of disambiguating between the meanings of *star*. ROBIN solves this problem by gated connections that feed evidential activation back from a frame to those concepts, and only those concepts, that are bound to its roles with signature activation. In the case of *The star saw the astronomer,* only the signature of *Movie-Star* reaches the Actor role of *See* (because *Celestial-Body* violates its selectional restrictions). *Movie-Star* therefore receives evidential activation that *Celestial-Body* does not, so that it becomes more highly activated and is chosen as the interpretation of *star*. This control of activation based on signature bindings is also done by structures of units and gated connections within the network; how crucial it is to the disambiguation process by controlling crosstalk is explained more thoroughly in Lange (in press).

3.2. Comparison of ROBIN and Hybrid Models

Signatures allow ROBIN to hold and propagate variable bindings much like symbolic markers allow marker-passing networks to. They are simply activation patterns that spread across normal numeric connectionist units and connections, thus they allow purely localist connectionist networks to have much of the functionality of hybrid localist and marker-passing networks. It is equally important that ROBIN retains the normal disambiguation abilities of localist networks, unlike other localist models that have demonstrated the ability to handle variable bindings (such as Ajjanagadde and Shastri (1989), Barnden (1990), and Holldobler (1990). ROBIN thus completes the circle; hybrid networks such as those of Lange, Hodges, Fuenmayor, and Belyaev (1989) and Kitano, Tomabechi, and Levin (1989) demonstrate that localist networks having marker-passing abilities are useful for language understanding, and ROBIN demonstrates that the abilities of these kinds of hybrid models can actually be embedded within a purely localist network.

As is generally the case when a mechanism is developed to give a specific connectionist level the capabilities of hybrid model, the signature mechanism for variable bindings in localist networks has both advantages and disadvantages in comparison to that of marker-passing in hybrid networks. Signatures have the weakness that each binding unit can hold only one signature activation at a given time, whereas each marker-passing unit can hold as many markers as its symbolic stack can hold. This is why each role of ROBIN's frames has multiple binding units to hold ambiguous bindings (such as of the word *pot*). In addition, signature activation patterns only represent the concept being bound, whereas markers can also hold complex symbolic information such as the type of the marker, the path it has followed, the time the marker arrived, and so on.

On the other hand, a purely localist connectionist model such as ROBIN has the advantage that its building-block elements are all relatively simple, numeric connectionist elements. This is in contrast to hybrid localist and marker-passing networks, whose elements must not only support normal connectionist activation functions, but must also be capable of holding lists of symbolic markers and acting on the sometimes complex symbolic information on those markers. The more important advantage of ROBIN's purely localist networks, however, lies in how naturally signature activation variable bindings interact with evidential activation as opposed to the variable bindings held in symbolic markers. For example, a signature matches a selectional restriction if its concept has been inferred to be an instance of the type of that restriction (e.g., if the *Dishwasher* in the phrase has been inferred to be an Instance of type *Opaque-Object*). This is calculated in the network by comparing the signature activation on the candidate binding unit to the signature activation on each of the binding units of the restriction type's Instance role (by units having opposite-signed weights from each and a low firing threshold). If any match, then the signature is of the right type, the restrictions are met, and the corresponding binding constraint unit becomes active. A multiplicative connection from this binding constraint unit to the connection on the evidential layer from one frame to the other is then all that is needed to gate the flow of evidential activation open and closed when necessary. The symbolic information held in the activations of the signature bindings thereby controls the disambiguating activations of the evidential layer by the normal spreading-activation process.

In a hybrid marker-passing/localist connectionist model, on the other hand, there is nothing akin to multiplicative connections to cleanly interface between the symbolic information on markers and the numeric information of evidential activation. Thus, to enforce selectional restrictions within the network, the weighted activation connections between frames would have to somehow query or be controlled by the symbolic marker-passing units (which would have to symbolically calculate whether the restrictions have been met). This is certainly possible in a hybrid model, but having such awkward communication between different processing paradigms makes the network more complex and violates the normal numerically based activation functions of connectionist units (Feldman & Ballard, 1982).

A more fundamental potential advantage to using activation-based signatures in a localist network as opposed to using a hybrid with marker-passing comes into play if signatures are uniquely identifying distributed patterns of activation (as shown in Fig. 10.4) rather than the arbitrary scalar values shown propagated in Figs. 10.5a and 10.5b. In this case, the distributed representations of similar concepts would have similar signature patterns and thereby carry a degree of semantic information that could be used locally in the network. Such a move toward a hybrid localist and distributed connectionist model would allow signature inferencing to automatically drive distributed learning of selectional restrictions and long-term instances (as proposed in Lange & Dyer, 1989), something not possible with the symbolic backpointers of markers. By finding a mechanism that allows localist networks to handle the variable-binding and inferencing of hybrid marker-passing and localist connectionist models, we have thereby moved closer to being able to naturally take advantage of the features of the third level—distributed connectionist networks.

4. HYBRID COGNITIVE MODELS

Most connectionist and artificial intelligence systems attempt to model one subtask of a single cognitive ability, such as of natural language understanding, planning, memory retrieval, or visual processing. Given the current relatively primitive understanding of how to model cognitive functions, this is generally the best way to explore an area in any depth. In people, however, processing of different cognitive functions are rarely completely separate, and the interaction of two or more cognitive functions can have dramatic effects on each other. What people see or read affects what they think, what plans they make, what they say, and what they remember. Different types of cognitive functions tend to range in the amounts of symbolic and perceptual (subsymbolic) processing they require, thus models that attempt to explore two or more cognitive functions and how they interact with each other are especially likely to benefit from a hybrid connectionist modelling approach.

For example, natural language understanding and memory retrieval are two tightly intertwined cognitive functions. When people understand a text, they are using their natural language understanding abilities to build a conscious interpretation of the text's meaning. This interpretation will often trigger a reminding of a similar or analogous episode from memory, which may in turn be used to aid in their understanding of the text, bolster an argument, or simply sidetrack the person to think of something more interesting. The language understanding process therefore affects the memory (or analogical) retrieval process, which, in turn, affects language understanding by changing the context in which the next pieces of text or speech will be disambiguated and understood.

Although there have been a number of symbolic and connectionist models of language understanding and analogical retrieval, few have dealt with how the two processes are integrated and affect each other. This section gives an overview of Spreading-Activation Analog Retrieval by Constraint Satisfaction (SAARCS) (Lange, Melz, Wharton, & Holyoak, 1990), a hybrid localist connectionist and marker-passing network that performs both language understanding and analogical retrieval in order to model the effects of inferencing and disambiguation on the memory retrieval process. The fact that SAARCS is a hybrid model that combines elements from both localist and marker-passing networks allows it to explore aspects of this problem that would currently be difficult to explore in a pure model from either level because it ranges from handling low-level priming and disambiguation (difficult to model in marker-passing networks) to large-scale comparison of symbolic structure (difficult for localist networks).

4.1. Analogical Retrieval

Human memory retrieval involves more than just matching text against items in memory. Comprehension processes, such as disambiguation and inferencing, will alter the effective retrieval cue. Thus a realistic model of episodic reminding must integrate the process by which the retrieval cue is understood with the process by which it is used to recall information from memory.

Considerable evidence indicates that a primary influence on reminding is the degree of direct semantic similarity between the cue and objects in memory (Holyoak & Koh, 1987; Ross, 1989). Though the evidence is not as compelling as for semantic similarity, some recent work has shown that structural consistency (i.e., analogy) also influences the retrieval process (Wharton, Holyoak, Downing, Lange, & Wickens, 1991). *Structural consistency* requires that if two frames are placed in correspondence, then their roles and fillers should also correspond (Holyoak & Thagard, 1989). Figure 10.8 illustrates a simple example of variation in structural consistency. Suppose a person has studied the sentences

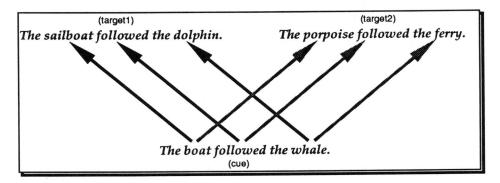

FIG. 10.8. Cue that shares similar concepts with two targets, but maps consistently to one only (heavy arrows). From Lange, Melz, Wharton & Holyoak (1990).

The sailboat followed the dolphin and *The porpoise followed the ferry,* and is then cued with *The boat followed the whale.* If the cue is viewed as being mapped to potential targets (or episodes) in memory, then the former target yields a consistent mapping in which similar objects fill the corresponding agent and object roles, whereas the latter target generates an inconsistent cross mapping in which similar objects play dissimilar roles. Ross (1989) found that cross mapping impaired retrieval of formulas to solve story problems when the analogs involved similar objects.

We believe, however, that the effect of analogy on reminding will be influenced by several other factors. First, cue/target semantic similarity is a necessary condition for structural consistency to affect reminding. If two situations are dissimilar, then the retrieval cue will likely fail to make contact with (activate) a stored representation of the individual concepts, in which case configural properties will be irrelevant. Second, there is considerable evidence that human memory is sensitive to retrieval interference effects (e.g., Nickerson, 1984). Because of retrieval competition, a stored potential analog that maps inconsistently to the retrieval cue may be less likely to be recalled if a rival analog with a consistent mapping to the cue is also stored in memory (see Fig. 10.8).

Finally, the impact of structural consistency and retrieval competition influences and is influenced by the comprehension processes involved in lexical disambiguation. The reversal of case role fillers, which can alter the structural consistency of a mapping, can also alter preferred interpretations of individual lexical items. For example, the fish in *The surfer ate the fish* is small, dead, and cut up, whereas the fish in *The fish ate the surfer* is very large, alive, and whole. In such cases, a role reversal can affect the interpretation of lexical items, which in turn can alter the similarity of individual concepts in the cue to the concepts in a stored potential analog, as well as altering configural resemblance. The inferences needed for the comprehension process are also crucial to retrieval—

without a minimal understanding of how the concepts and actions of a cue are related, it is unlikely that a reasoner will retrieve a proper analogy to a given cue. This is especially true if the potential memories are indexed in ways that can only be inferred indirectly from the cue.

4.2.   SAARCS: A Hybrid Connectionist Model of Understanding and Retrieval

SAARCS is a hybrid localist connectionist and marker-passing model that integrates language comprehension and analogical retrieval. Given the syntactic representation of an input sentence as a cue, SAARCS' network first disambiguates and infers an interpretation of the cue, and then retrieves and returns the sentence or episode from long-term memory that is analogically closest to that interpretation. The system combines the ROBIN localist connectionist model for disambiguation and inferencing (Lange & Dyer, 1989) with aspects of ARCS, a hybrid symbolic/localist connectionist model of analog retrieval (Thagard, Holyoak, Nelson, & Gochfeld, in press). Because we are interested in modelling the processes of disambiguation and inferencing and their effects on analogical retrieval, SAARCS combines marker-passing with a localist spreading-activation network in a single integrated model.

SAARCS consists of a localist connectionist network that encodes a knowledge base of concepts (e.g., objects, actions, plans, and goals) and general knowledge rules for inferencing between concepts, as in ROBIN (e.g., Fig. 10.6). Also indexed into this semantic network are units representing long-term memory episodes that are potential targets for retrieval. Using this network, the understanding and analog retrieval process consists of four major stages:

1. Activation is spread through the semantic network to disambiguate and infer an interpretation of the cue, as in ROBIN.

2. Symbolic markers are propagated from the units of the winning inference path to find the targets that are semantically similar in the current context to the cue's interpretation.

3. A network of units is dynamically built to represent the possible competing mappings between the cue's interpretation and the semantically similar targets found by the spread of markers. The excitatory and inhibitory connections between units of this new mapping network enforce semantic and structural consistency with the cue.

4. The new mapping network is settled by a constraint-satisfaction process similar to ARCS' that performs competitive retrieval; the mapping units active after settling constitute the most coherent match to the cue.

The units in the mapping network formed by the spreading-activation and marker-passing process feed back into the corresponding units in the semantic network, so the activation of the target most semantically and structurally similar to the cue increases. The target episode in the semantic network with the highest activation is retrieved.

4.2.1. Cue Disambiguation and Understanding. As previously mentioned, SAARCS is built upon the purely localist connectionist network of ROBIN (described in section 3.1). This allows SAARCS to perform lexical and pragmatic disambiguation and reinterpretation, while also being able to represent the variable bindings and perform some of the general knowledge rules necessary for high-level inferencing and understanding.

In addition to ROBIN's normal network structure encoding frames and rules for inferencing between them with signatures and evidential activation, SAARCS has conceptual units representing the episodes in its long-term memory. Each of the elements of these episodes is an instance of a frame in the semantic network, and so is connected (without signature binding paths) to the evidential units of those frames. The strength of those weights is relative to how well the episodes have been remembered: Particularly salient episodes will have high connection weights, and fading memories will have low connection weights.

Figure 10.9 shows an example of how a simple episode is connected to the network. This network shows a simplified view of a portion of the evidential units in the network. Shown are the frame and roles for phrase *P-Devoured* (as in *The shark devoured the diver*), for action *Ingest-Food,* and two of *Ingest-Food's* alternative concept refinements, *Carnivore-Ingest-Human* and *Human-Ingest-Food.* Also shown are some of the nodes and their connections for a relevant portion of the network's refinement hierarchy (roles and connections to many other frames not shown.) In Fig. 10.9, the episode *The crocodile ate the swimmer* is represented by the instance *Carnivore-Ingest-Human.1,* whose Actor is connected to *C-Crocodile.1* and whose Object is connected to *Swimmer.1. The sailor consumed the fish* is represented by *Human-Ingest-Food.2* and the connections of its Actor to *Sailor.2* and Object to *D-Fish.2.*

To start off the understanding and retrieval process, the input for a cue is presented to the network. Figure 10.9 shows the results of the spread of activation for the cue *The shark ate the diver.* In this network, the word *shark* has two alternative meaning senses, *C-Shark* (a large, carnivorous shark) and *D-Shark* (a cut-up dinner shark). The labels next to the role units in the figure (e.g., *C-Shark*) represent the bindings inferred by propagation of signatures along paths of binding units like those of Fig. 10.5. The result in Fig. 10.9 shows that the network has disambiguated the word *shark* to the large, carnivorous kind, and inferred that there has been a case of *Carnivore-Ingest-Human* where a *C-Shark* Actor has eaten a *Diver* Object.

4.2.2. Finding Similar Targets. The spread of activation used to understand the input has the side-effect of activating targets that are semantically similar to the interpretation of the cue. For example, in Fig. 10.9, the target

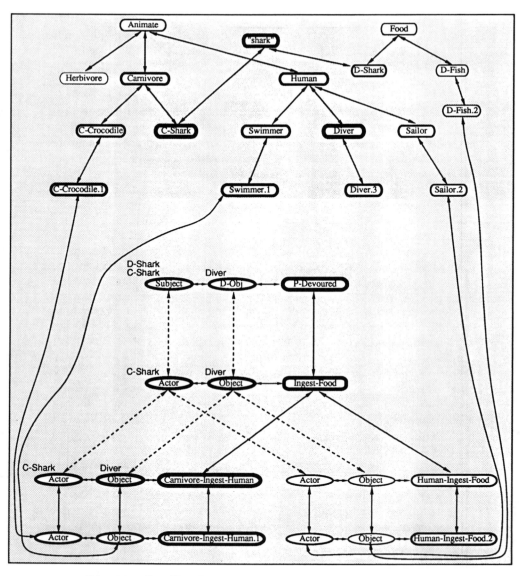

FIG. 10.9. Simplified SAARCS network segment showing some of the conceptual nodes on the evidential layer of the network. The network is similar to that of ROBIN's (e.g., Figs. 10.5a and 10.5b), except that long-term memory episodes, such as *Carnivore-Ingest-Human.1 and Human-Ingest-Food.2*, are connected to the network. Shown are the activation of the evidential layer's nodes after presentation of input for *The shark devoured the diver*. The labels next to roles (i.e., D-Shark, C-Shark, and Diver) show the concepts inferred over the binding nodes by propagation of signatures.

Carnivore-Ingest-Human.1 has become strongly activated due to activation from *Carnivore-Ingest-Human,* as a result of processing input for the sentence *The shark ate the diver* (Killer Shark).

To start memory retrieval, symbolic markers are spread from the frame and role units of the cue's winning interpretation. These markers hold both a symbolic backpointer to their originating unit and a strength equal to the numeric product of the connection weights they have propagated over. The frame and role markers only propagate over connections between corresponding frames and roles, respectively, and only over active portions of the network.

This propagation of markers finds, in parallel, all of the instances in memory that are semantically similar to the cue in the current context. Equally important is that the markers' backpointers tell exactly which part of the cue they are similar to. For instance, in Fig. 10.9, one marker will reach *Carnivore-Ingest-Human.1* from the inferred *Carnivore-Ingest-Human,* and another marker will reach *C-Crocodile.1* from *C-Shark.*[9]

This marker-passing naturally constrains the search for similar targets because of two features of the network: (a) instances not semantically similar to the cue in the current context will have little or no activation, and so will not be reached (e.g., *Herbivore*), and (b) instances that are active, but are semantically distant from a cue concept (such as *C-Crocodile.1* from *Diver*) will not be reached because of their separation in the network.

4.2.3. Building the Mapping Network. The marker-passing process finds large numbers of partially active long-term instances that are semantically similar to part of the cue. Each of these correspondences is a potential analog. However, to retrieve a single coherent episode most analogous to the cue, these isolated correspondences must compete against each other. This competition is driven by parallel satisfaction of the two main types of constraints, semantic similarity and structural consistency, that are believed to operate in both analogical retrieval (Thagard, Holyoak, Nelson, & Gochfeld, in press) and analogical mapping (Holyoak & Thagard, 1989).

To perform this competition, a mapping network is dynamically formed whose units represent the possible mappings between each pair of semantically similar concepts, as in the ARCS model of analogical retrieval (Thagard et al., in press). In SAARCS, these are the pairs found by propagation of the markers. For

---

[9]Markers are used here rather than signatures because each instance in the targets may be semantically similar to multiple concepts in larger cue stories, and thus need to hold several markers at once. Signatures are activation patterns, thus binding units can hold only one signature binding at a time. Although markers could also be used in place of signatures for the language understanding portion of the network, signatures are used because of the smoother integration of signature activation and selectional restrictions with the activations of the evidential portion of the network (see sect. 3.2). Future extensions of signatures may make it possible to eventually use them in place of markers throughout SAARCS.

example, in Killer Shark, markers hitting units for the target *The crocodile ate the swimmer* would cause mapping units to be created for the hypotheses that *C-Shark=C-Crocodile.1*, *Diver=Swimmer.1*, and *Carnivore-Ingest-Human=Carnivore-Ingest-Human.1*. Target roles that receive markers also create units representing the possible mappings between those roles and the markers' originating roles. This in itself enforces partial structural consistency because only corresponding roles that can be reached over signature inferencing paths (dashed lines in Fig. 10.9) will receive markers. The units created for the potential mappings between Killer Shark and *The crocodile ate the swimmer* are shown in Fig. 10.10.

As in ARCS, structural consistency is enforced by excitatory connections between corresponding mapping units. As shown in Fig. 10.10, excitatory connections are created between units mapping two roles (e.g., $C\text{-}I\text{-}H^\wedge Actor = C\text{-}I\text{-}H.1^\wedge Actor$) and the units mapping their frames (e.g., *Carnivore-Ingest-Human=Carnivore-Ingest-Human.1*). Units mapping two concepts that serve as the fillers of two mapped roles also have excitatory connections (e.g., between *C-Shark=C-Crocodile.1* and $C\text{-}I\text{-}H^\wedge Actor = C\text{-}I\text{-}H.1^\wedge Actor$).

All of the aforementioned types of connections between structurally consistent mapping units have a small positive value (0.05). Excitatory weights are also constructed to mapping units from the units in the semantic network that they map, with the connection weights being proportional to the total path weight product between the concepts (0.05 * strength of the marker that caused the

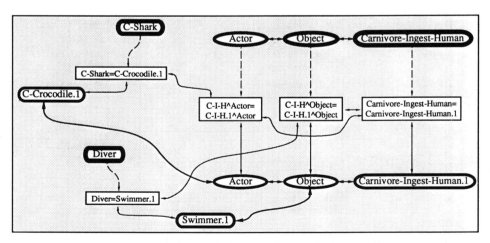

FIG. 10.10. Some of the mapping units (rectangles) created by passing of markers in Killer Shark. All links shown are excitatory. Unidirectional dashed lines have weights proportional to the total weight distance between that particular concept and the target being mapped. From Lange, Melz, Wharton, & Holyoak (1990).

mapping unit to be built). These weights thus give importance to both (a) semantic similarity, because the weights to mapping units for two very similar concepts will be higher than those for two less similar concepts, and (b) pragmatic relevance, because important and relevant goals will have more basic activation in the semantic network, thus biasing retrieval towards unit, mapping those goals.

Competition between potential mappings is facilitated by inhibitory connections between all rival mappings (−0.20 in the simulation). For instance, there will be an inhibitory connection between *Diver=Swimmer.1* and the mapping unit created for *Diver=Sailor.2* (from the target *The sailor consumed the fish*).

4.2.4. Competition and Retrieval.   During and after creation of the units representing candidate analogical mappings, the new mapping network is settled using a constraint-satisfaction algorithm. The mapping units that are most active after the network has settled will be those that constitute the most coherent match to the cue (Thagard et al., in press).

Mapping units are created with bidirectional connections from their target units in the semantic network (e.g., from *C-Shark=C-Crocodile.1* to *C-Crocodile* in Figure 10.10), so activation from the winning mappings feeds back into the targets. This boosts the evidential activation of targets most analogous to the cue, so that they tend to become highly activated. The target retrieved is the episode with the highest evidential activation.

4.2.5. Simulation Results.   SAARCS has been implemented in the DESCARTES connectionist simulator (Lange et al., 1989). The model has been tested on three different types of competitive and noncompetitive retrieval: Examples in which the targets can be retrieved solely on the basis of semantic similarity after interpretation, examples in which analogical similarity plays a crucial role, and examples in which plan/goal analyses of the cue must be made before retrieval is possible.

The first class simulated are retrievals in which a single target is clearly the most semantically similar to the cue after interpretation. In such examples, the interpretation process activates the similar target much more highly than any others. This is the case when *The crocodile ate the swimmer* and *The sailor consumed the fish* are the closest potential targets for *The shark ate the diver*. The carnivorous crocodile episode is so similar to Killer Shark that it becomes highly active just from the inferencing process, especially in relation to *The sailor consumed the fish* (see Fig. 10.9). Structural similarity pressures from the mapping network only marginally helps retrieval in these kind of cases.

In other cases, however, multiple targets can have approximately the same semantic similarity to the cue, so structural consistency plays a larger part in retrieval. An example of this is that the target *The sailboat followed the dolphin* (*Ptrans-Follow.1*) is a better analogy for *The boat followed the whale* than is *The*

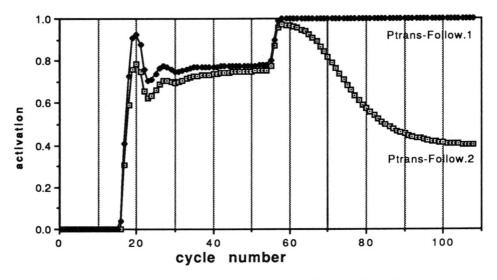

FIG. 10.11a.   Activation of target nodes *Ptrans-Follow.1* (*The sailboat followed the dolphin*) and *Ptrans-Follow.2* (*The porpoises followed the ferry*) after presentation of *The boat followed the whale.* From Lange, Melz, Wharton & Holyoak (1990).

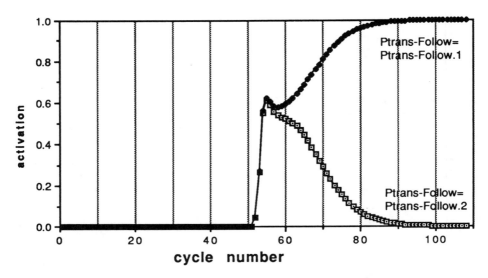

FIG. 10.11b.   Activation of mapping units *Ptrans-Follow=Ptrans-Follow.1* and *Ptrans-Follow=Ptrans-Follow.2* after they were created due to presentation of *The boat followed the whale.* From Lange, Melz, Wharton, & Holyoak (1990).

276

porpoise followed the ferry (*Ptrans-Follow.2*). In this kind of case, the pressures due to structural consistency allow the better analogy to be retrieved first.

Figure 10.11a shows the activations of these target episodes during retrieval in SAARCS. Activation reaches the two targets after presentation of the cue at cycle 16, and the semantic network settles by about cycle 39. Although activations of the cue (not shown) clearly indicate that a *Boat* was *Ptrans-Following* a *Whale*, the activations of the two targets are about the same, essentially because they both involve sea mammals and boats following each other. At this point, markers propagate from the cue's interpretation, so that at cycle 41 the competing mapping units for *Ptrans-Follow=Ptrans-Follow.1* and *Ptrans-Follow=Ptrans-Follow.2* are formed (Fig. 10.11b). Because of the excitatory connections enforcing structural similarity between them and the other newly created mapping units, *Ptrans-Follow=Ptrans-Follow.1* soon begins to win, dominating by about cycle 80. This activation feeds back into the semantic network, driving *Ptrans-Follow.1* to saturation and allowing *Ptrans-Follow.2* to decay. *The sailboat followed the dolphin* is thus retrieved as the best analogy for the cue.

The final set of simulations have tested SAARCS' ability to perform retrievals that require a plan/goal analysis of the cue. For instance, to understand *John put the pot inside the dishwasher because the police were coming*, the ROBIN portion of the network must first make multiple inferences to decide that John was most likely trying to hide his marijuana from the police inside the dishwasher, because he didn't want to get arrested. These inferences combined with ROBIN's spread of activation allow the network to disambiguate and form an interpretation of the cue (see sect. 3.1).

Once a reinterpretation has been made to *Hiding Marijuana* due to confluences of evidential activation from the inferred plan/goal analysis, SAARCS uses that inferred interpretation to retrieve the analogous episodes *Bill hid the cocaine in the stove so that he wouldn't be arrested,* as opposed to the previously most analogous episode *Mary put the cooking pot in the dishwasher to clean it.*

4.3. Comparing SAARCS to Nonhybrid Models

By integrating a localist connectionist network with marker-passing that allows the dynamic creation of a mapping network, SAARCS is able to combine parts of the language understanding and analogical retrieval processes in a network without an external supervisor (other than the one that created the network in the first place). It is thus a first pass at a model explaining the influence of the language understanding on memory retrieval and vice versa. Unlike models that concentrate primarily on memory retrieval, such as symbolic case-based reasoning models (cf. Schank & Leake, 1989) and connectionist retrieval models (Barnden & Srinivas, in press; Thagard et al., in press), SAARCS can potentially account for many psychological phenomena involving priming and language effects in human memory retrieval. These phenomena include increased retrieval due to repetition, recency, and prior semantic priming, all of which can be modelled by variations in evidential activation levels prior to presentation of the cue.

It will be desirable in the future to simplify SAARCS by removing the hybrid portions of the model. For example, it would be desirable to replace the marker-passing that SAARCS uses to find correspondences between semantically similar concepts with a purely spreading-activation approach, such as an extension to signatures. The dynamic creation of mapping units is also quite expensive computationally, so we are looking into ways to instead temporarily recruit preexisting mapping units. As we found when finding a way to handle some of the variable binding and inferencing abilities of hybrid marker-passing networks in ROBIN, we suspect that finding purely localist or distributed connectionist techniques to handle the hybrid portions of SAARCS will also proffer a number of advantages, such as learning and more natural integration of understanding and retrieval. For now, however, the hybrid connectionist modeling approach allows us to explore the effect of integration of cognitive functions that have not yet proven amenable to single-level solutions.

5. REMOVING UNREDUCED HYBRID MECHANISMS

It often goes unmentioned that most connectionist models, even those on a single level, are actually hybrid models that rely on human or symbolic intervention to succeed. For example, the researcher or a program must usually provide networks' inputs and examine their final outputs to see if they have completed their tasks as desired. This is generally quite reasonable because connectionist (and artificial intelligence) research is at far too early a stage to build cognitive robots that interact with their environments autonomously.

It is somewhat more troublesome that the human researcher must always specify the structure of the networks in advance. For distributed connectionist networks, this means specifying the number of units, their connectivity, the form of the input and output, and various network parameters. For localist and marker-passing networks it is even more difficult because the researcher must specify the knowledge representation to be encoded by units in the network, how those units are connected, and specify the connection weights between units. However, although specifying the network structure in advance is often tedious, it is also arguably reasonable to work with such networks, on the assumption that some learning or even evolutionary mechanism could be postulated to have come up with that structure in the first place.

Potentially the most problematic human and symbolic interventions in connectionist network processing are those which must often be used during network processing. Many models have such hybrid *unreduced mechanisms* that are crucial during network processing but are not handled by the units and connections of the network. For example, learning techniques for distributed networks, for the most part, require that all patterns to be learned are known in advance and continually presented to the network as training progresses incrementally. This requires that all of the patterns be stored outside of the network while learning occurs, generally in a symbolic buffer without which learning would fail. Other examples of unreduced mechanisms in connectionist networks are described by Lachter and Bever (1988) and Aizawa (chap. 4 in this volume).

If connectionist models are to be posited as comprehensive models of cognitive function, it will therefore be necessary to eventually find connectionist implementations of all such hybrid unreduced mechanisms, in much the same way as it is necessary to eventually implement hybrid models on a single connectionist level.

5.1. Short-term Sequential Memory

One cognitive function that has not yet been implemented in connectionist networks is that of *short-term sequential memory*. Short-term sequential memory is what people use to store short sequences of semantically unrelated items for a period of a few seconds or minutes. Examples of short-term sequential memory are remembering a phone number between the time a telephone operator says it until the time it is dialed, remembering the combination of a lock long enough to copy it down on paper, and so on. People in general are able to remember such ordering information for a maximum of around seven "chunks" of previously established concepts (Miller, 1956).

There have been a few models that implicitly learn and store sequential information in long-term memory, such as the recurrent backpropagation model of Pollack (in press). These models, however, store their sequential information by employing time-intensive methods for modifying connection weights, and so are models of long-term, rather than short-term sequential memory.

Besides being an important cognitive function in itself to model, short-term sequential memory is one of the unreduced hybrid mechanisms of distributed connectionist networks that deal with time. In order to learn an ordered sequence, a model must be able to store it temporarily. For example, several models have been able to handle and interpret sequential input by using recurrent networks, such as models that take sequential text as input (e.g., Miikkulainen & Dyer, 1989; Pollack, 1990; St. John, 1990). The basic training procedure of such models is often to present each element of the sequence in turn as input to the network while training each input (even the first element) to produce the desired output of the entire sequence. Of course, if the models are ever to work without supervision, they will have to have some means to compute the desired training output. Doing this will generally require seeing the complete sequence before training can begin—which means that the actual sequence itself will have to be stored temporarily. Currently that short-term sequential memory can only be done with the hidden hybrid mechanism of a symbolic buffer.

5.2. A Model of Short-term Sequential Memory

To model short-term sequential memory and potentially eliminate one of the unreduced mechanisms of distributed connectionist networks dealing with time, we have been working on a connectionist model of short-term sequential memory that uses only *activation changes* to temporarily store and recall the exact order of a single, novel short sequence of previously defined concepts (Lange & Allen, 1991).

The basic model consists of a network for *semantic memory* and a network of *responder groups* (Fig. 10.12). The semantic memory holds all of the previously known concepts, and would in theory hold the model's semantic knowledge and rules for use in short-term semantic reasoning. For simplicity, however, the semantic memory is simply a localist winner-take-all network, with a separate unit for each concept. The responder groups serve to temporarily store ordering information of the sequences presented. Each concept in the semantic memory is randomly connected to a subset of the responder groups, which each have a random output threshold.

5.2.1. Storing the Sequence.   An ordered sequence is presented to the model for storage by activating, in turn, each of the units in semantic memory representing that element in the sequence. When a given element in the sequence is activated, activation will propagate from it to its responder groups. This new activation will cause a subset of its responder groups to go over threshold and to be temporarily *recruited* to represent that element and its position in the sequence. The numbers of responders recruited for each element holds the ordering information.

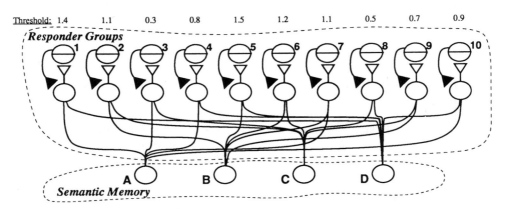

FIG. 10.12.   Random interconnections between units in semantic memory and responder groups. The thresholds on the top line are the thresholds of the top node of each responder group. The links with dark triangles are inhibitory, while the links with white triangles or no triangles are excitatory.

Figure 10.12 shows a limited network with 10 responder groups and 4 semantic units (A, B, C, and D). Each of the semantic units is randomly connected to half of the responder groups. The thresholds of the responders have been randomly chosen between 0 and 2. For simplicity, all excitatory connections are of unit weight. We now present this network with the sequence D-A-C.

To start the sequence, semantic memory unit D is clamped to an activation of 1 (Fig. 10.13a), with all other semantic units having activation 0. Activation spreads from D to each of its potential responders through the responders' input units (bottom layer of the responder groups). Responder 1's activation is now 1, but its threshold is 1.4, so it does not fire. The same is true with Responder 5, whose threshold is 1.5. Responders 4, 8, and 10, however, have thresholds under 1, and so do fire. These responders have been recruited to represent the fact that D was the first element in the sequence, with the inhibitory connection to their input units shutting them off from further input.

Unit D is then shut off, and the second unit in the sequence, A, is clamped to an activation of 1 and its activation propagated to its responder groups (Fig. 10.13b). Responder 1, which had an activation of 1 before (from D), now gets enough activation (2 overall) to fire, and is recruited by A. Responder 3 is likewise recruited by A, with Responder 7 gaining activation but not firing. A has no effect on Responders 4 and 10, however, because they have shut themselves off from further input after having been recruited by D. Finally, the third unit in the sequence, C, is clamped, and activation spread (Fig. 10.13c). C is only able to recruit one responder group, Responder 9.

A total of 6 of the responder groups in Fig. 10.13c were recruited during presentation of sequence D-A-C. The order of the elements in the sequence is implicitly represented by the activation of the responder groups, because 3 of the responders were required by D, 2 were recruited by A, and 1 was recruited by C. This ordering information of the network will also occur with other sequences that are presented. For example, if the sequence presented had instead been A-C-D, there would have been (a different) 3 responders recruited for A (3, 4, and 10), 2 for C (8 and 9), and 1 for D (1). As long as the thresholds of the responder groups are randomly set within a certain range, the number of recruited responders for each element will generally vary with its position in the sequence—the first element in the sequence will nearly always recruit the most responder groups, the second element the next most, and so on, as the pool of eligible responder groups becomes smaller for each element in the sequence. This ordering becomes increasingly likely with larger responder group networks.

5.2.2. Retrieving the Sequence. Once a sequence has been presented to the network and each of its elements recruited a decreasing number of responder groups, the sequence can be recalled by feeding activation back from the responder groups to the units in semantic memory. The first element in the sequence will generally win the competition because it has connections from all of its recruited responder groups (the largest group of recruited responders).

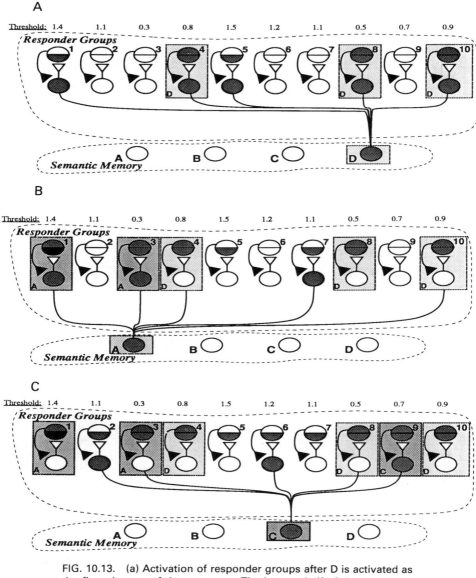

FIG. 10.13. (a) Activation of responder groups after D is activated as the first element of the sequence. The bottom half of the responder nodes shows their level of activation (grey = 1.0), and the top half shows their output (1 if activation greater than thresholds, 0 otherwise). Responder groups within the rectangles labeled D have been caused to fire and therefore be recruited by the first element in the sequence, D. (b) Activation of responder groups after A has been activated as the second element of the sequence. (c) Activation of responder groups after C has been activated as the third element of the sequence.

Unfortunately, such a simple scheme will all too often fail, especially on sequences with repeated elements. If the sequence *F-G-G* is presented, for example, and *F* recruits 30 responders, the first *G* recruits 20, and the second *G* recruits 15, then the total number of responders feeding back into *G* will be 35, causing it to be recalled first.

To handle these kinds of retrieval problems, the model has a network of *sequence clusters,* each of which is randomly connected to a subset of the responder groups (Fig. 10.14). The newly fired responder groups recruited by the presentation of a given element in the sequence will drive a winner-take-all competition between the sequence clusters. The cluster that best represents the space of newly recruited responder groups (because it happens to have connections to more of the responder groups than any other cluster) will win the competition and cluster those responders—into a group separate from the responders recruited by previous and future elements in the sequence.

At the end of the presentation of the sequence, there will be one sequence cluster active for each element in the sequence. There were more newly recruited responder groups for the first element than for any of the later elements, so the cluster representing the first will have input from the largest number of active responders. Similarly, the second cluster will have more active inputs than the

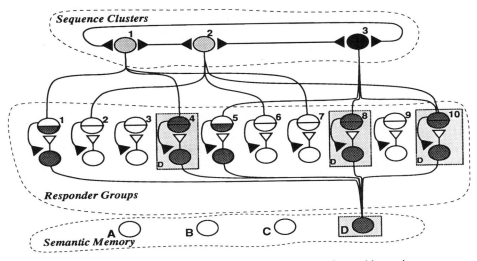

FIG. 10.14. Simplified version of sequence clusters formed in a winner-take-all network and randomly connected to responder groups. Here, Sequence Cluster 3 has inputs from more of the responder groups recruited by D (2) than the other sequence clusters, and so will win the winner-take-all competition and serve to cluster those responders. Sequence Cluster 3 will therefore control their feedback to semantic memory on retrieval.

third, and so on. An example run, implemented in the DESCARTES connectionist simulator (Lange et al., 1989) is shown in Table 10.3.

On recall, the active clusters will compete, and the cluster for the first element will win because of its greater number of responder groups (22 in Table 10.3). This cluster will then feed its activation back to its responder groups and through them down to the semantic memory—causing the first element in the sequence (*R*) to get the most activation and be recalled. The first cluster then removes itself from the competition (through gating not shown), allowing the cluster representing the second element in the sequence to win and recall the second element. The rest of the sequence is recalled in the same way. The complete sequence can be recalled repeatedly, until a new sequence is stored or all of the activation in the responder groups decays away.

5.3. On Removing Hidden Hybrid Mechanisms

The model we have just described is in the early stages of testing. As a model of human short-test sequential memory, it currently has several shortcomings. For example, because there are fewer and fewer responder groups available as elements are presented, it tends to remember the first elements of a sequence the best, and remember the last elements the worst. People, however, are worst at repeating elements in the middle of a sequence, and not the end (Miller, 1956). We plan to experiment with various changes in decay rates and the basic architecture to see if we can more closely match such psychological data.

TABLE 10.3
Responder Groups and Sequence Clusters Activated When the
Sequence *R* - *B* - *G* - *D* - *S* Was Presented to a Network Where
Each Semantic Element Was Randomly
Connected to 50 of the 100 Total Responder Groups.

Element Presented	Responders Recruited	Sequence Cluster #	Responders Clustered
R	36	4	22
B	28	33	18
G	10	29	9
D	8	25	8
S	6	41	5

The network had 50 sequence clusters, each of which had random connections to 50 of the responder groups. The first column shows the element presented, the second column shows the number of responder groups recruited by that element, the third column shows which sequence cluster won to represent that element, and the fourth column shows how many of the responders that cluster actually represents.

On the other hand, this model seems successful as a first pass at modeling short-term sequential memory in a distributed connectionist network, and therefore as a first step toward removing the hybrid symbolic buffer mechanism from long-term memory distributed models that operate on sequential data.

6. CONCLUSIONS

The distributed connectionist, localist connectionist, and marker-passing levels of connectionist processing each have a different set of strengths and weaknesses. There is a large gap between the low-level areas that subsymbolic (distributed connectionist) models are well-suited to modeling and the high-level areas that symbolic (marker-passing and traditional AI) models are well-suited to modeling. Consequently, it is often impossible to build a model of a given cognitive task solely from elements of a single connectionist level. The only possible solution in these cases is often to build hybrid models that combine elements and capabilities from multiple connectionist levels.

Besides allowing progress in problems that cannot be handled otherwise, hybrid connectionist models serve as useful guides to potentially valuable areas of future research in single connectionist levels. If a hybrid model is successful, then it serves as strong evidence that an attempt to map the abilities of the hybrid model into a single level might be a good way to solve the problem. On the other hand, if the hybrid model is unsuccessful, then the attempt shows that either a different approach is needed or that there are more facets to the problem than originally expected.

Of course, if hybrid connectionist models are to be of value to researchers ultimately interested in building models on a single connectionist level, then it must eventually be possible to at least roughly map the hybrid capabilities into that level. It is therefore preferable to use mechanisms that are as similar to each other as possible in building hybrid models to increase their chance of being implemented in a single level. When a hybrid model is actually mapped to a single connectionist level, it will likely have advantages over the hybrid because of better integration with the rest of the level than the sometimes awkward integration between elements in hybrid models. It is also important to note that most connectionist models are actually hybrids; even single-level models often use symbolic mechanisms (such as temporary storage buffers) to allow processing or training to succeed. These unreduced hybrid mechanisms must also be eventually mapped to units and connections in the connectionist level.

Our research has resulted in three models that illustrate the value of the hybrid connectionist modelling approach:

1. SAARCS, a hybrid localist connectionist/marker-passing model that is able to integrate aspects of the language understanding process with the analo-

gical retrieval process. Its use of hybrid capabilities allows it to model the influence of comprehension on retrieval in a way that single-level connectionist or symbolic models have not yet been able to, including potentially being able to account for many psychological phenomena involving priming on human memory retrieval.

2. ROBIN, a purely localist connectionist network that has many of the variable binding and inferencing abilities of hybrid marker-passing/localist connectionist models. ROBIN illustrates that the abilities of hybrid models can sometimes be mapped onto a single connectionist level, with the resulting model gaining advantages in both simplicity and processing abilities.

3. A purely distributed connectionist model of short-term sequential memory that is a start toward mapping one of the unreduced hybrid mechanisms necessary for training of sequential distributed connectionist networks.

ACKNOWLEDGMENTS

This research has been supported in part by grants from the W. M. Keck and ITA Foundations. I would like to thank John Dinsmore for his helpful comments and for the opportunity to present the arguments and models in this chapter. I would also like to acknowledge the contributions of Michael Dyer, Keith Holyoak, Eric Melz, Charles Wharton, and Colin Allen to the development of the models described here and for their valuable suggestions on earlier drafts of this chapter.

REFERENCES

Ajjanagadde, V., & Shastri, L. (1989, August). Efficient inference with multi-place predicates and variables in a connectionist system. *Proceedings of the 11th Annual Conference of the Cognitive Science Society,* (p. 396–403). Hillsdale, NJ: Lawrence Erlbaum Associates.

Barnden, J. (1990). Encoding complex symbolic data structure with some unusual connectionist data-structuring techniques. In J. A. Barnden & J. B. Pollack (Eds.), Advances in connectionist and neural computation theory. (p. 180–240). Norwood, NJ: Ablex.

Barnden, J., & Srinivas, K. (in press). Overcoming rule-based rigidity and connectionist limitations through massively-parallel case-based reasoning. *International Journal of Man-Machine Studies.*

Charniak, E. (1986, August). A neat theory of marker passing. *Proceedings of the Fifth National Conference on Artificial Intelligence.* (p. 584–588). Los Altos, CA: Morgan Kaufmann.

Diederich, J. (1990). Steps toward knowledge-intensive connectionist learning. In J. Barnden & J. Pollack (Eds.), Advances in connectionist and neural computation theory (pp. 284–304). Norwood, NJ: Ablex.

Dolan, C. P., & Smolensky, P. (1989). Tensor product production system: A modular architecture and representation. *Connection Science, 1* (1), 53–68.

Dyer, M. G. (1983). *In-depth understanding: A computer model of the integrated processing for narrative comprehension.* Cambridge, MA: MIT Press.

Dyer, M. G. (1990). Symbolic neuroengineering for natural language processing: A multi-level research approach. In J. Barnden & J. Pollack (Eds.), *Advances in connectionist and neural computation theory* (pp. 32–86). Norwood, NJ: Ablex.

Eiselt, K. P. (1987, July). Recovering from erroneous inferences. *Proceedings of the Sixth National Conference on Artificial Intelligence.* (p. 540–544). Los Altos, CA: Morgan Kaufmann.

Feldman, J. A., & Ballard, D. H. (1982). Connectionist models and their properties. *Cognitive Science, 6* (3), 205–254.

Fodor, J. A., & Pylyshyn, Z. W. (1988). Connectionism and cognitive architecture: A critical analysis. In S. Pinker & J. Mehler (Eds.), *Connections and symbols* (pp. 3–71). Cambridge, MA: MIT Press.

Fukushima, K., Miyake, S., & Ito, T. (1983). Neocognitron: A neural network model for a mechanism of visual pattern recognition. *IEEE Transactions on Systems, Man, & Cybernetics, SMC-13, 5,* 826–834.

Gasser, M. (1988). *A connectionist model of sentence generation in a first and second language* (Tech. Rep. No. UCLA-AI-88-13). Doctoral Dissertation, Computer Science Department, University of California, Los Angeles.

Granger, R. H., Eiselt, K. P., & Holbrook, J. K. (1986). Parsing with parallelism: A spreading activation model of inference processing during text understanding. In J. Kolodner & C. Riesbeck (Eds.), Experience, memory, and reasoning (pp. 227–246). Hillsdale, NJ: Lawrence Erlbaum Associates.

Hendler, J. (1988). *Integrating marker-passing and problem solving: A spreading activation approach to improved choice in planning.* Hillsdale, NJ: Lawrence Erlbaum Associates.

Hendler, J. (1989a). Editorial: On the need for hybrid systems. *Connection Science, 1* (3), 227–229.

Hendler, J. (1989b). Marker-passing over microfeatures: Towards a hybrid symbolic/connectionist model. *Cognitive Science, 13* (1), 79–106.

Holldobler, S. (1990, July). A structured connectionist unification algorithm. *Proceedings of the 8th National Conference on Artificial Intelligence.* Menlo Park: AAAI Press.

Holyoak, K. J. (in press). Symbolic connectionism: Toward third-generation theories of expertise. In K. A. Ericsson & J. Smith (Eds.), *Towards a general theory of expertise: Prospects and limits.* Cambridge, MA: Cambridge University Press.

Holyoak, K. J., & Koh, K. (1987). Surface and structural similarity in analogical transfer. *Memory & Cognition, 15,* 332–340.

Holyoak, K. J., & Thagard, P. (1989). Analogical mapping by constraint satisfaction. *Cognitive Science, 13,* 295–355.

Kintsch, W. (1988). The role of knowledge in discourse comprehension: A construction-integration model. *Psychological Review, 95,* 163–182.

Kitano, H., Tomabechi, H., & Levin, L. (1989). Ambiguity resolution in DMTRANS PLUS. In *Proceedings of the Fourth Conference of the European Chapter of the Association of Computational Linguistics.* Manchester University Press.

Lachter, J., & Bever, T. G. (1988). The relation between linguistic structure and associative theories of language learning—A constructive critique of some connectionist learning models. In S. Pinker & J. Mehler (Eds.), *Connections and symbols* (pp. 195–247). Cambridge, MA: MIT Press.

Lange, T. (in press). Lexical and pragmatic disambiguation and reinterpretation in connectionist networks. *International Journal of Man-Machine Studies.*

Lange, T., & Allen, C. (1991). *A connectionist model of short-term sequential memory.* Unpublished manuscript, Computer Science Department, University of California, Los Angeles.

Lange, T., & Dyer, M. G. (1988). Dynamic, non-local role-bindings and inferencing in a localist network for natural language understanding. In David S. Touretzky (Ed.), *Advances in neural information processing systems* (Vol. 1, pp. 545–552). San Mateo, CA: Morgan Kaufmann.

Lange, T., & Dyer, M. G. (1989). High-level inferencing in a connectionist network. *Connection Science, 1* (2), 181–217.

Lange, T., Hodges, J. B., Fuenmayor, M., & Belyaev, L. (1989, August). DESCARTES: Development environment for simulating hybrid connectionist architectures. *Proceedings of the 11th Annual Conference of the Cognitive Science Society.* (p. 698–705). Hillsdale, NJ: Lawrence Erlbaum Associates.

Lange, T., Melz, E., Wharton, C., & Holyoak, K. (1990). Analogical retrieval within a hybrid spreading-activation network. In D. S. Touretzky, J. L. Elman, T. J. Sejnowski, & G. E. Hinton (Eds.), *Proceedings of the 1990 Connectionist Models Summer School* (p. 265–276). San Mateo, CA: Morgan Kaufmann.

Lee, G., Flowers, M., & Dyer, M. G. (1990). Learning distributed representations of conceptual knowledge and their application to script-based story processing. *Connection Science, 2* (4), 313–345.

McClelland, J. L., & Kawamoto, A. H. (1986). Mechanisms of sentence processing: Assigning roles to constituents of sentences. In J. L. McClelland & D. E. Rumelhart (Eds.), *Parallel distributed processing* (Vol. 2, pp. 272–325). Cambridge, MA: MIT Press.

Miikkulainen, R., & Dyer, M. G. (1989, June). A modular neural network architecture for sequential paraphrasing of script-based stories. *Proceedings of the International Joint Conference on Neural Networks.* San Diego, CA: IEEE Neural Network Committee.

Miller, G. A. (1956). The magical number seven, plus or minus two: Some limits one our capacity for processing information. *Psychological Review, 63* (2), 81–97.

Nickerson, R. S. (1984). *Retrieval inhibition from part-set cuing: A persisting enigma in memory research. Memory & Cognition, 12,* 531–552.

Norvig, P. (1989). Marker passing as a weak method for text inferencing. *Cognitive Science, 13* (4), 569–620.

Pazzani, M. J., Dyer, M. G., & Flowers, M. (1987, August). Using prior learning to facilitate the learning of new causal theories. *Proceedings of the 10th International Joint Conference on Artificial Intelligence.* (p. 277–279). Los Altos, CA: Morgan Kaufmann.

Pinker, S., & Prince, A. (1988). On language and connectionism: Analysis of a parallel distributed processing model of language acquisition. In S. Pinker & J. Mehler (Eds.), *Connections and symbols* (pp. 73–193). Cambridge, MA: MIT Press.

Pollack, J. B. (1990). Recursive distributed representations. *Artificial Intelligence 46,* 77–105.

Riesbeck, C. K., & Martin, C. E. (1986). Direct memory across parsing. In J. Kolodner & C. Riesbeck (Eds.), *Experience, memory, and reasoning* (pp. 209–226). Hillsdale, NJ: Lawrence Erlbaum Associates.

Rose (1990). Appropriate use of hybrid systems. In D. S. Touretzky, J. L. Elman, T. J. Sejnowski, & G. E. Hinton (Eds.), *Proceedings of the 1990 connectionist models summer school* (p. 277–286). San Mateo, CA: Morgan Kaufmann.

Ross, B. H. (1989). Distinguishing types of superficial similarities: Different effects on the access and use of earlier problems. *Journal of Experimental Psychology: Learning, Memory, and Cognition, 15,* 456–468.

Rumelhart, D. E., Hinton, G. E., & McClelland, J. L. (1986). Learning internal representations by error propagation. In D. E. Rumelhart & J. L. McClelland (Eds.), Parallel distributed processing (Vol. 1, pp. 318–364). Cambridge, MA: MIT Press.

Rumelhart, D. E., & McClelland, J. L. (1986). On learning the past tenses of English verbs. In J. L. McClelland & D. E. Rumelhart (Eds.), *Parallel distributed processing* (Vol. 2, pp. 216–271). Cambridge, MA: MIT Press.

Schank, R., & Abelson, R. (1977). *Script, plans, goals and understanding.* Hillsdale, NJ: Lawrence Erlbaum Associates.

Schank, R. C., & Leake, D. B. (1989). Creativity and learning in a case-based explainer. *Artificial Intelligence, 40,* 353–385.

Shastri, L. (1988). A connectionist approach to knowledge representation and limited inference. *Cognitive Science, 12* (3), 331–392.

St. John, M. F. (1990). *The story gestalt: Text comprehension by cue-based constraint satisfaction* (Tech. Rep. No. 9004). Doctoral Dissertation, Department of Cognitive Science, University of California, San Diego.

Sumida, R. A., & Dyer, M. G. (1989, August). Storing and generalizing multiple instances while maintaining knowledge-level parallelism. Proceedings of the 11th International Joint Conference on Artificial Intelligence. (p. 1426–1431). San Mateo, CA: Morgan Kaufmann.

Thagard, P., Holyoak, K. J., Nelson, G., & Gochfeld, D. (1990). Analog retrieval by constraint satisfaction. *Artificial Intelligence, 46,* 259–310.

Touretzky, D. S. (1990). Connectionism and compositional semantics. In J. A. Barnden & J. B. Pollack (Eds.), *Advances in connectionist and neural computation theory* (p. 17–31). Norwood, NJ: Ablex.

Touretzky, D. S., & Hinton, G. E. (1988). A distributed connectionist production system. *Cognitive Science, 12* (3), 423–466.

Waibel, A. (1989). Consonant recognition by modular construction of large phonemic time-delay neural networks. In D. S. Touretzky (Ed.), *Advances in neural information processing systems* (Vol. 1, pp. 215–223). San Mateo: Morgan Kaufmann.

Waltz, D., & Pollack, J. (1985). Massively parallel parsing: A strong interactive model of natural language interpretation. *Cognitive Science, 9* (1), 51–74.

Wharton, C., Holyoak, K., Downing, P., Lange, T., & Wickens, T. (1991). Retrieval competition in memory for analogies. *Proceedings of the 13th Annual Conference of the Cognitive Science Society,* p. 528–533. Hillsdale, NJ: Lawrence Erlbaum.

Wermter, S., & Lehnert, W. G. (1989). A hybrid symbolic/connectionist model for noun phrase understanding. *Connection Science, 1* (3), 255–272.

Author Index